BETWEEN
JERUSALEM AND BENARES

Between Jerusalem and Benares

Comparative Studies in Judaism and Hinduism

edited by
Hananya Goodman

STATE UNIVERSITY OF NEW YORK PRESS

We gratefully acknowledge the permissions granted by authors and publishers to reprint several essays in this volume.

David Flusser's essay was originally published under the title "Abraham and the Upanishads" in *Immanuel* 20 (Spring 1986) 53–61, published by the Ecumenical Theological Research Fraternity in Israel and ADL of B'nai B'rith.

Francis Schmidt's essay was published under the French title "Entre Juifs et Grecs: Le Modèle Indien" in *Collection Purusartha* II (1988) published by the École des Hantes Études en Sciences Sociales.

Bernard S. Jackson's essay was published under the title "From *Dharma* to Law" in the *American Journal of Comparative Law* 23 (1975) 490–508 published by the American Association for the Comparative Study of Law.

Published by
State University of New York Press, Albany

Printed in the United States of America

For information, address State University of New York Press,
State University Plaza, Albany, N.Y., 12246

Library of Congress Cataloging-in-Publication Data

Between Jerusalem and Benares : comparative studies in Judaism and Hinduism / edited by Hananya Goodman.
p. cm.
Includes bibliographical references and index.
ISBN 0-7914-1715-8.—ISBN 07914-1716-6 (pbk.)
1. Judaism—Relations—Hinduism. 2. Hinduism—Relations—Judaism.
I. Goodman, Hananya, 1953– .
BM536.H5B47 1994
296.3'872—dc20 92-47229
CIP

10 9 8 7 6 5 4 3 2 1

Contents

PART TWO

Cultural Resonances

To my mother, Rita Goodman, and

To the memory of my father, Arnold Goodman, *zichrono levracha,* whose religion was caring about others.

The last conversation I had with my father took place en route to a meeting of the National Conference of Christians and Jews, where he was to be honored for his contribution to interfaith dialogue. He inclined toward me and shared with me the theme of his acceptance speech:

> "From what time may one recite the *Shema* in the morning?
>
> From the time that one can distinguish his friend at a distance of four cubits."
>
> Talmud *Brachot* 9b

At the other end of the day, after the bedtime recitation of the *Shema,* my children, Moshe and Meira, say:

> "HaShem give me some good dreams.
>
> Always protect me.
>
> Protect Adina.
>
> Protect Jakie.
>
> Protect the angels.
>
> Protect all the people.
>
> Protect the world.
>
> I love you.
>
> Goodnight.
>
> Amen."

Acknowledgments

I am grateful to my dear wife, Sharon, *yedidat nafshi,* for helping me apply Lamaze-like breathing techniques during the labor of this book, and for her spiritual nurturance and discipline of both author and book. I could not have done the book without her incisive commentaries and loving support.

I thank my editors—Riqi Kosovske, Kate Lebow, Noah Millman, and Justin Leites—who helped during the delivery. I especially thank Abbie Ziffren, a true friend, who helped me through a tough final editing.

I am fortunate in having devoted friends in Jerusalem, and abroad, who cheered me on over the years: Minna and Jacob Amsel, Yehudit Abinun, Eleazer and Raphaela Ben-Baruch, Naomi and Yoel Glick, Boris and Sarah Gottlieb, Alon and Tamar Goshen-Gottstein, Yossi and Sarah Klein Halevi, Dalia and Yehezkiel Landau, Ruthy and Yitzhak Muller, Moshe Reiss, and Sri Yogeshwar.

I welcomed ideas and advice from all directions but particularly from: David Appelbaum, Herbert Basser, Carmel Berkson, Mira Binford, John Carman, Francis Clooney, Joseph Dan, Richard Davis, Duncan Derrett, Evan Finkelstein, Eli Franco, Marc Galanter, Yehudah Gellman, David Goodman, Arthur Green, Deirdre Green, Wilhelm Halbfass, Hank Heifetz, Moshe Idel, Artur and Shirley Isenberg, Nathan Katz, Miles Krassen, Yohanan Lederman, Saul Levin, Judy Linzer, Charles Malamoud, Natan Ophir, Shlomo Pines, A. K. Ramanujan, Ben-Ami Scharfstein, Richard Solomon, Charles Vernoff, Sunthar Visuvalingam, Zwi Werblowsky and Elliot Wolfson.

I also wish to thank Bill Eastman, Director of SUNY Press, for his enthusiastic and immediate interest in the project and for his patience in waiting for a long overdue birth.

Preface

When we first went from Jerusalem to Benares, some twenty years ago, my wife and I met an old man on the Sarnath bus. Not knowing us, not knowing whence we had arrived, he began to speak to us in hushed tones, as if conveying a great secret. He loved Benares, and he told us: "There are two cities in the world that are truly alike, two ancient sisters—Jerusalem and Benares." He was thinking, surely, about a certain kind of continuous passion for an experience we sometimes call "holy," manifest in a single place; and he may also have meant something more than this, something connected to the varied and often paradoxical relations between this "holiness" or "otherness" and the life of a civilization unfolding around it. This book is devoted to exploring that venerable Banarsi's proposition.

The proposition is by no means axiomatic, and this is the first book that has thought it worthy of serious notice. Do the two cultures share anything basic? Is the comparison worth pursuing? At first glance, from the vantage point of Jerusalem, India seems to be immersed in what the Jews call *avodah zarah,* "alien worship," that is, a form of idolatry. (This has also been a prevalent Islamic perspective on Indian religion, as centuries of Muslim iconoclasm in India have shown.) The panoply of temples, with their stone or metal images; the richly sensuous modes of worship; the apparent proximity of god and man; the potential manifestations of the divine in any place or thing; the readiness of the mystic to proclaim, *so 'ham asmi,* "I am God"—all these are conducive to this rather hostile view. From Benares, on the other hand, Jerusalem may seem stubbornly, even perversely, fixated in a severely *nirguṇa* mode. The Jews insist on God's unity and transcendence and claim, at least, to deny him representation—although, for many Hindus, the Biblical use of language to speak of God as having thoughts, intentions, actions, attributes, not to mention metaphors or figures such as "a strong hand and mighty arm," is not qualitatively different from actual representation in visual images. Even metaphoric conceptualization fractures the infinite wholeness of the Absolute. Philosophic Hinduism is perfectly aware of this issue: Śaṅkara is said to have prayed on his deathbed for forgiveness (from whom?) for having worshipped God in his partial manifestations, in temples and mental images, with human language. Such limitations are no more than painful concessions to our weakness. This being so, the Hindu might well ask, why all the fuss about symbolization, why the monotheistic horror of the visible?

This first, impressionistic line of division could be formulated as a hypothesis: Is it true that the Jews worship a *saguṇa* god—a deity endowed with attributes—who cannot be symbolized, while Hindus worship a *nirguṇa* Absolute, without attributes, who can? But much more than the issue of symbolism is at stake. There are questions here of epistemology, of the relation to sacred texts and their explication, of the social and cultural construction of the self, of ethical philosophy, and of basic cultural intuitions that, however much they transform themselves over time, remain distinct. Let me give two examples from one year in Jerusalem. When our seminar on enigmas invited several Bible scholars to discuss the opening chapters of Genesis, and they proceeded to do so with their customary vigor and concern for the singular truth of the text, my Hindu colleague, V. Narayana Rao, whispered to me: "If I have to be reborn, I have only one request—let it not be into a monotheistic religion." Factuality is not, perhaps, the dominant Hindu interpretative mode for metaphysical utterance. Later he attended a lecture by my colleague Moshe Idel, who strove to prove, in the face of much skepticism, that the cherubim in the Second Temple carried a powerful erotic symbolism of male and female hypostases uniting within the godhead. Discussion was heated, and, for obvious reasons, the thesis had to be painfully and very meticulously argued. At its conclusion, my Hindu friend remarked: "So much effort to establish what should be taken for granted!"

Are Benares and Jerusalem really part of the same world? The possibility of communication suggests that the unlikely answer may, after all, be yes. Perhaps, in the end, comparison is impossible: Cultures live out their peculiarly organic lives, and it is usually all we can do to understand a little of even one of them, on its own terms. Yet without comparison, thought itself is probably impossible, and neither taxonomy nor history could exist. Moreover, the fact of cross-cultural resonances is established by experience. I teach Sanskrit and Tamil in Jerusalem. Each year I am amazed anew at the hunger for knowledge about India that animates a select group of young Israeli students. Many of my best students come to me from the study of Kabbalah; they seem to understand easily, intuitively, the inner world of Indian texts. *Bhakti* religion, in particular, perhaps partly because of my own affinities, awakens their response. Some find in India a vision of the repressed side of their own culture. Some seek relief from their own in the exotic; the self defines itself only in relation to an other, real or imagined. A few have come to me from the communities of Indian Jews, with their own intimate experience and personal or family memories of India. These same students will also draw in the boundaries, the profound and evident contrasts, between Benares and Jerusalem.

The essays in this volume open a discussion, long overdue. Some trace linkages rooted in actual contact, borrowed elements, the residue of historical ties. The anthropology of India's Jews presents a case of unconscious symbiosis and acculturation as well as powerful continuities with the imported Jewish past. The European romance of Jewish Indologists points to one type of charmed (and problematic) relations. The essays here constitute a fertile beginning. Whatever the similarities, the shared themes and tensions, this is no simple enterprise. Ultimately, it is less a matter of making comparisons, always partial and often frustrating, than of a certain kind of listening. The challenge is to hear the echoes that connect, however tenuously, two ancient civilizations, each richly endowed with experience of God and of the world, and not entirely without a history of intellectual, linguistic, and material interaction. To study them together is to provoke the overtones or resonances, *dhvani,* that—so Hindu poets tell us—are the vehicle of truth.

David Shulman

1

Introduction
Judaism and Hinduism: Cultural Resonances

Hananya Goodman

Personal Encounters

Growing up, I had no idea that one day I would become so immersed in the comparative study of Judaism and Hinduism. It all began when, as a teenager, friends introduced me to the practice of silent mantra meditation, vegetarianism, and Indian philosophy. During the same period my friendship with a Hasidic rabbi exposed me to a devotional community where the study of Jewish mystical texts and the zealous observance of *halakhah* were the norm.

When the experimental world of the 1960s arrived in my Midwestern hometown, I was ready. I came from a non-Orthodox but traditionally observant Jewish home. My liberal parents were devoted, professionally and personally, to "saving the world" through their work for international peace organizations, multicultural encounters, interreligious conferences. As a result of this family atmosphere, one of my brothers became a Japanese scholar, while the other brother became director of an educational institute in Jakarta, Indonesia. We each divided up the earth, like Noah's sons, and I took Israel and India as my provinces.

Although my exposure to Advaita Vedanta and associated meditation techniques is what first attracted me to Hinduism, I soon recognized that, just as a limb is attached to a larger organism, these formative experiences did not predeterminate the multitude of alternative approaches I could take to comparative inquiry. Jerusalem and Benares were fascinating and elusive sources of attraction, each side manifesting vast and untraversed regions of correspondence. They were living symbols of my encounter with exile in exile. They remained distant textual abstractions until I finally left exile by moving to a living Jerusalem. What had been unknown and exotic became elevated and concrete. Half of my pilgrimage has been realized, and I am still on the road to Benares.

A History of Comparative Scholarship

In the mid-1970s, I met Barbara Holdrege, who may well be the only person whose lifework centers on the academic study of Judaism and Hinduism. I was so impressed with her knowledge of and dedication to a topic of mutual interest, that I wrote Gershom Scholem for his opinion regarding the possibility of making further comparisons between the two traditions. He responded:

> I do not know of *scholarly,* critical studies comparing Indian and Jewish thought. Having read Patañjali on Yoga and some of Sankara's writings in English and German, I doubt very much whether this would be a good subject for a critical comparison. But I may be mistaken. I possess a work by Schrader, *Introduction to the Pañcarātra* (Madras, 1914) which has struck me as presenting a system not unsimilar to the Kabbalistic tree of the Sefiroth, and I suppose that there may be a number of systems presenting similar *structures* of Divine powers. This, of course, would be something to be expressed as *gnostic* structures of the world of Divinity [which] have an overall affinity in many religious systems in quite different religions (Tantra, Hindu later philosophy, Islamic gnosis of Ismailitic type, Christian theosophy like Jacob Boehme, etc.). In all these independent or not so independent systems you find certain *structural* affinities with Kabbalah—only the *contrary* would surprise me. . . . Therefore, I am not sure that such a study would do much to "illuminate Jewish and Indian scholarship" as you put it. See for instance my remarks on the Shekhinah and Shakti at the end of my (German) lecture on the concept of the Shekhinah in Kabbalism in the *Eranos-Jahrbuch* vol. XXI

(Zurich, 1953) (also contained in my book *Von der mystischen Gestalt der Gottheit,* 1962).[1]

Scholem's skepticism had a cautionary effect, but I continued to sound people out about the project. Negative reactions generally softened quickly as scholars I spoke to warmed to the idea, offering their own suggestions and referring me to literary sources, articles, and other people interested in the topic.

As I began to search I realized that a fuller presentation of the history of the idea of comparing Hinduism and Judaism was a desideratum for any future discourse between these two great traditions. The idea of comparing Judaism and Hinduism is not unique to this volume. In fact, such comparisons have been an important thread woven into the fabric of Western intellectual thinking for centuries. Placing Hinduism and Judaism side by side has played an important part in European discussions of spirituality, primitivism, idolatry, theories of language and race origins, universalism and particularism, comparative mythology, and oriental studies.

Although conscious comparisons between Hinduism and Judaism started at least two thousand years ago, as discussed by Francis Schmidt in our volume, the theme was only treated substantially from the eighteenth-century European Enlightenment onward, when direct exposure to Indian texts and culture became possible. The fascinating historical details of this European encounter with India can be found in the comprehensive works of Raymond Schwab, Donald Lach, Wilhelm Halbfass, and others.[2]

In these studies I found the juxtaposition of biblical and Indian ideas used for a variety of theological and ideological purposes. The role and meaning of biblical scriptures, and the Jewish and Christian conceptions of God, were the epistemological counterpoints or ontological foundations for much of the philosopher's constructions. For example, comparisons between Hinduism and Judaism in the Enlightenment were instrumental in arguing for a deistic worldview in which the authority and centrality of biblical revelation and chronology were pitted against the claimed antiquity of the Vedas and the original religious practices of the Indians. In 1704, La Crequiniere wrote a lengthy treatise entitled, *The Agreement of the Customs of the East-Indians with those of the Jews, and other Ancient People.*[3] This French author sought to reconcile Hindu spiritual practices with deistic concepts similar to John Toland's views of a universalistic deism substantiated through studies in comparative religion. La Crequinere sought a critique of contemporary thinking by highlighting the universality of superstitions to be found in the Bible and in recent discoveries of traditional Indian practices.[4] The approach was so close to Toland's that the English translation was attributed to Toland.[5]

Then, in 1760, with the appearance of the *Ezourvedam,* Voltaire argued that India was the cradle of civilization, and he questioned the historical and theological priority of biblical chronology. He claimed that Abraham and Brahma were identical.[6] Indian religion provided Voltaire with evidence of an alternative to Christianity and he held Hinduism to be the true religion which preserved the pure, natural, and original revelation from which biblical religions devolved.[7] His Enlightenment critique of Christian revelation had a tremendous impact on future comparative studies.

In contrast, the scientist and theologian, Joseph Priestley asserted in 1799 the superiority of the Bible over the pagan Hindus in his *A Comparison of the Institutions of Moses with those of the Hindoos and other Ancient Nations.*[8] He used the comparative approach to clarify and locate his version of the original, purified Christianity, as evidenced by Indian practices, and, in a counter to Voltaire, raised enlightened Christianity above all other religions.[9]

In the late 1700s, with the researches of Sir William Jones and others, Indian studies entered a period of intense and specialized scholarship. For our discussion, the studies of Karl Theodor Johannsen on *Die Kosmogonischen Antichten der Inder und Hebraer*[10] in 1833 and F. A. Korn's *Braminen und Rabbinen*[11] in 1836, serve to exemplify the more focused disciplinary approach taken. In 1868 Jacoillet synthesized many of the earlier comparative observations and wrote a popular study, *The Bible in India,*[12] which went through a dozen editions and several translations.

Despite the lineage of works we have drawn, it is clear that comparisons between Hinduism and Judaism were not the main concern of Indologists, Judaic scholars, and comparativists. Those comparisons were made when they served to highlight and contrast the principle elements of a larger research enterprise. Nevertheless, important scholars kept returning to the Hindu-Jewish theme in an effort to discover something new in their own disciplines and theories. In 1898, Henri Hubert and Marcel Mauss wrote their "Essai sur la Nature et la Fonction du Sacrifice." In introducing what was to become a seminal work, they explain their motives for choosing to compare Hinduism and Judaism over other possible cultures:

> We shall try to study thoroughly typical facts which we shall glean particularly from Sanskrit texts and from the Bible. We are far from having documents of equal value concerning Greek and Roman sacrifices. By comparing scattered pieces of

> information provided by inscriptions and writers, only an ill-assorted ritual can be built up. On the other hand, we have in the Bible and in the Hindu texts collections of doctrines that belong to a definite era. The document is direct, drawn up by the participants themselves in their own language, in the very spirit in which they enacted the rites, even if not always with a very clear consciousness of the origin and motive of their actions.[13]

Through a careful analysis of the social, textual, and material data in the two traditions, Hubert and Mauss explored the dynamics of sacrifice. They attempted to reconstruct and recreate the symbolic world of the ritual participant, arguing that the meaning of the ritual act is in its ability to transform reality for the participant. For both Hindus and Jews of the past, sacrificial rituals were held to transform the self and the world.

Other comparative themes were undertaken by Sanskrit scholars such as James Darmesteter, Sylvain Lévi, Moritz Winternitz, and Gustav Salomon Oppert.[14] Maurice Bloomfield wrote about "Joseph and Potiphar in Hindu Fiction" (1923),[15] while Walter Ruben explored the "Bible and Purana" (1966).[16] Recent doctoral dissertations include: Michael Futterman's "Judaism, Hinduism and Theodicy" (1977),[17] and Daniel Polish's "The Flood Myth in the Traditions of Israel and India" (1974).[18] Mention should also be made of Barbara Holdrege's recent work *Veda and Torah: Transcending the Textuality of Scripture.*[19] An interesting feature of these and other studies is the lack of awareness which each one shows for previous studies comparing Hinduism and Judaism, both within and outside of their own disciplinary field.[20]

Scholars within the traditional Jewish orbit also took an interest in making comparisons with the Indians. Although a fuller treatment of this material is desirable, let us mention that there have been, occasional, passing citations of India in Jewish medieval texts. For example, Sa'adya Gaon (tenth century),[21] Moses Maimonides (eleventh century),[22] Abraham Ibn Ezra,[23] and *Sefer ha-Ḥayyim*[24] illustrate how these rabbinic scholars peripherally imagined India and Indians to be sources of spiritual wisdom, sometimes pure, sometimes impure. The pattern continues later in the works of Isaac Abravanel (fifteenth century),[25] Manasseh Ben Israel,[26] and Shalom Shabazi (seventeenth century).[27] In the Jewish encounter with the Enlightenment we find Moses Mendelssohn (eighteenth century)[28] making direct use of Holwell's publications on India in his *Jerusalem.* In Orthodox Jewish responsa, we find a preoccupation with the application of the laws concerning idolatry and with the subtleties of spiritual impurity.[29] Then with strong Hegelian[30] influences we find liberal, enlightened Jews such as Moses Hess (nineteenth century),[31] Franz Rosenzweig (twentieth century),[32] and Martin Buber[33] struggling with the implications of Oriental thought for a renewal of Jewish theology.

When we turn to the image of Jews and Judaism in Indian thought, we discover a virtually unexplored topic. But an examination of Hindu reactions to Christian and Muslim ideas, some of which can be traced back to Jewish conceptions, is likely to reveal some fascinating if not peculiarly transformed images of Judaism.[34]

A critical analysis of Hindu-Jewish comparisons and their limitations provides the initial focus for the pieces collected in this volume. Preferably, serious discussions of Judaism and Hinduism ought to be founded on intimate familiarity with the texts, practices, and peoples of both cultures. This is not always possible. But close collaboration among scholars has the potential to rectify the situation and produce some unexpected results. This was the case with Hubert and Mauss. Therefore, I have made no claim for comprehensiveness regarding the possibilities for comparison, nor have I sought material limited to a uniform methodology of comparative religion. Hinduism and Judaism merit examination together from a variety of approaches, using methods appropriate to particular themes and fields, whether they be anthropology, history, philology, law, literature, or theology.

As a result of this orientation, I have found in Hinduism and Judaism two comprehensive traditions whose hermeneutic inventiveness has resulted in highly ramified and evolving traditions with extensive written and oral components. The intricate mappings of halakhic and shastric regulations covering every aspect of life engage the mind, while aggadic and mythological modes of discourse engage the heart, testifying to the encompassing nature of the two traditions. In developing this volume, my goal has been to stimulate further study and collaboration among scholars who will continue the process of elaborating and deepening the connections and resonances.[35]

This is what I found when I visited David Shulman at his home in Jerusalem. His unassuming and supportive friendship gave me the confidence to create this volume. He introduced me to Wendy Doniger, and she led me to others. Doniger's thoughts on the relevance of her Jewishness to her fascination with something so foreign as Sanskrit texts can lead to fruitful speculations about the phenomenon of Jewish interest in other cultures.[36] The need both to assimilate foreign cultures and to be assimilated by them without eliminating distinctions, epitomizes a Jewish paradigm. This paradigm is characterized by exile and survival on the periphery of diverse civilizations.

This volume begins with Wendy Doniger's personal essay in which she explores some of the factors that have attracted contemporary Jewish scholars to India. For her, a secularized Jew, India provided the path to rediscover her own culture. She needed to experience several foreign religions, as she writes, to "come to a more complex understanding of my own mythology as a Jew and as a scholar of Hinduism." In her scholarly work she claims a centrality for her Jewish identity. Just as her study of Hinduism has enabled her to discover previously unseen personal meanings in Judaism, her Jewish cultural heritage, whether expressed through active religious observance or not, has provided her with the tools to draw new meaning out of Indian texts. This cultivated habit of "cracking open" a text, this *gemara kop,* applied so assiduously by Jewish scholars such as Doniger and Shulman, represents an example of what I call the "culture of questions," which I consider to be a dominant Jewish mode of thought.

The Culture of Questions

The culture of questions confronts all aspects of life with an intense curiosity, an active receptivity, and an urgency to ask questions regardless of the answers. From the encouragement of curiosity in children to the struggle to understand nature and the human condition, the Jewish people partake of this culture.[37] More articulated examples of this approach are to be found in Anson Laytner's review of Jewish arguments with God,[38] Adin Steinsaltz's translation of Talmudic hermeneutics,[39] Abraham Abulafia's kabbalistic technique of *zerufim,*[40] Samuel Heilman's ethnographic study of contemporary Talmudic *lernen,*[41] Deborah Schiffrin's sociolinguistic observations concerning Jewish argument,[42] William Novak and Moshe Waldoks's anthology of Jewish humor,[43] or Edmond Jabes's *Book of Questions.*[44] Philosophical approaches to the nature of questioning are discussed by Michel Meyer and others.[45]

In traditional Jewish study, questions go beyond the reaffirmation of what is already known; they elicit new revelations of understanding, *hiddushei Torah.* The method of superactivated reflection allows the Jewish hermeneut to break the seal that masks our rootedness in divinity and see all of creation more clearly. The art and technique of questioning makes the world translucent. The great energy released from such interpretive acts spills over into all aspects of life, and then the questioning and interpretive capacity becomes suffused in the reading of other texts, other peoples. This culture of questions involves, to varying degrees, a mental state of rapid frame-switching and radical perspective-taking. George Steiner highlights the manner in which the questioning mode of rabbinic discourse emerges in other domains.[46]

Jewish scholars are, in Steiner's words, "meta-rabbis,"[47] expositors of the law outside the Law. Whether in a particularistic Jewish context or a universalistic mode of participation in larger culture, Jews find the law to be nurturing and life-promoting.[48] And in this mode, they have been interlocutors and translators for the Jewish community and others, purveyors in the world economy of ideas, exploring uncharted territories of the mind and soul.[49] Jewish scholars working in this culture of questions are a generative part of contemporary Western Indology, and their ethnoreligious heritage is an integral part of the translation of Indian culture to the West.[50] As such they are among the most frequent travelers between Jerusalem and Benares, among the first to articulate the mediation of Judaism and Hinduism.

Naturally, this encounter between the two traditions will develop with the help of scholars of both Indian and Judaic studies. The need for such an encounter and for comparative study was emphasized recently by Peter Berger in his provocative essay, "Between Jerusalem and Benares: The Coming Contestation of Religions."[51] Berger states:

> Put simply, western Asia and India have given birth to the two most comprehensive religious worldviews, and the antithesis between them constitutes the most important problem for contemporary ecumenicity.[52]
>
> *Contestation means an open-minded encounter with other religious possibilities on the level of their truth claims* . . . to enter into interreligious contestation is to be prepared to change one's own view of reality.[53]

I share Berger's enthusiasm but differ with him in his characterization of the mediational process. When Berger couches the encounter between Judaism and Hinduism in terms of the confrontation of truth claims he is perpetuating a "culture of answers." To illustrate one need only consider the mode of discourse employed by the major Western missionary religion, Christianity, in its interrelations with other religions. Historically, communication with other religions was framed and determined by the need of the missionary religion to spread convincingly a set of propositional truths about the nature of reality.[54] Centered around orthodoxy, Christianity has tended to generate a discourse of doctrinal theology, an ideology of faith. Certainly Judaism and Hinduism also have a corpus of answers, but I would suggest that the discourse of questions predominates in these two traditions, partly because both share a strong orientation towards orthopraxy as opposed to orthodoxy. In the Judaic and Hindu traditions great latitude is available in the realm of thought, while one's actions are more circumscribed.

The goal of this questioning process is not so much to find definitive answers as to enter more deeply into the phenomenal world of states of being, thoughts, texts, and people and then to create linkages and networks of meaning. I am therefore less interested in juxtaposing truth claims than in developing an emerging sense of cross-cultural resonances among two comprehensive ethnoreligious systems. In this regard, Judaism and Hinduism represent two highly developed cultural modes of being that comes from the reaches of ritual and meditation, study and prayer, service and sacrifice, charity and generosity, joyous dance and modesty, spontaneity and memory. An immersion in ritual and devotional acts, a zealousness for correct behavior, a passion for communal unity, a search for the remythologizing of lived events—all of this is part of the legacy that Jews and Hindus share.

The culture of questions provides us with a reasonable framework for an encounter between Jews and Hindus, an expanding encounter that this book hopefully will stimulate. Historically, whatever exchanges have taken place in the past have suffered from the mutual peripherality of the Jewish and Hindu worlds. Despite their interest in foreign cultures, Judaism and Hinduism are, in at least three senses, home religions. First, they share in common an appreciation of the symbolic power of seeing the home as a temple and consequently emphasize the role of the family and domestic rituals, while at the same time emphasizing the importance of ethnicity as the encompassing network of extended family relations. Second, motifs of exile and cyclic return in Judaism or of separation and union in devotional Hinduism express the desire to return to the home of being in and with God. The attempt to overcome the gap between the reality of exile or separation and the goal of godliness is an important element in these two religious cultures, cultures of searching, yearning, and questioning.[55] Third, Judaism and Hinduism are homes in the sense of being points of origin for spiritual descendants who have subsequently touched every corner of the world. Judaism is the necessary subtext for Christianity and Islam. Likewise, Hinduism is the subtext for Buddhism and Jainism. These descendants, as well as other, independent traditions, have historically bridged the physical and spiritual distance between Hindus and Jews, and consequently the interaction of the two traditions has been refracted or occluded but rarely appreciated. There exists an extensive and organized literature on the image of India in the

Christian West, as well as on the image of the West in India, but a systematic study of the Jewish literature in these areas is still lacking.

Historical Encounters

In investigating the history of Hindu and Jewish influences on each other for this volume, I encountered a warm and eager scholar at the Hebrew University in Jerusalem, Chaim Rabin, who urged me to look further into the historical connections between India and Israel. He showed me examples of Tamil loanwords in the Bible and explained the possible mechanism of transmission. Rabin found that Hebrew speakers were exposed to Tamil and Sanskrit words through the sea trade with southern Arabia during the period between the tenth and sixth centuries B.C.E. As discussed in Rabin's essay in this volume, these words were almost exclusively associated with the transfer of material rather than cultural goods.

In later periods the possibility of cultural exchange began to unfold. David Flusser's essay on comparative mythology examines the possible Indian origins of a Midrash explaining Abraham's discovery of divine unity. The story, which has roots in Jewish texts as early as the second century B.C.E., reflects a basic teaching of the early Upanisads dating from the sixth century B.C.E. Flusser conjectures that, arriving through the intermediary of Persian Zoroastrianism, the Indian version may have influenced the expression of Jewish monotheism.

The most frequent meeting place of Jewish and Hindu thought before the modern period, however, was in the country of the imagination. In the Greco-Roman period in Palestine, accounts of Hindu practice brought back by Alexander's expeditions were used more to facilitate understanding of Jewish relations in the Near East than of Indians themselves. Francis Schmidt's essay discusses how the Brahmins of India became for the Greeks a paradigm for understanding the Jews' relation to the Syrians around them, and how the story of two gymnosophists met by Alexander's envoy, one obstinate and the other cooperative, was used by the Sicarii to justify their ultimately suicidal resistance to Roman authority. Although appearing to illustrate Alexander's famous encounters with the Indian sages, the Jewish texts in fact dealt with the relationship between Hellenism and Judaism and raised a fundamental issue for the Jewish world: How to retain one's own identity despite foreign domination.

In his essay on Arumuga Navalar's influential Tamil booklet, *The Abolition of the Abuse of Saivism,* D. Dennis Hudson investigates the use of Jewish scriptures by a prominent nineteenth-century Hindu thinker. Navalar uses the Torah, available to him only as the Protestant Old Testament, to defend Saiva worship against the Protestant polemic. To him the Protestants were not living up to their own scriptures, which mandated practices surprisingly similar to those of the Saiva community. Hudson speculates on the conversation Navalar might have had with a rabbi about Protestant missionary intolerance and argues that, although their reasoning might be quite different, they would both make similar criticisms of the missionaries and would construct similar rationales for tolerating each other, but would do so within the view of foreign faiths in their respective traditions. This dialogue has taken place only in the imagination because the majority of Jews were exiled westward from the ancestral homeland. Had they gone eastward the very character of Judaism and the world might have been radically different.[56] Abraham Joshua Heschel observes:

> Had Jerusalem been located at the foot of the Himalayas, monotheistic philosophy would have been modified by the tradition of Oriental thinkers. Thus, our intellectual position situated as it is between Athens and Jerusalem is not an ultimate one. Providence may some day create a situation which would place us between the river Jordan and the river Ganges, and the problem of such an encounter will be different from that which Jewish thought underwent when meeting with Greek philosophy.[57]

There have of course been Jewish communities situated at just such a crossroads, since at least the tenth century C.E. Shalva Weil's essay treats the subject of Jewish communities in India, examining the ways in which the Bene Israel Jews' self-perception is affected by their Hindu environment. In celebrating the holiest day of the Jewish year, Yom Kippur, the Bene Israel, as out-of-caste Indians, reinforce the complementarity of Indian social structure and worship that is inherent in the caste system. Jewish attitudes and practices concerning atonement, purification, death, and sacrifice are integrated with comparable Hindu notions and practices in the Bene Israel's observance of Yom Kippur.[58]

Indian Jewish communities have not generally been as bookish as their counterparts in the Christian and Muslim worlds. Adaptations of their ritual norms have sprung not from new texts or interpretive strategies but from daily encounters at home with the surrounding Hindu culture. Their experiences of Yom Kippur and other festivals such as Passover resonate deeply with Hindu attitudes and behaviors. The idea of resonance is implicit in the work of Nathan Katz and Ellen Goldberg, who in their work on the Cochin Jews develop a useful concept of foregrounding and backgrounding to explain the manner in which Jewish cultural resources are amplified or attenuated as a means of creative adaptation to the dominant Hindu culture.

> In their *minhagim* the Cochin Jews have foregrounded the symbols of purity and nobility inherent in Judaism at the same time as they have adapted some of the priestly and royal symbols of Hinduism, making for one of the most exotic systems of Jewish observance found anywhere in the Diaspora. On the one hand, they have appropriated certain Brahmanical symbols of purity in their unique Passover observances. On the other hand, they have adapted aspects of the Nāyars' symbols of royalty and prosperity in their unique Simchat Torah observances as well as in their marriage customs. Moreover, they manage this syncretism judiciously so as not to contravene *halacha*. . . .
>
> Judaism has ample indigenous resources that could easily be assimilated to the Brahmanical priestly-ascetic symbols, including: (1) a hereditary priesthood of *kohanim,* paralleling the Brāhmans; (2) a fastidious system of laws of *kashruth,* or dietary regulations; (3) complex laws governing family purity; and (4) ascetic tendencies in certain holidays, especially Passover and Yom Kippur. At the same time, Judaism has other resources comparable to the noble-kingly symbols of the Nayars, including: (1) the royalty symbolism *(malchut)* of the High Holy Days; (2) the resemblances between the Torah processions (*haqafot* or rodeamentos) of Simchat Torah and Hinduism's deity processions; and (3) the royalty symbolism traditionally ascribed to brides and bridegrooms. The *minhagim* of the Cochin Jews represent a creative synthesis that accentuates Jewish traditions connected with these two symbol complexes, while at the same time incorporating comparable elements from Hindu traditions.[59]

Phenomenological Resonances

The essays in the second part of the volume are concerned primarily with cultural resonances among the Judaic and Hindu traditions, rather than with actual points of historical encounter. Much hair-splitting has been directed to the question of what are the reasonable, essential rules for comparing two apparently similar complexes of ideas or practices.[60] Is the mystical experience in Judaism the "same" as in Hinduism? Are the conceptions of purity and impurity comparable in the scriptures and practices of the two religions? While the debate goes on, I would like to take a less categorical approach by which we can avoid endless discussions of the point-by-point correspondences or disparities between the Judaic and Hindu traditions. It is sufficient that we learn about each tradition as much as possible on its own terms and then examine resonances as well as divergences among certain ideas and practices of the two traditions. One attains an understanding of the points of intersection among two traditions not so much through an awareness of the "totality" of each tradition as through a receptivity to specific meaningful resonances or counterpoints.[61]

Barbara Holdrege's essay is a comparative analysis of the role of scripture in the Brahmanical tradition and the rabbinic and kabbalistic traditions. She focuses in particular on cosmological conceptions of scripture in which Veda and Torah, respectively, are depicted not merely as a circumscribed corpus of texts, but as a multileveled cosmic reality that encompasses both historical and transmundane dimensions. She argues that the sacred status, authority, and function of scripture in these traditions are to a certain extent shaped by these conceptions, and thus such a study is essential to understanding the role of Veda and Torah as the paradigmatic symbols of their respective traditions.

Bernard Jackson's essay examines the extent to which legal regulations, customs, and royal ordinances in *halakhah* and *dharmaśāstra* are binding on members of their respective societies. Jackson suggests that both Jewish and Hindu law evidence a great sensitivity to the interplay of local custom and authoritative law. He evaluates this interplay by gauging when a law on the books was practiced and when it fell out of use and why. He finds that it is related, in both Jewish and Hindu legal texts, to whether a custom abrogates or suspends a religious duty and whether the law is able to unify a multiplicity of local customs. Given that *dharma* as defined in Hindu law codes is not necessarily legally binding, a central question must be asked regarding the comparison of Hindu and Jewish law: How does the ideal conform to or diverge from the actual in the Hindu and Jewish cases? Jackson observes that in both cases the writing down of a collection of norms did not necessarily mean that all or even most norms were even intended to be enforced; even the laws connected with royal authority were not necessarily statutory. Jackson thus concludes that authority should not necessarily be equated with legal enforcement in the ancient world.

The essays on union and unity in the Tantric and kabbalistic traditions represent a collaborative effort by Elizabeth Chalier-Visuvalingam and Charles Mopsik. While focusing exclusively on their own areas of expertise—the Tantric and kabbalistic traditions, respectively—they were asked nevertheless to keep in mind the comparative problematics of their project.

Chalier-Visuvalingam's study of union and unity in Tantric Hinduism examines the transformation of the concept of union from the absolute transcendent Other, beyond individuality and plurality, to its immanent contextualization in Tantric practices of sexual unity. The various processes of ascent and descent along the axis of *chakras* in the subtle physiology are examined in several highly charged contexts, with emphasis on the use of the body to reach an effective unification with the absolute. The ritualized sexual union of *kulayāga* is interpreted as an internalization of the Vedic fire-sacrifice.

Mopsik examines the Jewish aspiration for union within the kabbalistic mode. The seeker of unity with God engages himself in acts that parallel the sefirotic structure of the divine pleroma. The ascents and descents along the sefirotic ladder are accomplished by particular mental and physical acts of unification. Mopsik uses kabbalistic texts to show how the image of male-female coupling facilitates the process of connecting the seeker with a higher unity. This higher unity comes through a unification with the manifest emanations of the sefirotic realm rather than through a transcendence of the pluralistic phenomenal world. In this respect, the Tantric and kabbalistic models share a common interest in using the phenomenal world, structured by the hierarchical but dynamic ladders of *cakras* and *sefirot,* respectively, to ascend and descend into and out of unity. In both traditions this experience of unity is depicted as transforming both the individual and the world, raising them eventually to the highest possible level of union.

The volume concludes with Margaret Chatterjee's exploration of two of this century's most creative mystical teachers in India and Israel: Sri Aurobindo Ghose and Abraham Isaac Kook. Had Aurobindo and Kook encountered each other they would have had much in common to talk about: the mystical worlds they inhabited, their concepts of an evolving spirituality, their use of traditional religious discourse, and their simultaneous and energetic entrance into the course of modern history. Chatterjee's exploration of the shared spiritual landscapes of Aurobindo and Kook represents in some ways a culmination of all the separate strands contained in this volume. We are given a glimpse of what the future might look like if such great souls encountered each other at home, in Jerusalem and Benares.

2

The Love and Hate of Hinduism in the Work of Jewish Scholars

Wendy Doniger

Many great Jewish scholars of religion have been motivated not by love of religion but by hatred of religion, or at least by anger directed against religion, or fear or loathing of religion. Freud and Marx are the most outstanding examples of brilliant Jewish haters of religion but there are others. The strange *Hass-Lieb* relationship that has bound many important Jewish Indologists to their subject matter has long been apparent to scholars working in the field. Yet Jews have also been numbered among the great scholars who are sympathetic to religion: Emil Durkheim, Marcel Mauss, Lévy-Bruhl, Boaz, Sapir, Radin, and Claude Lévi-Strauss. Within the narrower field of Indology, one would think of Sylvain Lévi,[1] Moriz Winternitz, and, in our generation, Milton Singer, Charles Malamoud, and David Shulman. I would locate myself within this latter tradition, of Jews who love rather than those who hate religion in general and Hinduism in particular, and I would trace my lineage through the paternal line: my mother was a brilliant and passionate atheist and Marxist and my father a publisher of journals for the protestant clergy.

There are so many things that could account for both the hate and the love of Jews toward Hinduism. Both might be connected in some way to the same phenomenon: the law of physics that like repels like.

For Judaism and Hinduism are alike in all sorts of striking ways, in their depiction of the cunning malevolence of God (be it the god of Job or Shiva), in their tendency toward orthopraxy rather than orthodoxy (the emphasis on correct praxis allowing for greater doctrinal freedom)—every Jewish Indologist would doubtless have his or her own list. But another phenomenon would account better, I think, for the predominance of love over hate in the annals of Jewish Indology, and that is the traditional Jewish relationship with other religions.

There are two basic sets of question that one could ask about these Jewish Indologists. First, one could ask what it is that Jewish scholars have brought *to* the study of India, what Jewish "baggage" they have dragged through their Sanskrit texts, or what Jewish ways of thinking have proved fertile (or, indeed, barren) in foreign soil. But one could also look at the other side of the transaction, and ask what it is that Jewish scholars have gotten *from* India, what they have sought, and what they have found, in Hinduism. In this article I have chosen to set aside the first set of questions and to concentrate instead on the second, and, indeed, on one small aspect of that second question. I want to ask why Jews have taken Hinduism seriously as a source of personal meaning.[2]

Jews have always lived among Others—have always *been* the Others wherever they lived. The tendency to make use of other people's myths has long been a habit of the Jews, wandering or dispersed as they are. But this talent (or weakness, if you will) of a particular sort of Jew must be understood in the context of Judaism as a whole. The overwhelming majority of Jews are of a very different sort. They live and die in the religion of their birth and find it entirely sufficient unto their religious needs. I am not talking about religious conversion, let alone the anti-Semitic proselytizing of such groups as the Jews for Jesus. (It is indeed interesting to note the fascination that Indian gurus seem to have for American Jews, but this is another story.[3]) I have in mind, rather, the ways in which Jews have been forced, for their very survival, to *learn* other peoples' religions, and some cases to learn *from* them as well.

This is all the more true of Jewish scholars. On some deep level, I think, all truly creative scholarship in the humanities is autobiographical, but it is particularly true that people who traffic in foreign myths are caught up in them, *volens nolens.* The great Indologist Heinrich Zimmer retold a well-known Hasidic tale told by Martin Buber, a version of the story of the Jew among Others.

It is a brief story, told of the Rabbi Eisik, son of Rabbi Jekel, who lived in the ghetto of Cracow, the capital of Poland. He had remained unbroken in his faith, through years of affliction, and was a pious servant of the Lord his God.

One night, as this pious and faithful Rabbi Eisik slept, he had a dream; the dream enjoined him to proceed, afar, to the Bohemian capital, Prague, where he should discover a hidden treasure, buried beneath the principal bridge leading to the castle of the Bohemian kings. The Rabbi was surprised, and put off his going. But the dream recurred twice again. After the third call, he bravely girded his loins and set forth on the quest.

Arriving at the city of his destiny, Rabbi Eisik discovered sentries at the bridge, and these guarded it day and night; so that he did not venture to dig. He only returned every morning and loitered around until dusk, looking at the bridge, watching the sentries, studying unostentatiously the masonry and the soil. At length, the captain of the guards, struck by the old man's persistence, approached, and gently inquired whether he had lost something or perhaps was waiting for someone to arrive. Rabbi Eisik recounted, simply and confidently, the dream that he had had, and the officer stood back and laughed.

"Really, you poor fellow!" the captain said: "Have you worn your shoes out wandering all this way only because of a dream? What sensible person would trust a dream? Why look, if I had been one to go trusting dreams, I should this very minute be doing just the opposite. I should have made such a pilgrimage as this silly one of yours, only in the opposite direction, but no doubt with the same result. Let me tell you my dream."

He was a sympathetic officer, for all of his fierce mustache, and the Rabbi felt his heart warm to him. "I dreamt of a voice," said the Bohemian, Christian officer of the guard, "and it spoke to me of Cracow, commanding me to go thither and to search there for a great treasure in the house of a Jewish rabbi whose name would be Eisik son of Jekel. The treasure was to have been discovered buried in the dirty corner behind the stove. Eisik son of Jekel!" the captain laughed again, with brilliant eyes. "Fancy going to Cracow and pulling down the walls of every house in the ghetto, where half of the men are called

> Eisik and the other half Jekel! Eisik son of Jekel, indeed!" And he laughed, and he laughed again at the wonderful joke.
>
> The unostentatious Rabbi listened eagerly, and then, having bowed deeply and thanked his stranger-friend, he hurried straightway back to his distant home, dug in the neglected corner of his house and discovered the treasure which put an end to all his misery. With a portion of the money, he erected a prayer house that bears his name to this day.[4]

Both of the people in the story resist the idea that they must go abroad to find their treasures. The Captain laughs, not realizing that he is actually addressing "Eisik son of Jekel" when he repeats that phrase, three times, in mockery. The Rabbi experiences "surprise" when he has his dream—again, three times—but he does not experience (or, at least, reveal) any surprise at the Captain's words. Instead, he hastens to dig in the neglected dirt of his own home, to excavate his own tradition more deeply. As Zimmer comments on this myth, "Now the real treasure . . . is never far away; it lies buried in the innermost recess of our own home; that is to say, our own being . . . but there is the odd and persistent fact . . . that the one who reveals to us the meaning of our cryptic inner message must be a stranger, of another creed and a foreign race."

The moral of the story of the Rabbi from Cracow according to Rabbi Simha Bunam of Pzhysha (the original author of the story, according to Buber) is somewhat different from the moral drawn by Zimmer: "There is something you cannot find anywhere in the world, not even at the zaddik's, and there is, nevertheless, a place where you can find it."

I must apologize for using Heinrich Zimmer's version of this story here, when I have cited it before, in several other contexts, beginning in my very first book, about Shiva. Apparently it is for me, as the dream of the Christian on the bridge was for the Rabbi, a central source of truth to which I cannot help returning; or, in other words, it is one of my myths. More than that, it is, like the Rabbi's treasure, a native treasure that I found abroad: I had to read a book about India, by Zimmer (a Lutheran), to find that parable from my own Jewish tradition. And it played the same role for Zimmer himself, as he notes:[5] "When I first read this tale, some ten years ago, I realized that I had been living and acting along its lines for over a decade—ever since that moment when the millenary, spiritual treasure of Hindu myth and symbol had begun to reveal itself to me through my academic studies of Indian sacred diagrams and Mandalas."

That this is an enduring myth in real life, as well as in satirical literature, was demonstrated to me by an article in the *New York Times* (Sunday, 8 September 1985), stating that the Jews of Cracow, reduced by the Nazi Holocaust to a tiny community of old people, had sent to America to have a young boy come to Cracow to mark his bar mitzvah, the first bar mitzvah there in twenty years. The return of this young Jewish boy, whose great-great-grandparents had been killed near Cracow, in Auschwitz, is yet another variant of the myth, built out of the pieces of real life: the native treasure of Cracow had to be imported back from America.

Charles Long has characterized "creative mythology" (*contra* Joseph Campbell) as a genre that results when "the individual has had an experience of his own—of order, horror, beauty, or even exhilaration—which he seeks to communicate through signs."[6] The signs that one uses are derived from the myths that one already knows, and they may not necessarily belong to one's own culture. When J. Robert Oppenheimer witnessed the explosion of the first atomic bomb, he realized that he was part of the myth of doomsday, but not his own Jewish doomsday. (The remarks of other scientists present on that occasion, such as General Farrell, also tended to employ mythical and theological eschatological language, but from the Western traditions.) Oppenheimer, who liked to think that he knew some Sanskrit, said that as he watched the bomb go off he recalled the verse in the *Bhagavad Gita* when Krishna reveals himself as the supreme lord, blazing like a thousand suns. Later, however, when he saw the sinister clouds gathering in the distance, he recalled another verse, in which Krishna reveals that he is death, the devourer of men.[7] Perhaps Oppenheimer's inability to face directly his own shock and guilt, the full realization and acknowledgment of what he had helped to create, led him to distance the experience by viewing it in terms of someone else's myth of doomsday. The other side of the coin of this phenomenon was demonstrated by those contemporary American critics who faulted Peter Brook's recreation of the *Mahabharata* for projecting into the Indian text references to our own impending nuclear holocaust.[8] In fact, every word of the Peter Brook script was taken from the Sanskrit text, which tells of two great warring factions each of which possesses terrible weapons capable of destroying the world. It was the critics who projected our situation onto the Indian story, unconsciously demonstrating precisely the power that great myths have: to depict a great human story in which we are compelled to see ourselves, even across the barriers of cultures. Many of the dark truths of hate, as well as the sunnier truths of love, come to us from other peoples' myths.

This has certainly been true for me. In 1971, when I was struggling to come to terms with the death of my father (my first major experience of inexplicable and unjust evil), I failed to draw any comfort from Jewish or Christian approaches to the problem, not through any inherent inadequacy in them but simply because they were not *my* myth; I had never had them. I had grown up with a certain number of Jewish rituals, and with a great number of Jewish social attitudes, but with no myths (unless, of course, one were to count as myths Jewish jokes, which I had in abundance).

Perhaps I was unable to live the Jewish myths when I needed them because I had already unconsciously replaced them with the Hindu myths in which I had been steeped from the age of twelve, when my mother gave me a copy of E. M. Forster's *A Passage to India*. Perhaps I simply had an innate affinity for the Hindu myths, an immediate individual response. In any case, I found that I could in fact make some sense of my father's death in terms of the Hindu mythology of death and evil—the subject of the book that I was working on at the time, and had begun some years before the onset of my father's illness.[9] In a certain sense, I had been experiencing the same events that were narrated in the myth that I had been reading and writing about, though at first I did not realize that this was the myth that I was in, perhaps because I did not expect someone else's myth to be my myth.

But there was another good reason why I could not use Jewish myths to sustain me then, why, indeed, it would perhaps have been inappropriate to use them to understand my father's death: They had ceased to be his myths, too. Both of my parents were relentlessly assimilated, secularized, and enlightened Jewish refugees, he from Poland (a small town not far from Cracow) and she from Vienna (she lived on the street where Sigmund Freud had lived). My father, whose father had been a Talmudic scholar, knew much of Frazer's *The Golden Bough* by heart and taught it to me. He had learned it at New York University, where he had worked his way through school as a stringer for the *New York Times*, going around to all the major churches in Manhattan every Sunday and summarizing the sermons; he was paid by the inch. Eventually it dawned on him that it might be profitable to serve as a kind of matchmaker between those ministers who yearned to see their sermons in print and those ministers who were eager to have at their disposal every week the sermons of the first sort of ministers. Thus he founded in the late 1930s, and published throughout his life two magazines for the Protestant clergy, *Pulpit Digest* and *Pastoral Psychology*. And from time to time, when he was short of copy, he wrote, under various pseudonyms, sermons that were preached all over America by Protestant clergymen who little dreamed that their homilies had been composed by an East European Jew. He had already crossed over that bridge in Cracow long ago, and in crossing it myself I was, ironically, following traditionally in his footsteps, doing a very Jewish thing.

As a Jew teaching in a predominantly Christian divinity school, I continued to wrestle with my own manifestation of the archetypal problem of the Jew among others, and one day I had a dream about it. I dreamed that I was at a meal in the Commons Room of the Divinity School at the University of Chicago, sitting at one of the long tables as I have so often done at formal and informal dinners, with friends on either side and across from me. And suddenly I looked up and realized that I was inside the Leonardo da Vinci painting of the Last Supper, that Jesus and the disciples had come forward in time to join us now at the table in Chicago. As I realized this, the person sitting beside me said to me, "But Wendy, what is *your* religion?" and I replied, "My myths are Hindu, but my rituals are Christian."

This dream puzzled me when I awoke; why did I not say, "My rituals are Jewish?" For indeed, although, as I noted earlier, I have few Jewish myths, my sense of community is primarily Jewish, and I usually participate, albeit somewhat irregularly, in the Passover ritual. Instead, I had borrowed from Christianity to make the collage or bricolage of my dream image. Through this indirect path, my dream also incorporated the ceremony of the sharing of the leftovers (or *prasāda*) of the Hindu gods, the food distributed to the worshippers after the god has tasted them in the temple. This *prasāda* is also said to incorporate the substance of the god, so that the worshipper is, as in the Christian Eucharist, eating God.[10] (There is also a Hasidic tradition of gathering for the Third Meal on the Sabbath, when the Rebbe feeds his disciples from the leavings of his plate, the *sharayim.*) For the myth of the communal meal served me simultaneously as a Jewish Seder, a Christian Eucharist, a Hindu *prasāda,* and a University of Chicago dinner. My dream incorporated my four rituals (three religious and a transcendent fourth): Jewish, Christian, Hindu, and academic. The fourth, the academic, provided a kind of metareligion that transcended religions, a framework that made possible the bricolage of the other three. Of course, this was only a *dream* of a ritual, a story that I told myself about a ritual—a myth. I had not converted to a new ritual, merely dreamed that my usual rituals had taken on a new mythic dimension. But the Christian (particularly the Catholic) and Hindu myths had come to play a very important role in my religious thinking, to answer needs that were not answered by the ritual community into which I had been born, with implications that I had not yet not come to terms with until I had that dream. Like the Rabbi from Cracow, I needed to listen to the dream of a foreign religion—of several foreign religions—to come to a more complex understanding of my own mythology as a Jew and as a scholar of Hinduism.

PART ONE

Historical Encounters

3

Lexical Borrowings from Indian Languages as Carriers of Ideas and Technical Concepts

Chaim Rabin

India is a long way from Palestine and culturally very different, and therefore, especially for early periods, contacts are not sufficiently probable to assume, without further evidence, that mere similarity of words for more or less similar concepts is due to linguistic borrowing. Moreover, there were several different populations in India, who spoke different languages and had settled in that subcontinent at very different times.

A number of renowned linguists in the present century assumed the existence in prehistory of an "Indo-Mediterranean" culture as the source of certain connections in Indian and Mediterranean vocabulary. Even if we accept this idea, there is still the question whether the linguistic influence went westwards from India or eastwards from the Mediterranean. A further problem is: Which of the known Indian populations lived in India at that early period?

Artifacts of the pre-1000 B.C.E. Harappa and Mohenjo-Daro culture in the northwest of the historic Indian sub-continent have been discovered in Mesopotamia, possibly pointing to direct trade relations. A Buddhist story[1] tells us of Indian merchants visiting "Bāveru," that is,

Babylonia, and selling the locals a peacock, which was exhibited there for show. This is matched by a Mesopotamian piece of early literature about a monkey exhibited to the public.[2] These stories may go back to the period mentioned. However, insofar as the language of inscriptions on objects from that period has not been unanimously deciphered, we cannot know whether words were also borrowed.

The first penetration of words from an Indian language, Sanskrit, appears to have no connection with India. We find around the end of the second millennium B.C.E. in the Near East, including Palestine of the Tell-Amarna letters, names that seem to be Sanskrit, and are borne by soldiers connected with the use of horse-drawn light chariots—such as were brought by the Sanskrit-speaking Aryans to India—some of whom appear in the Tell-Amarna letters as rulers of Palestinian cities.[3] We find these warriors under the name of *maryannu,*[4] a Hurrian derivation[5] from Sanskrit *marya-* "young man," in Akkadian, Ugaritic, and Egyptian. It is widely accepted among scholars that the Aryans,[6] that is, the Persians and Indo-European Indians, lived in Southern Russia before they wandered eastwards to their present habitats, and the Maryannu may have broken away and crossed the Caucasus into Mesopotamia.

Out of a number of possible Indo-Aryan loanwords found in the Hebrew Bible,[7] we shall mention here only the few that imply concepts new to Semitic thought. Some are connected with horses and chariots. Thus the rare *daharot* (Judges 5.22) and the participle *doher* (Nahum 3.2), probably "to trot," may be a loan from the (late attested) Sanskrit *dor-*.[8] That *resen* "bridle" (also Aramaic, Arabic) is borrowed from Sanskrit *raśanā, raśmi* "rope, bridle," was discovered in 1866.[9]

As the Maryannu and their chariots are closely connected with horses (which in Vedic India were also offered as sacrifices), it was but natural that a number of scholars tried to derive the Semitic word for "horse": Hebrew *sūs,* Aramaic *sūsyā,* Akkadian *sisū,* attested already in the fourteenth-century Amarna tablets in the plural *zūzima* (letter no. 263, actually only *zu-u-* is preserved) as a Canaanite gloss to Akkadian *sisē,* from the Sanskrit word for "horse," *aśva,* cognate with Latin *equus,* in spite of the lack of similarity in sound. About 1911 Schrader suggested that the Semitic word was borrowed from *sa aśvas* "this is a horse." It is, however, more probably that *sūs,* with the long vowel at the end in Akkadian and Aramaic, is an original Semitic word from the root SWSW, "to go about," from which is derived Ethiopic *ĕnsĕsā* "animal, quadrupede, horse." This root also exists in the early stages of Egyptian as *š'ś* "to walk, to wander." The connection was first suggested by Albright in 1917, and again by Marcel Cohen and J. Nougayrol in 1948. N. H. Torczyner (Tur-Sinai) pointed out the existence of the verb *sūs* in Zechariah 14.20 *(mĕṣillath ha-sūs),* which he translates "shady garden for riding practice." In view of the abovementioned Egyptian verb *š'ś,* it seems probable that the late (eighteenth dynasty) Egyptian word for "horse," *smsm, ssmt, sst* was borrowed from Semitic. According to Erman-Grapow (*Deutsch-Aegyptisches Wörterverzeichnis,* vol. 6, 1950, p. 117b), all the words for "horse" in Egyptian are eighteenth dynasty and later, a fact which contrasts curiously with the warning in Deuteronomy 17.16, not to import horses from Egypt. The root SWS is represented in Akkadian *šušānu, šušannu,* "servant," "servant looking after horses or cattle," and Syriac *šaušāyā* "muleteer, caravan attendant," and other languages. Similarly Arabic, which does not have *sūs* "horse," has in the dialects of Syria and Lebanon *sās* "to look after horses," with the verbal noun *syēse,* also *sāwas, sāyas,* "to transport people."

Two terms of social importance are almost certainly of Sanskrit origin, and throw light upon the relations of the Maryannu with the local population. Maryannu names play an important role in the ruling class of Ugarit[10] and among the rulers of localities in Palestine as seen in the Tell-Amarna letters. Sisera, a typical Maryannu, bears a Sanskrit name, meaning "Evening coolness." In Sanskrit *ādṛta,* pronounced *ādrita,* means "honoured," and may well have been the title the Maryannu gave to themselves. This would provide an explanation to the line, "in a goblet of *addīrīm* she offered buttermilk" (Jud. 5.25): the wife of the Cainite metalworker offered the humble drink in a goblet such as is used by the honoured Maryannu—the addiction of the early Indo-Europeans to alcohol is well documented. In later biblical Hebrew the same term was used to mean the upper class among shepherds.

Another social marker is the verb *miggēn* "to give, to bestow" in Genesis 14.20, Hosea 11.8, and Proverbs 4.9, and probably also Genesis 15.1. The same root appears in Aramaic *maggān* "gratuitous," that is, a gift without expection of anything in return. W. von Soden has shown[11] that this is Sanskrit *magha* "gift," in the nominative and accusative *magham.* In the form *makanni* it occurs several times in a letter of the Hurrian king of Mitanni, found among the Tell-Amarna documents; *-nni* is a Hurrian noun-suffix. Through Hurrian, or directly from the Aryan language, the word was borrowed into Akkadian, both as "gift" and adverbially as "gratis." As a verb, in parallelism to *θṭy* "give," it occurs in Ugaritic epics, corresponding to the Hebrew *miggēn.* Probably from Aramaic, the word came into Arabic as *majjānan,* with an added adverbial ending. In a society where it was customary to respond to presents with presents, the manner of the *addīrīm* warriors, who did not respond, caused their word for this habit to be taken over.

Of course, this meeting with Aryans was only indirectly a contact with Indian civilization. Whether the Maryannu arrived as a split-off during the Aryan migration to India, or came on their own initiative from the European home of the Aryans, they represent a culture not yet touched by autochthonous Indian ideas and customs; on the contrary, such people were later in India separated as a warrior caste, as opposed to the more spiritual Brahmans.

Thus the first meeting of the ancient Israelites with the Indo-Aryans was, from a cultural point of view, rather negative, and even if the ten or so words for horse-colors, military equipment, items of clothing, and the word *tophet, tophteh,* "hell," are counted as coming from the early period, we can hardly count them as a cultural influence, and even less as an influence from India.[12]

Contact between ancient Israel and the Indian subcontinent is, in the view of the present author, recorded for the reign of King Solomon, tenth century B.C.E., in I Kings 10.22 (cf. II Chron. 9.21): "For the king had Tarshish ships in the sea together with the ships of Hiram; once every three years the Tarshish ships arrived, carrying gold and silver, elephant tusks, monkeys, and peacocks."

The most widely accepted view in Old Testament studies is that Tarshish was a city somewhere in the Mediterranean in a region where gold and silver were found. Few searched for a place where ivory, monkeys, and peacocks were available, or which only could be reached at certain times of the year. Both peculiarities point to India, where all those three animals existed, and where because of the necessity of sailing with the monsoon winds, one could only sail in one direction at a time, and had to wait for months before returning—a condition which necessitated a longish stay in India and enabled the sailors and traders to get to know the culture and art of the area where they had landed.

This is vividly described in a Tamil epic of the third century C.E.:[13] "in different places of Puhār the onlooker's attention was arrested by the sight of the abodes of Yavanas (i.e., Greeks and Romans), whose prosperity was never on the wane. Near the harbour seamen from far-off lands appeared at home." Tamil is a Dravidian language as opposed to Indo-European Sanskrit. The Indian word from which "Tarshish" is borrowed, is itself a hybrid of *toya-* "water," connected with Dravidian verbs meaning "to get wet," and the noun *rāši-*, "a heap," of uncertain origin.[14]

I Kings 10.22 contains three other words of presumably Indian origin: *šenhabbīm, qōphīm,* and *tukkiyīm, Šenhabbīm,* "ivory," means literally, "teeth of *habb-īm*"; the latter word no doubt means "elephants," and corresponds to Early Egyptian *'bw* "elephant," Middle Egyptian "ivory," Coptic *ebū,* Latin *ebur* ("ivory"), Greek *el-ephās,* and Sanskrit *ibha-* "elephant."[15] As this word-group has no further Indian cognates,[16] it may have been brought by the Aryans from Europe, where ivory would have been supplied by Egyptians.

Qōphīm, "monkeys," is found in Aramaic, Syriac, Mandaic as *qop-,* in Akkadian as *uqupu, ugubi, agubi, pagū* (the latter ones perhaps originally Sumerian), Egyptian *gf, gyf,* later *gwf,* late Egyptian *g'f,* all Egyptian forms said to mean "small monkey," a long-tailed variety brought from abroad; Sumerian *ugu-bi,* Greek *kēpos, kēbos,* in Germanic and Celtic forms without the initial k/g; Sanskrit *kapi-* (but in the Ṛg-Veda the monkey is only mentioned once, and under the name *harito mṛgaḥ* "the yellow animal"), may ultimately come from Dravidian (cf. Parji *kovva* "red-faced monkey," Gondi *kowwē* "red monkey").

The most interesting of the three is *tukkiyīm.* This word has been identified with different animals, but today most scholars accept "peacock," a translation found first in the Aramaic Targum and in the Vulgate and the Syro-Hexapla. This connects the word in the Hebrew text with Tamil *tōkai* "anything that hangs down, especially a peacock's tail," which seems also to have meant "a peacock."[17] Import of peacocks to the Middle East is mentioned in an early Buddhist text, the *Bāveru* ("Babylonia") *Jātaka.*[18] It is hardly imaginable that peacocks would be transported such distances overland, and their mention in connection with Solomon's trade expeditions proves that their destination was Dravidian-speaking Southern India. The long stops enforced by the monsoons in that land of poetry and music would have familiarized the merchants from Judaea with a poetic genre typical of Tamil literature in which maidens complained to their girl-friends or maidservants that their beloved young men were absent for long periods in order to gain fame or riches. These songs are also marked by frequent reference to plants and landscapes, and dreamed-up excursions to beautiful nature spots where the couple are unobserved.[19]

These themes play a prominent role in the "Song of Songs" included in the Bible. The girl complains of the long absences of her lover, in far-away and fearful places. These are not named, but described (2.17) as "cleft mountains," that is, paths passing between high crags, but in 8.14 as "mountains of incense," 4.6 "mountain of myrrh and hill of boswellia." The wares the lover's caravan carries are enumerated in 3.6: "who is that coming up from the desert, like pillars of smoke, perfumed with myrrh and incense and all the powders of the perfume merchant?" In other words, the lover is not a simple shepherd, but a merchant who brings his loads of perfumes from distant countries to Jerusalem from the east, via the Arabian desert.

Moreover, the description of love for the gods in terms of carnal love is a theme of Indian poetry, and however the Song of Songs was understood by later Jewish interpreters and modern biblical scholars, the very fact that it was included in the canon and treated as holy, may be taken to imply that its possible religious implications were accepted by at least some scholars in early post-biblical Judaism, though the absence of documents regarding views held in the Second Temple period prevents us from knowing what their views may have been.[20]

Trade connections between India and Palestine and Mediterranean Jewish communities did not cease, though we do not know whether Jewish traders visited India, or bought Indian goods from middlemen. Whatever the process, Indian names of wares passed into Hebrew and Aramaic. An outstanding example is the name of the fruit used in the ceremony of Sukkot, which in Leviticus 23.40 is called *pĕri 0 ēṣ hadar,* "fruit of a tree of splendor," and in the Mishna and afterward *ethrog.* That word comes from Tamil *mātulankam* or *mātulai,* meaning both "pomegranate" and "lemon"; already when it passed into Persian, the word lost the first syllable and became *turunğ,* in Mandaic *trungā,* and in Jewish Babylonian Aramaic *ethrogā.* According to Babylonian Talmud Kiddushin (fol. 70a), the Jews in Babylonia said *ethroga* (with the Aramaic definite article *-a*), the rabbis used the Hebrew form *ethrog,* and haughty characters said *ethrunga.* Thus a fruit with a South Indian name, and probably originated in India, came to play the role of a fruit named quite differently in the Bible. It is equally remarkable that no similar name appears in Sanskrit, thus confirming that the fruit was at the time shipped from Southern India only.

The same is true of rice: The Sanskrit name is *vrīhi,* which was taken over by Persian as *birinğ.* Another reproduction of Sanskrit *vṛ* in some Aryan dialect must have caused the late Akkadian word for rice to be *kurangu.* In the earliest form of Persian, the language of the Avesta, there is still a *v,* namely *verenğa,* in Middle-Persian or Pehlevi, written without vowels, *blnč.* We do not know whether the *-ang* represents some Indian form or was added in Persian. On the other side, east of India and across the sea, there are forms closer to *vrīhi,* such as

Javanese *pari,* Malay *bĕras.* A third way of reproducing the Sanskrit consonant *v* we find in Mishnaic Hebrew *orez,* Greek *oryza.* There appears to be no connection between the Sanskrit word and Tamil *ari,* "rice," *ariči,* "peeled rice," but it is possible that forms like *ruz, ruzz, rizz,* and others in the Arab countries go back to Tamil, especially as those countries received their rice by sea.

I would not dare to judge whether Sanskrit *vrīhi,* classified by Mayrhofer[21] as a *Kulturwort,* a loanword of unknown origin, can be connected with Tamil *vari,* meaning unpeeled rice. In Kurukh (Oraon), in northeastern India, the corresponding word is *maṇḍi,*[22] a form strikingly similar to *minnīt,* Ezekiel 27.17,[23] where Judah and the Land of Israel (the northern kingdom) are said to be suppliers of "wheat-grains of *minnīth* and *pannāgh*" to the Tyrian merchants. These goods were thus transported through Arabia to Judah, after being unloaded at ports along the Red Sea. The transport of rice on ships along the Red Sea is indicated in several passages of the Periplus Maris Erythraei.

In the Arabian peninsula and in Iraq the same word is used with transposition of its consonants: in Iraq *timman,*[24] in the peninsula *temn, temen.* In Khuzistan, at the southwest corner of Iran, *tamūna* and *tūmana,* both meaning "a grain of rice," were used as a weight unit.

If indeed *minnīth* does mean "rice" and Judaea was in the eighth century B.C.E. an entrepôt for this Indian produce, it would explain why later on, in the first century of Islam, the seventh century C.E., we hear about rice as a specifically Jewish article of food. One story accuses the Jews of having poisoned one of the first caliphs with rice, another tells how the Muslim conquerors were given raw rice by the Jews of Iraq, and after eating it uncooked, had stomach trouble. Whether these tales are true or not, the early acquaintance of Jews with rice might explain why Oriental Jews (Sephardim) eat rice during the days of Passover, while the Ashkenazi Jews do not.

This may well be the only provable and enduring connection with India. In the Middle Ages some Arabic moral stories were translated into Hebrew which were later found to have originated in India, but this was not known to their medieval Jewish readers. There are three groups of Jews who settled in India at different times: the "white Jews" of Cochin, on the Southwest coast of the Indian subcontinent, who are said to have settled there nearly 2,000 years ago, in an area which in those times was still part of the same country as that of the Tamils; the "Bene Israel" of the Marathi-speaking area east of Bombay; and the comparatively recent Jewish immigrants from Iraq. The latter group, who have a good Jewish education, played the most notable role. But none of these three groups have served as links between Indian thought or art and Jews outside India, or introduced any elements of Jewish thought into their Indian surroundings.

As against this, Indian culture attracted in the last two centuries a large number of outstanding Jewish scholars in Europe and America, some of whom also investigated the possibilities of Indian ideas having passed into Judaism. As Western knowledge of Indian literature of the formative period increases, such influences may be discovered, especially if Indian scholarly circles were to become interested in the same subject.

4

Abraham and the Upanishads

David Flusser

Abraham, "the father of a multitude of nations" (Gen. 17.4), is seen by the three monotheistic religions, Judaism, Christianity, and Islam, as their founder. This is not only because of the universalistic elements included in the faith of the Patriarch, but also because Abraham was the first to recognize God. Unfortunately, the Hebrew Bible itself does not indicate how Abraham discovered God and became the hero of the monotheistic faith. The recognition of the Creator by Abraham, the first believer, is depicted in the following parable told by R. Isaac (second half of the third century C.E.):

> This may be compared to a man who was travelling from place to place when he saw a building lighted. "Is it possible that the building lacks a person to look after it?" he wondered. The owner of the castle looked out and said to him, "I am the owner of the building." Similarly, because Abraham our father said, "Is it conceivable that the world is without a guide?" the Holy One, blessed be He, looked out and said to him, "I am the Guide, the Sovereign of the Universe."[1]

However, today another legend dealing with the same subject is much more famous.

> When the sun sank, and the stars came forth, he [Abraham] said, "These are the gods!" But the dawn came, and the stars

> could be seen no longer, and then he said, "I will not pay worship to these, for they are no gods." Thereupon the sun came forth, and he spoke, "This is my god, him will I extol." But again the sun set, and he said, "He is no god," and beholding the moon, he called her his god to whom he would pay Divine homage. Then the moon was obscured, and he cried out: "This, too, is no god! There is One who sets them all in motion."[2]

There is a basic difference between this legend and Rabbi Isaac's parable. According to the parable, Abraham took the first experimental step and then God looked out and told him that He was the governor of the world. The legend, on the other hand, describes how Abraham came to the conclusion, by means of a process of gradual deduction, that the true and only God is the "One who sets them all in motion."[3] The goal of Abraham's search had already been reached before he received the revelation of the One personal God. It is possible to assume that Rabbi Isaac was inspired by the legend, but this assumption cannot be based upon Rabbi Isaac's parable itself, because it is autonomous.

One significant fact should be better known: while our Jewish legend about Abraham evidently already existed in the second century B.C.E., it was largely ignored by the mainstream of rabbinic Judaism, and only much later did it become relevant for the explanation of monotheism. The legend appears neither in the Talmud nor in the classical collections of midrashim, with the one exception of Genesis Rabbah 33.11, where it appears in a secondary formulation.[4] Evidently, it did not form an authentic part of the original midrash but was added by the final redactor.[5] As we have already stated, the story appears only in later narrative rabbinic literature.[6]

However, as we have asserted, our legend already existed in the second century B.C.E. It is alluded to in the Book of Jubilees 11.16–18, and Josephus as well was evidently acquainted with the legend (*Ant.* I, 155–56). Finally, the legend appears in the Apocalypse of Abraham (chapter 7),[7] from the end of the first or the beginning of the second century C.E. Thus, our story is an outstanding example of a tendency in the history of Jewish literature, in which eminent narrative themes present in Jewish pseudepigraphic and Hellenistic literature are sometimes more or less absent in classical rabbinic sources, and then reappear in later narrative Jewish literature and in the Aramaic translations of the Bible. Often, it is precisely those stories which were incorporated into Christian and Muslim works which have also become popular among the Jews today. In fact, this particular legend about Abraham occurs in the Koran as well (3 Sura: 74–79).

According to the mainstream of rabbinic tradition, God revealed himself to Abraham only after the patriarch had discovered Him. As has already been mentioned,[8] according to Rabbi Isaac's parable, Abraham himself came to the conclusion that a world without a governor is unthinkable. Rabbi Simeon ben Yohai (second century C.E.) did not believe that Abraham had learned from his father or any other teacher, but that Abraham's kidneys became the fount of his knowledge—the kidney being the seat of understanding. Rabbi Levi (third century C.E.) stated simply that Abraham learned from himself.[9] While we see that the rabbinic sages were aware of the problem, the mainstream of rabbinic tradition did not refer to the gradual discovery of God by Abraham.

There is a parallel to our story in the apocryphal book of Ezra (I Esdras 3.1–4.63). The story centers around a contest among the three bodyguards of Darius. Each tried to correctly answer the question: What is the most powerful force in the world? The first youth claimed that wine is the most potent, while the second pointed to the power of the king. The third one observed that, although the king is great and wine is powerful, it is woman who dominates them all. He nonetheless asserted that truth is greater and incomparably stronger than all these things. It has already been rightly suggested that they story of the competition in I Esdras is Persian.[10] The similarity between this legend and that about Abraham raises the possibility that Abraham's quest for God had a Persian source. But can we proceed further?

There is an amusing Indian short story called "The Mouse Maiden,"[11] found in a work called *Panchatantra,* in which an Indian sage saved a young mouse and changed it into a maiden. When the maiden reached the appropriate age, the sage wished to find her a powerful husband who would be worthy of her. He summoned the venerable sun and said, "You are powerful; marry this my daughter!" But the sun replied to him, "Reverend sir, the clouds are more powerful than I, they cover me so that I become invisible." Then the sage said to a cloud, "Take my daughter!" But he answered, "The wind is stronger even than I am. It blows me hither and thither in all directions." Then he summoned the wind, but the wind replied to him, "Reverend sir, the mountains are more powerful than I, since I cannot move them so much as a finger's breadth." But when the sage summoned a mountain, he was told, "The mice are stronger than we, they make us full of countless holes on all sides." Thus, the sage turned the girl back into a mouse and found a mouse to take her as his wife.

The German translator of *Panchantantra,* T. Benfey, already made the connection between this Indian short story and our legend about Abraham.[12] Indeed, the similarity between the Indian tale and the Jewish legend is striking. Even without additional Indian material, it is clear that the story about the mouse maiden is a kind of parody on a serious theme. We may even be able to guess how this parody came into existence. Among the Aesopian fables there is one which is pertinent to our theme,[13] namely, the fable of "The Weasel as Bride." Once a weasel fell in love with a handsome young man and Aphrodite changed it into a beautiful maiden. When the time for their wedding came, the goddess wanted to know whether the weasel's character had changed when it was metamorphosed into the maiden. In order to test her, Aphrodite sent a mouse into the midst of the wedding party. The bride paid no attention to the guests present, but began to pursue the mouse in order to eat it. The goddess became angry and turned the girl into a weasel again.

Even with the help of a specialist in Indian culture, I have been unable to discover any Indian fable similar to the Greek fable of the weasel. Nevertheless, I assume that there must have been such a fable, which stimulated the creation of the parody, "The Mouse Maiden," included in the *Panchatantra.* But even if we cannot find a parallel to the *Panchatantra* tale within the Indian tradition, its parodistic intention is patent. The similarity of this tale to the legend about Abraham also makes it probable that the tale about "The Mouse Maiden" is a humerous joke on a highly theological theme—the very same theme reflected in the legend about Abraham's search for God. Fortunately, it is undisputed that this is precisely one of the main themes of the old Indian Upanishads,[14] which are generally thought to have originated in the sixth century B.C.E.

It would be both tedious and unnecessary to describe here the aims of the theology of the Upanishads, as any reader of these sacred texts can easily recognize them. The One Presence, which was experienced as the Self *(ātman),* or the Holy Power *(brahman)* absorbed their entire interest.[15]

> Whatever is expressed in divine *personae*—or, for that matter, in any tangible, visible, or imaginable form—must be regarded as but a sign, a pointer, directing the intellect to what is hidden, something mightier, more comprehensive and less transitory than anything with which the eyes or emotions can become familiar. . . . In India the quest for the primal force reached, in soaring flight, the plane of reality whence everything proceeds as a merely temporal, phenomenal manifesta-

> tion. This ultimate power in the universe, and in man, transcends both the sensual and the conceptual spheres. . . . The crucial problem for a theologian is to make contact with the right divinities for the purposes of the time, and to ascertain, if possible, which among the gods is the most powerful in general. . . . The highest principle is to be discovered and mastered through wisdom.[16]

I have quoted here the words of one important scholar in support. However, as already stated, the message of the Upanishads themselves is obvious, as is its similarity to the meaning of the legend about Abraham. What is said there about Abraham's search for God is a central concept in Upanishadic religiosity.[17] Brahma is "the maker of everything, for he is the creator of all; the world is his: indeed, he is the world itself."[18] He is also "the source and origin of the gods."[19] God's transcendence is described in the following stanza:

> The sun shines not there, nor the moon and stars,
> These lightnings shine not, much less this (earthly) fire!
> After Him, as He shines, doth everything shine,
> This whole world is illuminated with His light.[20]

Another stanza describes the superiority of God in the following way:

> Through fear of Him the Wind (Vāyu) doth blow.
> Through fear of Him the Sun (Sūrya) doth rise.
> Through fear of Him both Agni (Fire) and Indra
> And Death (Mṛityu) as fifth do speed along.[21]

One can easily discover parallels in the Upanishads to the Abraham legend.[22] The most striking one is the following:[23]

> But [once] when Janaka, [king] of Videha, and Yājñavalkya were discussing together at an Agnihorta, Yājñavalkya granted the former a boon. He chose asking whatever question he wished. He granted it to him. So [now] the king, [speaking] first, asked him: "Yājñavalkya, what light does a person here have?" "He has the light of the sun, O king," he said, "for with the sun, indeed, as his light one sits, moves around, does his work, and returns." "Quite so, Yājñavalkya. But when the sun has set, Yājñavalkya, what light does a person here have?" "The moon, indeed, is his light," said he. . . . "Quite so, Yājñavalkya. But when the sun has set, and the moon has set, what light does a person here have?" "Fire, indeed, is his light," said he. . . . "Quite so, Yājñavalkya. But when the sun

> has set, Yājñavalkya, and the moon has set, and the fire has gone out, what light does a person here have?" "Speech, indeed is his light," said he. . . . "Therefore, verily, O king, where one does not discern even his own hands, when a voice is raised, then one goes straight towards it." "Quite so, Yājñavalkya. But when the sun has set, Yājñavalkya, and the moon has set, and the fire has gone out, and speech is hushed, what light does a person here have?" "The soul *(ātman),* indeed, is his light," said he, "for with the soul, indeed, as his light one sits, moves around, does his work, and returns."

We must remember that in the Upanishads *ātman,* the Self, is identified with *brahman,* the Holy Power.

I hope that it has now become clear that nobody would find it strange or inappropriate were the hero of the story of Abraham's discovery of God changed from the biblical Patriarch to an ancient Indian sage. It is true that the Jewish legend tends to be overly iconoclastic for an Indian; Abraham denies the divinity of the heavenly bodies, which would surely be considered too extreme in Indian eyes. But, on the other hand, the Upanishads often betray a similar, though somehow not so radical, revolutionary spirit. Sacrifice and works of merit towards hypostatized divinities are considered as futile in the light of metaphysical knowledge. The entire religious doctrine of different gods and the necessity of sacrificing to the gods is seen as a stupendous fraud by the man who has acquired metaphysical knowledge of the monistic unity of self and world in Brahman or Atman. "This that people say, 'Worship this god! Worship that god!'—one god after another—this is his creation indeed! And he himself is all the gods."[24] But even so, the existence of lesser divinities is not questioned—which is precisely the message of the Jewish legend, even if its theme per se does not completely exclude the possibility that the heavenly bodies, created by God, possess some divine power.

I admit that our "Indian hypothesis" will seem adventurous to some readers, but I did not reach India as a kind of new Sinbad. The Indian roots of this legend about Abraham are not so improbable as would seem at the first glance. I venture that the theme reached the Jews via Persia, through a Zoroastrian medium. In our sources, the legend about Abraham's quest for God was connected from the beginning with his fight against idolatry, his rescue from the fiery furnace and the death of his brother Haran by fire. Variants of these motifs already appear in the Book of Jubilees (11.16–18; 12.1–6, 12–14) from the second century B.C.E. Moreover, it is not improbable that these sources attest to an older written legendary epic about Abraham's earlier days, perhaps similar in contents to the narratives told about Daniel.[25]

However, this problem is beyond the scope of the present study. What is significant for our purposes is that the main aim of this entire cycle of legends is to describe how Abraham discovered the theological truth of monotheism and demonstrated the futility of idolatry. The spiritual monotheistic and iconoclastic kerygma of the legends admirably fits the atmosphere of the post-exilic, Persian and Pre-Maccabaean period.[26] One may speculate that these legends later constituted a special genre used to inculcate monotheistic beliefs among "God-fearers" and potential proselytes to Judaism in the Hellenistic world. If I am correct, its theology is common to both Judaism and Zoroastrianism. In this light, the path from India to Persia and from Persia to the Jews is easy to follow, both from the historical and from the geographical point of view.

My first step on the journey to India was when I recognized the similarity between Abraham's quest for God and the story in the Indian *Panchatantra.* Later, by mere chance, I was confronted with the Upanishads, as a consequence of which my initial assumption was strengthened. I have found that in the Upanishads one can find, not only numerous more-or-less similar parallels to the Jewish legends, but that its subjacent idea is essential for their own theology. It became clear, moreover, that although the story of Abraham's quest for God may be traced as far back as the second century B.C.E. in ancient Jewish pseudepigraphic and Hellenistic literature, it was not accepted into the mainstream of rabbinic tradition. Thus, the legend is contained only in later rabbinic narrative literature. I hope to show elsewhere that this paradoxical situation is by no means restricted to the legend about Abraham's quest for the one God. In our case, one point seems to me to be the most important, far more so than the pedigree and literary history of the legend. The probable foreign roots of the story about Abraham's search and the eminent importance of the legend for the understanding of the Jewish (and Christian and Muslim) faith are each meaningful. The god whom Abraham discovered was the impersonal cosmic supreme God, the Creator of the world and its Governor. While this is the essence of the God of Israel, he is also a personal and merciful God who answers and communicates his nature by revelation, as he has already done to Abraham himself. Thus God responded to Abraham's quest for him. According to Rabbi Isaac's parable, God looked out and said to Abraham, "I am the governor, the lord of the whole world."

Both these elements are likewise present in our legend about how Abraham came to recognize the creator through contemplation of the Creation, as it appears in *Barlaam and Ioasaph,* written by St. John Damascene (675–749).[27] There, the story concludes, "therein he recognized the true God, and understood him to be the maker and sustainer of the whole. And God, approving his fair wisdom and right judgment, manifested himself unto him and planted in Abraham more perfect knowledge; he magnified him and made him his own servant." Thus, philosophical monotheism is united with the revelation of the personal God.

And what was Abraham's reaction? The oldest witness of the legend also seems to contain the earliest reference to the post-biblical concept of the kingdom of heaven. According to the Book of Jubilees 12.19, after having attained knowledge of the one and only God, Abraham prayed to Him and said, "My God, the Most High God, you alone are God to me. And you created everything, and everything which is was the work of your hands, and you and your kingdom I have chosen."[28] Is there already an allusion here to the famous biblical verse, "Hear, O Israel, the Lord our God is one Lord" (Deut. 6.4), by whose recital one proclaims God's oneness, and by which very act one takes upon oneself the yoke of the kingdom of heaven?[29] In any case, Abraham's proclamation in the Book of Jubilees supports the rabbinic view[30] that, until Abraham came, God ruled only in the heavens. It was Abraham who made God king over both the heaven and the earth. After having found God, Abraham accepted Him as his King.

5

Between Jews and Greeks: The Indian Model

Frances Schmidt

When the three sons of Noah divided the earth among themselves, the eastern sector of the inhabited world, stretching from the Euphrates to the Indian Ocean, was allotted to the descendants of Shem. Easternmost Asia was assigned to the thirteen sons of Yoqtan, a great-great-grandson of Shem: "These, proceeding from the River Cophen [or Kabul, a tributary of the Indus] inhabited parts of India and of the adjacent country of Seria." This, at least, is how Flavius Josephus, in his *Antiquities of the Jews* (I.143–47), interprets Genesis 10.26–30. For the ancient Jews, India was at the ends of the earth, watered by the Pishon, one of the four streams issuing from Eden, "a name meaning multitude," and which the Greeks call the Ganges (*Antiquities* I.38). It was also to India, "anciently called Sōpheir, but now the Land of Gold," that Solomon's fleet sailed in search of the gold required for the Temple ornaments (*Antiquities* VIII.164). When Josephus sought to underscore the vast extent of the Persian Empire, whose 127 satrapies stretched from the eastern to the southern margins of the inhabited world, he borrowed a formula of the Achaemenid chancery: "from India to Ethiopia" (cf. *Antiquities* XI.33, 186, 216, 272).

Nevertheless, for the Jews of the Hellenistic and Roman period, India did not remain the farthest corner of the world or the fabulously wealthy realm of Ophir whither Solomon had sent for gold and precious gems. Jews and Indians could have come into direct contact through the commercial and diplomatic overland and maritime intercourse between India and the countries of the eastern Mediterranean.[1] Strabo reported around the year 24 B.C.E. that Alexandrian merchants fitted out ships that annually weighed anchor from the Red Sea port of Myos-Hormos and set sail for India (*Geography* II.5, 12). Egypt, according to Josephus, is "the port for India" (*Jewish War* II.385). A more probable and more direct avenue for contact between Jews and Indians was the Great Silk Road. When, in the second half of the third century B.C.E., the ambassadors of Asoka crossed the Hindu Kush in order to disseminate the teachings of the Buddha as far as the countries of the eastern Mediterranean, they followed the Silk Road as far as Palmyra, proceeding from there towards Antioch, Macedon, Epirus, and Corinth in the north, and towards Alexandria and Cyrene in the south.[2] During Augustus' reign, Nicholas of Damascus—who was an advisor to Herod the Great, and whose *Universal History* was one of the chief sources for Josephus' *Antiquities*—encountered the ambassadors sent by Porus to Augustus in Antioch. They were accompanied by a gymnosophist named Zarmanochegas, who later immolated himself in Athens (cited by Strabo, *Geography* XV.1.4, and 73; see also Plutarch, *Life of Alexander* 69.8).

I am not concerned here with the historicity or even with the probability of contacts between India and Judaism. My theme is quite different: namely, Jewish perceptions of India. To repeat what François Hartog said in his introduction to a recent study of Greek images of Egypt, my perspective does not involve the degree of historicity or truthfulness of Jewish appreciations of India, but of the internal logic within Judaism itself that structured and gave meaning to them.[4] This is because in terms of the creative imagination the Jews had another, indirect acquaintance with India: through the intermediacy of the Greek historians who wrote on India. Philo of Alexandria, citing an apocryphal letter from Calanus to Alexander (*Quod omnis probus* 93–96), repeats and interprets certain traditions of Greek historiography relating to Alexander. Flavius Josephus mentions the histories of India by Megasthenes and Philostratus (*Antiquities of the Jews* X.227–28; *Contra Apion* 1.144).[5] In *Contra Apion,* he also quotes Clearchus of Soles, who viewed the Jews as the "descendents"—*apogonoi*—of the Indian philosophers (I.179). An aggadic passage in the Babylonian Talmud (BT) reports ten questions that Alexander asked of "the ancients of the southern regions"; these are borrowed from one of the Greek versions of the conversation between Alexander and the gymnosophists (BT Tamid 31b–32a).[6] From these Greek histories of India we see that the Jews had taken over mainly the narratives of the first contacts between the Greeks and the Indians, and particularly the traditions about the first interview between Alexander and the Brahmans. How do these Jewish texts deviate from or transform the Greek sources? Why were they modified and transformed? The main question is whether, under the guise of narratives about the first contacts between Alexander and the sages of India—an encounter perceived as the foundation of the future relations between Hellenism and Indian wisdom—these Jewish texts do not in fact speak of something quite different: not of the relations between Greeks and Indians, but of those between Hellenism and Judaism.

Calanus and Mandanis

The Greek traditions concerning the first encounter between Alexander and the Indian sages are contradictory. They usually involve two Brahmins, Calanus and Mandanis.[7] One is old, the other younger; one is open to dialogue, the other refuses to participate. But the sources differ as to which of the two sages adopted which of these opposing attitudes, as well as about the arguments adduced by them. These divergent accounts can be traced back to two archetypes, each of which has its variants: the accounts of Onesicritus and those of Megasthenes.

Onesicritus the Cynic, the chief pilot of Alexander's fleet of which Nearchus was the admiral, wrote a work about Alexander. Strabo, who incidentally dubs him the "arch-pilot of the incredible" (*Geography* XV.1.28), reports the discussion between Onesicritus and the two ascetics (XV.1.63–65). Alexander had learned that the gymnosophists of Taxila refused to disturb themselves for anyone, believing that it was incumbent upon those who wanted to question them to seek them out, so he sent Onesicritus as his emissary. One of the ascetics, named Calanus, lay naked on a pile of stones. At the sight of the stranger, he laughed at his Greek garments and told him the following myth: In olden times the world was full of barley meal and wheaten meal; water, milk, honey, wine, and oil flowed from the fountains. But, irritated by human insolence, Zeus put an end to this golden age and subjected mankind to a life of toil. The practice of wisdom *(sôphrosyne)*, however, made abundance return. It was to be feared, concluded Calanus, that insolence might once again make these bounties disappear. If Onesicritus wanted to participate in the discussions of the gymnosophists, he should remove his garments and lie down naked on the pile of stones. Mandanis, the oldest of the ascetics, reproached

Calanus for demonstrating hubris just when he was condemning human insolence. Speaking to Onesicritus, Mandanis congratulated the king his master for behaving as a philosopher-warrior. Only the need to have recourse to interpreters prevented him from expounding his thought further for the stranger.

This narrative of Onesicritus is also known from a summary given by Plutarch (*Life of Alexander* 65.1–3). Plutarch underscores Calanus' insolence and rudeness, which is contrasted to Mandanis' more courteous attitude.

The second archetype is represented chiefly by Megasthenes. An Ionian from Asia Minor, a contemporary of Seleucus Nicator, Megasthenes was charged with several embassies to India, where he spent a number of years between 302 and 288 B.C.E. For Greek readers of the Hellenistic and Roman era, his *Indica* was one of the chief sources of knowledge about India.[8] He too is quoted by Strabo (*Geography* XV.1.68). When Alexander's messengers came to ask Mandanis to appear before the king, "the son of Zeus," "and promised that he would receive gifts if he obeyed, but punishment if he disobeyed," Mandanis refused: Alexander, who ruled over only a small part of the earth, was not the son of Zeus; the sage did not receive his gifts and was not afraid of his threats. As long as he lived, India would supply him with sufficient food; if he died, "he would be released from the flesh wasted by old age and be translated to a better and purer life" *(apallaxaito tês tetruchômenês apo gêrôs sarkos, metastas eis beltiô kai katharôteron bion)*. This proud response earned him Alexander's praise. As for Calanus, his attitude was quite different—he agreed to follow the king. The gymnosophists themselves passed a severe judgement on his self-immolation, calling him "a man who was without self-control and a slave to the table of Alexander."

Megasthenes' account is also repeated by Arrian (*Anabasis* VII.II.2–4). Mandanis, the oldest among the sages of Taxila—the others are his disciples—repulsed Alexander's offer:

> While he lived, the land of India was all he needed . . . ; and when he died, he would merely be released from an uncomfortable companion, his body. Renouncing, then, any resort to compulsion, the king recognized this man as a being "truly free." Calanus, on the other hand, accepted Alexander's invitation. Hence the other sages regarded him "as most uncontrolled in his desires, reproaching Calanus because he had deserted the happiness which they had, while he served a master other than God."

Aristobulus, originally from Chalcidis, a member of Alexander's expedition, is one of Arrian's principle sources.[9] He too tells of the encounter between the king and the two "sophists" of Taxila: Of the two Brahmins, "the younger showed a far greater self-mastery than the elder; . . . but . . . the elder accompanied the king to the end, and when he was with him changed his dress and mode of life" (quoted by Strabo, *Geography* XV.1.61). Even though the names of the two sages are not specified, there is no doubt that we should identify the older, who agreed to follow Alexander at the cost of losing his identity, as Calanus.

Retracing the main narrative threads, then, we find two series: one originating with Onesicritus (cited by Strabo and Plutarch), the second originating with Aristobulus (quoted by Strabo) and Megasthenes (cited by Strabo and Arrian). In both series, the two Brahmins follow diametrically opposed paths vis-à-vis Alexander: one of refusal, the other of acceptance. But whereas in Onesicritus the intransigence of Calanus is in contrast with the courtesy of Mandanis, in Megasthenes it is Mandanis who refuses to follow the king while Calanus agrees to do so.[10]

Strabo stresses the disagreement among the Greek historians who had written about India; he nevertheless notes that all agree that Calanus followed Alexander and that he died voluntarily, burned on a pyre before the king's eyes. He adds that the causes and the circumstances of this death differ from one historian to another (cf. *Geography* XV.1.68). For some it was a glorious death: thus Onesicritus, for whom he died "in accordance with ancestral custom" (*tôi patriôi nomôi:* quoted by Strabo, *Geography* XV.1.64); or Arrian, for whom the account of this death is useful to "anyone who cares to realize how stalwart and unflinching is human resolution to carry out that which it desires" (*Anabasis* VII.3.6; cf. Diodorus Siculus, XVII.107.1–5; Plutarch, *Life of Alexander* 69.6–7). For others it was a shameful death: thus Megasthenes: "Suicide is not a dogma among the [Indian] philosophers, and . . . those who commit suicide [like Calanus] are adjudged guilty of the impetuosity of youth" (quoted by Strabo, *Geography* XV.1.68).

Calanus' Letter to Alexander

The *Quod omnis probus liber sit* of Philo of Alexandria is probably a youthful work, composed at the beginning of the Common Era.[11] To illustrate his theme—that every virtuous man is free—Philo offers various examples: the Seven Sages of Greece, the Persian magi, the Indian gymnosophists, the Essenes among the Jews. Other illustrations of his theme are represented by individuals who maintained their freedom of speech in the face of oppressors or who preferred death to slavery. To begin with Calanus:

> Calanus was an Indian by birth of the school of the gymnosophists. Regarded as possessed of endurance more than any of his contemporaries, by combining virtuous actions with laudable words he gained the admiration, not only of his fellow countrymen, but of men of other races, and, what is most singular of all, of enemy sovereigns. Thus Alexander of Macedon, wishing to exhibit to the Grecian world a specimen of the barbarians' wisdom, like a copy reproducing the original picture, began by urging Calanus to travel with him from India with the prospect of winning high fame in the whole of Asia and the whole of Europe; and when he failed to persuade him declared that he would compel him to follow him. Calanus's reply was as noble as it was apposite. "What shall I be worth to you, Alexander, for exhibiting to the Greeks if I am compelled to do what I do not wish to do?" What a wealth of frankness there is in the words and far more of freedom in the thought. But more durable than his spoken are his written words and in these he set on record clear signs of a spirit which could not be enslaved. The letter he sent to Alexander runs thus:—
>
> "Calanus to Alexander
>
> Your friends urge you to apply violence and compulsion to the philosophers of India. These friends, however, have never even in their dreams seen what we do. Bodies you will transport from place to place, but souls you will not compel to do what they will not do, any more than force bricks or sticks to talk. Fire causes the greatest trouble and ruin to living bodies: we are superior to this: we burn ourselves alive. There is no king, no ruler, who will compel us to do what we do not freely wish to do. We are not like those philosophers of the Greeks, who practice words for a festal assembly. With us deeds accord with words and words with deeds. Deeds pass swiftly and words have short-lived power: virtues secure to us blessedness and freedom." (*Quod omnis probus* 93–96)[12]

Of the various Greek traditions about the interview between Alexander and the gymnosophists, Philo presents here that transmitted by Megasthenes. For Philo, as for Megasthenes, Alexander is ready to resort to threats if persuasion fails to convince the sages to follow him. In both accounts the gymnosophist follows the same line of argumentation: threats have no effect on an Indian sage, who can always find in death the means to escape a destiny he would not have freely chosen.

Nevertheless Philo, far from simply paraphrasing Megasthenes, makes a number of modifications in his model. Philo says nothing about the Brahmin who is receptive to the king's proposal. Only the attitude of refusal remains. Another innovation is that by fabricating this apocryphal letter—for which the text of *Quod omnis probus* is the only evidence—Philo gives countenance to Calanus' noble refusal as a real deed. On the other hand, the intransigent gymnosophist is not Mandanis, as in Megasthenes, but Calanus. Having transferred to the latter the intransigence that Megasthenes ascribed to Mandanis, Philo suggests that, if subsequently Calanus did follow Alexander, he was forced to do so. If he committed suicide by self-immolation, it was not to escape old age or sickness,[13] but rather to free himself from a strange manner of life that had been imposed upon him against his will. As he declares in his letter to the king, the sage, in choosing death, chooses liberty. Philo's Calanus is thus a compound character. He combines the capacity for refusal of Megasthenes' Mandanis with the heroic death of the Calanus of Greek tradition. By conflating these two characters into one Philo sets up Calanus as a paradigm of the Indian rejection of Hellenism.

The Jewish Brahmins

But Philo's rewrite of Megasthenes was not limited to the narrative of the first encounter between Alexander and the Brahmins. Thanks to a fragment quoted by Clement of Alexandria (*Stromatos* I.15.72.5), we know that Megasthenes held that "all the opinions expressed by the ancients about nature *(ta peri physeôs eireména)* are found also among the philosophers outside Greece, some among the Indian Brahmans and others in Syria among those called Jews *(ta men par' Indois hypo tôn brachmanôn, ta de en têi Syriai hypo tôn kaloumênon Ioudaiôn).*"[14] In other words, when it comes to speculations about nature, the philosophers are to Greece what the Brahmins are to India and the Jews to Syria. Around 300 B.C.E., a contemporary of Megasthenes, Clearchus of Soles, a disciple of Aristotle, took up these parallels. Flavius Josephus quotes a passage from Clearchus' *Dialogue on Dreams,* which recounts an interview between Aristotle and a Jew of Coele Syria.[15] The Jews, says Aristotle, "are descended *(apogonoi)* from the Indian philosophers. The philosophers, they say, are in India called *Calanoi,* in Syria *Ioudaioi*" (*Contra Apion* I.179). Louis Robert has proposed identifying the Clearchus who had Delphic sayings engraved on a stele of the *temenos* of Kineas at Aī Khanoum—Alexandria on the Oxus in Bactria—with the author of this *Dialogue on Dreams.* A great traveller who was curious about barbarian wisdom, Clearchus could have gained his knowledge of India and the Brahmins during his stay in Bactria.[16]

By making the Jews the "descendants" of the Indian philosophers, Clearchus goes farther than Megasthenes. Here the *apogonoi* indicates the relationship of teacher to student and suggests an intellectual kinship; the Jews are presented as the heirs and torch-bearers of the Indian sages, whose disciples they were.[17] For Megasthenes and Clearchus, the Jews are not a people like the Greeks, the Persians, the Indians, or the Syrians, but rather constitute a community of sages like the magi or the gymnosophists. These two accounts are typical of the Greeks' initially laudatory estimation of the Jews, whom they viewed as priest-philosophers. Later, of course, towards the end of the second century before the Common Era, the Greeks' regard for the Jews changed and became openly hostile.[18]

When Philo of Alexandria included among his exemplars of the freedom conferred by true wisdom the Seven Sages of Greece, the Persian magi, the gymnosophists of India, and the Essenes in Syria-Palestine, he is repeating the analogies drawn by Megasthenes (*Quod omnis probus* 73–75). But at the same time he modifies and corrects them. It is no longer the Jews as a whole among the Syrians, but the Essenes among the Jews, who constitute a community comparable to that of the gymnosophists. Moreover, unlike in Megasthenes' text, their similarity does not have to do with speculations about nature; it is rather that the Essenes (like Calanus, whose story is related immediately after that of the Essenes), when confronted by foreign rulers who endeavored to subjugate them by cruelty or deceit, have always conducted themselves as free men, escaping any form of slavery by means of their virtuous deeds (*Quod omni probus* 89–91).

The Self-immolation of Wise Men

Born in Jerusalem to a priestly family, Joseph ben Matthias became a Roman citizen after the events of the year 70 CE: thereafter he called himself Titus Flavius Josephus. Between 76 and 79 he published in Rome his Greek *War of the Jews,* an apologia before God and posterity of his passage from Jerusalem to Rome: "Since fortune has wholly passed to the Romans, . . . I take thee to witness that I go, not as a traitor, but as thy minister" (*War of the Jews* III.354).[19] Josephus himself took over the Indian model, but not in order to cast himself as a new Calanus. For Josephus, it was Eleazar ben Yair who cited the example of the self-immolation of Indian sages.

The time is May of the year 73. The last Jewish insurgents have taken refuge in the fortress of Masada. Built on a rocky promontory, it dominates the western shore of the Dead Sea. Led by Eleazar ben Yair, the Sicarii have endeavored to continue the resistance. In August of the year 70 the Temple in Jerusalem had been burned; the following month Titus entered the ruined city as a conqueror. At Masada the situation is desperate. The Roman legions of Lucius Flavius Silva have blockaded the citadel. They have constructed an assault ramp against the western slope and have succeeded in breaching the wall. Fires are raging throughout the fortress.

At this juncture Eleazar ben Yair addresses his companions twice. We are actually talking about two speeches composed by Josephus (*War of the Jews* VII.323–88). The essence of Eleazar's first speech is that it is better to die with honor and freedom than to live in slavery: "Long since we determined neither to serve the Romans nor any other save God" (VII.323). This refers to the ideal of freedom which the Sicarii had made their watchword, ever since the year 6 when Judah the Galilean incited the Jews to refuse to pay tribute to the Romans so as not to recognize any other master than God (*Antiquities of the Jews* XVIII.4–10; 23–25; *War of the Jews* II.118; 433; VII.353–54). Eleazar then delivers his self-criticism: "From the very first, having chosen to assert our liberty, . . . we ought to have read God's purpose and to have recognized that the Jewish race, once beloved of Him, had been doomed to perdition" (VII.327). Here Josephus seems to be using Eleazar as his own mouthpiece. This criticism is exactly that addressed by the historian, throughout his *War of the Jews,* against the Zealots, the Sicarii, or members of the Fourth Sect, all of whom he calls "brigands": they were unable to understand that God had abandoned His people, that fortune had abandoned the camp of the Jews and resettled in Italy.[20]

In conclusion, Eleazar exhorts his companions to submit to divine punishment and kill themselves rather than surrender to the Romans: "We [choose] death rather than slavery."

But his first speech fails to sway all his listeners; so Eleazar tries again, this time targeting especially those deterred by the thought of death—their own and that of their families. This time his theme is the immortality of the soul, and his intended audience is somewhat different from that of the earlier speech. Eleazar first turns to those for whom it is life that is a calamity, not death (VII.343–57); then he addresses those for whom, on the contrary, life is preferable to death (VII.358–88). He begins by recalling the teaching of the Sages: death liberates the soul. During life the soul is imprisoned in a mortal body *(en sômati thêntôi dedemenai).* After death, however, freed from the weight that drags it down to earth *(apolutheisa tou kathelkontos autên barous epi gên),* the liberated soul can return to its own abode *(eis ton oikeion . . . apallassesthai),* where it will live with blessed power and unfettered strength (VII.344–48). This belief in the immortal soul, liberated by death from the durance of the mortal body, does not accord with traditional Jewish doctrine. To judge by what Josephus himself reports, it corresponds neither to the Pharisaic doctrine of the reincarnation of the souls of the righteous in "another body" (*War of the Jews* II.163; III.374; *Antiquities of the Jews* XVIII.14; *Contra Apion* II.218)[21] nor to the Sadducean teaching that denies the survival of the soul (*War of the Jews* II.165; *Antiquities of the Jews* XVIII.16). On the other hand, its exposition agrees exactly, in form and content, with what Josephus attributes to the Essenes. Strongly Hellenized in their formulation, both take over the Platonic theme of death as liberation, *apallagê.*[22] According to Josephus (*War of the Jews* II.152–53), the Essenes, when tortured during the war against the Romans, demonstrated that they were ready to die in order to observe the Law:

> They cheerfully resigned their souls, confident that they would receive them back again. For it is a fixed belief of theirs that the body is corruptible and its constituent matter impermanent, but that the soul is immortal and imperishable. Emanating from the finest ether, these souls become entangled, as it were, in the prison-house *(hôsper heirktais)* of the body, to which they are dragged down *(kataspômenas)* by a sort of natural spell; but when once they are released from the bonds of the flesh *(tôn kata sarka desmôn),* then, as though liberated from a long servitude *(makras douleias apêllagmenas),* they rejoice and are borne aloft. (II.153–55)

Thus this teaching of the Sages, which Eleazar invokes in order to persuade those among his hearers who are afraid to surrender life, is the Essenian doctrine of death as the liberation of the soul.[23]

Eleazar continues: if it is necessary to adduce the testimony of foreign peoples,

> let us look at those Indians who profess the practice of philosophy. They, brave men that they are, reluctantly endure the

> period of life, as some necessary service due to nature, but hasten to release their souls from their bodies; and though no calamity impels nor drives them from the scene, from sheer longing for the immortal state, they announce to their comrades that they are about to depart. Nor is there any who would hinder them: no, all felicitate them and each gives them commissions to his loved ones; so certain and absolutely sincere is their belief in the intercourse which souls hold with one another. Then, after listening to these behests, they commit their bodies to the fire, that so the soul may be parted from the body in the utmost purity, and expire amidst hymns of praise. Indeed, their dearest ones escort them to their death more readily than do the rest of mankind their fellow-citizens when starting on a very long journey; for themselves they weep, but them they count happy as now regaining immortal rank. (VII.351–56)

Finally, addressing those for whom death rather than life is the calamity, Eleazar returns to and develops the self-criticism he had sketched out in his previous speech. "Long ago . . . God issued the warning to the whole Jewish race together that life would be taken from us if we misused it" (VII.359). Hence there is only one way out for those besieged in the burning citadel: to die, as free men, by the sword and the flames,[24] and not become slaves of the hated enemy.

Nothing in the passage about the Indian ascetics indicates that Eleazar is alluding to Calanus, whose self-immolation made such an impression on the Greek imagination. For Eleazar, no foreign presence or external compulsion pushes these ascetics to liberate their soul from the body by ascending the pyre. The voluntary self-cremation under discussion is more like that of Zarmanochegas—the *sraman* "Khegas"[25]—one of the gymnosophists who accompanied the Indian embassy sent to Augustus, known to us from Nicholas of Damascus:

> Some [of the Indian philosophers] commit suicide when they suffer adversity, seeking release from the ills at hand, [but] others do so when their lot is happy, as was the case with that man [Zarmanochegas]; for . . . although that man had fared as he wished up to that time, he thought it necessary then to depart this life, lest something untowards might happen to him if he tarried here. (Strabo, *Geography* XV.1.73)[26]

Thus the persuasive force of the two discourses on suicide is based entirely on the cumulative effect of arguments borrowed from various currents of Jewish thought. Eleazar mentions the Sicarii's watchword of liberty, the Essene doctrine of death as liberation, and speaks on his own account Josephus' criticism of the insurgents' actions: God has abandoned His people. In this speech, as in Philo, the Indian example is associated with the exposition of an Essene doctrine. But Josephus, by placing in Eleazar's mouth an "apocalypse of death" that leads to the destruction of the Jewish people, links the folly of those who deliver their bodies to the raging furnace of Masada and their Indian model in a single condemnation.[27]

The image of India and Indians created by Philo and Josephus is based on information transmitted by the Greek historians of India. The most ancient Greek interpretation of Judaism and the Jews, which saw them as the descendants of the Indians or as the Brahmins of Syria, led the Jews to inquire into the identity of that people and, more particularly, of that class of philosophers among them whom the Greeks saw as their kindred, or at least their analogues. Taken over by hellenized Jews, this Greek image of India was transformed. To what end? For these Jews it was not so much a matter of spreading knowledge about these inhabitants of the far ends of the Earth by depicting, in the manner of Herodotus, the wonders *(thaumata)* of these distant peoples; rather, it was a matter of posing, through them, a question that was fundamental for Judaism in the Hellenistic and Roman era: how can one remain true to one's own identity in the face of foreign domination? The Indian sages, represented by Mandanis and Calanus, offered two incompatible answers: acceptance or refusal, openness to acculturation or resistance to it. In the age when Judea became a Roman province, when the Jews were deeply divided as to the attitude to take towards Rome, when Judah the Galilean founded the "Fourth Sect," the young Philo of Alexandria, offering to his contemporaries only the model of Calanus, supported the latter attitude against the former. Similarly, when the fall of Masada in 73 signalled the failure of the policy of resistance, it was still the heroic death of the Indian sages that was offered by Eleazar ben Yair, in Josephus' dramatic rendition of the event, as an example to his companions.

But we must not be led astray by this. Face to face with Hellenism or the Roman *imperium,* Philo and Josephus, who were neither apocalyptics nor Essenes, and even less Sicarii or Zealots, did not chose this model for themselves. For them, it was stamped with a profound ambiguity: simultaneously esteemed to the extent that it exalted loyalty to the ancestral tradition, and condemned as leading to death.[28] In their eyes, a particular community within Judaism incarnates a type of resistance to acculturation comparable to that which the Brahmins represent for the Indians. Borrowing and transforming the analogies of

Megasthenes and of Clearchus, for whom the Jews were the Brahmins of Syria, Philo and Josephus see the Essenes, those philosophers, those ascetics who preached loyalty to the ancestral doctrines in the face of the risk of the loss of identity that the Roman presence in Judea posed to Judaism as a whole, as the true Brahmins of the Jews.[29]

6

A Hindu Response to the Written Torah

D. Dennis Hudson

In January of 1854, in the midst of a busy life opposing Christian missions to the Hindus in northern Sri Lanka (Ceylon), Ārumuga Nāvalar (1822–79) published a major refutation of Protestantism. He wrote it in Tamil prose and printed it on his own press. The booklet, *The Abolition of the Abuse of Śaivism,* was reprinted in Madras in 1868 and again in 1890 and has appeared various times since.[1] It, and the vigorous career of its author, were decisive factors in the growth of a Hindu—specifically a Śaiva—self-consciousness that has fed opposition to missionaries among the Tamils since the latter half of the nineteenth century until today.

This essay will explore one element in Ārumuga Nāvalar's opposition to the missionaries: his response as a devout worshipper of Śiva to the written Torah as recorded in *The Abolition of the Abuse of Śaivism.*[2] Nāvaler encountered the written Torah in the form of the Old Testament of the Christian Bible, which he studied with Methodist missionaries from Britain. His written response was occasioned by the severe verbal attacks that Christian preachers and teachers in Sri Lanka and India had made for years on Śiva and his worship in temples. Śiva, they stated baldly, is a demon. His worshippers are ignorant heathens. To refute such painful attacks, Ārumuga Nāvalar used his extensive knowledge of the books that compose the Old Testament to show that far from being heathenish, the worship of Śiva is fundamentally similar to the worship of God prescribed in the Old Testament and followed by Jesus at the Temple in Jerusalem.[3]

Now, Nāvalar's argument in *The Abolition of the Abuse of Śaivism* is intended to refute Protestants, not to discuss comparative religion. Yet it reveals the way a learned, articulate, and devout worshipper of Śiva in the middle of the nineteenth century actually did respond to biblical religious practice as he encountered it Tanakh—the books of Moses, of the prophets, and of the canonical writings—as embodied in the English Christian Bible. Although his response was to the written Torah within the context of Protestant interpretation and not in the interpretive context of the oral Torah (Talmud), his response nevertheless began what could be an interesting conversation today between Śaivas and Jews. Because he did respond to the written Torah in a nineteenth-century Protestant context, I will retain his use of terms born of that context, for example, *Jehovah* as the name of God.

What emerges in the booklet is a sophisticated analysis of Śaiva and Jewish temple cults that argues for strong similarities between the two. Since there are such similarities, Nāvalar asks, what justification do the missionaries have for opposing the worship of Śiva in temples? After all, Jesus himself worshipped in the Temple in Jerusalem, which means that he worshipped in many ways like a Śaiva. By denying that temple worship as prescribed by the Old Testament is of fundamental authority, the missionaries, he asserts, have abandoned central biblical precepts without any warrant from the teachings of Jesus found in the New Testament and built a false religion that is not even supported by their own sacred books. By sneeringly and ignorantly judging Śaiva worship as devilish, they do not see the similarities between the Temple in Jerusalem and the Śiva temples in India and Sri Lanka. If they did, he concludes, they could not reasonably assert that the worship of Śiva is ignorant heathenism.

The effect of Ārumuga Nāvaler's work was notable. Hindu preachers and teachers used the analysis of the Old Testament and New Testament in *The Abolition of the Abuse of Śaivism* to oppose Christian preachers vigorously in public. Indeed, Protestant missions in northern Sri Lanka never fully recovered from the results of Nāvalar's lifetime of work to purify and revitalize the worship of Śiva among the Tamils.[4]

Ārumuga Nāvalar's extensive knowledge of the Old Testament derived from his work during an eight-year period (1841–48) assisting with the translation of the Christian Bible into Tamil. Peter Percival, principal of the Wesleyan Seminary in Jaffna where Nāvalar had studied, was a British Methodist and a noted Tamil scholar. When Nāvalar completed his studies at the age of nineteen, Percival employed him to teach Tamil and English in the school and invited him to serve as his Tamil referee for the Bible translation. Nāvalar worked closely with Percival and received his high respect. He was in his twenties at the time, unmarried, and in the throes of defining his own identity as a Śaiva.

In 1848 Nāvalar left Percival's employ to begin his own career as a Śaiva educator and reformer, adapting successfully the methods of the Methodists. He produced what might be called an "evangelical Śaivism," launching preaching sessions at Śiva temples with a circuit of preachers, a Śaiva school system with a Śaiva curriculum, a Śaiva printing press to publish his own compositions and his many editions of Tamil religious classics, and a supporting organization of Śaiva laymen called the Splendor of Śiva Society. He also attacked those Śaiva practices he thought in violation of the Śaiva scriptural canon. His educating and reforming efforts produced numerous tracts and pamphlets that he wrote in a clear prose that shaped the development of modern Tamil. The most significant of these was *The Abolition of the Abuse of Śaivism.*

Nāvalar's ideas about the Old Testament found in the booklet had been developing since the age of twenty when he sent a letter to a newly launched bilingual Protestant journal, *The Morning Star (Utaya Tārakai).* In that anonymously signed published letter, he raised questions about the Bible that contain the germ of the analysis he would develop more fully later in *The Abolition of the Abuse of Śaivism.* The Protestant editors of the journal had recognized that in the writer they had a serious opponent and had spent three issues of the paper responding.[5] Their arguments, however, did not satisfy him. Twelve years later he printed and distributed his fully developed analysis and argument, a weapon for Śaivas to use against the missionaries.

Description of the Booklet

Ārumuga Nāvalar opened *The Abolition of the Abuse of Śaivism* with a poem by a Śaiva poet. Then, in a twelve-page essay, he addressed Śaivas living in the Tamil region of India and in Sri Lanka (Īḻam). He defined Śaivism as the true religion *(satsamaya),* for it is based on the scriptures *(Veda-Āgama)* revealed by God. God is the Supreme Śiva *(Paraśivan),* who emanates, protects, and resorbs the universe and obscures and emancipates souls.[6] He described the intolerable abuse Śaivism has received from missionaries who view Śiva as one of many gods *(deva),* not as the God of gods, and presents the scriptural basis in Śaivism for vigorous opposition to its abusers. He concluded with seven specific nonviolent measures Śaivas can take against the abuse, including prayer to Śiva and the use of this booklet and other publications to educate themselves for public disputation with Christian propagandists.

Nāvalar then began the body of the work with a preface, balanced at the end by a short address to Śaivas reminding them of the urgency in following the path of Śiva for their own salvation. In the preface he described the context for the main text that follows. Barbarian missionaries, Nāvalar says, have entered the "noble island" *(āryakhānda)* and attacked the true religion of Śaivism verbally and in print. Some people, who are ignorant of the Śaiva scriptures and have not read the false Bible of the missionaries completely and have little sense of sound reasoning, have in confusion agreed with their abuses and have fallen into the pit of Christianity. Out of compassion for them and to rejuvenate Śaivism, members of the Splendor of Śaivism Society in Jaffna have prepared this booklet.

The body of the work, which is our concern here, consists of twenty-two chapters that demonstrate parallels between worship by Śaivas and worship by the people of Israel and two discussions of those parallels. Ārumuga Nāvalar wrote those chapters and discussions in the clear Tamil prose for which he is noted and addressed them to an anonymous missionary—*pāttiri* from the Portuguese *padre*—toward whom he sustained an aggressive and combative tone throughout.

Each chapter discusses a category in Śaiva worship that Nāvalar will show has its counterpart in worship as prescribed by God through Moses and as enacted by the people of Israel. The categories are grouped in two sets, each set followed by a discussion.[7] The first set develops the theme of temple liturgy in the worship of the one God and includes chapters one through fourteen. The second set treats specific personal and institutional practices related to that liturgy and includes chapters fifteen through twenty-two.

In this essay I shall summarize Ārumuga Nāvalar's comparative study chapter by chapter, though combining some chapters together, and I shall summarize the relevant points he makes in the two discussions. The summaries are meant to render Ārumuga Nāvalar's relevant arguments concisely just as he develops them. Nāvalar ends each chapter with a pointed remark addressed to the missionary, frequently a rhetorical question, and these will be included when they make a useful point. He also provides many and often lengthy citations from the Bible, mostly from the Old Testament, sometimes as translations and sometimes as summaries. I have included them all in summary form, but have placed most of the citations from the New Testament, which are relatively few in the first and longest set of chapters, in the notes. Besides making his argument precise, the citations reveal his knowledge of the text and the creative way he handled it. Nāvalar's major attention is on the phenomena he finds in the Hebrew scriptures and they will be the center of our attention too.

Liturgical Parallels

The Lord Is One

Ārumuga Nāvalar begins his discussion with monotheism. Śaivism, he insists, teaches a monotheistic doctrine quite different from what he sees is the polytheism of the Christians. Out of great compassion the one Lord *(pati),* who is Śiva, creates, protects, and destroys the world, entangles souls within it and releases them from it. Śiva performs those five acts not for his sake but for the sake of souls. Nāvalar will return to that doctrine at the end of the work.

The Vedas and the Āgamas, which he refers to as the "true scriptures," explain that Śiva alone contains the six qualities of omniscience, infinite happiness, innate consciousness, self-dependence, faultless power, and infinite power. For that reason, he says, we follow only Śiva and are called Śaivas. "But you," he says to the anonymous missionary, "do not understand this matter in the slightest and despise us as heathen who worship many gods *(deva).* Yet you worship Jehovah, the Holy Spirit, and Christ as gods; it is *you* who are the heathen."

It is true, he continues, that Śaivas worship other gods than Śiva, but they do so because those other gods are the servants or slaves of the supreme Lord. Śiva considers the worship or the disparagement of his servants to be the same as the worship or disparagement of him, and he bestows blessings or punishments accordingly.

Nāvalar briefly turns to the Bible for the parallel idea of venerating or worshipping the servants of the Lord and cites two examples from the Old Testament: Abraham bowed down and served the three divine messengers (Genesis 18.2) and Joshua fell on his face near Jericho and worshipped a man with a drawn sword, the commander of the army of Jehovah (Joshua 5.14).[8] What basis is there then, Nāvalar asks, for the missionary to despise Śaivas who worship the various gods who are the servants of Śiva?

It is also true, he continues, that the Vedas and Āgamas speak of Siva having a form, but that form is not to be confused with the Christian idea of God as flesh, blood, and bone, and born from a woman.

Śiva's body is made only from the power of his grace *(aruḷ śakti).* It exists for specific purposes: to perform the five acts for souls, to facilitate the meditative visualizations and other acts of worship performed by those who follow him, and to reveal the scriptures. Since this form is pure grace, how can there be any defect in it?

Moreover, the stories found in the Purāṇas about the male and female aspects of the Lord, about Śiva and Pārvati, are not to be taken literally. They are symbolic of mysteries unknown to the uninitiated. Nāvalar provides a glimpse of those mysteries by introducing here the distinction between the absolute *Śivam* on one hand and the male Śiva and female Pārvati on the other. The beginningless Lord known as *Śivam,* he says, is beyond male, female, and neuter. To bring forth all souls, *Śivam* becomes the male gender called Father and *Śivam*'s power *(śakti),* which is not different from it, becomes the female gender called Mother. By a resolution of will, that *Śivam* and that *śakti* together bring forth souls. The act of will is called their union; the absence of the act of will is called their separation. That mystery *(rahasya)* reveals itself to the direct perceptions that ecstatic union *(samādhi)* bestows. The scriptures give various esoteric meanings of the stories of Śiva, but, he insists, they cannot be taught to anyone who abuses Śiva, eats the flesh of cattle, and commits other grievous sins.

Holy Places and Temples

Nāvalar turns next to holy places and temples. Invoking the simile of the king who makes himself available to his subjects throughout his kingdom, he says that Śiva, the infinite Lord of all worlds who pervades and rules everything graciously, takes up residence in different finite places. He does this in order to receive worship and to give blessings to his followers who are limited by finite bodies and minds. The places where he dwells are holy or meritorious.[9]

The Bible, of course, provides parallels. Nāvalar cites seventeen passages to make the point, thirteen of them from the Old Testament. He cites them in a sequence building up to the Temple in Jerusalem: the mount of God called Horeb which Elijah reached (1 Kings 19.8) and where Moses had to remove his shoes on the holy ground (Exodus 3.1 and 5); Mount Sinai, which, Moses warned, would kill those who touched it (Exodus 19.2 and 12); Mount Zion, where the Lord dwells (Psalms 9.11) and the holy place where he is to be worshipped (Psalms 99.9); Bethlehem, where David's family conducted a yearly sacrifice (1 Samuel 20.6); Bethel, where God was worshipped, the hill of God garrisoned by Philistines (1 Samuel 10.3 and 5);[10] Jerusalem, chosen by Jehovah (1 Kings 11.13) as the place where he dwells forever

(1 Chronicles 23.25), the place of his house (Ezra 1.2–3),[11] the house where his name dwells and which he watches day and night to hear the prayers directed to it (2 Chronicles 6.18–21) from the people Israel and from foreigners (2 Chronicles 6.32–33), the house built by Solomon whose rites and priests he established according to the commandments of Moses and the ordinance of David (2 Chronicles 7.12–19).

The Āgamas, he observes, also say that it is meritorious to build and consecrate abodes for the Transcendent Being *(kaṭavuḷ)* in holy places according to the rules. Those abodes or temples enable both the learned and the ignorant to have true life by worshipping with love. The Bible says the same. Moses built and consecrated a dwelling place for God according to his commands (Exodus 35–40). David intended to build a house for God, but it was his son who did it (2 Chronicles 6.7–9). Solomon built and consecrated the house for God in Jerusalem (2 Kings 6 and 8) and it was later rebuilt and consecrated according to God's will (Ezra 6).

The Liṅga

The sculpted icon that represents Śiva in the most sacred part of the temple is called the *liṅga.* Ārumuga Nāvalar explains that there are three types of linga, the manifest, the unmanifest, and the partially manifest. The manifest linga is an icon that portrays the full body of Śiva, and he notes twenty-five versions. The unmanifest linga is a plain shaft sculpted without any bodily parts and rises vertically from a platform. The partially manifest linga is the shaft portraying Śiva's face and shoulders, but not his full body.

The Āgamas, Nāvalar says, explain that a sculpted linga is to be understood in two ways. It is the symbol of Śiva, functioning in the way a written character symbolizes an articulated sound. It is also a residence for Śiva. Śiva takes up residence in the linga when he is invoked with mantras in accord with the rites. Even though Śiva pervades the entire manifest universe, he bestows grace through the delimited icon of the linga when he is worshipped and served there. Nāvalar uses the simile of the cow and her calf to explain the mystery of the conjunction of the infinite and the finite: even though the milk of a cow permeates her entire body, when she sees her calf, she pours it out through her teat. Similarly, the compassionate and loving Śiva pours out his all-pervasive grace through the finite linga.

What parallels to this are found in the Hebrew scriptures? Nāvalar finds fifteen, all having to do with the ark of the covenant. He cites them in a narrative sequence leading from Moses and the ark at Sinai to Solomon's temple in Jerusalem.

Jehovah instructed Moses to construct the box of acacia wood, to cover it with pure gold, to place the record of the covenent inside, to fashion on its top a mercy seat of gold with the image of a cherub at each end, and to conduct ritual worship there at all times (Genesis 25). Accordingly, Moses had a tabernacle built, had the ark constructed and consecrated, and began the ritual service of it by priests *(ācārya)*[12] under the leadership of Aaron. Jehovah rejoiced in the offerings and was gracious (Exodus 35–37, 40). Jehovah said, "In the middle of the two cherubim on the box of the covenant, above the mercy seat, I will appear to you *[darśaṇam-āki]* and I will tell you all that I shall command for the people of Israel" (Exodus 25.22). Whenever Moses wanted to speak to God he did so between the two cherubim (Numbers 7.89). The ark of God bears the name of Jehovah, the Lord of Hosts, who sits in the middle of the cherubim (2 Samuel 6.2). The Psalms rejoice in that presence of God: May he who sits in the middle of the cherubim, shine forth (Psalms 80.1), and may the people tremble as he rules from the midst of the cherubim (Psalms 99.1).

One day, Nāvalar continues, a plague suddenly came upon the Jews *(yūtarkaḷ).* Aaron quickly ran and waved incense before the ark and performed ritual worship and the plague stopped (Numbers 16.46–48). The people followed the ark when it was carried by the *ācāryas,* keeping a distance between themselves and it (Joshua 3.2–4). The *ācāryas* carrying the ark approached the Jordan River, its waters parted, and they walked across it on a dry riverbed (Joshua 3.11–17). When the *ācāryas* carried the ark around the city of Jericho, its walls fell down (Joshua 6). Once when the people of Israel suffered a defeat in a battle, Joshua and others fell before the ark and the Lord gave them the boon of victory over their enemies (Joshua 7). When the Israelites' enemies captured the ark and put it in their own temple, the image belonging to that temple fell face down before it and its head and hands broke off. Suffering from plagues because of the ark, those enemy peoples sent it back to the people of Israel (1 Samuel 5–6). David processed the ark in a new cart and the Lord killed a man who touched it. Now afraid to take the ark home, David took it to another's house but the Lord blessed that household for three months. When he learned this, David brought the ark to his own city, sacrificed, and performed ritual worship before it (2 Samuel 6). David's son, Solomon, later built a temple in Jerusalem, placed the ark inside it, sacrificed many goats and cattle, and conducted ritual worship before it (1 Kings 6 and 8).

Now, Nāvalar asks the missionary, given this understanding of your god *(deva)* Jehovah and of the ark of the covenant in your own scriptures, and given your own eating of bread and wine as symbols of the body and blood of your god *(deva)* Christ, is it not demented on your part to claim that Śaivas are heathens who worship stone and gold? The Transcendent Being *(kaṭavuḷ),* he says, is not demented. He reveals himself for worship through the iconic linga, using it as a symbol of himself and as a finite place to reside. He does not take the worship offered there to be the worship of the linga, but as the worship of himself.

The Liturgy of the Liṅga

Ārumuga Nāvalar next discusses three modes of serving the Transcendent Being who bestows grace through the lingas in which he resides. One is to anoint him in the linga. One is to offer him food in the linga. And a third is to venerate him with incense and light in the linga.

The Āgamas, he explains, declare it meritorious *(puṇya)* to anoint God with oil, milk, curds, ghee, honey, tender coconut milk, and other things in accord with the rites. He cites one parallel to this in the Old Testament, the instructions Jehovah gave Moses for the compounding and use of a holy anointing oil by all generations (Exodus 30:22–33). It is to be compounded like a perfume from liquid myrrh, cinnamon, aromatic cane, cassia, and olive oil. It is to be used to anoint the tent of meeting, the ark of the testimony, the table and its utensils, the lampstand and its utensils, the altar of incense, the altar of burnt offerings and its utensils, and the laver and its base. The oil will make those objects holy and whatever touches them will in turn become holy. The oil shall also be used to anoint Aaron and his sons, consecrating them as the Lord's *ācāryas.* No one is to compound an anointing oil like it nor spread it on the body of an ordinary man or on an outsider.

Now, Nāvalar asks the missionary, seeing that instruction about anointing in your own scriptures, when you see us anoint, is it right on your part to rave like a blindman that it is vain for us to anoint images?

The Śaiva scriptures, he goes on to explain, declare it meritorious to offer boiled rice, milk, fruit, balls of cooked rice, and other such things to the Transcendent Being who bestows grace by residing in lingas. Nāvalar cites three parallels to those food offerings in the Old Testament. First, the Lord instructed Moses, "You shall set the bread of the Presence on the table before me always" (Exodus 25.30). Second, in the ritual for completing the separation of the Nazirite, the Nazirite is required to bring to the door of the tent of meeting a male lamb as a burnt offering, a ewe lamb as a sin offering, a ram as a peace offering, a basket containing breads, cakes mixed with oil, and wafers spread with oil, and offerings of cereal and drink. These items the *ācārya* is to present before the Lord and offer to him (Numbers 6.14–17). Third, every sabbath Aaron and his sons are to make food offerings on behalf of the people of Israel and as a covenant forever. They are to set two rows of six cakes baked from fine floor on a table of pure gold. They are to place pure frankincense on each row to be burned as a memorial portion. Aaron and his sons shall eat the bread in a holy place as their perpetual due, a most holy portion out of the offerings by fire to the Lord (Leviticus 24.5–9). Nāvalar notes that the details of other offerings are described in Exodus (chapter 29) and in Leviticus (chapters 2, 3, and 4), and in other places, but that those are the major examples.

Addressing the anonymous missionary, Nāvalar then says, You see those instructions for offerings in your own scriptures, yet knowing that we make offerings to our God you despise us and say, "Hey, you who offer cooked rice, fruit and other things before the linga, does it eat them?" That question reveals, in fact, your own belief that in ancient times *your* Jehovah was hungry and ate the offerings set before him.

The Śaiva Āgamas, finally, declare it meritorious to venerate the Transcendent Being who bestows grace by residing in lingas with incense and light. Nāvalar provides four examples from the Hebrew scriptures of the use of incense and light in the worship of the Lord.[13] Jehovah told Moses how to prepare incense to be placed before the ark in the tent of meeting, a compound that is very holy to the people of Israel (Exodus 30.34–36). Aaron is to burn that incense within the veil so that a cloud of incense may cover the mercy seat placed on the ark (Leviticus 16.12–13). Moses ordered Aaron to burn incense in fire taken from the altar and to run quickly with it to an assembly of people to make atonement for them (Numbers 16.46). And Jehovah commanded Moses to construct an altar of incense and have Aaron burn incense on it every morning when he dresses the lamps and every evening when he sets the lamps, throughout the generations (Exodus 30.7–8).

Therefore, Nāvalar says to the missionary, seeing that your own scriptures say Jehovah ordered incense to be burnt for himself and that his devotees did so, it is stupid for you to despise us for presenting incense and light to our Transcendent Being.

Liturgies in the Presence of God

Ārumuga Nāvalar next compares elements in temple rites. In three chapters he discusses the burning of lights in temples, the playing of musical instruments and dancing, and the observance of auspicious times.

Śaiva scriptures say it is meritorious to light lamps in Śiva temples. The Bible, Nāvalar points out, says the same thing. The Lord told Moses to have a light from olive oil kept burning continually. Aaron is to keep a light outside the curtain of the ark from evening to morning, for all generations. And he is to keep the lamps upon the lampstand of pure gold before the Lord continually (Leviticus 24.1–4 and Exodus 27.20–21). The Lord instructed Moses to have Aaron set up seven lamps to give light in front of a lampstand made with a pattern of hammered gold from its base to its flowers (Numbers 8.1–4).

Nāvalar then addresses the missionary: Even when you see that command to burn lamps in temples right in your own scriptures, still you say to us, "Do you spend so much money to burn lamps in your temples? Is your Transcendent Being blind?" That abuse is ignorant, is it not?

Nāvalar next observes that according to Śaiva texts, when conducting such events as an unction of a linga, a ceremony of worship, and a festival, it is meritorious to play various instruments and to perform dances in the presence of Śiva. He lists similar declarations and practices in the Bible. Following the command of Moses, Levites carried the ark upon their shoulders with poles and David told their leaders to appoint their brothers as singers who should play loudly on musical instruments (harps, lyres, cymbals) to raise sounds of joy (1 Chronicles 15.15–16). Some singers were to sound bronze cymbals, some were to play harps, and some were to lead with lyres (1 Chronicles 15.19–21). All of Israel brought the ark this way, with shouting and to the sound of the horn, trumpets, and cymbals, making loud music on harps and lyres (1 Chronicles 15.28). Two priests are to blow trumpets continually before the ark (1 Chronicles 16.6). The sons of Aaron, the *ācāryas,* shall blow trumpets as a remembrance before God throughout the generations. The Lord told Moses, When at war in your land, the trumpet alarm will be a remembrance before God and you will be saved from your oppressors. The trumpet shall be blown over the burnt offerings and the peace offerings on the day of your gladness, at appointed feasts, and at the beginnings of the months (Numbers 10.8–10). A psalm proclaims, With the lyre and with songs and the lyre, sing to the Lord. With trumpets and horns make a joyful noise before the King, the Lord (Psalms 98.5–6). And David and all the house of Israel made merry with all their might before the Lord, with lyres, harps, tambourines, castanets, and cymbals (2 Samuel 6.5).

The Śaiva scriptures, he continues, delineate certain days as auspicious, for example, Monday, Wednesday, Friday, Sunday, the new moon, the full moon, the fourth of the lunar month, the sixth of the lunar month, the full moon of Kārttikai, the Night of Śiva, the birth of the month, the birth of the year, and those of a festival. On such auspicious days it is particularly meritorious to turn the mind inward from the senses, to limit food, and to worship the Transcendent Being ritually in a special way.

Similar observances of auspicious times are found in the Bible. When a woman asked her husband to give her a servant and ass so she might quickly visit a man of God and return, he replied, Why go today since it is neither a new moon nor a day of rest (2 Kings 4.22–23)? David said the sons of Levi shall praise and thank the Lord whenever burnt offerings are offered on days of rest, on new moons, and feast days (1 Chronicles 23.31). And the Lord told Moses that the day of rest, the birth of the month, the new moon, the full moon, and the days of festivals are auspicious times; that on those days the Lord's convocations are to be held, ordinary work is not to be done, and burnt sacrifices of flesh and other things are to be offered in the eternal fire; and that each according to his resolution is to fast and perform his vow right on the appointed days (Leviticus, chapter 23 and other places).

Even though you see these sayings in your own Bible, Nāvalar says to the missionary, and even though you celebrate Sunday as an auspicious day just like us, you tell us that all times are equal but we set some aside and call them auspicious, and the vows we observe and the festivals we celebrate are worthless. Is that kind of raving attractive?

Śiva Ācāryas

According to the Āgamas, those who have the authority to establish a linga for others to worship, to conduct ceremonial worship and festivals for others, to perform initiations, and to perform all other such ritual acts are the Śiva *ācāryas (Śivācārya).* They are Śiva Brahmins known as Ādiśaivas, "the first Śaivas," born in the lineages of the five Seers, Kauśika, etc.[14] They renounce sins, perform meritorious acts, receive all three initiations *(samaya, viśeṣa, nirvāṇa),* recite and understand the Āgamas, possess the various qualities enjoined in the Āgamas, and receive the anointing as an *ācārya.* All others of the four classes—the Brahmins, Kṣatriyas, Vaiśyas, and Śudras—who have received the anointing as *ācārya* as mentioned above have the authority to establish a linga and to perform initiations and all other such things for private worship. They do not have the authority to establish a linga for public worship or to perform other acts of public worship as mentioned above. All of these men are born human, but they are to be thought of as gods. Whoever worships them, worships Śiva. Whoever abuses them, abuses Śiva. To serve them and to act according to their instruction is highly meritorious.

Similarly, in the Bible the Lord commanded Aaron and his sons to be anointed *ācāryas,* prescribed the way to do it (Exodus 29), and Moses anointed them accordingly (Exodus 40). The Levites were separated from the people of Israel and anointed to serve the Lord (Numbers 8). Aaron, his sons, and the Levite *ācāryas* in the lineage of his father were to receive no portion or inheritance among the people of Israel. The Lord alone was to be their inheritance (Numbers 18.20 and Deuteronomy 18.1–2). From the offerings that the people of Israel bring to the Lord (flesh, breads, etc.), a portion is to be given Aaron, to his sons, and to the Levites (Deuteronomy 18). The Levite must not be forsaken (Deuteronomy 12); everyone should hear his word and follow it (Deuteronomy 17). The Lord punished those who spoke against Aaron (Numbers 16). The generations of the sons of Aaron are qualified to become *ācāryas* and those among them who possess the necessary qualities have the right to become *ācāryas* (Leviticus 21).[15] Seeing all that in your own scriptures, Nāvalar asks the missionary rhetorically, why do you rave on that all men are equal, but that Śaivas, out of their ignorance, call some men among themselves *ācāryas* and Brahmins, say that they alone are supreme, and wander around worshipping them and serving them?

We note parenthetically that Nāvalar is right in drawing the parallel between the Śaiva and the Israelite notions of priesthood over against the missionary's denial of priesthood, but that he ignores a fundamental difference in those notions. The texts he cites from the Bible do not urge the worship of priests as gods as the Āgamas do.

Bodily Purity and Pollution

Ārumuga Nāvalar moves on to treat the purity and pollution of the body in two chapters. When Śaivas perform meritorious acts each day—the daily rites of the initiated, softly uttered prayers, formal worship, temple service, the study of the Vedas, Āgamas, and Śāstras, and so on—they must do them only after the body has been purified and while wearing clean clothes. If they do them without such purification, the Śaiva scriptures declare, it is a sin. Similar prescriptions are found in the Bible. The Lord told Moses that on the third day he would appear to all the people on Mount Sinai. Therefore, he said, go to the people, have them wash their clothes today and tomorrow and purify them so they may be ready on the third day (Exodus 19.10–11). The Lord told Moses to wash Aaron and his sons with water at the door of the tent, to dress Aaron in pure clothes, and to anoint him as *ācārya* and make him pure. Moses did so. When Moses and Aaron and his son went into the tent and approached the altar, they washed their hands and feet (Exodus 40.12–13, 16, 31–32). The Lord told Moses to put a bronze laver with water between the tent and the altar for washing. Aaron and his sons are to wash their hands and feet when they go into the tent or when they come near the altar to burn an offering to the Lord. The washing of hands and feet is to be a statute forever, to them and to all their descendants throughout all generations (Exodus 30.17–21).

Śaiva scriptures declare that bodily pollution arises from birth and death. After a designated period of time the uncleanness is removed by purifications. Pollution arises during the three days of a woman's menstruation and is removed by purification on the fourth day. Polluted people are not to be touched. The Bible contains similar declarations. The Lord told Moses that a woman who bears a male child shall be unclean seven days, as at her menstruation. After the child's circumcision, she shall be unclean for thirty-three days and shall not touch any holy thing or enter the holy place until purified. If she bears a female child, she shall be unclean two weeks, as in her menstruation, and then again for sixty-six days (Leviticus 12.1–5). The *ācāryas,* the sons of Aaron, are not to defile themselves by the dead except for their nearest of kin (Leviticus 21.1–3). Whoever touches the carcass of an animal that is permitted for eating shall be unclean until evening (Leviticus 11.39). When a woman has her menstrual discharge of blood, she shall be unclean for seven days, and whoever touches her shall be unclean until evening. During her impurity, everything on which she lies and sits shall be polluted. Whoever touches her bed or anything on which she sits shall wash his clothes and bathe in water and be unclean until evening. Any man who lies with her receives her pollution and shall be unclean for seven days; and every bed on which he lies shall be polluted (Leviticus 15.19–24). Other details on pollution are found in Leviticus 11–15 and 21.

Donated Properties

Nāvalar concludes the theme of liturgical parallels with a consideration of property donated to the temple. Donating properties to temples as far as one is able is meritorious, according to the Āgamas. A similar teaching is found in the Bible. The Lord told Moses he was ready to receive offerings given willingly: gold, silver and bronze, various cloths and skins, acacia wood, oil and spices, and precious stones (Exodus 25.1–7 and 35.4–9). Men and women came willingly, bringing brooches, earrings, signet rings, armlets and all sorts of gold objects as offerings to the Lord (Exodus 35.22). The leaders of the people of Israel brought six covered wagons and twelve oxen (Numbers 7.3). The first offering made at the tent was of one silver plate and one silver basin, both full of fine flour mixed with oil for a cereal offering; one golden dish full of incense; one young bull, one ram, one male lamb a year old, for a burnt offering; one male goat for a sin offering; and two oxen, five rams, five male goats and five male lambs a year old for the peace offerings (Numbers 7.13–17). When making atonement for oneself, the rich shall not give more and the poor shall not give less than a half shekel as offering (Exodus 30.15). Money brought into the house of the Lord was given to the workmen who were repairing the house of the Lord with it. Money from guilt offerings and sin offerings belonged to the priests (2 Kings 12.13–14, 16).[16]

The First Discussion

Having concluded his discussion of the liturgical aspects of Śaiva and Israelite temple worship, Nāvalar pauses to point out their implications to the anonymous Protestant missionary. His comments reveal his response to the Bible as he encountered it. Nāvalar never discussed these ideas with an observant Jew, but his critique of the Protestant position in the mid-nineteenth century resembles in part the stance a Jew might have taken toward a nineteenth-century Protestant missionary who similarly sought to convert him.

Nāvalar first addresses the fact that Protestants do not follow the prescriptions for worship given in their own scriptures. Śaivas still perform the acts of worship their scriptures prescribe, but the missionary has given up the rites prescribed for him. Moreover, the missionary asserts that none of the ritual acts the Śaiva performs has any value and that the Transcendent Being who prescribed them therefore is not truly the Transcendent Being. If that is so, Nāvalar observes, then Jehovah who prescribed rites very similar to those of the Śaivas is not truly the Transcendent Being either.

The New Testament, he goes on to argue, provides the missionary no basis for abandoning those prescriptions for worship. The missionary says that Jehovah, who is the Transcendent Being, is Father, Son, and Holy Spirit, three persons. Among them, the Son became the human avatar named Jesus Christ. He renounced all those ritual acts and therefore we do not perform them. But, Nāvalar responds, Jehovah had repeatedly said that those ritual acts are to be performed for all generations.[17] If Jesus Christ did in fact renounce as useless the ritual acts that his Father Jehovah had enjoined for ever, then it shows him to be smarter than his Father and in rebellion against him. How, he asks, can anyone believe that two persons who disagree like that are equal in knowledge and power?

The missionary may say, however, that all along Jehovah the Father thought these ritual acts of worship should be given up in later days, but that in the meantime they should serve as symbols of the future crucifixion. But, Nāvalar replies, the statement, "an everlasting statute," does not suggest ever abandoning it. And, if Jehovah commands ritual acts that will be fruitful for earlier people but that for later people will be fruitless and abandoned, then he is not innately intelligent. Moreover, the four Gospels show that Christ the Lord himself followed the "everlasting statute" of Jehovah and participated in the commanded rites, beginning with his own circumcision, and did not believe they should be given up.

The missionary says that Jesus Christ was born as a man to be crucified on a cross and to die for the sins of all people. Jehovah, he says, instituted the ritual acts of the Old Testament as symbols of that future event. A symbol is useful so long as the thing it symbolizes is not present, but when it is at hand, the symbol has lost its usefulness and can be discarded. Similarly, the missionary says, once the crucifixion occurred, the ritual acts that symbolized it were useless and should be discarded.

Now if that were true, Nāvalar responds, as soon as Christ died, all those ritual acts would have been given up as useless, but that was not the case. Paul and other Apostles continued to practice them.[18] When Paul did abandon circumcision, he abandoned only that and nothing else.[19] In any case, Paul was only a man, not a god. If you say, however, that Paul gave circumcision up in accord with the words of Christ, who was a god, where do you find Christ saying that? There is no place in the New Testament where Christ the Lord says he would have all those ritual acts abandoned as soon as he died. Therefore, whoever abandons them acts directly against the eternal statute of Jehovah.

The missionary says that all ritual acts commanded in the Old Testament are symbols. But, Nāvalar responds, symbolic acts are useless if one does not know what they symbolize. Nowhere does the Lord explicitly give their meanings as symbols. If Moses and others who performed those ritual acts thought them to be symbolic but did not know what they symbolized, then they received no benefits from performing them. The missionary, he concludes, makes no sense.

Ārumuga Nāvalar ends this discussion by presenting the Śaiva view of ritual acts and of their symbolic meaning. He explains that the

Āgamas are divided into two parts. The first teaches ritual acts, the second teaches direct knowledge of Śiva, *Śivajñāna*. Śivajñāna is the direct cause of release from birth and death, *mukti*. Ritual acts make one fit for Śivajñāna and create the lineage of gurus by which one attains mukti. All of those ritual acts symbolize Śivajñāna. At the emanation of the world Śiva himself revealed the meaning of each ritual act in the Āgamas. All of the rituals appropriate to a person and as taught by an *ācārya* are to be followed until Śivajñāna appears. Once Śivajñāna has appeared, however, one may abandon ritual acts altogether or one may continue to observe them for the sake of others. Śaivas thus perform ritual acts that have come down to them in the Āgamas through the lineage of gurus for the sake of obtaining the direct knowledge of Śiva.

But, Nāvalar says to the missionary, you do not know the slightest thing about that. You think of yourself as the ruling colonialist and spend your days vainly thinking your job is to go on despising us and our religion as you please, just as you have done until now. Give up that idea, understand the truth, and be free, be free.

Ārumuga Nāvalar now turned to eight elements that Śaivas and Israelites share in their respective ways of life.

The Insignia of Śiva

Vibhūti is cowdung that has been burned to ash and ritually consecrated with Śiva mantras. Similarly, the beads called the "eye of Rudra" *(rudrākṣa)* are consecrated with Śiva mantras. With its animal defilement removed, *vibhūti* symbolizes the nature of Śiva *(Śivatva)*, which removes defilement from the soul. The "eye of Rudra" beads symbolizes the grace that appears in Śiva's eyes. When those who think of themselves as Śiva's slaves *(aṭimaikaḷ)*[20] wear those symbols and commit their mind, speech, and body to his service, others recognize them as devotees. Such true slaves of Śiva are themselves objects of devotion. The Vedas and Āgamas declare that all those who believe the Śaiva religion alone is the true religion and enter into its way of life are to wear these insignia of Śiva always and in accord with the rites.

In the Bible we find similar insignia. The Lord told Moses and Aaron that the ashes from the skin, flesh, blood, and dung of a burnt heifer shall be kept in a clean place outside of camp for the people of Israel to use for the removal of sin (Numbers 19.5, 9).[21] The Lord told Moses to have the people of Israel put tassels on the corners of their garments, each tassel with a cord of blue, as a reminder of his commandments (Numbers 15.37–40). And Moses told the people of Israel in Egypt to put the blood of the passover lamb on the lintel and doorposts of their houses so the destroyer would not enter and slay them (Exodus 12.22–23).[22] He ends the chapter admonishing the missionary: Since you read those commands in your own scriptures and you eat bread and wine, meditating on them as the insignia of Christ's flesh and blood, it is unjust for you to despise us for wearing *vibhūti* and *rudrākṣa* beads as insignia of Śiva.

Visualizing God

According to Śaiva texts, it is meritorious to worship Śiva while visualizing him. The devotee first learns a Śiva mantra from the guru and then everyday uses the eyes to visualize Śiva while the mind dissolves lovingly, like wax dissolves in the midst of a fire radiating joy. The devotee ritually repeats the Śiva mantra softly while pondering its meaning. Then he recites Śiva's names, sings him songs, and offers him praise. Nāvalar cites only one parallel from the Old Testament. David appointed a thanksgiving to be sung before the ark which begins, Praise the Lord, call on his name, make his deeds known among the people. Sing of him, praise him, *visualize* all his glorious deeds and speak of them. Praise the greatness of his holy name (1 Chronicles 16.8–10).

We note parenthetically that the parallel may not be exact.[23] The act of remembrance called for here by the word "visualize" *(dhyānittu)* may not have meant the same as *dhyāna* in the Śaiva context he describes. In the Śaiva context, *dhyāna* is performed by creating inner mental visions of Śiva in precise forms like those sculpted on temples.[24] It is a mode of yoga, an exercise in visual and mental self-control more akin to the meditational techniques of ecstatics than to the more generalized remembrance or recollection suggested by the biblical text.

Prostration and Circumambulation

The Śaiva scriptures proclaim it meritorious to prostrate before God ritually, to circumambulate him by walking, and to circumambulate him by rolling one's body on the ground. Nāvalar cites three parallels from the Old Testament. The admonition, Come, let us worship and bow down, let us kneel before the Lord (Psalms 95.6); the report that when fire came from the Lord and consumed the offerings on the altar, all the people shouted and fell on their faces (Leviticus 9.24); and the report that when Joshua saw the commander of the army of the Lord, he fell on his face to the earth and worshipped (Joshua 5.14).[25]

The missionary himself kneels in prostration and regards it as meritorious, Nāvalar then observes, so why does he say that our prostrations and circumambulations before our Transcendent Being are useless? If it is meritorious to prostrate on the ground before the Creator on only two limbs, is it not more meritorious to prostrate on eight? Is it not still more meritorious to circumambulate once and then to prostrate? And is it not of even greater merit to circumambulate by rolling one's whole body and then to prostrate?

The Śiva Purāṇas

The Śiva Purāṇas are books that tell of Śiva's greatness, of the meritorious acts to be performed for him and for creatures, of the way to perform those acts and the benefits that come to those who do, and of sins and the punishments that come to those who commit them. The Purāṇas stimulate aversion towards sins, desire for merits alone, and devotion to Śiva. Therefore, the Śaiva scriptures declare it meritorious to worship those Purāṇas ceremonially with love and the proper rites in temples, monasteries, and other such holy places, and to read them aloud, to expound them, and to listen to them.

Nāvalar again cites only one parallel from the Old Testament.[26] On the twenty-fourth day of the seventh month, the Israelites stood in their place and read from the book of the law of the Lord for a fourth of the day (Nehemiah 9.3). But he makes his point clearly. If reading, expounding, and hearing books is a fruitful rule for one, may we not say it is also a fruitful rule for another?

Holy Bathing Places

Holy bathing places, like the Ganges of Śiva, the Ganges River, and the Bridge of Rāma at Rameshvaram, are infused with Śiva's power of grace. The Śaiva scriptures declare that those who bathe there according to the rites and with love lose their sins and diseases such as leprosy. Again Nāvalar cites only one parallel from the Old Testament. At the instruction of the prophet Elisha, Naaman bathed in the Jordan River and his leprosy disappeared (2 Kings 5).[27] To counter the objection that it was not the water of the Jordan that healed Naaman but the words of Elisha and thus the parallel is false, Nāvalar tells the reader about the Śaiva understanding of holy bathing places. They receive their power from the energy of grace *(aruḷ śakti)* that has infused them. Those who bathe there with love and according to the rites that Śiva has established will be cleansed of sin and disease through the grace that infuses the water.[28]

Gifts of Gold and Food

According to the Śaiva scriptures, it is meritorious to give gold, silver and other such things to the slaves of Śiva and to the learned, and to others such as the blind, the lame, and the sick. Gifts *(dāna)* providing for the slaves of Śiva possess an endless increase of merit.

Nāvalar selects four statements from the Old Testament as parallels.[29] The man who fears the Lord is blessed: He has given freely to the poor, his righteousness endures forever, and he is honored (Psalms 112.9). He who closes his ear to the cry of the poor will himself cry out and not be heard (Proverbs 21.13), but he who is kind to the poor lends to the Lord who will repay him for his deed (Proverbs 19.17). And Daniel advised the king of Babylon to practice righteousness and to show mercy to the oppressed so that his tranquility might lengthen (Daniel 4.27).

Similarly, the Śaiva scriptures declare as supremely meritorious the gift of food *(annadāna)* to the slaves of Śiva and the learned, and to others such as the blind and the lame. As a parallel from the Old Testament Nāvalar selects only one passage: The true fast of the Lord is to share your bread with the hungry and to bring the homeless and poor into your house and to clothe the naked. If you pour yourself out for the hungry and satisfy the desire of the afflicted, your light shall rise in the darkness and your gloom shall be like the noonday (Isaiah 58.7, 10).[30]

When you see these teachings in your own scriptures, he asks the missionary, why do you stupidly say that our gifts of gold and food have no merit and are useless?

Asceticism

Nāvalar ends his description of parallels with the subject of asceticism or *tapas.* Obstacles to the freedom that is eternal and joyous, he explains, are desires for land, gold, and women. It is therefore meritorious, the Śaiva texts declare, to renounce all three desires completely, to put on the cloth of asceticism, to take up residence in the forest, to limit one's food, to control all five senses, and in this ascetic practice to think of Śiva. Nāvalar then subdivides the subject into four topics. Renunciation of land, gold, and women is the first. These objects are impermanent and bring sorrow, he explains, and desire for them is incompatible with love for Śiva. Since desire for even a single object will inevitably inflame desire for them all and ruin one's resolution, they all must be renounced. He cites no parallel passages from the Old Testament for this topic.[31]

The wearing of the cloth of asceticism is the second. It benefits the wearer, he says, for it reminds him of his renunciation and places him among other forest dwellers. It also benefits those who see him wear it, for it singles him out as an object of their own devotion. Nāvalar cites two parallels from the Old Testament. One is the vow of a Nazirite: He shall not cut his hair during the days of the vow and shall be holy (Numbers 6.5).[32] The other is the penance of the people of Israel at the time of Ezra: On the twenty-fourth day of the seventh month the people assembled with fasting and in sackcloth and with earth upon their heads (Nehemiah 9.1).

Reduction of food as an aid to meditation is the third topic. Nāvalar cites no parallel from the Old Testament.[33] The fourth is the control of the mind so that it does not move outward through the physical senses but is kept in a continuous visualization *(dhyāna)* of the Transcendent Being. The single parallel he gives from the Old Testament is brief: Elijah wore a garment of haircloth with a girdle of leather around his loins and practiced asceticism (2 Kings 1.8).[34] His brief attention to that parallel suggests that in his mind Elijah may not have practiced a form of yoga that included visualizations *(dhyāna).*

The Second Discussion

So far in *The Abolition of the Abuse of Śaivism,* Nāvalar has been addressing questions to the anonymous Protestant missionary whom he knew had ready answers. He now addresses those answers, arguing against Protestant justifications of their nonobservance of the commandments transmitted through Moses. I shall summarize only those arguments that suggest his response to the Old Testament.

He begins by repeating the point he has made throughout: Śaivas know from all sources of knowledge that Śiva is the supreme Lord, that the Vedas and Āgamas he has graciously provided are the true scriptures, and that everything commanded in them is meritorious and will bear great results. The missionary, however, believes that those commanded acts are not meritorious and do not bear results, that the scriptures that say they do are false, and that the god who says that such and such will be the results of those acts is likewise false. Since, as has been demonstrated, the missionary's own scriptures command similar meritorious acts, his scriptures too must be false and the god he follows must also be false.

Nāvalar then takes up the Protestant insistence that faith in Christ is the only means for emancipation (*mokṣa*). Citing the New Testament, he argues that like mercy and patience, faith is itself a meritorious mental act that does not exist apart from other meritorious acts.[35] Emancipation cannot be attained, therefore, without meritorious acts.

Even if the missionary agreed to that, Nāvalar continues, he would then reply that nevertheless only meritorious acts performed according to the Christian religion produce results. Similar acts performed according to other religions are actually polluted, like the defiled garments of menstruating women, and go against the will of the Creator and lead to eternal pain in hell. Nāvalar replies that if faith in Christ depends upon the work of the Holy Spirit in the hearts of those who hear about Christ, if anyone does not have such faith it is then the fault of the Holy Spirit. If anyone goes to eternal hell for lack of such faith it is likewise God's fault. It does not make sense, he concludes, to say that everyone will go to eternal hell who does not have faith in Christ.

What does make sense, he insists, is the Śaiva point of view. The Vedas and Āgamas say that only Śaiva Siddhānta is the true religion. Only those who follow it will attain the supreme and absolute freedom *(parama mukti)* from birth and death.[36] Those who believe other scriptures to be true and follow their paths will experience the fruits caused by their various actions *(karma)* in heaven *(svarga)* and other such places. If the quality of their meritorious acts allows, they will later join Śaivism. But anyone who knows that Śaivism alone is the true religion and nevertheless joins another religion, that person will suffer in hell.

Yet, the missionary may reply, the Śiva Purāṇas say that many trifling acts of merit will lead one to emancipation *(mokṣa)* and that is unreasonable. To that Nāvalar responds with the doctrine of Śiva's authority. In the beginning, the Transcendent Being divided between meritorious and sinful acts and the respective fruits of each. Whatever he declared to be merit is merit; whatever he declared to be sin is sin. All else is neither merit nor sin. Among the merits, some trifling acts bear great results and some difficult acts bear trifling results. The same is true with sins. Those who perform meritorious or sinful acts will obtain the pleasure and pain *(sukha-duḥkha)* ordained. It is therefore true that emancipation may be attained by acts of merit that are very easy to perform. And, he reminds the missionary, the New Testament says the same thing; for example, the robber on the cross who first reviled Christ and then took refuge in him and attained emancipation.[37] Besides, if one may attain eternal hell because of a trifling act of sin, one may attain emancipation because of a trifling act of merit. If punishment comes through sin, delight comes through merit.[38]

The missionary may then say that our god Christ grants emancipation and forgiveness of sins in response to acts of faith made in full consciousness, but the Śiva Purāṇas say that emancipation may be obtained merely by repeating the name of Śiva, by wearing *vibhūti* and *rudrākṣa* beads, and by remaining for a while in holy places. Nāvalar responds by pointing out that things, places, times, and acts that the Transcendent Being has appointed are made meritorious because he infuses them with his own energy *(śakti)*. Alluding to the concept of mantra, he notes that Śiva's names are holy because they are connected to him.[39] *Vibhūti* and *rudrākṣa* beads are themselves worn by Śiva and are pervaded by his energy and are thus holy things. Those among his devotees who are his slaves are also pervaded by his energy and are also holy. Parallels are found in the missionary's own Bible, he says, especially in the New Testament.[40] From the Old Testament he cites only two examples. Elisha took the mantle of Elijah, struck the Jordan River with it, and the waters parted and he crossed over (2 Kings 2.13–14). A psalm proclaims the Lord's name as great and terrible (Psalms 99.3), suggesting to Nāvalar that the Lord's name is, like Śiva's name, a mantra.

The missionary, he continues, may then reply that the Śiva Purāṇas do not say that to attain emancipation one must have the conscious belief *(viśvāsam)* that if this is done that will result. All that is necessary, they say, is to touch *vibhūti, rudrākṣa* beads, sacred bathing places and other such things with the body.

Nāvalar agrees, but he makes a distinction between conscious belief *(viśvāsam)* and implicit faith *(śraddhā)* in the rituals and teachings of tradition. Implicit faith is the supreme ordinance *(dharma)* and the root of all meritorious acts, he says. Only with implicit faith will meritorious acts produce their appropriate results. Therefore, even if a person implicitly trusts but does not consciously believe that "by touching this holy thing my sin will disappear and I will be meritorious," still if that person touches it, the appropriate result will emerge. As a parallel from the Old Testament, he gives the instance of the corpse that revived when it touched the bones of Elisha (2 Kings 13.21).[41]

After considering several topics not germane to our discussion,[42] Nāvalar moves on to the troubling question of divine justice. Responding to the missionary's claim that except for those who have faith in Christ, all are condemned to hell eternally no matter their deeds, Nāvalar insists that there are distinctions among sins, as there are among merits, and that punishments vary accordingly. No subject would view his king as just who gives all wrongdoers the same punishment, he observes.[43] The Bible itself makes clear that those who reside in emancipation *(mokṣa)* have differing statuses reflecting differing merits, for example the commander of the army of the Lord (Joshua 5.14).[44] It also shows that differing sins receive differing punishments, for example an eye for an eye, a tooth for a tooth, a hand for a hand, and a foot for a foot (Deuteronomy 19.21).[45]

It is also not just, Nāvalar argues, for souls to be condemned to hell eternally for sins. The Transcendent Being, like a father and a king, punishes those who go wrong because he loves them. Once the limit of punishment has been reached, he tells them to go on and live rightly. Similarly, souls suffering in hell return to live again once their punishment is complete.

Moreover, he says to the missionary, if you say that our sin is so offensive to the Transcendent Being that we deserve to be in hell eternally, that makes no sense. The fruits of pleasure and pain that come from our merits and sins have to do only with us, not with the Transcendent Being. Our sin is an offense against ourself, not against him. Moreover, if someone who is both meritorious and sinful is in hell eternally for his sins, how can he experience the fruit of his merits? If the Transcendent Being does not reward both, he is not compassionate, nor true, nor just. We do not owe it to the Transcendent Being always to do the good according to his command. If we commit a trifling sin, we do not deserve eternal hell. Whatever good we do comes to us, not to him, otherwise he would not be eternally joyous.

We note parenthetically that with his statement, "We do not owe it to God always to do the good according to his command," Nāvalar has exposed a crucial difference between Śaiva and Israelite thought. The convenant idea of the Old Testament says exactly the opposite. The entire sacrificial system of the Temple in Jerusalem is based on the idea that it makes an enormous difference to God what his people do, individually and collectively. Nāvalar did not himself point that fact out, although he must have been aware of it. His purpose in *The Abolition of the Abuse of Śaivism,* after all, was to refute the Protestant missionary by showing parallels between Śaivism and the Temple worship of the Bible, not to give him ammunition by showing where the Bible and Śaivism part company. Yet we note that without the covenant there is no concept of the peoplehood of Israel that is at the heart of the Temple worship he finds so familiar in the Old Testament. Without the covenant there would only be individual destinies, which is the Śaiva position Nāvalar now turns to in his consideration of the doctrine of individual rebirth.

What is the basis for saying that souls are reborn? he asks rhetorically. The Śaiva Āgamas declare that after souls die, they experience the pleasure and pain due them from their merits and sins in heavens or in hells *(svarga-narakaṅkaḷ).* The fruits remaining from the experiences of heaven and hell cause them to be born on earth in various kinds of wombs to experience the pleasure and pain of those residual fruits. The fruits of acts performed in previous lives determine one's nature at birth, for example whether one will be ugly or beautiful, healthy or crippled, and so forth. Everyone otherwise would be born the same. To say that the Transcendent Being decides at birth how each person shall be makes no sense. It denies the orderly consequences of merits and sins and it denies his compassion towards all souls. To say that the world would not run if the Transcendent Being had not created differences between the superior and the inferior also makes no sense. If he is skilled in everything, the Transcendent Being could run the world without those differences.

To say, moreover, that differences at birth arise from the sins of the parents contradicts observed facts. In any case, is it just that a child should suffer from the karma of its mother or father? In fact, it is the way the Bible says it is: A father shall not be put to death for the children and the children shall not be put to death for the fathers; every one shall be put to death for his own sin (Deuteronomy 24.16); and the proverb, "The fathers have eaten sour grapes, and the children's teeth are set on edge," shall no longer be used in Israel (Ezekiel 18.2).

Nāvalar then explains that people do not remember their previous lives because the trauma of birth removes the memory. Like a man holding something in his hand who with full knowledge stores it away in his house and suddenly cannot remember where, we forget the actions of previous lives that have caused our birth. Even though we do not remember them, the Transcendent Being causes us to experience the pleasure and pain produced by them so that by experiencing them we will exhaust them and attain eternal freedom *(mukti).*

Continuing his exposition of Śaiva metaphysics, Nāvalar presents a vision of reality for which the only parallel that could be found in the Old Testament would be through esoteric interpretation, say, for example, in the Kabbalah. There is no beginning to the Lord *(pati),* he explains, nor to souls *(paśu),* nor to their material fetters *(pāśa).* Nor is there a beginning to the Lord's fivefold activity to free souls from those fetters and to give them transcendent joy. They are all beginningless. That is not to say, however, as the missionary no doubt would, that there is thus no difference between the Lord and souls. Both have beginningless intelligence, but the Lord's intelligence is free of imperfection while the soul's is bound to it. The Lord's intelligence bestows grace on the soul while the soul's intelligence receives it. The Lord's intelligence performs the five acts of emanation, preservation, resorption, entanglement, and release, while the soul's intelligence dependently experience those acts. The Lord's intelligence knows what cannot be known by anyone, while the souls' intelligence understands only relatively, by knowing the small in relation to the great, for example. One cannot say, therefore, that because both the Lord and the soul are beginningless that they are not different. The Lord performs his fivefold action on the soul without beginning and ceaselessly, like a person who breathes, never stopping to rest.

When does a soul whirled around like that in birth and death attain eternal freedom *(mukti)?*, he asks. When the soul is ready, he answers. After many births in which the soul has performed meritorious acts without desire, Śiva begins the infusion of divine grace into it in a sequence of four stages. Śiva then appears in the form of an *ācārya* and administers initiations to the soul, establishing it first in the path of *cārya,* and then in the paths of *kriya, yoga,* and *jñāna.* Each path respectively confers a specific goal to the faithful initiate upon death: residence with Śiva *(sāloka),* residence near Śiva *(sāmīpa),* residence with Śiva's form *(sārūpa),* and residence yoked to Śiva *(sāyujyam).* The final goal, attained by the follower of the path of *jñāna* who has received the final *(nirvāṇa)* initiation, is the only goal from which there is no rebirth. Those goals are all explained to the initiate by a guru who follows the Āgamas.

Nāvalar ends the discussion by addressing a common question raised by Protestants who spend time and money to translate the Bible and to put printed portions of it into the hands of anyone who wants it. Why, they ask, when we go to such efforts to make the Bible openly available, do you Śaivas keep your scriptures closed to public scrutiny? What are you afraid of having exposed?

Nāvalar explains that Śiva does not give permission to teach the Āgamas to anyone belonging to a religion that disparages him. As Jesus said, You shall not cast pearls before swine (Matthew 7.6). But not even all Śaivas have the right to read the Āgamas, he continued. Those who have received both the *samaya* and the *viśeṣa* initiations have the right to read the texts on ritual action. Only those who have received in addition the *nirvāṇa* initiation have the right to read the texts on esoteric wisdom. But all must enter their study through a guru, otherwise they might destroy themselves. The Āgamas may be studied only by worshipping them under the guidance of a Śaiva *ācārya.* Nāvalar then draws a parallel with the Torah scrolls kept in the Temple. The *ācāryas* of the Jews *(yūtarkaḷ),* he notes, kept their scripture in the Temple, worshipped it, and taught the people what to do from it. It does not seem, he says, that each had their own written copy to study.[46]

Conclusion

What may we conclude from Ārumuga Nāvalar's response to the written Torah as he encountered it through the Protestant missionaries? To begin, we may note the limits set for him by the context of his response. He was a devout Śaiva who had studied the written Torah as the Old Testament and within a Protestant missionary context. The audience he addressed in his booklet consisted of Tamil-speaking Śaivas whom he sought to educate and Tamil-speaking Protestant missionaries whom he sought to refute. He was not responding to Jews or to the written Torah as interpreted by the oral Torah of the Talmud. Not surprisingly, therefore, Nāvalar paid no attention to rabbinical Judaism. Although he used the words "Jews" *(yūtarkaḷ)* several times, all he probably knew about rabbinical interpretations derived from the missionaries and was most likely distorted. In any case, response to Jews was not his purpose.

We also note that he paid no attention to the differences between the Śaivism of temples in Sri Lanka and India and the Temple cult in Jerusalem, to the *lack* of parallels between them. He did not, for example, say anything negative about the animal sacrifices prescribed for the rites in the Temple even though it was an issue very close to his heart. He tried vigorously to eliminate them among the Śaivas in Jaffna, even though they were customary, because they were contrary to the prescriptions of the Āgamas. As we observed, he paid no attention to the chasm between Śaivism's idea of individual karma on one hand and Israel's idea of a collective covenant on the other.

Moreover, there is a weakness in the parallels he drew in his second set of topics. He found little in the Old Testament to suggest the value of asceticism. He cited no parallel for the absolute renunciation of land, gold, and women, no parallel for the restriction of food to enhance meditation, and no parallel attention to techniques of meditation. The parallel he cited for the practice of the visualization of God is questionable. He did take note, however, of certain ascetic modes of dress and behavior: the ascetic treatment of hair by the Nazirite, the practice of fasting by everyone on certain days, and the ascetic garb of Elijah. Those do not, however, match the crucial role of asceticism in Śaiva thought and practice. Hebrew ascetic traditions during late biblical times, as found in the Qumran Community for example, perhaps would have given him more exact parallels, but not being included in the Old Testament they were not known to him. The lack of explicit discussion of the Kabbalah tradition in the Bible likewise meant that possible metaphysical parallels to Śaiva theology were not known to him.

Nevertheless, Nāvalar did perceive clear parallels and his discussion of them points us in interesting directions for the comparative study of Judaism and Śaivism. His major point, of course, is the similarity of worship in the temple cultus of both traditions. Further examination of the two modes of temple worship will reveal considerable differences hidden within the many similarities he cites, but an exploration of the phenomenological catalogue he made does reveal the way he understood both temple traditions and the views of the world they imply. His view prompts comparative questions, of the oneness of God in both traditions, for example. Is Śaivism as he understood it idolatrous from the point of view of the written Torah? How does the linga as symbol and residence of Śiva in fact compare to the mercy seat on the ark? Such questions lead us into to a comparative study of the Temple in Jerusalem before its destruction in 70 C.E. and the contemporary Śaiva temple, the one in Cidambaram for example. Each is acknowledged as *the* temple of their respective traditions, and in each the *absence* of a visible icon of God's personhood is the symbol of his presence.

It is striking to me how comfortable Nāvalar seems to have felt with Israelite temple worship. Unlike the Protestant missionary who found it an alien realm, part of a world no longer relevant to God's plan, Nāvalar the Śaiva found it familiar, part of the realm he lived in day to day. He viewed it as part of the plan of the Transcendent Being and easily recognized features of his own tradition in it.

Yet he must also have felt decidedly uncomfortable with some of it, though he did not say so. The animal sacrifices and the use of blood in Temple rites,[47] which he did not disparage, no doubt reminded him of the slaughter of animals in local cults around him in Sri Lanka. Indeed, Israelite temple worship must have appeared to him to be an elaborate version of the local worship of Śiva's servants, the gods *(deva)* and demons *(pēy)* who delight in the blood and flesh of goats, chickens, and buffaloes. To his mind such local cults have a limited validity, but are of an inferior status and not at all to be confused with the scriptural worship of Śiva, for whom the Āgamas prescribe only vegetarian offerings. In contrast to the Temple rites of the Old Testament, no flesh or blood is ever to cross the boundary of a temple of Śiva consecrated according to the Āgamas. The Jehovah that Nāvalar saw in the Old Testament must have looked to him like one of Śiva's many servants whom he uses for his own purposes, a god *(deva)* worshipped by unclean and alien foreigners *(mleccha)* whose ritual impurity (though not their colonial power) resembled the low-caste and untouchable worshippers of the created gods and demons around him in the "land of the noble" *(āryadeśa)*. Indeed, his consistent use of the word *mukti* for the eternal freedom from birth and death conferred by Śiva in contrast to the word *mokṣa* for the heaven of emancipation taught by the missionaries indicates his belief that Jehovah in his heaven is part of the world of birth and death, just like all the other gods and their heavens that Śiva has created.

Nāvalar's explanation of the Śaiva basis for religious tolerance suggests another point of comparison. Śaiva Siddhānta is the only fully true religion, he asserted, but others have their place in Śiva's scheme. What is Śiva's scheme? During the course of each soul's countless lives, he said, human birth may occur in barbarian lands *(mlecchadeśa)* where the worship of Śiva is not found and where the embodied soul might live and worship according to the religions found there (for example as a Jew or a Christian or a Muslim). Due to positive fruits harvested by meritorious actions in those lives, the soul might eventually be born in the noble lands *(āryadeśa),* India or Sri Lanka. After living according to one or another *āryan* tradition in various lives, the soul's meritorious fruits might result in birth as a Śaiva. It is while the soul is embodied as a Śaiva, indeed probably after many lives as a Śaiva, that it then receives the rare opportunity to attain eternal freedom from all births through a combination of its own efforts and the grace of Śiva.

Now, in that scheme, the religions of the West are barbarian traditions of lower status, but they serve a useful purpose as stepping stones to rebirth among Śaivas. Though they are polluted traditions and based on significant areas of ignorance, they are nevertheless useful in Śiva's organization of the universe. Nāvalar therefore never demanded that Christianity be dismantled or even removed from Sri Lanka and India. He demanded only that missionary abuse of Śaivism and the conversion of ignorant Śaivas cease. He believed, then, that there is a Śaiva basis for the tolerance of other religions: They are propaedeutics for rebirth as a Śaiva, the final stage before eternal and transcendent freedom *(mukti).* The missionaries Nāvalar encountered had no such basis for tolerance, because they believed that all people must become Christians if they are to attain emancipation. In their view, all other religions should disappear.

If Nāvalar had discussed his missionary problem with a rabbi, he might have learned of a functionally similar tolerance of other religions, but from a very different basis, the rabbinical interpretation of the covenant with Noah.[48] Accordingly, Jews and Śaivas living, let us say, in mid-nineteenth-century Sri Lanka, could have tolerated each other for religious reasons, but for very different ones. Jews could have viewed the Śaiva community as valid as long as it fulfilled the seven commandments of Noah's covenant, while the Śaivas could have viewed the Jewish community as a valid preparation for rebirth as a Śaiva. The result would be a mutual tolerance based in their respective traditions. Likewise, both would have been offended by the intolerance of proselytizing Christians who sought to end those traditions through conversion.

That brings us to a final comparison suggested by Nāvalar. He drew the distinction between conscious belief *(viśvāsam)* and implicit faith *(śraddhā).* Although the Protestant missionary whom Nāvalar addressed insisted on conscious belief in Christ as the only valid basis for a relationship to God, Nāvalar argued that the Bible contains examples where implicit faith also constitutes a basis for a valid relationship. The argument, it seems, is not only about the nature of emancipation, but also about the validity of one's own received tradition in effecting that emancipation. Jews and Śaivas in mid-nineteenth-century Sri Lanka might have agreed that conscious belief is extremely important for one's relationship to God, but that the fundamental root of that relationship is an implicit faith in the tradition that has given one birth. Tradition received in the family and affirmed through behavior is the beginning. Education should mature conscious belief in a manner consonant with tradition and should deepen understanding of it, but conscious belief is based on traditional practice. Over against that shared view is the anonymous Protestant missionary whom Nāvalar addressed. To him, it seems, conscious faith in Christ is the criterion for emancipation regardless of one's received tradition. Even birth into a Christian community and implicit faith in its tradition presumably will not bring emancipation without conscious belief in Christ.

As I hope I have demonstrated, Ārumuga Nāvalar's *Abolition of the Abuse of Śaivism* is no casual apologia. It reflects the thoughtful reflections and responses of a well educated man who gave his entire life to the devoted service of Śiva. Written in his mother tongue of Tamil, it reveals the way he talked to fellow Śaivas about what they were forced by Protestant missionaries to confront. It is remarkable that he found the Old Testament so familiar and the teachings of the Protestant missionaries so alien. His response to the written Torah as he found it, whatever its limitations, identifies issues that from a Hindu point of view, at least, could begin a fruitful comparative study of Hindu and Jewish traditions.

7

Yom Kippur: The Festival of Closing the Doors

Shalva Weil

Introduction

C. J. Fuller provides fresh insight into the relationship between the polytheistic pantheon and Indian social structure, arguing that the worship of deities at the lower levels of the pantheon legitimates the hierarchical nature of the caste system, whereas the worship of Sanskritic deities at the upper levels of the Hindu pantheon actually eliminates relationship with inferiors.[1] Paradoxically, then, it is not the substantial "Sanskritic" divinities which symbolize caste society, but the village deities which reinforce complementarity and hierarchy. Fuller reaches this conclusion by an examination of the deities' cults and the rituals surrounding them, rather than by an analysis of the deities in the abstract.

In this paper, I wish to take Fuller's hypothesis one step further by analysing the relationship between Indian social structure and worship enacted not at the fringes of the Hindu pantheon but beyond it: by "out-of-caste" Indians who belong to another religion. The nature of complementarity in Indian society will thus be explored by analysing a complex ritual, central to Jewish worship and religion and focal to Bene Israel (literally, "Children of Israel") Indian Jews' self-perception as an out-of-caste minority in a dominant Hindu society.

The Bene Israel, who numbered only 15,000 at their height in India,[2] claim that they originated in the Kingdom of Israel and, according to their own tradition, arrived in India in the year 175 B.C.E. Their origin myth relates that they were shipwrecked off the Konkan coast and retained their faith in monotheism and memories of the major festivals and the sabbath. They were incorporated in the caste system in the Konkan villages as *Shanwār Talīs* or "Saturday oilmen" since, as Jews, they refrained from work on the sabbath.[3] By the nineteenth century, the majority of Bene Israel lived in Bombay. Since 1947, with the withdrawal of the British from India and the founding of the State of Israel in 1948, Bene Israel have begun to emigrate to the Jewish homeland. In 1993, approximately 50,000 Bene Israel and Israelis of Bene Israel origin were living in Israel, with 4,000 remaining in India.

As opposed to the small group of Cochin Jews from the Malabar coast who were in contact with other Jewish communities in Europe and elsewhere for centuries,[4] the Bene Israel were cut off from other Jews until relatively recently, and therefore maintained a different pattern of adaptation to Indian society. Certain scholars place the first meeting of the Bene Israel with a representative of world Jewry in the eighteenth century,[5] but it must be pointed out that some Bene Israel only came into contact with other Jews during this century.

In this paper I shall enquire into the Bene Israel worship on the holiest day of the Jewish calendar, Yom Kippur, in order to demonstrate a paradoxical contention: that out-of-caste Indians, in their worship of the Jewish religion, actually reinforce the complementarity inherent in the caste system.[6] My examination relies upon historical data from India, and proceeds with a general analysis of Yom Kippur motifs as reflected both in the enactment of Jewish ritual on the day itself and in similar themes in the Hindu religion. The paper then turns to an analysis of attitudes and behavior among the Bene Israel towards the outlined motifs, and concludes with a description of Yom Kippur worship among Bene Israel Indian immigrants in Israel.[7]

Bene Israel Worship on Yom Kippur

The Bene Israel in India observed Yom Kippur or the Day of Atonement on the tenth of the Hebrew month of Tishri,[8] in accordance with the commandment in Numbers 29.7. The fast was known in Marathi as *Darfalnicha San,* or "Holiday of the Closing of the Doors." Reverend Wilson, a nineteenth-century missionary among the Bene Israel, described the day thus: "They spend much time, both during the night and day, in confessing their sins, and supplicating the divine mercy, agreeably to the forms of their liturgy. In the course of the night, they offer up prayers to God, for the sovereign of Britain, the Governor of Bombay, and all the authorities of the country. The day following the Kippur is distinguished for the exercise of hospitality and charity."[9]

On the day prior to the fast, the Bene Israel anointed their bodies with coconut oil and bathed in cold water; they dressed in white clothes. They believed that the souls of the dead visited their relatives on that day and departed on the day after Yom Kippur. Prior to the fast they held a memorial service for the dead and made a *melida* calling upon three generations of ancestors to join them over the fast day. They then partook of a festive meal and fasted from sundown to sunset the following day, according to Jewish custom.

In the Konkan villages, the Bene Israel would stay at home until nightfall. They would not work or even communicate with the local Hindus. As one ex-villager related: "None of us did any chores on that day. We did not even milk our cows. Our Hindu neighbours quietly took care of that for us. The Hindus of the village knew and respected our custom and would say 'Today the Bene Israel will not talk.' "[10] In the towns, the Bene Israel would remain in synagogue until the end of the fast, having arrived for the morning service during the night.

The Yom Kippur service was performed in the synagogue[11] in perfect accordance with Sephardic Jewish liturgy. The evening or *Kol Nidre* service was recited the first evening, and morning, additional, afternoon, and *Ne'ilah* services were recited the following day. The service was led by a *hazan* (cantor) who sang melodies familiar to other Jewish communities.

At the termination of the fast, the Bene Israel made a benediction for the new moon. In the villages "our neighbors would very unobtrusively come to our courtyard, leave the milk, which they, on our stead, had collected from our cows, and then they would silently go away."[12]

The following day was known as *Shila San,* or "Festival of Stale Things," since all the food was prepared prior to the fast. On the morning of *Shila San* the Bene Israel prepared a memorial service during which the souls of the ancestors were believed to depart. The rest of the day was spent in rejoicing, visiting friends and relatives, and giving alms to the poor.

Analysis of Yom Kippur Motifs

Yom Kippur is the most solemn day of the Jewish calendar. Literally translated, it means the "Day of Atonement," on which Jews pray while fasting for the atonement of their sins. The basic elements of the fast are of biblical origin, but the ritual has developed over the centuries. The evening liturgy of the Yom Kippur festival known as *Kol Nidre* was probably incorporated in medieval times. The liturgy for the whole day includes declarations of faith, memorial prayers for the dead, poems requesting forgiveness, quotations from selected passages in the Bible, and recitations of the order of service of the High Priest in the Temple on the Day of Atonement. The major motifs inherent in the Yom Kippur service are the themes of atonement, purification, death, and sacrifice.

Atonement

Yom Kippur, or the "Day of Atonement," derives its name from the injunction in Leviticus 16.30: "For on this day He shall atone you of all your sins, you shall be cleansed before God." The theme of atonement from sins is conveyed throughout the day, expressed continuously in the liturgy and in other symbolic actions. Atonement for all types of transgressions are included, ranging from speaking badly about other people to adultery or murder; for example: "We have trespassed; we have dealt treacherously; we have stolen; we have spoken slander; we have committed iniquity and have done wickedly; we have acted presumptuously; we have counselled evil; we have uttered lies. . . ."[13]

The ultimate quest is redemption from sins both on an individual level, so that a person may start the new year with a clean slate, and on a collective level, in the hope that all human ills will be rectified in an era of redemption. This is manifest during the course of the day when worshippers confess to a long list of sins nine times: four times communally and five times individually.

Purification

Atonement is associated with purity and the attainment of a pure state through fasting and other abstentions. Wearing leather shoes is forbidden, as are sexual relations. The body is bathed prior to Yom Kippur, but no washing is permitted on the day itself. Judaic Oral Law[14] details these and other preparations incumbent upon the individual worshipper prior to the fast. Custom dictates the wearing of clean, white clothes by women. Such practices reinforce the status of the day as a time when people retreat from daily routine to achieve a state of ultimate purification through atonement. As it is reiterated in the liturgy in the morning, afternoon, and evening services: "For on this day shall atonement be made for you to purify you; from all your sins shall you be pure before the Lord."[15]

Death

The liturgical symbolism on the Day of Atonement often evokes death. One of the most moving prayers recited on the day recalls different forms of death and natural disasters which could befall man if he does not repent. The prayer is as follows:

> On the first day of the year it is inscribed, and on the fast day of atonement it is sealed and determined how many shall pass away and how many will be born; who shall live and who die; who shall finish his allotted time, and who not; who is to perish by water, who by fire, who by the sword and who by wild beast; who by hunger and who by thirst; who by an earthquake, or who by the plague; who by strangling and who by lapidation; who shall be at rest and who shall be wandering; who to remain tranquil and who be disturged; who shall reap enjoyment and who be painfully afflicted; who become poor and who grow rich; who shall be cast down and who exalted.[16]

Then in unison the congregation shouts out: "But penitence, prayer and charity can avert the evil decree."[17]

God is conceived as the Supreme Judge who weighs and finally decides who should live and who should die on this day. Some worshippers even wear shrouds as white garments on this solemn day.

Sacrifice

One of the highlights of the Day of Atonement is reciting the sacrificial service which was carried out in Temple times. Details of the sacrifices are given in explicit detail with worshippers symbolically dipping their fingers in the animal blood and sprinkling it in imitation of the High Priest of the ancient Temple. A prayer is recited expressing the hope that the ancient sacrificial cult will be revived when the Messiah comes in the era of redemption.

The notion of *self*-sacrifice is also a central theme of Yom Kippur. As Deshen shows, the worshipper, through liturgy, "identifies himself as a sacrifice and prepares to offer himself on the holy day."[18] This theme is heightened by references to the *akedah* (sacrifice), the biblical story of the near-sacrifice of Isaac by his own father recited on the New Year (ten days previously), and to descriptions of the scapegoat banished to the desert by the High Priest in Temple times "so that it might carry away the sins of this people to an uninhabited country."[19]

Symbolic expression of self-sacrifice can be found in the custom of *kaparot* (atonements) performed on the morning before the fast. This custom, though opposed by certain rabbinic authorities, is surprisingly pervasive among Jews today.[20] A male Jew takes a rooster while a female Jew holds a hen and they swing it around their heads while reciting, "This is my substitute, this is my redemption. This fowl will go to its death and I shall be admitted and allowed to live a long, happy, and peaceful life." The fowl is slaughtered and its monetary equivalent is given to the poor.[21]

Yom Kippur Themes in Hinduism

The motifs which form the core of Yom Kippur belief and practice and are central to the Jewish religion are also of focal significance in Hinduism. I examine here these same themes with the full knowledge that Hinduism is in no way a monolithic religion; nor, for that matter, is Judaism. Nevertheless, the comparative approach serves to highlight the differences in emphasis between the two religions while acknowledging that one must clearly avoid "characterising a whole civilization in terms of a single value."[22]

Atonement

The idea of atonement is bound up in Hindu thought with karma and conduct in this world which will lead to ultimate redemption. In its classic formulation, the individual passes in this life through four stages *(asramas).* In the final stage, he may "free his soul" from material matters by meditation and penance.

Associated with the notion of atonement, then, is the elevation of asceticism as a desirable virtue and the idealization of the *sannyāsin* as a rootless wanderer. The theme of other-worldliness (as developed by Dumont as the "individual-outside-the-world")[23] is familiar in Hindu tradition, not as a one-day-a-year rite, but as a permanent condition. The *sannyāsin* renounces this world and, as an ascetic, afflicts his body through fasting and prayer in order to achieve redemption. The ascetic sometimes lives as a solitary individual, but at other times he may also dwell in groups. He may inflict upon himself extraordinary pain in order to free himself from life. The ultimate aim of the ascetic is transcendental knowledge *(mokṣa)* and ultimate salvation.

Purification

According to Dumont, purity and pollution are fundamental and complementary opposites which constitute the underlying ideology of

Hindu society.[24] Although this scheme has been criticized for its simplicity,[25] it still remains true that negative events such as illness or misfortune are attributed to the past impure actions of individuals. By this ideology, people must practice austerity and purify themselves through means such as cleansing the body or observing restrictions such as fasting or sexual abstinence in order to obtain reprieve.

Since man is born in an impure state, according to Hindu thought, he also returns to an impure state at death. This impurity, however, is always relative according to caste.[26] As Pocock has put it:

> One *mata* might be pure for this caste and impure for that; a custom or practice that is today the mark of a high caste can tomorrow become the distinctive trait of a low caste; but always the elements, from whatever source they derive, are subordinate to the pattern in which the structure of caste arranges them.[27]

Relative purity is thus established through caste affiliation and adherence to acts, such as stricter observance of dietary practices, which over a period of time represent hierarchical changes.

Death

The doctrine of reincarnation, which is central to Hindu thought, involves belief in the passage of the soul from life to life. It attributes to all living things souls which are linked in a unified system.

The course of the passage from life to life is defined by the conduct of a person in this world. Thus, an individual who has behaved in exemplary fashion will be exalted, while a bad person will be reincarnated at a lower level of existence. The doctrine of karma links all forms of life, as well as deities, into a single system spanning past, present, and future. Thus, the souls of the departed are also part of the unitary system and can be reborn at some time in the future. As Babb has pointed out, the evidence suggests that although the karmic doctrine may be modified, "the essential idea, that of action determining the subsequent destiny of the actor, is well understood, even by people who have little direct contact with textual religion."[28]

Death is considered one of the most ritually polluting events. *Antyesti,* or the funeral ceremonies, are the final sacraments marking man's life stages. Mourners must avoid all contact with others for fear of polluting them; they must abstain from particular foods, sleep on the ground, abstain from sexual relations, and not shave their hair. At the end of the *antyesti* (after the cremation of the corpse among Hindus) the mourners must bathe to remove the pollution.

Sacrifice

Sacrifice was traditionally the theme of the Aryan cult.[29] The sacrificial food was used to gratify the gods, who partook of the food together with the worshippers. The priests, who had mastered the rituals whereby the gods participated in the sacrifice, were the key to the gains which would be incurred as a result of the sacrifice. However, there was a historical progression from sacrifice as a physical act to the internalization of sacrifice as inner purification against the evil outside.

The act of sacrifice in contemporary times came to be associated with non-Brahmanical worship of local deities of divinities, which was not sanctioned by authoritative scripture. It led to a state in which "certain religious customs (such as animal sacrifice), which are predominantly non-Brahmanical and for which textual section is allegedly absent, have tended to be designated and denigrated as superstitious."[30]

The notion of self-sacrifice in Hindu thought is even more complex. Theoretically, through sacrifice man's soul is purged of outside evil; hence, the victims of human sacrifice were often criminals.[31] Voluntary human sacrifice became quite common in medieval India, and *sati,* whereby a widow immolates herself on her husband's funeral pyre, is also a form of human sacrifice.

Bene Israel Yom Kippur Worship

The Day of Atonement can be viewed as a transitional rite: people are transposed to a unique spiritual state and returned to daily life at the end of the holy day. Deshen finds this to be a key to the question of why Jews have attributed such importance to the *Kol Nidre* prayer in the ritual of the Day of Atonement itself. He writes:

> On this day, man confronts dramatically some of the central contradictory themes of his cultural being—such as sin and redemption, defilement and purity, justice and mercy, the meaning of death and the essence of life. In the course of the ritual, he comes to realize that these cultural contradictions can be bridged. With this realization he has reached a higher state of knowledge; he has attained a deeper understanding of the essence of the culture in which is embedded all that is seemingly so contradictory and confusing.[32]

The Bene Israel, like other Jews, confront the central contradictory themes of their existence on this day. Individually, the Bene Israel Jew comes to terms with existential questions which affect his day-to-day life, family, relationships, and personal status. Communally, the Bene Israel face a central contradiction in that they merge, in one community, two world religions whose doctrines appear to be opposed. In Judaism, atonement can be sought annually on a specific and dramatic holiday; in Hinduism, the quest for atonement is perpetual. In Judaism, forgiveness is a this-worldly concept; in Hinduism, salvation through *mokṣa* in other lives is an ongoing process. In Judaism, redemption from sins is a feasible possibility; in Hinduism, only the person who renounces the world can be redeemed, while the deities can only mitigate the effects of karma. In Judaism, man can continuously purify himself; in Hinduism, a pure state can only be achieved by altering caste status over the course of more than one lifetime, or through renunciation.[33] In Judaism, death on earth until the messianic era is usually considered "final" (although an after-life *is* acknowledged), while in Hinduism, the soul passes from life to life eternally. Finally, Judaic notions of sacrifice are allied to extinct Temple practice, while in Hindu thought, past Brahmanic sacrifice is idealized at the same time that low-caste sacrifice is perpetuated.

On Yom Kippur the Bene Israel work through reversals, like other Jews, in order to be absolved as a community of individual transgressions. As Deshen notes: "The major thrust of the Day of Atonement customs, from the anthropological angle, is that these customs sharpen the worshipper's awareness that atonement here is bound up with departure from worldliness and human routine."[34] In brief, Yom Kippur, analyzed as a transitional rite in which existential contradictions are confronted, entails "liminality" in the Turnerian sense of the word.[35] However, I would argue that on this day, the Bene Israel, by conforming to standard Jewish practice and strictly observing the most important Jewish fast of the year, actually intensify their Jewish worship by incorporating Hindu modes, despite their "out-of-caste" status. Let me explicate this idea with reference to special Bene Israel observance of the Yom Kippur motifs outlined above.

Atonement

In order to atone for their sins and achieve redemption, the Bene Israel become "*sannyasin*-like" for a day, renouncing the world and cutting themselves off from other, "impure" people. The attitude of one who renounces is symbolically and literally expressed in the semantics of the day's name. For the Bene Israel, this awesome day is called in Marathi "Darfalnicha San" or literally, "Holiday of Closing the Doors." Kehimkar describes it thus: "They did not stir out of their doors which they kept locked throughout the day."[36]

Now it could be maintained that the "Holiday of Closing the Doors" could also be attributed to other Jews. In particular, the concluding service of Yom Kippur entitled *Ne'ilah* or *Ne'ilat She'arim* literally means "Closing of Gates."[37] The service is so called because at that time the gates of the Temple were closed to worshippers;[38] on another level, the idea is that at this final hour God closes the gates of heaven and seals man's fate.

However, the practice of seclusion to the point of the abrogation of physical and verbal contact with non-members of the group is not part of "normal" Yom Kippur observance for Jewish communities outside India. Historically, this unique practice has been remarked upon by non-Indian writers. For example, when the emissary Sapir (1822–85) visited the Bene Israel in 1860 from Palestine, he wrote: "The Bene Israel sit indoors . . . ,"[39] and he indeed conjectured that the name they attributed to this festival derived from the *Ne'ilah* service. However, this appears unlikely in view of the fact that the appellation refers to the whole day, and given the differing emphasis attributed to the idea by the Bene Israel.

Another description comes from Reinemann (1815–80), a Galician Jewish trader who travelled to India in the middle of the nineteenth century. He described the fast among the Bene Israel thus: "On Yom Kippur, from time immemorial, from the time of their arrival in India unto the present day, they secluded themselves in their rooms and afflicted themselves throughout the day and nobody would pass a word but each man sits and fasts."[40]

It is thus on this day that the Bene Israel, as a community, withdraw from normal interaction with others and emphasize their exclusiveness by creating symbolic and literal barriers between themselves and their neighbors. As "renouncers" on Yom Kippur, they afflict their bodies and their souls in order to achieve reprieve and redemption.

Purity

Prior to the fast the Bene Israel cleanse themselves, chastise their bodies, and dress in white clothes, representing austerity. A nineteenth-century description of this Bene Israel practice can be found in the *Bombay Gazetteer:*

> In the afternoon (before the fast) they bathe in cold water or *tebila,* plunging in seven times and repeating prayers, or pouring water on their heads 7 times with bathing pots, and being struck by the minister 7 times across the back with a cord. When the bath is over and before lamplight, they finish their meals. Dressing in white clothes with the women and children

> in their richest robes, they go to the synagogue. This is beautifully lighted, and all the Law books are taken out of the ark by the elders, and portions are read. The atonement fast or kippur on the tenth day is kept strictly.[41]

There is little question that other Jewish communities took similar steps prior to the fast to cleanse themselves. Nevertheless, among the Bene Israel the attainment of purity was stringently observed. For example, although wearing white clothes is considered a *minhag* (custom) among some other Jewish communities, here it is meticulously observed by every member. Similarly, the self-abnegation, although observed by some Jewish communities, is somewhat unusual. Kehimkar conforms the chastisement prior to the fast, mentioning that "some devout Bene Israel subject themselves to the whip or twisted cloth correction."[42]

However, the key to the real difference between the Bene Israel and other Jews in the emphasis placed on Yom Kippur is to be found in the continuation of the *Bombay Gazetteer*'s description: "They blow trumpets in their houses, and shutting themselves in their houses till the evening of the next day, they do not talk to or even touch people of other *castes*."[43]

Kehimkar gives a similar account, stating "They did not touch the people of other *denominations*,"[44] which he later changed to the following rendition: "They did not touch people of other *religions*, nor did they exchange words with them, from the time they took the bath till the next evening"[45] (Italics mine). In other words, from the time they became pure, all contact, physical or verbal, with members of other castes (or religions) was forbidden. Clearly, these practices are not familiar in Judaism and I know of no other Jewish community that tried to preserve its seclusion on that day to the same extent.

The main factor influencing Bene Israel behavior on Yom Kippur derived from attitudes associated with the caste system, namely prohibitions against polluting contact between one person and another. Caste attitudes encompassed total external symbolic behavior in imitation of Hindu high-caste members: dress (white and symbolically pure), non-pollution by touch and even by interchange, fasting and bathing. Together, all of these elements were designed to ensure purity and caste exclusivity on the holiest day of the Jewish year.

Death

Bene Israel believe that on Yom Kippur they are united with all members of their community, both past and present, in a reaffirmation of their exclusivity. Kehimkar writes: "There is a pecular notion among the Bene Israel, that the souls of the departed, visit their habitation on the day known as Erev Kippur i.e. the day previous to Atonement Day, and leave on the night of Simḥat Cohen i.e. of the day immediately succeeding the Atonement Day."[46] Kehimkar himself justifies the notion by referring to current normative Jewish practices of visiting graves and praying for the dead on Yom Kippur.

Once again, however, the emphasis appears to be slightly different. In other Jewish communities, it is customary for Jews both to visit cemeteries and to pray for the souls of the departed during the actual Yom Kippur service. Among the Bene Israel, by contrast, the dead actually return to the community and reunite with the living for a single day in the year.

The dead are introduced to the Bene Israel community on the eve of Yom Kippur, known as *malma* in Marathi, at a sacrificial meal that morning. In this ritual feast each family offers up a *melida* dish containing pieces of *gharis* (in Marathi, cakes of rice flour fried in oil), *puris* (tarts of wheat flour and sugar and coconut), pieces of liver and gizzards, fruits, *subja,* a cup of wine, and other delicacies. "Prayers are first offered over it, and then some wine is poured on the ground as a libation; while the rest is sipped by the adult members of the family."[47] The names of dead ancestors are recalled patrilineally and matrilineally up to three generations. It is believed that the ancestors of the Bene Israel join them until the day after Yom Kippur. They depart immediately upon termination of the fast to their normal place, where they will remain until next year. On the day after Yom Kippur, known as *Shila San* in Marathi, life is resumed: the dead have departed, and interaction with Hindus is reconfirmed. Bene Israel consume food that was prepared prior to the fast and visit friends and relatives. They also give alms to the poor.

Sacrifice

Although the Judaic practice of *kaparot* (Hebrew, atonement) was first introduced in the eighth century C.E.[48] and only became popular in later times, it is significant that the Bene Israel actually practice this rite, which they connect with the sacrifice offered immediately before the fast. According to Kehimkar, the Bene Israel first recite the *seliḥot* (Hebrew, propitiatory prayers) and then perform the *kaparot* ceremony, wherein a fowl is swung round the head of a person and sacrificed in his stead.[49] This custom fits in with a widespread local practice in Konkan of presenting fowl as offerings to village deities.[50] In particular, waving rice, coconut, fowls, or money around the head and throwing it away is common in local Hindu rites; the practice also constitutes one of the themes of the Bene Israel prenuptial *mehendi* ceremony.[51] Immediately after the ceremony, the Bene Israel sit down to the sacrificial meal, where the dishes outlined in the previous section are offered up, prayers are delivered, and wine is poured on the ground as libation.

Bene Israel prepare a large number of offerings, which have their equivalents in biblical prescriptions of similar sacrifices, yet they rarely sacrifice animals or regard the offerings as sacrifice per se. For example, a thanksgiving offering called (in Marathi) *khundache nave tabak* ("dish offered in the name of God") is the equivalent of the (Hebrew) *zebah toda* prescribed in Leviticus; the free-will offering is similar to the *korban nedaba;* and the Bene Israel even have a Naziritic offering, whereby a woman who has no male offspring makes a vow to keep a future son as a "Nazir" for six or seven years.[52] Usually, the sacrifices take the form of the *pūjā* rites, whereby the worshippers receive *prasāda* in return. In the case of the Yom Kippur meal, the offerings are embodied in the sweet mixture of *melida,* the cakes and the meat, while the meat element was sometimes removed, particularly from the last century on.

There appears to be a progression in the Bene Israel's Yom Kippur rites from the substitute self-sacrifice of the *kaparot* to the sacrificial meal to the attainment of ultimate purity, not by refraining from meat sacrifice but by abstaining from food altogether. Simultaneously, the Bene Israel endorse the equivalent of the *bali* or animal sacrifices which were carried out in Temple times, by attributing utmost importance to the *avodah* (Hebrew, work, i.e. of the High Priest in the Temple) service and reciting this section with great piety during the Yom Kippur prayers.[53] During this part of the service, the Bene Israel "become" the highest and most absolute caste, independent of others and able to conduct sacrificial services without polluting their hands. As "Brahmins" they perpetuate the ultimate surrogate animal sacrifice: recitation of the order of service in the Temple. In this context, the ideal of self-sacrifice, of human sacrifice whereby Abraham offers to sacrifice Isaac, his son, becomes an ultimate value; in brief, it is the ideal of one who renounces the world.

Conclusion

It is on the holiest day of the Jewish calendar that the Bene Israel reaffirm the contradictions inherent in their unique religious life. By celebrating Yom Kippur in India, they are proclaiming annually their adherence to the Jewish religion. Since the beginning of the nineteenth century, the Bene Israel have increasingly practiced the Yom Kippur order of service as other Jewish communities do. Nevertheless, by their special observance of the day, and particularly by their self-imposed exclusivity, they demonstrate simultaneous affiliation to a hierarchical order of things.

As "out-of-caste" individuals incorporated into a larger caste framework, I would argue that the Bene Israel are an even more extreme case than lower castes of a group legitimating the caste system through ritual enactment. Precisely because their deity is not incorporated into the Hindu pantheon and because they believe in a monotheism which could be interpreted as the ultimate in a hierarchical theistic order, the Bene Israel, as Indian Jews, actually legitimate the relational aspects of Hinduism. This is effected in the case of Yom Kippur worship through the liminal phase which emphasizes reversals of everyday behavior and the self-validation of the rites which reinforce hierarchy.[54]

It is the "bracketing" of the Day of Atonement which is of essential significance here. During the year, the Bene Israel are not only meat-eating, accepting the superior purity of vegetarian castes, but they eat meat permitted by another religion. In addition, as traditional *Shanwar Talis,* they deal with an occupation which squeezes life out of vegetable matter in order to make oil. However, as Yom Kippur, the purest day of the year, approaches, they enact surrogate self-sacrifice *(kaparot)* and subsequently partake of a substitute sacrificial meal (with the *melida*).

On the fast itself, the Bene Israel not only become vegetarian but swing to the opposite extreme, expressing their purity by abstaining from food altogether. On this day they are reunited with their ancestors in a single Indian Jewish community, enacting the major motifs of Yom Kippur—atonement, purity, death, and sacrifice—in an exclusive manner. In the annual reversal that occurs on Yom Kippur, these outsiders to the caste scheme manage to reinforce a hierarchical ideology. By "closing the doors" on other castes, they perpetuate the status of the absolute purity of the Brahmin who retains exclusivity and independence in relation to a tainted world.[55] In effect, for one day in a year, the Bene Israel "become" Brahmins, preserving the barriers between ideal values and hierarchical realities. Shulman has noted the "gatekeeper" qualities of the Brahmin, who essentially maintains the system. He writes (with reference to South India) that

> his place [is] the threshold of a gateway that opens in two directions: to the world and away from it. But this gateway is placed at the cultural center, a monument of samskaric form.

> On the one side, lies the perfect, deathless world of the sacrifice without remnant, without evil, without end. . . . On the other side lies crude, uncontained impurity, a vital mixture of dyings and rebirths, and the unmediated emotions of terror, joy, and love. Yet, strange to say, these two realms, reached through opposite movements, soon flow together; to go through the gateway in either direction is ultimately to return, through a baffling circularity, to the same, literally "liminal" spot. This *limen* is the point of departure and of return, a boundary made center.[56]

At the termination of the fast, the Bene Israel bless the new moon, a practice well known to other Jews but interpreted by the *Bombay Gazetteer* as a relic of ancient moon-worship.[57] The following day, on *Shila San,* Bene Israel reaffirm their caste position in India, though officially "out-of-caste." They dispel the souls of their ancestors—who represented the community's exclusivity—and they reemphasize their exact place in the hierarchical order of things by reestablishing contact with Hindu neighbors and giving alms to lower-caste Hindus. The temporality of their exclusive status on Yom Kippur thereby serves to emphasize the preeminence of hierarchical relationships on a daily basis. This claim has even stronger legitimation because it comes precisely from a group affiliated with a quotidian contradictory ideology.

Postscript

Even in Israel, where 50,000 Bene Israel today reside, Bene Israel perpetuate patterns of non-interaction with other people on Yom Kippur. In the town of Lod, where I conducted fieldwork among the Bene Israel in the 1970s, I noted the following:

> In Lod, today, the Bene Israel pray in the Indian synagogue on Yom Kippur. The synagogue opens at 3 a.m. and the service begins half an hour later when it is still pitch black. From 1 a.m. onwards Bene Israel wend their way to the synagogue in the dark, and by the time the service begins at 3 a.m. the synagogue is nearly full. Bene Israel say that they arrive so early—at least six hours before all the other synagogues begin—to reserve a place. Whilst it is true that there is a severe shortage of room in the synagogue on High Holidays, the synagogue management could arrange for seats to be bought or for seats to be numbered and reserved for Yom Kippur as in other synagogues. However, the reluctance to introduce such a system

> relates to India where Bene Israel rushed to the synagogue in the middle of the night, covered in cloth all over their bodies except for their eyes, in order to avoid contact with defiling castes on such a holy day. One Bene Israel informant explained to me that she arrives at the synagogue while it is still dark in order to avoid meeting "other castes."[58]

Outstanding is the permanence among some Bene Israel of what Dumont calls "psychological dispositions" to the extent that each individual has something of the Hindu in him.[59] The salient question, however, is to what extent groups on the lower levels of the hierarchical order in a so-called egalitarian society which only has a "residuum of hierarchy" can continue to operate and legitimate complementarity.

As I show elsewhere, Bene Israel rituals on Yom Kippur seems to be part of a wider pattern of persisting caste orientations on the part of Bene Israel currently residing in Israel, who have actually transferred their fear of pollution with Hindus to other Jewish ethnic groups.[60] However, as ethnicity replaces caste and Bene Israel come to regard themselves as ideologically equal to other Jews, then we may find that the interpretation of worship and ritual enactment on the holiest day of the Jewish calendar takes on alternative symbolic meanings in line with the "egalitarianism" of Judaism, as practiced by the dominant ethnic groups of the Judaic social order. It is then that the "closed doors" will open and the Bene Israel will begin to cross the threshold.

PART TWO

Cultural Resonances

8

Veda and Torah
The Word Embodied in Scripture

Barbara A. Holdrege

The differences between the Hindu and Jewish traditions have often been emphasized, so much so that these two traditions have generally been characterized as representing opposite ends of the spectrum of world religions. Indeed, "Hinduism" and "Judaism" have been thought to have so little in common that prior to the essays in the present volume few scholars have attempted substantive comparative analyses of these traditions. "Polytheistic," iconocentric "Hinduism" vs. "monotheistic," iconoclastic "Judaism" have been characterized as further set apart by their cyclical vs. historical views of existence. However, such characterizations represent gross oversimplifications that fail to take into account the rich diversity of perspectives within the traditions themselves.

The categories "Hinduism" and "Judaism" are themselves problematic in this regard, for like the category "religion" they represent abstract theoretical constructs that attempt to impose unity on a myriad of different religious systems. The complex amalgam termed "Hinduism" encompasses a variety of "Hinduisms." Beginning in the Vedic period and throughout Indian history the orthodox brahmanical tradition has been continually challenged by competing traditions and movements—local village traditions, ascetic groups, devotional *(bhakti)* sects, tantric movements, and, more recently, modern reform movements. While the centripetal force of brahmanical power structures has sought to absorb and domesticate competing currents, the centrifugal force of these countervailing centers of power has persisted, giving rise to that uneasy conglomerate of heterogeneous tendencies which Western scholars term "Hinduism." Similarly, "Judaism" represents a composite category within which are subsumed a variety of "Judaisms." Following the biblical period a diversity of competing movements flourished in the Second Temple period, including the Sadducees, Pharisees, Zealots, Essenes, and various Hellenistic traditions. After the destruction of the Second Temple in 70 C.E., the Pharisaic trend prevailed in the form of rabbinic orthodoxy, which itself encompassed a variety of different schools. The medieval period saw the emergence of a number of contending currents, including the newly burgeoning kabbalistic and philosophical traditions. The modern period has similarly given birth to a variety of new "Judaisms"—Reform, Conservative, Orthodox, Zionist, and so on.[1]

Within this array of "Hinduisms" and "Judaisms" the present essay focuses on those traditions for which scripture is a constitutive category: the brahmanical Sanskritic tradition and the rabbinic tradition, with some attention also to kabbalistic traditions that have absorbed and elaborated rabbinic conceptions of scripture. Both the brahmanical and rabbinic traditions constitute elite "textual communities"[2] that have sought to shape and articulate the central norms of their respective societies through codifying symbol systems and practices in the form of scriptural canons of which they are the custodians. In the process of delineating the normative tradition and its standards of orthodoxy, these textual communities have accommodated, domesticated, and at times muted the multiplicity of voices representative of the competing trends in any particular period.

Most of the major religious traditions have elite textual communities that have fulfilled a comparable function of codifying the norms of their respective traditions in the form of scriptural canons. A comparative study of the categories of scripture in the brahmanical and rabbinic traditions is of particular significance because of the ways in which these categories reflect the broader structural affinities that connect these religious traditions. Contrary to the stereotypical characterizations that emphasize the oppositions between "Hinduism" and "Judaism," it could be argued that the brahmanical and rabbinic forms of "Hinduism" and "Judaism" represent two species of the same genus and provide a model of "religious tradition" that is distinctly different from the prevailing Christian-based model that has tended to dominate the academic study of religion. The paradigm of "religious tradition" that has developed out of a Christian context gives precedence to such categories as belief, doctrine, and theology and delineates notions of tradition-identity that are rooted in the missionary character of "Christianities." The brahmanical and rabbinic traditions, on the other hand, provide an alternative paradigm of "religious tradition," in which priority is given to issues of practice, observance, and law, and notions of tradition-identity are delineated primarily in terms of ethnic and cultural categories that reflect the predominantly nonmissionary character of these traditions.[3] These religions of orthopraxy have developed elaborate legal systems, sacrificial traditions, purity codes, and dietary laws that serve to inscribe and perpetuate the sociocultural taxonomies of their respective communities.[4] The manner in which the brahmanical and rabbinic traditions construct categories of sacred language, knowledge, and canon is also closely linked to their conceptions of communal identity. Each tradition defines itself in relation to a particular sacred language and to a particular corpus of sacred texts that is held to be linguistically, ethnically, and culturally tied to a particular people. The mechanisms through which the scriptural canon is circumscribed and subsequently expanded in the brahmanical and rabbinic traditions serve as a means of circumscribing the ethnic-cultural identity of their respective communities in relation to other peoples, of delineating a hierarchical differentiation of roles within each community, and of accommodating competing currents within the tradition.

Canonical authority is thus constitutive of both the brahmanical and rabbinic traditions. The authority of the brahmin priests and the rabbinic sages themselves is to a large extent derived from their privileged role as the preservers and transmitters of the scriptural canon. In each canon a certain corpus of texts has been set apart as having special sacrosanct and authoritative status: the Veda in the brahmanical tradition and the Torah in the rabbinic tradition. In the brahmanical tradition acceptance of the authority of the Veda has been the primary criterion for distinguishing orthodox from heterodox systems since at least the period of the early Dharma-Sūtras and Dharma-Śāstras (ca. third or second century B.C.E.).[5] Acceptance of the authority of the Torah has constituted one of the few dogmas of the rabbinic tradition since as early as the Mishnah (ca. 220 C.E.).[6] The authoritative status of Veda and Torah is connected to their symbolic function in which they assume the role of the encompassing, paradigmatic symbols of their respective traditions. A comparative analysis of the symbol systems associated with Veda and Torah can thus serve to illuminate the unique *Gestalt* that gives each tradition its distinctive character, as well as to highlight the resonances among these scriptural traditions.

From Text to Symbol

Veda and Torah are generally classified as types of "scripture," and thus any inquiry into the multivalent significations of these terms must begin with a consideration of the category of scripture as conceptualized by Western scholars during the last two centuries. The study of scripture since the nineteenth century has been almost exclusively the domain of biblical and orientalist scholars, who have used the tools of critical analysis in order to determine the cultural, historical, and literary influences that have given rise to individual texts. These historical and literary studies have primarily focused on the *content* of particular religious texts and on questions of *Entstehungsgeschichte,* or the "history of origins"—the history of causes and conditions that have produced specific texts. More recently, with the newly emerging interest in canon, scholars have begun to focus also on the *form* of particular scriptural traditions.

In recent years historians of religions such as Wilfred Cantwell Smith and William A. Graham have emphasized the need for more inquiries into the *concept* of scripture as a general religious category to supplement the study of particular texts and canons.[7] What does it mean for a text to be regarded as "scripture" or for religious communities to "scripturalize"? Scripture as a concept in the history of religions is primarily a relational category, which refers not simply to a text, but to a text in its relationship to a religious community for whom it is sacred and authoritative. The study of scripture as a relational category is concerned not only with questions of *Entstehungsgeschichte,* or history of origins, but also with *Wirkungsgeschichte,* the "history of effects," which encompasses the ongoing roles that a sacred text has assumed in the cumulative tradition of a religious community both as a normative source of authority and as a prodigious living force.[8]

One of the purposes of the present inquiry is to call into question the very category of scripture as it has generally been conceptualized by Western scholars. Graham's recent studies of the oral aspects of scripture in the history of religions have challenged scholars to stretch the boundaries of the concept beyond the limitations posed by the term "scripture" itself (which literally means "a writing") and its common equivalents such as "sacred writings" and "holy writ."[9] My study of Veda and Torah suggests that it is not sufficient simply to expand the concept to encompass the oral-aural dimensions of sacred texts. Rather, the category of scripture needs to be further exploded and the very notion of textuality implicit in the concept reexamined. For in certain traditional representations of Veda and Torah, scripture is depicted not simply as a textual phenomenon but as a cosmological principle that is inherent in the very structure of reality. The functional status of scripture within a particular religious community is to a certain extent shaped and informed by the community's conceptions of its cosmological status, and yet relatively little attention has been given to this important dimension of scripture.

The purpose of the present study is threefold. First, I attempt to demonstrate that scripture, as represented in the symbol systems associated with Veda and Torah, is not a unidimensional textual phenomenon, but is rather a multileveled cosmic reality that encompasses gross and subtle, mundane and supramundane dimensions. Second, I seek to demonstrate that these representations of Veda and Torah are not merely lifeless concepts embedded in the traditional texts, but have functioned as living, activating symbols that reflect and inform practices with respect to the modes of transmission, study, and appropriation of these two scriptures. Finally, I suggest that the ways in which the categories of Veda and Torah are constructed reflect the more fundamental structural affinities that connect the brahmanical and rabbinic traditions as representatives of a distinctive paradigm of "religious tradition."

In discussing the category of canon in the history of religions, Jonathan Z. Smith has suggested that "canon is best seen as one form of a basic cultural process of limitation and of overcoming that limitation through ingenuity."[10] He further suggests that the task of overcoming the limitation posed by a closed canon is accomplished through the exegetical enterprise, in which the task of the interpreter is "continually to extend the domain of the closed canon over everything that is known or everything that exists *without* altering the canon in the process."[11] In order to test the applicability of this model of canon to the cases of Veda and Torah, two types of questions need to be addressed. First, if indeed Veda and Torah do constitute closed canons, what are the criteria and mechanisms by which each canon has been delimited? Second, what strategies have been used to overcome this limitation? Are they primarily exegetical in nature?

Both Veda and Torah would appear to conform to at least one aspect of Smith's model in that each functions within its respective tradition as an encompassing, paradigmatic symbol that is simultaneously delimited and potentially unlimited. At the center of each canon is a fixed corpus of texts, whether oral or written, that has been meticulously preserved in strictly unaltered form: the Vedic Saṃhitās and the Sefer Torah. At the same time the domains of both Veda and Torah have been extended through a variety of strategies so that each functions as an open-ended, permeable category within which can be subsumed potentially all texts, teachings, and practices authorized by the religious elite. In the case of Torah these strategies, in accordance with Smith's model, have been to a large extent exegetical, involving endless reinterpretations, applications, and extensions of the content of the core text. In the case of Veda, on the other hand, the mechanisms for expanding the canon generally involve an extension of status with little reference to the content of the Saṃhitās. Irrespective of whether the content of the Saṃhitās is known or understood, their status as transcendent knowledge is acknowledged by orthodox exponents, and it is this status that subsequent texts and teachings seek to acquire through various modes of assimilation.

Veda

The term "Veda," derived from the root *vid,* "to know," means "knowledge." The term is used in the brahmanical tradition to designate a corpus of texts or teachings in at least four different senses. (1) The term is used in its narrow sense to designate the four Saṃhitās ("collections"), Ṛg-Veda, Yajur-Veda, Sāma-Veda, and Atharva-Veda, which constitute collections of verses (*ṛc*s), sacrificial formulae (*yajus*es), chants (*sāman*s), and incantations and imprecations (*atharvāṅgiras*es or *atharvan*s), respectively.[12] The versified portions of the Saṃhitās are termed *mantras*.[13] (2) The term is subsequently extended to include not only the four Saṃhitās, but also the Brāhmaṇas, sacrificial manuals attached to the Saṃhitās; the Āraṇyakas, "forest books" that reflect on the inner meaning of the sacrificial rituals; and the Upaniṣads, the latest speculative portions of the Vedas.[14] (3) In post-Vedic speculations the term is at times extended even further to include the Itihāsas or epics (the Mahābhārata and the Rāmāyaṇa of Vālmīki) and Purāṇas, which are respectively designated as the "fifth Veda."[15] (4) Finally, Veda becomes an encompassing symbol within which can be subsumed potentially all brahmanical texts, teachings, and practices.

In order to understand the mechanisms through which this expansion of the purview of the term Veda occurred, we need to examine more closely the distinction that is made in the brahmanical tradition between two categories of sacred texts: *śruti,* "that which was heard," and *smṛti,* "that which was remembered." The core *śruti* texts are the four types of *mantras*—*ṛcs, yajuses, sāmans,* and *atharvāṅgirases* or *atharvans*—that are collected in the Saṃhitās.[16] The domain of *śruti* was subsequently extended to include not only the Saṃhitās, but also the Brāhmaṇas, Āraṇyakas, and Upaniṣads. Although the canon of *śruti* is technically closed, the category of Upaniṣads has remained somewhat permeable, with new Upaniṣads being added to the traditionally accepted 108 Upaniṣads up to as late as the medieval period.[17] While the domain of *śruti* is thus in principle circumscribed, *smṛti* is a dynamic, open-ended category, which includes the Dharma-Śāstras, Itihāsas, and Purāṇas, as well as a variety of other texts that have been incorporated within this ever-expanding category in accordance with the needs of different periods and groups.[18] The primary criterion for distinguishing between *śruti* and *smṛti* texts is generally characterized by both Indian and Western scholars as an ontological distinction between "revelation" and "tradition."[19] *Śruti* texts—Saṃhitās, Brāhmaṇas, Āraṇyakas, and Upaniṣads—are traditionally understood to have been directly cognized—"seen" and "heard"—by inspired "seers" (*ṛṣis*) at the beginning of each cycle of creation. The formal schools of Vedic exegesis, Pūrva-Mīmāṃsā and Vedānta, maintain that the *śruti* or Vedic texts are eternal *(nitya),* infinite, and *apauruṣeya,* not created by any human or divine agent, while the Nyāya, Vaiśeṣika, and Yoga schools of Indian philosophy view the Vedic texts as the work of God.[20] All other sacred texts are relegated to a secondary status as *smṛti,* for they are held to have been composed by personal authors and are therefore designated as "that which was remembered" rather than "that which was heard." On the basis of this criterion the Itihāsas and Purāṇas are classified as *smṛti* texts, even though they may assimilate themselves to *śruti* by claiming the status of the "fifth Veda."

According to the above definitions, the term Veda refers strictly speaking only to *śruti* texts and not to *smṛti* texts. However, Sheldon Pollock has recently brought to light an essential mechanism whereby the domain of the Veda was extended to include not only *śruti* but also *smṛti.* He locates this mechanism in the definition of the terms *śruti* and *smṛti* themselves, which he argues have been incorrectly construed as representing a dichotomy between "revelation" and "tradition." He maintains rather that, according to the etymology derived from the Pūrva-Mīmāṃsā school that is still prevalent among certain traditional brahmanical teachers, *śruti* refers to the extant Vedic texts that can be "heard" in recitation, whereas *smṛti* is an open-ended category that encompasses any teachings or practices pertaining to *dharma* that have been "remembered" from lost Vedic texts. Understood in this way Veda becomes a limitlessly encompassing symbol that includes not only *śruti* but also *smṛti.* The meaning of the term Veda is extended beyond the circumscribed boundaries of the *śruti* texts—Saṃhitās, Brāhmaṇas, Āraṇyakas, and Upaniṣads—and through a process of "vedacization" comes to include within its purview not only the Itihāsas and Purāṇas, but potentially all śāstric teachings—as enshrined in practices as well as texts—that are promulgated by brahmanical authorities.[21]

While the original etymology of the term *śruti* may be debated, and may indeed be interpreted by certain strands of the brahmanical tradition to mean "that which is heard" in ongoing recitations of the Vedic texts, it is also clear that the related term *śruta* was used as early as the Ṛg-Veda to refer to the cognitions of the *ṛṣis*[22] and that the term *śruti* itself still retains this association among contemporary Hindu thinkers: Veda as *śruti* is "that which was heard" by the ancient *ṛṣis* as part of a primordial cognition in the beginning of creation. Moreover, Veda is that which was seen by the *ṛṣis*, who as "seers" are traditionally designated as those who "see the truth" (*satyadarśin).*[23] The transcendent status attributed to the Veda is itself constitutive of the Veda's legitimating authority as the encompassing symbol of the brahmanical tradition. The core *śruti* texts, the Vedic *mantras*, are represented in the mythological speculations of Vedic and post-Vedic texts as having a transhistorical dimension, in which they constitute that eternal, suprasensible knowledge which exists perpetually on the subtle level of creation as the source and "blueprint" of the universe.[24] The *ṛṣis* are portrayed as having the ability to station their awareness on that subtle level where they could "see" and "hear" the impulses of knowledge reverberating forth from the Transcendent as the fundamental rhythms of creation. They subsequently "recorded" on the gross level of speech that which they cognized on the subtle level, and in this way the *mantras* assumed a concrete form on earth as recited texts. The Vedic *mantras* are thus granted the status of transcendent knowledge. Any subsequent text or śāstric discourse can participate in that status only by assimilating itself to the Vedic *mantras* through a variety of strategies, including (1) claiming to form part of *śruti,* the original cognitions of the *ṛṣis*, in the case of the Brāhmaṇas, Āraṇyakas, and Upaniṣads; (2) claiming the status of the "fifth Veda," in the case of the Itihāsas and Purāṇas; (3) establishing a genealogy that directly links the text's teachings to the Veda or to some form of divine revelation; (4) claiming that the text's teachings derive from lost Vedic texts, a claim that could apply to potentially all *smṛti* texts; or (5) otherwise conforming to the model of the Veda.[25]

Brian K. Smith has emphasized that such strategies, including a variety of other modes of assimilation, have been used not only by exponents of the brahmanical hierarchy but also by nonbrahmanical Hindu groups in order to invest their sacred texts with the transcendent authority of the Veda.[26] He goes so far as to claim that "the Veda functions as a touchstone for Hindu orthodoxy" and that Vedic authority is constitutive of "Hinduism" itself, including not only the brahmanical tradition but also devotional sects and tantric movements: "Hinduism is the religion of those humans who create, perpetuate, and transform traditions with legitimizing reference to the authority of the Veda."[27] Jan Gonda similarly defines Hinduism as "a complex of social-religious phenomena, which are based on that authority of the ancient corpora, called Veda."[28]

The paradigmatic function of the Veda is evidenced in the way in which certain devotional sects have sought to imitate the Veda by elevating their own vernacular texts to a quasi-*śruti* status. For example, the Tamil hymns of the *Tiruvāymoḷi* by the poet Nammāḷvār (ca. ninth century C.E.), a low-caste exponent of the Vaiṣṇava Āḷvārs, are said to represent the four Vedic Saṃhitās and are designated as the "Dravidian Veda" or "Tamil Veda."[29] The *Rāmcaritmānas* of the poet Tulsīdās (ca. sixteenth century C.E.), a Hindi version of the Rāmāyaṇa popular throughout North India, has been granted a similar status as the "fifth Veda" or "Hindi Veda" that is said to represent the concentrated essence of all the Hindu scriptures.[30]

While some devotional sects have thus sought to legitimate their texts through assimilating them to the Veda, the claim that all Hindu groups—nonbrahmanical as well as brahmanical—accept the authority of the Veda does not hold true in the case of certain *bhakti* and tantric movements. For example, the *vacana* poets of the Vīraśaiva sect, which originated in the Kannada-speaking region of South India in the tenth century C.E., were leaders of a protest movement that rejected the Vedic texts and rituals because of their association with the caste system and other brahmanical institutions.[31] Certain left-handed tantric sects such as the Kashmir Śaivas have not only rejected Vedic authority, they have treated the Veda as a symbol to be subverted by actively adhering to teachings and practices that directly transgress orthodox brahmanical traditions.[32]

Whether the Veda is revered or rejected, appropriated or subverted, it remains a symbol invested with authoritative power that must be contended with by all those who wish to position themselves in relation to the brahmanical hierarchy. As J. C.

Heesterman emphasizes, "The crux of the matter is that the Vedas hold the key to ultimate legitimation. Therefore, even if the Vedas are in no way related to the ways of human life and society, one is still forced to come to terms with them."[33] Heesterman's remark points to an observation often made by Indologists: the authoritative power of the Veda does not lie in the content of the Vedic Saṃhitās themselves, for their content is primarily concerned with sacrificial rituals and is not directly relevant to the teachings and practices of post-Vedic Hinduism.[34] Louis Renou has observed that "even in the most orthodox domains, the reverence to the Vedas has come to be a simple 'raising of the hat', in passing, to an idol by which one no longer intends to be encumbered later on." He further remarks that "the term [Veda] tends to serve as a symbol."[35]

The critical point to be emphasized here is that the Veda serves as a symbol precisely because it transcends the confines of textuality that limit the term to a circumscribed body of texts and comes to represent the totality of knowledge, thus reclaiming its original etymology as "knowledge." Pollock remarks,

> As "Knowledge" *tout court,* as the *śāstra* par excellence, and as the "omniscient" text (Manu-Smṛti 2.7) and the "infinite" text (Taittirīya [Brāhmaṇa] 3.10.11.4, et al.), Veda is the general rubric under which every sort of partial knowledge—that is, the various individual *śāstras*—is ultimately subsumed.[36]

The legitimating authority of the Veda is thus inextricably linked to its symbolic function as knowledge—not the ordinary knowledge derived through the powers of human reasoning, but that transcendent, infinite knowledge which is held to be the essence of ultimate reality and the source and foundation of creation.[37] This knowledge is said to have been cognized by the *ṛṣi*s and preserved by them in the form of oral texts, but, as we shall see, certain brahmanical texts insist that the Veda, the limitless Word, cannot be limited to its finite expressions in the texts preserved by human beings on earth. Moreover, the power of the Veda as embodied in the recited texts is held to lie not in the discursive meaning of the texts, but rather in the sounds through which the primordial impulses of knowledge are expressed. In this view the content of the Vedic Saṃhitās will always be of secondary value, as Indologists have observed, because the primary concern of the brahmanical exponents of the Vedic recitative tradition is to preserve the purity of the Vedic sounds irrespective of whether their semantic content is understood.[38]

Torah

The term "Torah," according to the general consensus of most modern scholars, is connected with the hiphil conjugation of the root *yrh,* "to point out, direct, teach," and thus means "teaching" or "instruction."[39] In rabbinic literature the term is used to refer to a corpus of teachings or texts in at least four different senses. (1) The term is used in its narrow sense to refer to the Pentateuch, the Five Books of Moses or Sefer Torah (Book of the Torah), as distinct from the other two sections of the Hebrew Bible, Nevi'im (Prophets) and Ketuvim (Writings). (2) The term is subsequently extended to refer to the Hebrew Bible, the Tanakh, as a whole. (3) The meaning of the term is expanded further to include not only the Pentateuch, Nevi'im, and Ketuvim, which constitute the Written Torah *(tôrāh še bi-ḵṯāḇ),* but also the Mishnah, Talmud, and Midrash, which contain the halakhic and aggadic teachings that constitute the Oral Torah *(tôrāh še b^e-ʿal peh).* (4) Finally, Torah becomes an encompassing symbol that includes potentially all of the laws, teachings, and practices of the normative rabbinic tradition.

This progressive expansion of the term Torah is reflected in the ways in which the categories of Written Torah and Oral Torah are defined and distinguished. The Written Torah is a fixed, bounded text, whether understood in its narrow sense as the Pentateuch or in its broader sense as the entire Hebrew Bible. The Oral Torah, on the other hand, is a fluid, open-ended category, which in its broadest sense includes not only the teachings contained in the Mishnah, Talmud, and Midrash, but also all the laws and teachings that are introduced by the rabbinic sages in each generation as part of the oral tradition. The distinction between Written Torah and Oral Torah is traditionally held to derive from the original revelation at Mount Sinai, in which God gave to Moses two Torahs: a written text, consisting of the Pentateuch, Nevi'im, and Ketuvim, and an oral tradition of interpretation that was destined to be preserved in the Mishnah, Talmud, and Midrash, as well as in the teachings of subsequent generations of rabbis.[40]

The legitimating authority of the Torah is linked in particular to the Pentateuch, which is granted a special status as divine revelation in that its every word is traditionally believed to have been directly dictated by God to Moses, who acted as a scribe and recorded the words of God verbatim in the Sefer Torah. The authority of all subsequent texts and teachings is legitimated by establishing a connection between those texts/teachings and the Sefer Torah, either through (1) granting them a subsidiary status as part of the Written Torah, in the case of the books of the Nevi'im and Ketuvim; (2) allotting them a designated place as part of the Oral Torah, in the case of the teachings of the Mishnah, Talmud, and Midrash; (3) linking them to the revelation at Mount Sinai as part of the open-ended category of Oral Torah; or (4) otherwise aligning them with the model of the Sefer Torah.

In discussing the documentary history of the term Torah, Jacob Neusner has delineated the various strategies adopted by rabbinic texts to assimilate their teachings to the Torah. In the process the Torah was transformed from a limited, bounded text—the Sefer Torah—into a limitless, encompassing symbol, "the single critical symbol of the Judaism of the dual Torah," that represents the entire system of rabbinic Judaism.

> [The] documentary history [of this symbol] traces the story of how "the Torah" lost its capital letter and definite article and ultimately became "torah." What for nearly a millennium had been a particular scroll or book came to serve as a symbol of an entire system. When a rabbi spoke of torah, he no longer meant only a particular object, a scroll and its contents. Now he used the word to encompass a distinctive and well-defined world view and way of life. . . . In the Judaism of the dual Torah as it emerged from its formative age, everything was contained in that one thing, "Torah." It connotes a broad range of clearly distinct categories of noun and verb, concrete fact and abstract relationship alike. . . . As symbolic abstraction, the word encompasses things and persons, actions and statuses, points of social differentiation and legal and normative standing, as well as "revealed truth." . . . Every detail of the religious system at hand exhibits essentially the same point of insistence, captured in the simple notion of the Torah as the generative symbol, the total, exhaustive expression of the system as a whole.[41]

The critical question is why the Torah, and not something else, was singled out to serve as the generative symbol of rabbinic Judaism. For the answer we must return to the original referent of the term: the Sefer Torah. The Sefer Torah was granted an especially sacrosanct and authoritative status as "revealed truth," and therefore any text, teaching, practice, or person that wished to attain normative standing within the rabbinic tradition could only do so through becoming incorporated within the ever-expanding domain of Torah. While the Torah as a circumscribed written text constitutes a bounded category, in its status as revealed truth it becomes an open-ended symbol that extends beyond the boundaries of the text and is capable of absorbing a host of candidates whose linkage to the revelation, however tenuous, has been established.

The encompassing nature of the Torah as a symbol is linked in particular to its identification with the Word of God, for while the Sefer Torah might be held to be the most perfect, concentrated expression of the Word of God on earth, the Word itself is not limited to that expression. The divine Word through which God manifested himself at the time of revelation is also represented as the creative power through which God manifested himself at the time of creation. In its identification with the Word of God the Torah is thus at times portrayed as existing prior to the revelation, since the beginning of creation, as the instrument through which God brought forth creation. In certain representations of the Torah found in seminal form in rabbinic texts and subsequently elaborated in medieval kabbalistic texts, the Torah is personified as that primordial wisdom which had existed in heaven "from the beginning" as a living aspect of God and the immediate source of creation. At the time of the revelation at Mount Sinai the primordial Torah is said to have descended from its supernal abode and to have become embodied on earth in the concrete form of the Sefer Torah. It assumed the finite form of the Book of the Torah, but the book itself is understood in this context as simply the outer body in which the primordial reality of wisdom ever resides as its innermost soul. In this perspective the Sefer Torah itself becomes a symbol with transcendent significations in that it continually points beyond its own textuality to the divine reality enshrined within.

In rabbinic texts such speculations are not systematically developed as part of any consistent cosmology, and therefore it is difficult to assess whether such notions reflect a genuine interest in cosmological speculation or whether they are simply literary metaphors adopted in homiletical praise of the Torah.[42] It is also difficult to determine to what extent a particular view represents a consensus of opinion, or to what extent it represents the opinion of specific individuals or schools of rabbinic thought. Rabbinic texts do not present a single homogeneous perspective but rather a multiplicity of voices representing a variety of different schools with distinctive viewpoints and approaches. For example, Abraham Heschel has suggested that there were at least two contending schools among the second-century Tannaim with fundamentally different conceptions of the Torah's status: the school of R. Akiba, which emphasized the transcendent significance of every word and letter of the Torah, and the school of R. Ishmael, which maintained the more pragmatic stance that the Torah speaks in the language of human beings.[43] R. Akiba appears to be representative of certain more mystically oriented circles within the early rabbinic tradition that were concerned not only with more traditional matters of halakhah and aggadah, but also with the "secrets of the Torah" *(siṯrê tôrāh, rāzê tôrāh),* in particular with the mysteries of creation (*maᶜăśēh bᵉrē'šîṯ,* literally, "works of creation") described in Genesis 1 and the mysteries of the throne-chariot (*maᶜăśēh merkāḇāh,* literally, "works of the chariot") depicted in Ezekiel 1. Although the Mishnah placed certain restrictions on speculation and public discourse about *maᶜăśēh bᵉrē'šîṯ* and *maᶜăśēh merkāḇāh,*[44] it is clear from rabbinic texts that such speculation did indeed take place in certain circles.[45]

In contrast to the rather fragmentary nature of the rabbinic material, in which aggadic speculations about the Torah are interspersed throughout the texts, in medieval kabbalistic texts such speculations are generally presented as part of a grand cosmological scheme. The conceptions found in seminal form in rabbinic texts are fully elaborated and cosmologized by certain kabbalists, going beyond metaphorical personification to clear hypostatization. Although we thus recognize a difference in perspective and emphases with respect to the representations of Torah found in rabbinic and kabbalistic texts, we also discern sufficient threads of continuity to warrant juxtaposing these two different approaches.[46]

The Word Embodied in Scripture

The cosmological status ascribed to Veda and Torah can be fully understood only on the basis of their respective traditions' theories of language, in which scripture represents the embodiment of the Word. This Word cannot be delimited to the written word, as the term "scripture" itself and its common equivalents—for example, "sacred writings" or "holy writ"—might suggest. Nor is it sufficient simply to expand the meaning of scripture to encompass its oral-aural dimensions as spoken word. The Word as embodied in Veda and Torah also has a cosmological dimension, in which on one level it is represented as a cosmic reality that is a living aspect of the divine, while on another level it is depicted as the subtle plan of creation containing the elements of the divine language through which the creator brings forth the manifold forms of the universe.

The concept of the Word, as expressed in the theories of language developed by the brahmanical tradition and the rabbinic and kabbalistic traditions, encompasses not only the gross level of vocalized speech, but also the subtler levels of nonvocalized speech as expressed in the entire range of development of thought. The Word is conceived as encompassing both unspoken thought and spoken utterance and thus has two aspects: (1) a *cognitive dimension,* which is the unspoken thought or idea in the mind that constitutes the conceptual content of the word, and (2) a *phonic dimension,* which encompasses both the internally perceived sound of mental discourse and the vocalized speech through which thought finds expression in externally audible sound. When translated onto the cosmic level, as described in certain strands of the traditions, the distinction between unspoken thought and vocalized speech is understood as a distinction between knowledge and speech. The unspoken thought in the cosmic mind is knowledge or wisdom,[47] which is the cognitive *content* of the Word. The Word is spoken by means of speech, which is the vehicle for the *expression* of the Word. Knowledge and speech—both of these aspects of the Word are necessary in order for the process of manifestation to be complete. On the one hand, without speech the content of the Word, which is knowledge, would remain hidden, undisclosed; on the other hand, without knowledge speech would have no content to express. Knowledge and speech, or unspoken thought and vocalized speech, are represented as two phases in the single continuum of the Word.

In certain representations of Veda and Torah, as will be discussed in the following analysis, scripture is depicted as a multileveled cosmic reality, its different levels corresponding to the different levels of creation and to the different levels of the Word, in which the principles of knowledge and speech both come into play: (1) *scripture as the totality of the Word,* which is the essence of the ultimate reality, particularly as it manifests itself in creation; (2) *scripture as knowledge,* which is identified with the creator principle as the immediate source of creation; (3) *scripture as divine language,* its constituent sounds or letters representing the archetypal plan or "blueprint"[48] from which the creator structures the forms of creation; (4) *scripture as concrete text,* represented by the oral texts of the Vedic Saṃhitās, on the one hand, or the Written Torah together with an oral tradition of interpretation, on the other.

In the case of both Veda and Torah, the structure of relations that connects these symbolic complexes is twofold: spatial and temporal. The spatial relation is at times represented as a hierarchy of levels corresponding to the levels of creation on a continuum from subtle to gross, each symbolic complex representing a discrete level of the hierarchy. These symbolic complexes are also at times connected in a temporal set of relations in which each complex is correlated with a particular stage of manifestation in the process of creation.

Although there are significant structural affinities in the symbol systems associated with Veda and Torah, we shall see that there are also significant differences between these scriptural traditions, particularly with respect to the theories of language that underlie their conceptions and practices. My study highlights in particular three fundamental points of divergence. (1) With respect to the *oral and written channels of language,* the brahmanical tradition gives precedence to the oral channel, while the rabbinic and kabbalistic traditions assign special status to the written register. (2) These diverging emphases on the oral vs. written channels of language result in a corresponding divergence in *modes of perception,* what Walter Ong has termed the "ratio of the senses," in which brahmanical conceptions of language and text give primary emphasis to the auditory channel and rabbinic and kabbalistic conceptions to the visual channel.[49] (3) With respect to the *cognitive and phonic dimensions of the word,* the brahmanical tradition gives priority to the phonic dimension, while the rabbinic and kabbalistic traditions emphasize the cognitive dimension. These divergent emphases are particularly evident, as we shall see, in the traditions and practices that have evolved concerning the proper modes of transmission and study of the Vedic Saṃhitās and the Sefer Torah.

The present essay presents a schematic overview of the results of my extended study of cosmological conceptions of Veda and Torah.[50] In the longer study I employ a method of comparative historical analysis that involves three main phases: (1) history of interpretations,[51] (2) comparative analysis, and (3) cultural interpretation. Parts I and II of the following analysis present a synchronic overview of the results of the history of interpretations phase of my study. Within the scope of the present essay it is obviously not possible to provide a differentiated, contextualized treatment of the programmatic concerns of each stratum of texts. Rather, the major trends of speculation will be briefly indicated through reference to select examples from the various strata.[52] Part I focuses on brahmanical representations of Veda in Vedic and post-Vedic mythology.[53] The analysis of Vedic texts is drawn primarily from the mythological portions of the Saṃhitās (ca. 1500–800 B.C.E.), Brāhmaṇas (ca. 900–650 B.C.E.), and Upaniṣads (ca. 800–200 B.C.E.),[54] while the post-Vedic section of the analysis derives from the cosmogonic speculations found in the Manu-Smṛti (ca. 200 B.C.E.–200 C.E.), Mahābhārata (ca. 400 B.C.E.–400 C.E.), and selected Purāṇas (ca. 300–1000 C.E.). Part II examines certain symbolic complexes associated with the Torah in rabbinic and kabbalistic texts.[55] The rabbinic portion of the analysis is drawn from aggadic speculations found in the Mishnah (ca. 220 C.E.), Tannaitic Midrashim (up to 400 C.E.),[56] classical Amoraic Midrashim (ca. 400–640 C.E.),[57] Babylonian Talmud (ca. 500–600 C.E.), and certain post-Talmudic Midrashim (ca. 640–1200 C.E.).[58] The kabbalistic portion is based primarily on the cosmogonic speculations of the Zohar and the theosophical Kabbalah of thirteenth-century Spain.[59] Part III, which represents the comparative phase of the analysis, discusses the structural affinities in the symbol systems associated with Veda and Torah and then highlights some of the essential differences in the conceptions and practices of these scriptural traditions.

I. VEDA

Among the network of symbols associated with Veda in Vedic and post-Vedic mythology, four complexes persist through the various strata of literature: (1) the Veda is described as the Word (*brahman*), which is the essence of Brahman, the ultimate reality, and is at times designated more specifically as Śabdabrahman, Brahman embodied in the Word; (2) the Veda as the totality of knowledge is also at times identified with the creator principle as the immediate source of creation; (3) the Veda*s* (plural) are depicted as the plan or blueprint of creation containing the primordial expressions of the divine speech that the creator utters in order to manifest the forms of creation; (4) the Vedas in their earthly, transmitted form are the *mantra* collections, or Saṃhitās, of the Ṛg-Veda, Yajur-Veda, Sāma-Veda, and Atharva-Veda that are recited by human beings on earth as part of the Vedic sacrificial rites. The following analysis will be primarily concerned with the first three conceptions, since it is these conceptions that point to the cosmological status of Veda. With respect to the fourth conception, it is important to note that references in Vedic and post-Vedic mythology to the mundane manifestation of the Vedas as recited texts do not generally include the Brāhmaṇas, Āraṇyakas, and Upaniṣads but rather pertain solely to the Saṃhitās.

Veda as the Word: The Essence of Brahman

The brahmanical conception of Veda as the essence of Brahman must be understood against the background of the development of the term *brahman* itself. In the Ṛg-Veda and later Saṃhitās the term *brahman* is used, depending on the context, at times to refer to Veda, in the general sense of "Word," and at other times to refer more specifically to the Vedic *mantras*. The term is also used in the Saṃhitās to signify the power inherent in the Word or in the Vedic *mantras*. In the

Atharva-Veda Saṃhitā the meaning of the term *brahman* is extended to encompass that cosmic power or principle which underlies and gives rise to the universe.[60]

In the metaphysical speculations of the Upaniṣads the conception of *brahman* as a cosmic principle takes precedence over other meanings of the term. Brahman and Ātman (Self) are the most common Upaniṣadic designations for the ultimate reality, with the two terms becoming identified at times in certain Upaniṣads and used interchangeably to refer to the universal ground of all existence. In its identification with the ultimate reality Brahman-Ātman is depicted as both transcendent and immanent, formless and formed. On the one hand, Brahman-Ātman is declared to be transcendent, beyond the phenomenal creation, and completely unmanifest, formless, distinctionless, and nonchanging in its essential, absolute nature. On the other hand, Brahman-Ātman is depicted as that immanent, all-pervading reality which dwells in all aspects of the manifest, ever-changing relative creation.[61]

In post-Vedic literature the transcendent and immanent aspects of Brahman are termed, respectively, Nirguṇa Brahman, Brahman without attributes, and Saguṇa Brahman, Brahman with attributes. In post-Vedic texts that reflect the influence of sectarian devotionalism, such as the Mahābhārata and the Purāṇas, Brahman generally assumes a personalized aspect through becoming identified with the particular deity that is upheld as the ultimate reality. The Mahābhārata generally identifies Brahman with the supreme Godhead Viṣṇu, although the epic also contains Śaiva sections in which Brahman is identified with Śiva. Vaiṣṇava Purāṇas such as the Viṣṇu and Bhāgavata Purāṇas revere Viṣṇu as Brahman, while Śaiva Purāṇas such as the Liṅga and Śiva Purāṇas glorify Śiva as Brahman.

With respect to the relationship between Veda and Brahman, the Veda is described as an aspect of Brahman in at least two different senses in Vedic and post-Vedic mythology: (1) the Veda, as the Word that is undifferentiated knowledge, is the very essence of Brahman, the nature of which is knowledge, while (2) the Vedic *mantras*, as the differentiated impulses of knowledge contained in the expressions of speech, form the cosmic body of Brahman. The Veda as Śabdabrahman, Brahman embodied in the Word,[62] thus represents the totality of the Word in both its aspects—knowledge and speech—and participates in the reality of Brahman as both its inner essence and its outer form. As such the Veda is particularly associated with Saguṇa Brahman, that aspect of Brahman which possesses a form and various attributes and which manifests itself in creation.

Vedic Texts

In the Saṃhitās, as mentioned above, the term *brahman* is itself used at times to refer to Veda, in the sense of Word, and at other times to refer to the Vedic *mantras*. Taittirīya Saṃhitā VII.3.1.4, for example, uses the term *brahman* to refer to that limitless totality of the Word, Veda, of which the Vedic *mantras*—*ṛcs*, *sāmans*, and *yajuses*—are but a limited manifestation.

> The *ṛcs* are limited, the *sāmans* are limited, and the *yajuses* are limited, but of the Word *(brahman)* there is no end.

The conception of *brahman* as a cosmic principle first appears in the Atharva-Veda Saṃhitā, and it is in this Saṃhitā that we first find the notion that the Vedic *mantras* are constitutive of the cosmic body of Brahman. In Atharva-Veda X.7.20 the *ṛcs*, *yajuses*, *sāmans*, and *atharvāṅgirases* are depicted as forming various parts of the body of Skambha, the cosmic principle that is identified with Brahman as the foundation of the entire universe.[63] In Atharva-Veda IX.6.1–2 the Vedic *mantras* are similarly described as constituting different parts of the body of Brahman, with the *ṛcs* forming the spine, the *sāmans* the hairs, and the *yajuses* the heart.

The Upaniṣads develop this notion further, reinterpreting it in light of the Upaniṣadic concept of Brahman-Ātman.[64] The Taittirīya Upaniṣad, for example, describes the Ātman consisting of mind *(mano-maya)* as having the form of a person (Puruṣa), of which the Yajur-Veda constitutes the head, the Ṛg-Veda the right side, the Sāma-Veda the left side, and the *atharvāṅgirases* the foundation.[65] In the Kauṣītaki Upaniṣad the cosmic body that is constituted by the Vedic *mantras* is that of Brahman, the Imperishable.

> He whose belly is the *yajus,* whose head is the *sāman,* whose form is the *ṛc,* yonder Imperishable *(avyaya)* is to be known as Brahman, the great seer *(ṛṣi),* consisting of the Word *(brahma-maya).*[66]

This passage points to two levels on which the Veda participates in the reality of Brahman: (1) the Veda as *brahman,* the Word, constitutes the very fabric of which the cosmic principle of Brahman is made, while (2) the Vedic *mantras*—*ṛcs*, *yajuses*, and *sāmans*—each form a different part of the cosmic body.

Post-Vedic Texts

Post-Vedic texts further elaborate on the twofold manner in which the Veda is an aspect of Brahman. According to the sectarian emphasis of the text, Viṣṇu or Śiva is generally upheld as that ultimate reality which is identical with Brahman, and the Veda is correspondingly depicted as an aspect of Viṣṇu or Śiva.

In a number of passages in the Mahābhārata Viṣṇu is directly identified with the Veda, and the Vedic *mantras* in particular.[67] He is said to be the embodiment of the *ṛcs*, *yajuses*, *sāmans*, and *atharvans*.[68] In the Śaiva sections of the epic Śiva becomes identified with the Veda, and the Vedic *mantras* are described as forming different parts of Śiva's body.[69]

The Purāṇas emphasize the the nature of Viṣṇu or Śiva, as the ultimate reality identified with Brahman, is knowledge, and the Veda constitutes both the inner essence and the outer form of this reality. The Viṣṇu Purāṇa, for example, celebrates Viṣṇu as the supreme Brahman, whose essence is knowledge, who is knowledge incarnate *(jñāna-mūrti)*,[70] and who is one with the Vedas,[71] his form being composed of the *ṛcs*, *yajuses*, and *sāmans*.

> He is composed of the *ṛcs*, of the *sāmans*, of the *yajuses*, and he is the Self (Ātman). He whose Self is the essence of the *ṛcs*, *yajuses*, and *sāmans*, he is the Self of embodied beings. Consisting of the Veda *(veda-maya)*, he is divided; he forms the Veda and its branches *(śākhās)* into many divisions. Creator of the *śākhās*, he is the *śākhās* in their totality, the infinite Lord, whose very nature is knowledge *(jñāna-svarūpa)*.[72]

The Veda, as represented in this passage, participates in the nature of Viṣṇu/Brahman on at least two levels. (1) As the undifferentiated totality of knowledge, the Veda constitutes the very essence of Viṣṇu/Brahman, whose nature is knowledge and who thus consists of the Veda *(veda-maya)*. (2) While Viṣṇu/Brahman's inner essence is Veda, knowledge, his outer form is composed of the Vedic *mantras*—*ṛcs*, *yajuses*, and *sāmans*. As Veda he is undivided, encompassing the totality of knowledge, while as the Vedas he is divided into parts composed of the Vedic *mantras* and their numerous branches (*śākhās*). Another passage in the Viṣṇu Purāṇa describes the Vedas and their supplements, the Vedāṅgas and Upavedas, together with the Itihāsas, Dharma-Śāstras, and other sacred texts, as the body of Viṣṇu in the form of sound/word *(śabda-mūrti)*.[73] The Veda as such is Śabdabrahman, Brahman embodied in the Word.

Viṣṇu-Nārāyaṇa is extolled as the embodiment of knowledge, whose form is composed of the Vedas, not only in Vaiṣṇava Purāṇas such as the Viṣṇu Purāṇa and Bhāgavata Purāṇa, but also in nonsectarian

Purāṇas such as the Mārkaṇḍeya Purāṇa and in cross-sectarian Purāṇas such as the Matsya and Kūrma Purāṇas that contain both Vaiṣṇava and Śaiva material.[74] For example, the Matsya Purāṇa in its account of creation eulogizes Viṣṇu-Nārāyaṇa, who is identified with the supreme Brahman, as the secret essence of the Vedas *(vedānām rahasya)*[75] who is composed of Veda *(veda-maya)*.[76]

In Śaiva Purāṇas such as the Śiva Purāṇa it is Śiva who is identified with the supreme Brahman, and as such he is extolled as the embodiment of knowledge *(jñānātman)* who is composed of the three Vedas *(trayī-maya)*.[77] Moreover, Śiva in his *saguṇa* form is described in the Śiva Purāṇa as Śabdabrahman, Brahman embodied in the Word, his body constituted by the forty-eight *varṇa*-sounds of Sanskrit and the three Vedas—Ṛg, Yajur, and Sāma.[78]

Veda as Knowledge: The Creator Principle

In Vedic and post-Vedic mythology the Veda and its differentiated expressions are associated not only with Brahman, the ultimate reality, but also with the creator god, the demiurge principle, who is responsible for giving shape to the manifest forms and phenomena of the material creation.

In the Ṛg-Veda Saṃhitā the personal creator god who is the fashioner of the three worlds—earth, midregions, and heaven—and the lord of all beings is variously designated as Prajāpati ("lord of created beings") or Hiraṇyagarbha ("golden embryo/germ") in Ṛg-Veda X.121 or as Viśvakarman ("maker of all") in Ṛg-Veda X.81 and X.82. Ṛg-Veda X.90, the famous Puruṣa-Sūkta, presents a more monistic perspective, in which the one, all-pervading principle that is the source and basis of creation is Puruṣa, the cosmic Man. In the Atharva-Veda Saṃhitā, Vājasaneyi Saṃhitā (White Yajur-Veda), and Taittirīya Saṃhitā (Black Yajur-Veda) Prajāpati is singled out as the paramount creator god.

The cosmogonic speculations of the Brāhmaṇas, like the later Saṃhitās, center around Prajāpati, who is celebrated as the supreme god and creator and is explicitly identified with Puruṣa, Hiraṇyagarbha, and Viśvakarman. In the Upaniṣads, in contrast, the ultimate reality, Brahman-Ātman, is given precedence over the creator principle, and the figures of Prajāpati and Puruṣa are either identified with that reality or subordinated to it.

In post-Vedic cosmogonies the primary designation for the creator principle is Brahmā, who is explicitly identified with both Puruṣa and Prajāpati. As in the Upaniṣads, in post-Vedic accounts the creator principle is generally relegated to a subsidiary role as a manifestation of the supreme reality of Brahman, who is identified in these texts with either Viṣṇu or Śiva.

Vedic Texts

Ṛg-Veda X.90, the Puruṣa-Sūkta, describes the emergence of creation through a primeval sacrifice *(yajña)* in which the different parts of the body of Puruṣa, the cosmic Man, are offered up to form the different aspects of the universe. The hymn describes the *ṛcs*, *yajuses*, and *sāmans* as emerging from the cosmic body of Puruṣa[79] along with the four basic orders that are fundamental to the Vedic conception of reality: the sacrificial order, the human order, the natural order, and the divine order.

The cosmogonies of the Brāhmaṇas, building on the speculations of the Puruṣa-Sūkta, identify the creator Prajāpati with that supreme Puruṣa who is the source of the sacrifice, the first performer of the sacrifice, and the sacrifice itself. The Veda is at times identified with Prajāpati: "In the beginning Prajāpati was the Veda" *(Prajāpatir vedaḥ).*[80] The Veda is described as constitutive of Prajāpati's being, with the Vedic *mantras*, meters, and various components of the sacrifice forming different parts of his body or self *(ātman).*[81] At the same time the Veda is said to be derived from Prajāpati *(Prājāpatyo vedaḥ),*[82] for it is Prajāpati who brings forth the Veda in the beginning of creation.[83] These two notions—the Veda as constitutive of Prajāpati and the Veda as derived from Prajāpati—are brought together in the Jaiminīya Brāhmaṇa, which describes Prajāpati as bringing forth certain *stomas*, *sāmans*, and meters from various parts of his body.[84] The Veda is more specifically represented as the expression of Prajāpati's speech.[85]

A number of passages in the Upaniṣads similarly depict the Vedic *mantras* as not only derived from the creator principle but as constitutive of certain aspects of his being. Muṇḍaka Upaniṣad II.1.1–10 describes the *ṛcs*, *sāmans*, and *yajuses* as emerging from Puruṣa along with the various parts of the sacrificial, human, natural, and divine orders. The manifest *(vivṛta)* Vedas are identified in particular with his speech.[86] Although the passage recalls the language of the Puruṣa-Sūkta, the concrete imagery of the sacrifice is stripped away and the creation narrative is recast in light of the Upaniṣadic metaphysical perspective by establishing the identity of Puruṣa with Brahman-Ātman.[87] Taittirīya Upaniṣad II.3, mentioned earlier, correlates Puruṣa more specifically with the Ātman consisting of mind *(mano-maya)* and identifies the four Vedas with different parts of Puruṣa's body. The Chāndogya Upaniṣad goes even further and asserts that Puruṣa *is* the *ṛc*, the *sāman*, and the *yajus*.[88]

Post-Vedic Texts

In post-Vedic cosmogonies the creator Brahmā is described as that manifest form which Brahman—whether identified with Viṣṇu or Śiva—assumes for the purpose of fashioning the forms of creation. Brahmā himself thus participates in the nature of Brahman, and in his role as creator he is particularly extolled as the embodiment of knowledge and Veda incarnate.

In the Mahābhārata Brahmā is celebrated as the guru of the worlds and of the gods[89] whose very substance is Veda *(veda-maya).*[90] He is also described as "the one with the four Vedas *(catur-veda),* the four forms *(catur-mūrti),* the four faces/mouths *(catur-mukha).*"[91] Brahmā is at times depicted as bringing forth the Vedas in the beginning of each new cycle of creation, although the epic is careful to emphasize that it is Viṣṇu who is the ultimate source of the Vedas and who assigns Brahmā his role as the intermediate instrument by means of which the Vedas are manifested and promulgated.[92]

The Purāṇas celebrate the creator Brahmā as the embodiment of Veda. The Viṣṇu Purāṇa describes Brahmā as "Hiraṇyagarbha, that form of Brahman which consists of Lord Viṣṇu and which is composed of the Ṛg-, Yajur-, and Sāma-Vedas."[93] The Kūrma Purāṇa declares the *ṛcs, yajuses, sāmans,* and *atharvans* to be the inherent form *(sahaja rūpa)* of Brahmā,[94] and he in turn is said to be the embodiment of the Vedic *mantras (chando-mūrti)*[95] as well as their repository *(veda-nidhi).*[96] In the Bhāgavata Purāṇa it is the creator Brahmā who is called Śabdabrahman, Brahman embodied in the Word,[97] and he is thus identified with Veda and is said to be composed of Veda *(veda-maya)*[98] and the abode of Veda *(veda-garbha).*[99] The body of Brahmā, as Śabdabrahman, is described as constituted by the Sanskrit *varṇas* and the Vedic *mantras* and meters.[100]

Veda as Divine Language: The Blueprint of Creation

Vedas as the Expressions of Divine Speech

While on one level the creator is depicted as Veda incarnate, on another level, as we have seen, he is said to be the source of the Vedic *mantras*. From the Veda, as identified with the creator principle, come forth the Vedas. The Vedic *mantras* are often depicted in Vedic and post-Vedic cosmogonies as emerging from the creator at the beginning of creation as the expressions of his speech. The Vedas thus become associated with Vāc, speech, who is depicted in the Brāhmaṇas as the consort of the creator Prajāpati. In post-Vedic cosmogonies the role of

Prajāpati is assumed by Brahmā, and correspondingly the role of Prajāpati's consort Vāc is assumed by Brahmā's consort, Sarasvatī or Gāyatrī/Sāvitrī, who becomes identified with the goddess of speech. In the Mahābhārata Sarasvatī and Gāyatrī/Sāvitrī generally retain their distinctive identities as two separate goddesses, with Sarasvatī portrayed as the daughter of Brahmā and Gāyatrī/Sāvitrī as his wife. In the Purāṇas the two goddesses become identified, as do the roles of daughter and wife.

Vedic Texts

The conception of Vāc in the Ṛg-Veda Saṃhitā is already quite complex and multidimensional, encompassing both a divine dimension, in its hypostatization as the goddess Vāc, and an earthly dimension, in its diversified expressions in human language.[101] The connection between Veda and Vāc is primarily expressed in the Ṛg-Veda in terms of the notion that the *ṛṣis*, the seers of the Vedic *mantras*, are especially beloved of Vāc, upon whom she bestows the power of *brahman*.[102]

In the Brāhmaṇas, as in the Saṃhitās, Vāc has both a divine dimension as a goddess and an earthly dimension as human language. Within the divine dimension we can discern at least two different levels. (1) On the subtlest level, Vāc is hypostatized as the divine consort of the creator Prajāpati. On this level she is unexpressed *(anirukta)*, transcendent speech and is identified with the primordial waters in which Prajāpati implants his seed in order to bring forth creation. (2) On the more manifest level, the waters of Vāc flow out in differentiated streams as the expressed *(nirukta)*, vocalized speech of the creator himself.[103] The Veda as the undifferentiated Word, *brahman*, is at times correlated with the first level, while the differentiated Vedic *mantras* are correlated with the second level. The *ṛcs*, *yajuses*, and *sāmans* are said to be the threefold form of Vāc.[104] From Vāc, who is designated as the "Mother of the Vedas,"[105] the Vedic *mantras* go forth in the beginning of creation as her "thousandfold progeny."[106]

As the expressions of Vāc the Vedic *mantras* are associated in particular with the speech of the creator Prajāpati, which is the vehicle through which the phenomenal world is projected into manifestation. The original utterances by means of which Prajāpati brings forth the three worlds are generally identified in the Brāhmaṇas with the three *vyāhṛtis* ("utterances")—*bhūḥ*, *bhuvaḥ*, and *svaḥ*—which are consistently represented throughout the Brāhmaṇas as the essences of the three Vedas—Ṛg-Veda, Yajur-Veda, and Sāma-Veda.[107] For example, Śatapatha Brāhmaṇa XI.1.6.3 declares,

> He uttered (root *hṛ* + *vi-ā*) *"bhūḥ"*—that became this earth; *"bhuvaḥ"*—that became the midregions; *"svaḥ"*—that became yonder heaven.[108]

In a number of passages in the Brāhmaṇas the words that Prajāpati speaks in order to manifest the phenomena of creation are explicitly identified with the words of the Vedic *mantras*. Prajāpati is portrayed as the primordial *ṛṣi* who originally "sees" (root *dṛś*) specific *ṛcs* and *sāmans*,[109] as well as the sacrificial rituals in which the *mantras* are used.[110] He then performs the various sacrifices, assuming the functions of the different priests: as the *hotṛ* priest he recites the *ṛcs*, as the *udgātṛ* priest he chants the *sāmans*, and as the *adhvaryu* priest he utters the *yajuses*.[111] For example, in Pañcaviṃśa Brāhmaṇa VI.9.15, and the corresponding variant in Jaiminīya Brāhmaṇa I.94, Prajāpati is depicted as chanting the words of a *sāman* (Sāma-Veda II.180 = Ṛg-Veda IX.62.1) in order to bring forth not only the gods, human beings, ancestors, and other beings, but also various aspects of the sacrificial order, including the Soma libations, *stotras* chanted by the *udgātṛ*, and *śastras* recited by the *hotṛ*.

> [Saying] *"ete"* ("these") Prajāpati brought forth the gods; [saying] *"asṛgram"* ("have been poured out") he brought forth human beings; [saying] *"indavaḥ"* ("Soma drops") he brought forth the ancestors; [saying] *"tiraḥ pavitram"* ("through the filter") he brought forth the [Soma] libations; [saying] *"āśavaḥ"* ("swift") he brought forth the *stotra;* [saying] *"viśvāni"* ("all") he brought forth the *śastra;* [saying] *"abhi saubhagā"* ("for the sake of blessings") he brought forth the other beings.[112]

In the Upaniṣads, as in the Brāhmaṇas, the Vedic *mantras* are associated in particular with the speech of the creator principle. As mentioned above, the Muṇḍaka Upaniṣad identifies the manifest Vedas with the speech of Puruṣa (= Brahman-Ātman).[113] Vāc, speech, is the uniting-point *(ekāyana)* of all the Vedas, as the ocean is the uniting-point of all waters.[114] Vāc, by means of which the four Vedas and other sacred texts are made known, is ultimately identified in the Upaniṣads with Brahman.[115]

Like the Brāhmaṇas, the Upaniṣads emphasize the creative power of speech as the vehicle through which the creator brings forth creation. For example, a passage in the Maitri Upaniṣad describes how in the beginning the world was unuttered *(avyāhṛta)* until Prajāpati, having practiced *tapas,*[116] uttered (root *hṛ* + *anu-vi-ā*) it in the words *bhūḥ, bhuvaḥ, svaḥ.*[117] Although the passage invokes the imagery of the Brāhmaṇas, in accordance with the Upaniṣadic metaphysical perspective it interjects a new element into the creation narrative by identifying Prajāpati with the Self (Ātman) of all. The Vedas are not explicitly mentioned in this passage, although they are represented metonymically by the three *vyāhṛti*s, *bhūḥ, bhuvaḥ, svaḥ,* an identification that had already been well established by this period and is developed elsewhere in the Upaniṣads, as will be discussed below.

A passage in the Bṛhadāraṇyaka Upaniṣad depicts the Vedic *mantra*s as the first manifestation of that speech by means of which the creator brings forth the entire universe.[118] Another passage in the Bṛhadāraṇyaka Upaniṣad describes speech as the differentiating principle through which the creator—here identified with the Imperishable *(akṣara)*—introduces distinctions in the originally distinctionless totality.[119]

Post-Vedic Texts

As in Vedic cosmogonies, Vāc assumes a dual role in post-Vedic cosmogonies as, on the one hand, the feminine principle with which the creator unites, and, on the other hand, the vocalized speech that he utters in order to bring forth the Vedas and manifest creation.

In the Mahābhārata both Sarasvatī and Gāyatrī/Sāvitrī, as the daughter and consort of Brahmā, respectively, are associated with Vāc, speech, and, like Vāc in Vedic cosmogonies, both are celebrated as the "Mother of the Vedas."[120] It is as speech that Sarasvatī and Gāyatrī/Sāvitrī fulfill their role as the Mother of the Vedas, for speech provides the vehicle by means of which the Vedic *mantra*s issue forth in the beginning of creation from the creator—whether in his supreme reality as Viṣṇu or in his relative manifestation as Brahmā.

In accordance with the Vaiṣṇava emphasis of the Mahābhārata, the Vedas are particularly associated with the speech of Viṣṇu, the lord of speech *(vācas pati),*[121] who is the ultimate source and abode of the Veda. Viṣṇu is depicted as bringing forth speech, Sarasvatī, along with her progeny, the Vedas, at the beginning of creation[122] and as reciting the *mantra*s in contexts outside of the creative process as well.[123] The Vedas are also at times depicted as emerging in the beginning from the demiurge Brahmā as the expressions of his speech.

> In the beginning knowledge *(vidyā),* without beginning or end, divine speech (Vāc), consisting of the Vedas *(veda-mayī),* from which all manifestations are derived, was sent forth by Svayambhū [Brahmā].[124]

The passage goes on to describe how by means of the primordial impulses of speech contained in the Vedic *mantras* the creator Brahmā projects the phenomena of creation into manifestation.[125]

In the Purāṇas Sarasvatī and Gāyatrī/Sāvitrī become identified as a single goddess, who is depicted as issuing forth from the body of Brahmā as his female half, or daughter, with whom he then unites as his wife and from whom he brings forth the Vedas.[126] While Brahmā is the master of the Vedas, Sarasvatī/Gāyatrī is their mistress.[127] Like her progeny, the Vedas, Sarasvatī as the goddess of speech is at times associated in the Purāṇas with the mouths of Brahmā, which are her special abode.[128]

The Purāṇas describe the Vedic *mantras* as the primordial utterances of Brahmā by means of which he brings forth the forms of creation. A number of the Purāṇas contain a standardized description of the four types of Vedic *mantras*—*ṛcs*, *yajuses*, *sāmans*, and *atharvans*—issuing forth from the four mouths of Brahmā—eastern, southern, western, and northern, respectively—along with certain Vedic *stomas*, *sāmans*, meters, and sacrifices.[129] The Bhāgavata Purāṇa, which provides a variant of the standard account, declares,

> While he was contemplating, "How shall I bring forth the aggregate worlds as before?" the Vedas issued from the four mouths of the creator. . . . From his eastern and other mouths he brought forth in succession the Vedas known as Ṛg, Yajur, Sāma, and Atharva. . . .[130]

Vedas as the Blueprint of Creation

There is creative power in the divine speech of the creator that issues forth as the Vedic *mantras*. When the creator wishes to call the forms of creation into being, he simply recites the Vedic *mantras*, which are depicted in Vedic and post-Vedic accounts as the subtle plan or blueprint of creation that contains the basic sound impulses that structure the manifold phenomena of the universe.

Vedic Texts

The Vedic *mantras*, as the expressions of the divine speech of the creator Prajāpati, are depicted in the Brāhmaṇas as part of the very fabric of reality and as reflective of the structures of the cosmos. The realm of concrete phenomena is held to have been brought forth through the sound impulses contained in the Vedic *mantras*, and thus the Vedic words are viewed as the subtle correlatives of the forms of creation. In this context the three Vedas—Ṛg-Veda, Yajur-Veda, and Sāma-Veda—

are incorporated into the Brāhmaṇas' cosmological system as part of an elaborate set of correspondences (*bandhus*) that, building upon the speculations of the Puruṣa-Sūkta, correlate the various orders of reality—sacrificial order, human order, natural order, and divine order.

At the basis of this system of correspondences are the three primordial utterances, or *vyāhṛtis*—*bhūḥ, bhuvaḥ, svaḥ*—which constitute the seed syllables of creation corresponding to the three worlds—earth, midregions, and heaven[131]—and which are identified, respectively, with the Ṛg-Veda, Yajur-Veda, and Sāma-Veda, representing their essences (*śukras* or *rasas*).[132] With these three primordial utterances, as discussed above, Prajāpati brings forth not only the three worlds,[133] but also other aspects of creation.[134] A number of passages in the Brāhmaṇas establish correspondences between the three *vyāhṛtis, bhūḥ, bhuvaḥ, svaḥ;* the three Vedas, Ṛg, Yajur, and Sāma; the three worlds, earth, midregions, and heaven; and the three elements fire, wind, and sun, together with their presiding deities, Agni, Vāyu, and Sūrya/Āditya.[135] This system of homologies is at times extended to include the three constituent sounds of the sacred syllable Om, *a, u,* and *m,*[136] as well as certain human faculties. The standard tripartite schema generally correlates the *ṛc, yajus,* and *sāman* with speech, breath, and the eye, respectively,[137] although alternative schemas are also presented.[138]

Primordial Utterances			Natural Order		Divine Order	Human Order
a	*bhūḥ*	Ṛg-Veda	earth	fire	Agni	speech
u	*bhuvaḥ*	Yajur-Veda	midregions	wind	Vāyu	breath
m	*svaḥ*	Sāma-Veda	heaven	sun	Sūrya/Āditya	eye

This tripartite taxonomy establishes a series of correlations between, on the one hand, the realm of sound, represented by the primordial utterances, and, on the other hand, the realm of form, represented by the human, natural, and divine orders. Implicit in this schema, as well as in the more general Vedic conception of the creative power of the divine speech, is the notion that an intrinsic relation exists between the Vedic word and the object that it signifies, between the name *(nāma)* and the form *(rūpa)* that it designates. In this conception *bhūḥ* is not simply a conventional designation, it is the natural name of the earth, and thus it represents the subtle correlative that contains the "reality" of the earth within its structure. The primordial utterances *bhūḥ, bhuvaḥ,* and *svaḥ* are like potent seeds containing the entire tree of creation about to sprout. These three seed syllables represent the concentrated essences of the divine speech, which are in turn elaborated in the three Vedas.

The Vedas in this perspective contain the primordial sounds from which the phenomenal creation is structured. Taittirīya Brāhmaṇa III.12.9.1–2 describes the *ṛcs, yajuses,* and *sāmans* as the sources of form, motion, and light, respectively, and then declares, "All this *(sarvam idam)* indeed was brought forth through *brahman* [Veda]." A passage in the Śatapatha Brāhmaṇa depicts the three Vedas as containing the entire universe in potential form.[139] While the three Vedas together correspond to the creation in its entirety, each Veda separately, in its correlation with one of the three worlds, represents the plan for that particular world.[140]

The Upaniṣads develop further the series of correlations established in the Brāhmaṇas between the realm of sound—represented by the three Vedas (Ṛg, Yajur, and Sāma) and their concentrated essences in the three *vyāhṛtis* (*bhūḥ, bhuvaḥ,* and *svaḥ*) and the three constituent sounds of Om *(a, u, m)*—and the human, natural, and divine orders.[141] In accordance with the earlier view of the Brāhmaṇas, several Upaniṣadic passages depict the intrinsic connections between these orders of reality as manifesting through the demiurgic activity of Prajāpati.[142] However, in other passages the Upaniṣadic monistic perspective is superimposed on the inherited paradigm by identifying the various aspects of the natural, divine, and human orders as different manifestations of Brahman-Ātman. Thus while the Brāhmaṇas, in their emphasis on the relative material creation, are concerned with establishing correspondences between specific aspects of the macrocosm and the microcosm, the Upaniṣads, in their focus on the ultimate reality, are above all concerned to establish a more fundamental identity among all aspects of the universe as simply different expressions of the unitary ground of existence, Brahman-Ātman. For example, a passage in the Maitri Upaniṣad describes the constituent elements of Om, *a, u,* and *m,* as the sound-form *(svana-vati)* of Ātman; the Ṛg-Veda, Yajur-Veda, and Sāma-Veda as its knowledge-form *(vijñāna-vati);* the earth, midregions, and heaven as its world-form *(loka-vati);* and fire, wind, and sun as its light-form *(bhās-vati).*[143] The Taittirīya Upaniṣad, in addition to the three *vyāhṛtis* and their corresponding triads, includes a fourth utterance, *mahaḥ,* which is identified with Brahman-Ātman and which constitutes the "transcendent fourth" that transforms the triadic structure into a

"3 + 1" structure that becomes paradigmatic in post-Vedic texts. In this schema the transcendent fourth that corresponds to *mahaḥ* in the triad of *ṛcs*, *yajuses*, and *sāmans* is *brahman,* the Word, which represents the undifferentiated totality of Veda that is beyond the Vedic *mantras*.[144]

Post-Vedic Texts

In post-Vedic texts, particularly in the Purāṇas, the primordial utterances described in Vedic accounts—the three constituent sounds of Om, the three *vyāhṛtis*, and the three Vedas—are represented as different stages in the sequential unfoldment of the divine speech. A number of new elements are incorporated, which can be schematized in six main stages: (1) the syllable Om, which as the sound-embodiment of Brahman is the fundamental, all-encompassing sound at the basis of all creation; (2) the three sounds *a, u, m,* which are the constituents of Om; (3) the three *vyāhṛtis*—*bhūḥ, bhuvaḥ, svaḥ*—which are the seed syllables of the three corresponding worlds; (4) the forty-eight *varṇas*, or *akṣaras*, of Sanskrit, which are the basic structural elements of creation; (5) the three-lined *gāyatrī mantra,* also called *sāvitrī,* which incorporates and expands on the three *vyāhṛtis* preceded by Om; and (6) the four Vedas—Ṛg, Yajur, Sāma, and Atharva—which are composed of various configurations of the forty-eight Sanskrit *varṇas*.[145] The notion that the Vedas, as the most developed expressions of the divine speech, contain the primordial sounds that structure the forms of creation is formulated in post-Vedic accounts in terms of the image of an archetypal plan that the creator Brahmā consults at the beginning of each cycle of creation in order to fashion the names, forms, and functions of all beings.

The cosmogonic account of the Manu-Smṛti maintains that in each new cycle of creation each class of beings is allotted the same function that it had assumed in the previous cycle.[146] In the midst of the endless cycles of creation and dissolution the Vedas are said to exist perpetually as "the eternal *(sanātana)* eye of the ancestors, gods, and human beings."[147] The eternal Vedas, unaffected by the ebb and flow of time, are drawn forth by the creator Brahmā at the beginning of each new cycle and serve as the plan that he employs in order to assign each being its respective name, nature, and function.

> In the beginning he [Brahmā] formed from the words *(śabdas)* of the Vedas alone the particular names, activities, and conditions of all [beings].[148]

In another passage the Manu-Smṛti describes the Vedas as not only the blueprint but also the source of creation. Moreover, in accordance with the Manu-Smṛti's preoccupation with *varṇāśrama-dharma,* the Vedas are depicted as the source not only of the three worlds and all beings, but also of the social order, as represented by the system of four classes (*varṇas*) and four stages of life (*āśramas*).[149]

A number of passages in the Mahābhārata point to the cosmogonic role of the Vedas as the means by which Brahmā brings forth the phenomenal world.[150] It is the demiurge Brahmā to whom Viṣṇu assigns the role of the "ordainer *(dhātṛ)* of all created beings," for it is Brahmā who manifests the various classes of beings anew in each cycle of creation and reassigns to them their designated names and allotted duties.[151] The names, forms, and functions of all beings are said to be eternally preserved in the Vedic *mantras*, which reappear at the beginning of each new cycle as the blueprint that the architect Brahmā consults in order to fulfill his function as demiurge.

> In the beginning the Lord forms from the words (*śabdas*) of the Vedas alone the names of the seers (*ṛṣis*), the creations in the Vedas, the various forms of beings, and the course of actions.[152]

The notion that the creator Brahmā structures the names and forms of all beings from the Vedic words is found in the Purāṇas in the form of a standardized description that is regularly incorporated in Purāṇic accounts of creation.

> In the beginning he [Brahmā] formed from the words (*śabdas*) of the Vedas alone the names, forms, and functions of the gods and other beings. He also formed the names and appropriate offices of all the *ṛṣis* as heard *(śruta)* in the Vedas.[153]

As indicated in the above passage, Purāṇic accounts, like those of the Manu-Smṛti and Mahābhārata, point to name, form, and function as the three fundamental aspects of created beings that have their source in the Vedas. (1) The Vedas contain the *names* of all beings. These names are considered to be the natural names—rather than conventional designations—of the forms that they signify, and therefore the same names are assigned to each class of beings at the beginning of each new cycle of creation. (2) The *forms* of creation are brought forth through the names contained in the Vedas. The form is considered to be already inherent in its natural name and thus represents a more precipitated, consolidated expression of that name. Therefore, Brahmā need only recite the words of the Vedas in order to generate the corresponding forms. (3) The words of the Vedas also determine the *functions* of all beings in that the special character and function of each type of being is said to be contained in its name. For example, when Brahmā utters the Vedic word *"gandharva"* a special group of celestial beings spontaneously comes forth whose function is to serve as heavenly musicians through "drinking speech" *(gām dhayantaḥ)*. When he utters the word *"sarpa"* a type of serpent emerges whose nature is to "creep" (root *sṛp*) on the ground.[154]

Stages of Manifestation

Thus far our analysis has been concerned with three aspects of Veda as depicted in Vedic and post-Vedic mythology: (1) Veda as the Word, which is the essence of Brahman, particularly in its manifestation as Śabdabrahman; (2) Veda as the totality of knowledge, which is identified with the creator principle, who serves as the immediate source of creation; and (3) Veda*s* as the subtle impulses of divine speech that constitute the plan or blueprint from which the creator structures the forms of creation. These various aspects of Veda are represented not only as corresponding to different levels of creation, but also as different stages of manifestation in the cosmogonic process.

F. B. J. Kuiper, in his attempt to reconstruct the Vedic cosmogonic myth, has suggested that this myth comprises two different stages. (1) In the first stage the primordial world was "an undivided unity, a *rudis indigestaque moles*," which consisted of the primordial waters and the undifferentiated totality of the cosmos—frequently represented by the image of the cosmic egg—floating on the surface of the waters. (2) In the second stage heaven and earth were separated out of the originally undifferentiated unity, either through an autonomous process of division or through the demiurgic act of a god.[155] Although the details of Kuiper's thesis need not concern us here, my own research confirms that this basic two-stage pattern of creation is fundamental to both Vedic and post-Vedic cosmogonies. Beyond the elements emphasized by Kuiper, this two-stage process involves two phases of manifestation of the three primary agents in the creative process: the male principle, who is the embodiment of knowledge; the female principle, who is the embodiment of speech; and the Veda.

Vedic Texts

With respect to Vedic texts, my reconstruction of the two-phase process of creation is based on several accounts in the Brāhmaṇas, in which Prajāpati and Vāc both participate in each stage. (1) In the first stage the creator Prajāpati has a desire to reproduce and unites with his consort Vāc. The Vāc with which Prajāpati unites at this stage is the unexpressed, transcendent level of speech that is generally identified with the primordial waters. Prajāpati implants his seed in the waters of Vāc and the seed becomes an egg, which represents the totality of the universe in yet undifferentiated form. (2) In the second stage of creation a child, representing the "second self" of Prajāpati, is born and speaks. This speech, which represents the second phase of Vāc, is the expressed, vocalized speech by means of which the creator introduces distinctions in the originally distinctionless totality of creation represented by the egg, dividing it into the three worlds and manifesting various types of beings. The creator simply speaks—simply utters the names—and the corresponding forms are set apart, differentiated out of the primordial state of unity.

Corresponding to these two stages of creation are two levels of Veda: (1) in the first stage the Veda is *brahman,* the undifferentiated Word that serves as the foundation of the creator and of his creation, while (2) in the second stage the Veda differentiates into the three Vedas, which are connected with the speech of the creator. The progression from the first stage of creation to the second stage is thus represented as a move from an unmanifest state of undifferentiated unity to a manifest state of differentiation: the primordial waters of Vāc, which represent the unexpressed level of speech, begin to flow out in streams of expressed, vocalized speech that issue forth as discrete utterances; the one Veda divides into the three Vedas; the undivided totality of creation represented by the egg differentiates into the three worlds.[156] The essential elements of these two stages of creation are schematized below.

	Male Principle	Female Principle	Veda	Creation
Stage 1	creator Prajāpati →	waters of Vāc	Veda as *brahman*	undivided egg ↑
Stage 2	"second self" of Prajāpati →	vocalized speech →	three Vedas →	three worlds

Post-Vedic Texts

In post-Vedic cosmogonies the basic structure of the two-stage process of creation is retained, although the designations of the male and female principles change to accord with the particular discursive framework of these texts. (1) In the first stage of creation the unmanifest Brahman (Nirguṇa Brahman) assumes a manifest form as Nārāyaṇa (Saguṇa Brahman), who provides the spur for creation to begin by implanting his seed in the womb of the female principle, depicted in mythological terms as the waters or in metaphysical terms as Prakṛti (primordial matter). The seed bears fruit, emerging as the golden egg of creation. (2) In the second stage Nārāyaṇa himself enters the egg and is born from it as Puruṣa. The Puruṣa who is born from the egg is identified either with the creator Brahmā (according to the Manu-Smṛti, Mahābhārata, and most Purāṇic accounts) or with Nārāyaṇa in his second manifestation (according to the Bhāgavata Purāṇa). With the infusion of the life principle into the cosmic egg, the primordial undivided unity begins to differentiate, giving rise to the three worlds and all animate and inanimate beings. In accordance with Vedic accounts of creation, in post-Vedic cosmogonies it is only after the creator emerges from the egg that he speaks, reciting the Vedic *mantras* in order to project the forms of creation into manifestation. In Purāṇic cosmogonies these two stages of creation correspond to the cycles of primary creation *(sarga)* and secondary creation *(pratisarga),* respectively.

As in Vedic texts, different levels of Veda correspond to these two stages of creation: (1) in the first stage the Veda is that totality of knowledge which is the essence of Brahman, while (2) in the second stage the Veda manifests as the Vedic *mantras*, which constitute the blueprint containing the words spoken by the creator Brahmā in order to bring the forms of creation into being.[157]

	Male Principle	Female Principle	Veda	Creation
Stage 1	Saguṇa Brahman (Nārāyaṇa) →	waters/ Prakṛti	Veda as the essence of Brahman	undivided egg ↑ (from waters/Prakṛti)
Stage 2	Puruṣa (creator Brahmā or second manifestation of Nārāyaṇa) →	vocalized speech →	four Vedas as blueprint →	three worlds

II. TORAH

Among the various representations of the Torah in rabbinic and kabbalistic texts, four main complexes can be distinguished: (1) the Torah is identified with the Word *(dāḇār)* of God or Name *(šēm)* of God, which participates in the reality and essence of God himself; (2) the Torah is personified—or hypostatized, in the case of kabbalistic texts—as primordial wisdom, Ḥoḵmāh, which serves as the architect of creation; (3) the Torah is depicted as the subtle plan or blueprint of creation, which contains the primordial elements of the divine language through which God brings forth the creation; and (4) the Torah in its earthly, transmitted form is a concrete written text composed of words and sentences inscribed on parchment, together with an oral tradition of interpretation that seeks to clarify and elaborate the implications of its laws and teachings for subsequent generations. The following analysis will focus on the first three conceptions, which are most germane to our discussion of the cosmological status of Torah.

Torah as the Word: The Word of God or Name of God

Rabbinic Texts

A number of passages in rabbinic texts take it for granted that the Torah is the Word *(dāḇār)* of God, although the meaning of this identification is not generally explained.[158] For example, several Midrashim interpret Psalm 105.8 (= 1 Chron. 16.15), "Remember His covenant for ever, the word *(dāḇār)* that He commanded for a thousand generations," as referring to the Torah.[159] This verse is interpreted to mean that the Torah, as the Word of God, was to have been commanded or revealed after one thousand generations. However, in actuality it was revealed after twenty-six generations (ten generations from Adam to Noah, ten from Noah to Abraham, and six from Abraham to Moses—Isaac, Jacob, Levi, Kohath, Amram, and Moses). What happened to the other 974 generations (1000 – 26 = 974)? According to a Midrash in Genesis Rabbāh, attributed to R. Huna in the name of R. Eliezer b. Jose the Galilean, they were blotted out—that is, they remained uncreated.[160] This notion is explicitly connected in several Talmudic Midrashim to the preexistence of the Torah, which is said to have remained hidden as God's "secret treasure" *(ḥămûḏāh gᵉnûzāh)* for 974 generations before the world was created.[161]

An anonymous Tanḥûmā' Yᵉlammᵉḏēnû Midrash, through reference to the same proof text (Ps. 105.8 = 1 Chron. 16.15), connects the Torah as the Word of God with the plan of creation that God had contemplated for a thousand years prior to bringing forth the world. The Midrash then establishes another implicit connection between the Torah and the creative power of God's Word by citing Psalm 33.6, "By the word *(dāḇār)* of the Lord were the heavens made."[162] The role of the Word in bringing forth creation will be discussed in more detail below.[163]

The Torah is also at times connected with the Name *(šēm)* of God, although the nature of this connection is not generally elaborated upon in rabbinic texts.[164]

Kabbalistic Texts

In medieval kabbalistic texts, particularly as represented by the Zohar and the theosophical Kabbalah of thirteenth-century Spain, the conceptions of Torah as the Word of God or Name of God are cosmologized, and the Torah becomes hypostatized to the point of being identified with God himself. These conceptions must therefore be understood with reference to the theosophical kabbalists' conceptions of divinity, in which God is represented as having both an unmanifest and a manifest dimension. The unmanifest aspect of God is generally termed 'Ên-Sôp̄ (literally, "without limit") and is described as the Godhead in itself, in its own absolute nature, as a formless, limitless, transcendent reality that is distinct from the relative phenomenal world. When the time of creation dawns the unmanifest 'Ên-Sôp̄ emerges from its hidden abode and progressively manifests itself in ten spheres of divine emanation, which are termed *s^ep̄îrôṯ:* (1) Keṯer ᶜElyôn ("supreme crown"), (2) Ḥoḵmāh ("wisdom"), (3) Bînāh ("intelligence"), (4) Ḥeseḏ ("love"), (5) G^eḇûrāh ("power"), (6) Tip̄'ereṯ ("beauty"), (7) Neṣāḥ ("lasting endurance"), (8) Hôḏ ("majesty"), (9) Y^esôḏ ("foundation"), and (10) Malḵûṯ ("kingdom"). The ten *s^ep̄îrôṯ* function together as a single, unified organism, representing the manifest, dynamic, pulsating life of the Godhead in relation to creation. In their totality the *s^ep̄îrôṯ* are often depicted in the form of a supernal Man, each *s^ep̄îrāh* constituting a different part of the body of the divine anthropos.[165]

The realm of the *s^ep̄îrôṯ* is often represented in kabbalistic texts as the hidden world of divine language, the ten *s^ep̄îrôṯ* being identified with the ten divine names as well as with the ten primordial words *(ma'ămārôṯ)* through which God brings forth creation.[166] The Torah is at times described as encompassing the influence of all of the ten *s^ep̄îrôṯ* and is thus correspondingly depicted as that totality of divine unity which is the one Name containing all names, the one Word containing all words. The Torah as the Name of God or Word of God expresses that aspect of God which is revealed in and through creation. It encompasses the totality of God's manifestations in the world of emanation, the realm of the *s^e^pîrôṯ*, and in the created worlds.

The conception that the Torah is the one great Name of God first appears among the thirteenth-century Spanish kabbalists of Gerona. Moses b. Naḥman (Naḥmanides), the eminent Talmudist who was the most authoritative representative of the circle of kabbalists in Gerona, provided the basis for this notion by maintaining, in the preface to his commentary on the Torah (Pentateuch), that the Torah can simultaneously be read on two levels: in the traditional manner as historical narratives and commandments, or according to a more subtle level of interpretation as a series of divine names.[167] Naḥmanides's colleagues in Gerona, in particular Ezra b. Solomon and Azriel b. Menaḥem, went beyond this conception by asserting that the Torah is itself the one great Name of God and constitutes a perfect divine edifice *(binyān 'ĕlôhî)*.[168]

The Zohar, the classical text of Spanish Kabbalah, expressly assumes the identity of the Torah and the Name of God, declaring that the Torah is the one supernal Name of the Holy One.[169] The Zohar ultimately proclaims that "the Torah and the Holy One, blessed be He, are one,"[170] for God and his Name are one.[171] The full significance of this declaration can only be understood on the basis of kabbalistic conceptions of the creative power of language, which in turn are founded on the traditional rabbinic notion that an intrinsic relationship exists between the word and what it signifies, between the name and the object that it designates.[172] Understood in this context the notion that the Torah is the Name of God leads to the conclusion that God and the Torah are one, for the Torah as God's Name represents the total manifestation of the divine essence and power, which are concentrated in his Name.

The identity of the Torah and God is asserted not only by the author of the Zohar, but also by other theosophical kabbalists in the last third of the thirteenth century who were undoubtedly influenced by the Zohar. For example, Joseph Gikatilla, a prominent thirteenth-century Spanish kabbalist, writes,

> His Torah is in Him, and that is what the Kabbalists say, namely, that the Holy One, blessed be He, is in His Name and His Name is in Him, and that His Name is His Torah.[173]

The letters of God's Name, according to Gikatilla, are the mystical body of God, while God is the soul of the letters.[174]

Torah as Wisdom: The Architect of Creation

In the conception of Torah as the Word of God or Name of God, the Torah is represented as participating in the essence of God. In another type of conception found in both rabbinic and kabbalistic texts, the Torah is depicted not as the manifestation of God's essence, but rather as a particular aspect of God—God's wisdom, Ḥoḵmāh, which serves as the architect of creation.

Rabbinic Texts

The Torah is personified as God's architect or co-worker in creation in a number of passages in rabbinic literature. Underlying such rabbinic speculations is the assumption that the Torah is identical with the figure of personified wisdom, Ḥoḵmāh, in Proverbs 1–9, especially as she appears in the wisdom hymn in Proverbs 8.22–31. In Proverbs 8.22–31 wisdom is personified as a feminine figure who speaks of her own primordial beginnings as the first of God's works: "The Lord made me as the beginning *(rē'šîṯ)* of His way, the first of His works of old" (v. 22). "When He established the heavens I was there, . . . when He marked out the foundations of the earth, then I was beside Him as an *'āmôn,* and I was His delight day after day" (vv. 27, 29, 30). The term *'āmôn* in verse 30 has generally been vocalized in rabbinic and kabbalistic interpretations, as well as by many modern scholars, as *'ûmān or 'ommān,* "artisan, craftsman."[175] Rabbinic speculations about the preexistence of the Torah and its role in creation frequently invoke verses 22[176] and 30[177] of Proverbs 8.22–31 as proof texts. Proverbs 3.19–20, "The Lord by wisdom *(ḥoḵmāh)* founded the earth; by understanding *(tᵉḇûnāh)* He established the heavens; by His knowledge *(daᶜaṯ)* the depths were broken up," is also at times cited in discussions of the Torah's cosmogonic role.[178]

The opening proem of Genesis Rabbāh, attributed to R. Hoshaiah, begins and ends with the wisdom hymn in Proverbs 8.22–31, establishing the role of the Torah as the instrument of creation through incorporating the two most crucial verses, 30 and 22, and linking them through a series of interpretations to the base verse of the pericope, Genesis 1.1.

> R. Hoshaiah opened: "Then I was beside Him as an *'āmôn,* and I was His delight day after day" (Prov. 8.30). . . . [*'Ā*]*môn* is an artisan *('ûmān).* The Torah declares, "I was the working instrument *(kᵉlî)* of the Holy One, blessed be He." In the normal course of affairs, when a mortal king builds a palace he does not build it by his own skill, but by the skill of an architect. Moreover, the architect does not build it out of his head,

> but makes use of plans and tablets in order to know how to make the rooms and the doors. Thus the Holy One, blessed be He, looked *(hibbîṭ)* into the Torah and created the world. And the Torah declares, "With *rē'šîṯ* [E.V. 'In the beginning'] God created" (Gen. 1.1), and *rē'šîṯ* means nothing other than the Torah, as it is said, "The Lord made me *rē'šîṯ* [E.V. 'as the beginning'] of His way" (Prov. 8.22).[179]

The proem offers four possible interpretations of *'āmôn* in Proverbs 8.30, culminating in a fifth interpretation, in which *'āmôn* is vocalized as *'ûmān,* "artisan." The proem takes for granted that the Torah is identical with the personified wisdom of Proverbs 8.22–31, and hence it is the Torah that served as the artisan or "working instrument *(keli)*" of God.[180] The proem goes on to depict the role of God's artisan, the Torah, in terms of the dual image of the architect whom the king employs to build and the blueprint that the architect consults in building—although the interrelationship between these two images is not clarified. The proem concludes with an exegesis of the first verse of the Torah, *berē'šîṯ bārā' Elohim,* which it interprets in light of the expression *rē'šîṯ darkô* in Proverbs 8.22, understanding *berē'šîṯ* in Genesis 1.1 to mean *be-ḥoḵmāh:* "By means of wisdom/ Torah God created [heaven and earth]."[181]

An anonymous Midrash in Exodus Rabbāh II declares that it was with the aid of the Torah that God created heaven and earth and then invokes Proverbs 3.19–20 as proof of the role of the Torah, as primordial wisdom, in creation.[182] In other Tanḥûmā' Yelammeḏēnû Midrashim the nature of the Torah's cosmogonic role is more specifically delineated, using a variety of images. Several passages in the Tanḥûmā' depict the Torah as a counselor with whom God consulted when he created the world.[183] In the opening Midrash of the Tanḥûmā' the Torah is described not only as God's counselor in creation, but it is also portrayed as assuming a more active role as the artisan of creation. Vocalizing the *'āmôn* of Proverbs 8.30 as *'ûmān,* "artisan," the Midrash invokes the language and imagery of Proverbs 8.22–31 to describe how through the aid of his artisan, the Torah, God established the heaven and earth, fixed the boundaries of the deep, brought forth the sun and moon, and formed all of the works of creation.[184] Another Midrash in the Tanḥûmā' similarly invokes Proverbs 8.22–31 to describe the Torah's role as the artisan of creation, vocalizing *'āmôn* in verse 30 as *'ûmān.*[185]

In Pirqê de-R. Eliezer the cosmogonic role of the Torah as personified wisdom is primarily depicted in terms of the image of God's counselor. Having established that the Torah, as the primordial wisdom of Proverbs 8.22, had existed from "the beginning" as one of the first of God's works,[186] the text goes on to describe how God took counsel with the Torah concerning the creation of the world.[187]

Kabbalistic Texts

Rabbinic conceptions of the Torah as primordial wisdom are reinterpreted in kabbalistic texts in light of the doctrine of the *s*ᵉ*p̄îrô*ṯ. While the Torah as the Name of God is generally identified with the totality of the manifest Godhead, encompassing all of the ten *s*ᵉ*p̄îrô*ṯ, the Torah as wisdom is identified more specifically with the second *s*ᵉ*p̄îrāh,* Ḥoḵmāh, which is the demiurge principle in the sᵉp̄îrôṯic scheme.

As in rabbinic texts, the Torah as Ḥoḵmāh is identified in the Zohar with the primordial wisdom of Proverbs 8.22–31 and Proverbs 3.19–20 and is celebrated as the artisan of creation.[188]

> "The Lord by wisdom founded the earth; by understanding he established the heavens" [Prov. 3.19]. When God . . . created the world, He saw that it could not exist without the Torah, as this is the only source of all laws above and below, and on it alone are the upper and lower beings established. Hence, "the Lord by wisdom founded the earth; by understanding he established the heavens," inasmuch as it is through Wisdom that all things are enabled to exist in the universe, and from it all things proceed.[189]

Whereas in rabbinic texts the Torah as wisdom is personified as a female figure, the Torah as Ḥoḵmāh is hypostatized as a male principle in the Zoharic cosmology of the *s*ᵉ*p̄îrô*ṯ. The Torah as Ḥoḵmāh is the Father, who unites with the Mother, Bînāh ("intelligence"), the third *s*ᵉ*p̄îrāh,* in order to bring forth creation.[190] It is as Ḥoḵmāh that the Torah assumes its role as the architect of creation. The Zohar declares,

> When the Holy One resolved to create the world, He guided Himself by the Torah as by a plan, as has been pointed out in connection with the words "Then I was by him as [an] *amon*" [Prov. 8.30], where the word *amon* (nursling) may also be read *uman* (architect). Was the Torah, then, an architect? Yes; for if a King resolves to build him a palace, without an architect and a plan how can he proceed? Nevertheless, when the palace has been built, it is attributed to the King: "here is the palace which the King has built", because his was the thought that has thus

been realized. Similarly, when the Holy One, blessed be He, resolved to create the world, He looked into His plan, and, although, in a sense, it was the plan which brought the palace into being, it is not called by its name but by that of the King. The Torah proclaims: "I was by Him [as] an architect, through me He created the world!"[191]

Torah as Divine Language: The Blueprint of Creation

Torah as the Blueprint of Creation

The Torah is depicted in certain rabbinic and kabbalistic texts, as illustrated by the passages cited above from Genesis Rabbāh and the Zohar, not only as the architect of creation, but also as the blueprint that the architect employs in order to fashion his creation.

Rabbinic Texts

In rabbinic texts the notion that the Torah constitutes the plan or blueprint of creation is generally depicted in three ways: (1) as the plan that God "looked into" *(hibbîṭ),* as an architect consults his blueprint, in order to create the world; (2) as the mental plan of creation conceived in the mind of God; or (3) as the plan that reflects the laws and structure of the universe.

The use of the blueprint analogy in the opening proem of Genesis Rabbāh, cited earlier, obviously conforms to the first image, although scholars have debated whether the portrayal of God "looking into" the Torah might be understood as a cognitive act of contemplation rather than as simply a perceptual act involving the sense of sight—in which case it would also partake of the second image of a mental plan of creation.[192]

Irrespective of whether the blueprint in Genesis Rabbāh can be interpreted as a mental plan, the notion that creation was first conceived as a plan in the mind of God, which was then brought to fruition in the concrete forms and phenomena of the manifest world, is expressed in a number of other Midrashim.[193] An anonymous Tanḥûmā' Yᵉlammᵉḏēnû Midrash, mentioned earlier,[194] directly links the Torah, through reference to 1 Chronicles 16.15 (= Ps. 105.8), to the plan of creation that had been conceived in the mind of God for a thousand years. When the time of creation came, the plan effortlessly—in one day—materialized as the multiple forms of creation.

> "My hand laid the foundation of the earth" (Isa. 48.13). The Holy One, blessed be He, said, "For My thoughts (*maḥšᵉḇôṯ*)

are not your thoughts. . . . For as the heavens are higher than the earth, so are My ways higher than your ways and My thoughts than your thoughts" (Isa. 55.8–9). A person sits and plans (*ḥiššēḇ*), saying, "In this manner I shall build, in this manner I shall make it." He plans (*ḥāšaḇ*) in one hour what he does not produce in ten years. But the Holy One, blessed be He, is not so, for [what] He plans (*ḥāšaḇ*) in a thousand years He builds in one day, as it is said, "Remember His covenant for ever, the word (*dāḇār*) that He commanded for a thousand generations" (1 Chron. 16.15). [The heavens] were created in one day, as it is said, "By the word (*dāḇār*) of the Lord were the heavens made" (Ps. 33.6).[195]

The notion of the Torah as a plan that reflects the structure of the universe is pointed to in several Midrashim. An anonymous Midrash in Leviticus Rabbāh identifies the laws of Torah with the laws of nature by means of which God brought forth the universe, implying that the social and moral order laid out in the Torah reflects the cosmic order. Commenting on Leviticus 26.3, "If you walk in my statutes *(ḥuqqōṯ),*" the Midrashist connects *ḥuqqōṯ* by word analogy to a number of proof texts and thereby establishes that it was by means of the statutes of Torah that God marked out the heaven and earth (Jer. 33.25), the sun and moon (Jer. 31.35), the sea (Prov. 8.29), the sand (Jer. 5.22), and the deep (Prov. 8.27).[196] A tradition that appears in Pᵉsîqtā' dᵉ-R. Kahana and in the Babylonian Talmud suggests that the laws of Torah reflect the structure of both the macrocosm and the microcosm. Of the 613 commandments *(mitzvot)* in the Torah, the 365 negative precepts are said to correspond to the number of days in a solar year, while the 248 positive precepts correspond to the number of members in the human body.[197]

Kabbalistic Texts

Rabbinic conceptions of the Torah as the plan or blueprint of creation are elaborated in the Zohar. In discussing the nature of the Torah as the architect and plan of creation, the Zohar seeks to clarify in what way God "looked into" the Torah when creating the world. It suggests that the Torah served as the plan of creation in that it is composed of the words that God looked into, in the sense of "contemplating through seeing" *('istakkēl),* in order to bring forth the corresponding forms.

When the Holy One resolved to create the world, He guided Himself by the Torah as by a plan. . . . [W]hen He resolved to

> create the world He looked into the Torah, into its every creative word, and fashioned the world correspondingly; for all the worlds and all the actions of all the worlds are contained in the Torah. Therefore did the Holy One, blessed be He, look into it and create the world. . . . God looked at His plan in this way. It is written in the Torah: "In the beginning God created the heavens and the earth"; He looked at this expression and created heaven and earth. In the Torah it is written: "Let there be light"; He looked at these words and created light; and in this manner was the whole world created.[198]

In another passage God is described as not only looking into *('istakkēl)* the words of the Torah, but also uttering them aloud in order to bring forth the phenomenal world.[199]

The Torah, as the primordial plan of creation, is said to be the source of all the laws through which the various worlds and beings, above and below, were created.[200] The Zohar elaborates on the rabbinic notion that there is a correspondence between the structure of the Torah and the structure of the macrocosm and microcosm. The microcosm, the human body, is patterned after the macrocosm, and both in turn are organized in accordance with the plan of the Torah, which itself consists of different parts that combine to form a single body.

> Everyone who studies the Torah sustains the world and maintains every individual thing in its proper form. For every part that exists in man there is a corresponding element created in the world. Just as man is composed of separate parts, all of them with their own specific levels, arranged one above the other, and yet all comprising a single body, so it is with the world: all the created elements are separate parts, situated one above the other, and when they are all arranged they actually form one body. Everything is patterned on the Torah, for the Torah is all limbs and joints, and they are positioned one above the other, and when they are all arranged they become a single body.[201]

The "limbs and joints" of the body of Torah are described in the Zohar as reflecting the structure not only of the human body and of the cosmos-body, but also of the body of the divine anthropos. More specifically, the commandments are described as the "limbs and joints" that join together to form the mystery of the supernal Man, encompassing both the masculine and feminine aspects of the Godhead.[202]

As will be discussed below, the notion that the Torah constitutes a plan that reflects the laws and structure of the cosmic order is elaborated in the Lurianic school of Israel Sarug (ca. 1600 C.E.), which maintains that there are different forms of the Torah corresponding to the different worlds that exist between the unmanifest 'Ên-Sôp̄ and the gross material world. Implicit in this conception is the notion that the Torah in all its manifestations constitutes a comprehensive blueprint for all levels of existence.[203]

Torah as Divine Language

The Torah that constitutes the plan of creation is composed of the twenty-two letters *('ôṯiyyôṯ)* of the Hebrew alphabet that are the fundamental elements of the divine language. The role of the Torah in creation is thus at times linked in rabbinic and kabbalistic texts to notions of the creative power of the divine language.

Rabbinic Texts

The Torah is connected with the divine language in a number of different ways in rabbinic texts: in its identification with the Word of God,[204] in its association with the divine Name,[205] and in its role as the repository of the Hebrew letters.

The role of the divine speech in bringing forth creation is embodied in the rabbinic epithet for God, "He who spoke *('āmar)* and the world came into being."[206] "And God said, 'Let there be light,' and there was light" (Gen. 1.3)—and what he spoke, according to the sages, was Hebrew. Hebrew is the holy tongue *(lᵉšôn ha-qôḏeš),* the language of God himself, which he inscribed in the Torah and which he used to create the world. A tradition in Genesis Rabbāh declares, "Just as the Torah was given in the holy language *(lᵉšôn qôḏeš),* so the world was created with the holy language."[207]

The cosmogonic role of the divine language is often depicted in rabbinic texts in terms of the twenty-two consonants of the Hebrew alphabet that compose the Torah, which constitute the basic structural elements of creation. Speculations regarding the creative power of the Hebrew letters received their most elaborate expression in the early rabbinic period in the *Sēp̄er Yᵉṣîrāh* ("Book of Creation") (third to sixth century C.E.), the earliest extant Hebrew text of a speculative nature, which describes the process of creation as arising through different permutations and combinations of the twenty-two letters.[208] The origins of this mystical text are obscure, and rabbinic literature does not contain anything comparable to its complex cosmology of numbers *(sᵉp̄îrôṯ)* and letters. Rabbinic texts do, however, contain a number of homilies on the Hebrew letters, which focus in particular on the shape of the letters, their semantic significance, their numerical value, and their cosmic role in creation, with less emphasis on their sound value. With respect to their cosmogonic role, a tradition in the Babylonian Talmud speaks of "the letters *('ôṯiyyôṯ)* with which heaven and earth were created."[209] An anonymous Tanḥûmā' Yᵉlammᵉḏēnû tradition describes the twenty-two letters of the Torah as God's "twenty-two workmen *(pô ᶜălîm)*" who assisted him in bringing forth creation.[210] A number of Midrashim confront the problem of why the world was created with *bêṯ,* the second letter of the Hebrew alphabet, and not with *'ālep̄,* the first letter. *Bêṯ* is the first letter of the first word of the Torah, *bᵉrē'šîṯ,* and thus some rabbis assume that God must have created the world with *bêṯ.*[211] According to an alternative interpretation, this world was created with the letter *hē,* while the world to come was created with the letter *yōḏ.*[212]

While rabbinic homilies on the letters generally emphasize the written and cognitive dimensions of Hebrew—that is, the shape and semantic significance of the Hebrew letters—we do find occasional references to the phonic dimension of the divine language. When viewed from the perspective of their sound the letters become intimately linked with the creative power of the divine speech. The fact that God simply spoke and the different aspects of creation came into being is, according to a number of Midrashim, an indication of the complete effortlessness with which he created. Psalm 33.6, "By the word *(dāḇār)* of the Lord were the heavens made," is invoked as a proof text to show that the process of creation required no labor or effort on the part of God.[213] He simply said, "Let there be light," and there was light. God speaks and it is accomplished; he commands and his will is done.[214]

What were the words by which God called the world into being? A number of Midrashim invoke the Mishnaic tradition, "By ten words *(ma'ămārôṯ)* was the world created,"[215] giving different interpretations of what these ten words were.[216] According to one enumeration in Genesis Rabbāh XVII.1, the ten words were the first word of the Torah, *bᵉrē'šîṯ;* the spirit/voice of God upon the waters; and the eight commands "And God said" that appear in the account of creation in Genesis 1.3–26.[217] In this interpretation *bᵉrē'šîṯ,* the first word of the Torah, constitutes the original unspoken Word that was the vehicle through which the undifferentiated totality of heaven and earth were created.[218] As discussed earlier, this primal unspoken Word, *bᵉrē'šîṯ,* is directly linked in the opening proem of Genesis Rabbāh to the creative role of the Torah as primordial wisdom.[219] The second creative utterance was the voice, yet unexpressed, that hovered as the spirit of God over the waters (Gen. 1.2).[220] Then the voice became vocalized and burst forth onto the expressed level of speech: "And God said, 'Let there be light' " (Gen. 1.3). This is the first of eight commands[221] that progressively unfolded the details of creation from the primordial totality. With each command, "Let there be. . . . ," it was so. The Lord spoke the name and the corresponding form appeared. In this portrayal of creation we find a progressive development from unspoken thought to spoken utterance to concrete form. The Torah as the Word of God embraces both the cognitive and phonic dimensions of the Word, both unspoken thought and spoken utterance.

Kabbalistic Texts

In certain kabbalistic texts the ten primordial words *(ma'ămārôṯ)* through which the world was created are hypostatized, becoming identified with the ten *sᵉp̄îrôṯ*. The realm of the *sᵉp̄îrôṯ* is depicted as the world of divine language, in which the successive emanation of the *sᵉp̄îrôṯ* is the process through which the divine language unfolds. The stages of unfoldment of the divine language are ultimately correlated with the stages of manifestation of the Torah, as will be discussed in the following section.

The unfoldment of the divine language begins with the emergence of a primordial point of divine thought—Ḥoḵmāh, wisdom, the second *sᵉp̄îrāh*. The mechanics of creation are described in a number of passages in the Zohar as the mechanics through which thought develops, for creation is viewed as simply a process of unfolding the original seed-thought of wisdom, Ḥoḵmāh, through progressive stages of development until it finds expression on the level of vocalized speech. The Zohar describes four main stages in the manifestation of the divine language—thought, inaudible voice, audible voice, and vocalized speech—which correspond to the four *sᵉp̄îrôṯ* Ḥoḵmāh, Bînāh, Tip̄'ereṯ, and Malḵûṯ, respectively.

In order to understand the role of these four *sᵉp̄îrôṯ* in the unfoldment of the divine language, we must first briefly examine the Zohar's characterizations of them as hypostatized entities that play a key role in the creative process. When the time of creation dawns, according to the Zohar, the unmanifest 'Ên-Sôp̄ descends into the realm of manifestation in the form of a supernal Man, Keṯer ("crown"), the first *sᵉp̄îrāh,* who is the supreme will that sets the process of creation in motion. With the "decision of the King" to create, the effulgence of Keṯer withdraws into itself and a hidden supernal point shines forth,[222] which is the *rē'šîṯ,* "beginning," of creation.[223] This primordial point is the thought of the creator, in which he enfolds himself and the totality of the universe in potential form. From this single concentrated impulse of thought, which is identified in the Zohar with the second *s^e^pîrāh,* Ḥoḵmāh, the entire creation unfolds.[224] Ḥoḵmāh thus assumes the role of the Father of creation in the s^e^p̄îrôṯic scheme.

The Zohar describes how Ḥoḵmāh, the primordial point of wisdom, makes for himself a refulgent "palace" (*hêḵālā'*) or "house" (*bayiṯ*) for his honor and glory and there he sows "the holy seed in order to beget offspring for the benefit of the world."[225] This house built by wisdom, Ḥoḵmāh, is at first uninhabited and is only extended enough to make room for the seed. Then the house conceives and expands sufficiently to become habitable. Ḥoḵmāh subsequently enters the house and makes it his abode, "just as the silkworm encloses itself, as it were, in a palace of its own production which is both useful and beautiful."[226] This "inhabited house" is called Elohim and is identified with Bînāh ("intelligence"), the third *s^e^p̄îrāh,* who is the Mother in whose womb the seed of Ḥoḵmāh, the Father, is implanted.[227]

The child that is born from the impregnated "house," Bînāh, is identified in the Zohar with Tip̄'ereṯ ("beauty"), the sixth *s^e^p̄îrāh,* who as the lower Ḥoḵmāh represents the second phase of manifestation of the Father. Just as the upper Ḥoḵmāh has his counterpart in the lower Ḥoḵmāh, Tip̄'ereṯ, so the Mother above, Bînāh, has her counterpart in the Mother below, Malḵûṯ ("kingdom"), the tenth *s^e^p̄îrāh,* which is the Shekhinah, the divine presence. Tip̄'ereṯ and Malḵûṯ are the son and daughter who are the king and queen of the world below, mirroring the reality of the king and queen above.[228] Bînāh, the Mother above, forms a house for the upper Ḥoḵmāh, while Malḵûṯ, the Mother below, forms a house for Tip̄'ereṯ, the lower Ḥoḵmāh.[229]

Each of these four *s^e^p̄îrôṯ*—Ḥoḵmāh, Bînāh, Tip̄'ereṯ, and Malḵûṯ—is associated in the Zohar with a particular stage in the manifestation of the divine language. The process through which Ḥoḵmāh unites with Bînāh and gives birth to the son, Tip̄'ereṯ, and the daughter, Malḵûṯ, is thus sometimes described in terms of the process through which the divine thought (Ḥoḵmāh) progressively develops from an inaudible voice (Bînāh) to an audible voice (Tip̄'ereṯ) to vocalized speech (Malḵûṯ). (1) From the divine will, represented by Keṯer, issues a thought, Ḥoḵmāh. (2) This concentrated impulse of thought expands and creates an abode for itself in the throat as the inaudible Great Voice, which is Bînāh. (3) From this inaudible Great Voice issues forth an audible voice, the voice of Jacob, which is Tip̄'ereṯ. (4) The voice of Jacob, striking against the lips, emerges in the open and finds expression in vocalized speech, which is Malḵûṯ, the Shekhinah.[230]

The first two stages in the unfoldment of the divine language—thought (Ḥoḵmāh) and the Great Voice (Bînāh)—are said to be inaudible, taking place in silence,[231] and correspond to the expression *b^e^rē'šîṯ bārā' Elohim* in the first verse of the Torah, which is understood to mean "By means of Ḥoḵmāh [= *rē'šîṯ*] it ['Ên-Sôp̄] created Bînāh [= Elohim]."[232] Among the ten words *(ma'ămārôṯ)* by which the world was created, *b^e^rē'šîṯ* is included as the original unspoken Word, for as the Zohar explains, "even though *bereshith* is a 'saying' [*ma'ămār*], 'and He said' is not written in connection with it."[233] The last two stages in the manifestation of the divine language—the voice of Jacob (Tip̄'ereṯ) and vocalized speech (Malḵûṯ)—are said to be audible[234] and correspond to the words "And God said" in the Genesis 1 account.

> Hence "and God said" means that now the above-mentioned palace [Bînāh] generated from the holy seed with which it was pregnant. While it brought forth in silence, that which it bore was heard without. That which bore, bore in silence without making a sound, but when that issued from it which did issue, it became a voice which was heard without, to wit, "Let there be light."[235]

The four stages in the unfoldment of the divine language thus ultimately constitute a two-stage process of creation, one unmanifest and inaudible, the other manifest and audible, in which the male and female principles both participate. (1) In the first stage Ḥoḵmāh, the Father, makes a house for himself—Bînāh, the Great Voice—in which he sows his seed. The voice at this stage is still inaudible. (2) In the second stage the child, Tip̄'ereṯ, who represents the second phase of Ḥoḵmāh, issues forth from the womb of Bînāh as a voice that is heard without through the agency of Malḵûṯ, vocalized speech, who represents the second phase of the Mother. It is this audible voice that is responsible for unfolding the details of creation from the original totality by means of the series of specific commands that are introduced in the Genesis account by the words "And God said."

After having called the light into being, the voice, as described in Genesis 1, commands: " 'Let there be a firmament in the midst of the waters, and let it divide the waters from the waters.' . . . and it was so."[236] The upper waters, according to the Zohar, are heaven, while the lower waters are the earth, with the firmament forming a third world between the two.[237] The voice, having established the earth, firmament, and heaven, creates all animate and inanimate beings through its successive commands, bringing forth plants, the sun, moon, and stars, animals, and human beings, each in turn.[238]

Stages of Manifestation

Our analysis thus far has focused on three different conceptions of the Torah found in rabbinic and kabbalistic texts: (1) Torah as the Word of God or Name of God, which is the manifestation of God's essence; (2) Torah as primordial wisdom, which serves as the architect of creation; and (3) Torah as the plan or blueprint of creation, which contains the elements of the divine language through which the forms of creation are brought forth. These various aspects of the Torah are at times represented in kabbalistic texts as different stages of manifestation in a single process. Just as creation unfolds in stages, so the Torah, the instrument of creation, unfolds in stages, which are correlated with the stages of unfoldment of the divine language and the various levels of creation.

Rabbinic Texts

The relationship between the various aspects of the Torah's role in creation is generally not discussed in rabbinic texts. Rabbinic speculations about the Torah appear rather as isolated fragments throughout the texts and are not developed in terms of a consistent cosmology. It is only on the basis of the Midrashim concerning the ten words by which the world was created[239] that we can begin to develop an interpretive scheme in which the different aspects of the Torah's cosmogonic role—as architect, as blueprint, and as divine language—can be viewed as progressive manifestations of a single process. The Torah conceived as God's architect is a living, organic entity, which in its identification with primordial wisdom almost appears to take on an existence independent of God. Yet at the same time it is *God's* wisdom, which contains within itself the ideal plan of the universe. This plan conceived in the mind of God contains the "ideas" of all the forms in creation. These ideas are then spoken out by God, expressed by him in speech utterances, which are then precipitated to form the concrete phenomena of creation. From unspoken thought to vocalized speech utterances to concrete forms: this is the progressive process of creation in which the Torah participates at every stage.

Kabbalistic Texts

The notion of the sequential unfoldment of the divine language, found in incipient form in certain rabbinic texts, is developed in kabbalistic texts in terms of a series of clearly demarcated stages corresponding to the emanation of the *s^e^p̄îrôṯ*. In the Zoharic scheme, as we have seen, the various stages in the manifestation of the divine language—thought, inaudible voice, audible voice, vocalized speech—are identified with the four *s^e^p̄îrôṯ* Ḥoḵmāh, Bînāh, Tip̄'ereṯ, and Malḵûṯ, respectively. These various stages, with their corresponding *s^e^p̄îrôṯ*, are in turn identified with the different stages in the manifestation of Torah.

The Zohar and other thirteenth-century kabbalistic texts generally distinguish at least three main manifestations of the Torah: (1) *tôrāh q^e^ḏûmāh,* the primordial Torah, which is generally identified with Ḥoḵmāh, the second *s^e^p̄îrāh,* and which is also at times associated with Bînāh, the third *s^e^p̄îrāh;* (2) the supernal Written Torah, which is identified with Tip̄'ereṯ, the sixth *s^e^p̄îrāh;* and (3) the supernal Oral Torah, which is identified with Malḵûṯ, the Shekhinah, the tenth *s^e^p̄îrāh.* A threefold set of correspondences is thus established in which four *s^e^p̄îrôṯ* are primary.

S^e^p̄îrāh	Stage of Divine Language	Stage of Manifestation of Torah
Ḥoḵmāh (Father)	thought	Primordial Torah
Bînāh (Mother)	inaudible voice	
Tip̄'ereṯ (Son)	audible voice	Written Torah
Malḵûṯ/Shekhinah (Daughter)	vocalized speech	Oral Torah

In the Zohar all three aspects of the Torah are allotted a role in creation. The primordial Torah, Ḥoḵmāh, the point of divine thought, contains the totality of creation in potential form and is said to be the source of both the Written Torah and the Oral Torah.[240] From the primordial Torah, Ḥoḵmāh, the supernal letters of the Hebrew alphabet issue forth and become crystallized as the engravings of the Written Torah, Tip̄'ereṯ.[241] The Written Torah, Tip̄'ereṯ, is said to have produced the world from the power of the writing that issues forth from Ḥoḵmāh, while the Oral Torah, the Shekhinah, is responsible for completing and preserving the world.[242] The Written Torah and Oral Torah, as the divine hypostases Tip̄'ereṯ and the Shekhinah, complement and support one another,[243] representing the unity of the male and female principles,[244] the unity of the upper and lower worlds,[245] and the unity of the Holy Name.[246] The Written Torah, which remains hidden and undisclosed in the supernal realms, is manifested through the Oral Torah.[247] The Written Torah on high rejoices in the Oral Torah below.[248]

While the different stages of manifestation of Torah are correlated with particular *s*ᵉ*p̄îrôṯ,* the Torah is also described as encompassing all of the *s*ᵉ*p̄îrôṯ.*[249] In its stages of unfoldment from the unmanifest 'Ên-Sôp̄ through Ḥoḵmāh and Bînāh to Tip̄'ereṯ and Malḵûṯ, the Torah encompasses all of the *s*ᵉ*p̄îrôṯ,* all of the spheres of the Godhead, and thus, in the final analysis, the Zohar declares that God and the Torah are one.[250]

The various stages of manifestation of the Torah are correlated by certain kabbalistic schools with the different levels of creation. As mentioned earlier, texts originating in the Lurianic school of Israel Sarug describe the Torah as emerging from the unmanifest 'Ên-Sôp̄ in stages in which it progressively assumes different forms corresponding to each of the four worlds that exist between the unmanifest 'Ên-Sôp̄ and the gross material world. These texts describe how the unmanifest 'Ên-Sôp̄, in self-rapture, begins to move within itself, generating the movement of language and weaving a texture *(malbûš)* of the twenty-two letters of the Hebrew alphabet in the substance of 'Ên-Sôp̄ itself. This constitutes the original Torah, in which the letters, in their original sequence, contain within themselves the seeds of all possibilities for further linguistic expression. In the next phase the Torah assumes different forms corresponding to the four worlds. In the highest world, *'ăṣîlûṯ,* the world of emanation, which is the abode of the ten *s*ᵉ*p̄îrôṯ,* the Torah manifests as a sequence of combinations of the Hebrew consonants. In the second world, *b*ᵉ*rî'āh,* the world of creation, which is the abode of the throne, the Merkabah (throne-chariot), and the highest angels, the Torah appears as a sequence of holy names of God. The Torah manifests as a sequence of angelic names in the third world, *y*ᵉ*ṣîrāh,* the world of formation, which is the main domain of the angels. Finally, in the fourth world, *ᶜăśiyyāh,* the world of making or activation, which is the spiritual archetype of the material world, the Torah appears in its traditionally transmitted form.[251] The particular configuration of letters in each form of the Torah is said to reflect the laws and structure of the corresponding world, thus constituting a plan for that world.

All these concrete and subtle forms of the Torah are in the final analysis modifications and elaborations of the one great Name of God, for in the kabbalistic perspective it is the Name of God that is the source of all language, the source of all letters, and hence the source of all possible combinations of letters that form names, words, and sentences. In this context certain kabbalists, in particular the Lurianic school, correlate the four letters of the Tetragrammaton—Yōḏ-Hē-Wāw-Hē—with the four worlds—*'ăṣîlûṯ, b^e^rî'āh, y^e^ṣîrāh,* and *^c^ăśiyyāh,* respectively—and by implication with the four forms of the Torah in the four worlds. The four letters and the four worlds are in turn correlated with the four *s^e^p̄îrôṯ*—Ḥoḵmāh, Bînāh, Tip̄'ereṯ, and Malḵûṯ, respectively—that correspond to the major stages of manifestation of the Torah discussed earlier. Our previous schema can thus be expanded to incorporate a number of new elements.

S^e^p̄îrāh	World	Letter of Tetragrammaton	Stage of Manifestation of Torah	Form of Torah
Ḥoḵmāh	'Ăṣîlûṯ	Yōḏ	Primordial Torah	letters
Bînāh	B^e^rî'āh	Hē		names of God
Tip̄'ereṯ	Y^e^ṣîrāh	Wāw	Written Torah	angelic names
Malḵûṯ/ Shekhinah	^c^Ăśiyyāh	Hē	Oral Torah	words with earthly referents

III. VEDA AND TORAH

Structural Affinities in Symbol Systems

From our analysis of the symbol systems associated with Veda and Torah we have seen that in certain strands of the brahmanical tradition and the rabbinic and kabbalistic traditions, scripture is represented as a multileveled cosmic reality that is correlated with the different levels of the Word and the different levels of creation. We can distinguish at least four types of symbolic complexes that are structurally parallel: (1) scripture as the Word, which is the essence of the ultimate reality; (2) scripture as knowledge, which is an aspect of the creator principle; (3) scripture as divine language, which constitutes the blueprint of creation; and (4) scripture as a concrete corpus of oral and/or written texts.

While the seminal expressions of these conceptions are found in Vedic and rabbinic texts, the most extensive discussions are found in post-Vedic and kabbalistic texts, which reformulate and elaborate the seed speculations contained in the earlier texts, embedding them in complex cosmologies. It is in these later texts that we find the most significant parallels among representations of Veda and Torah.

1. Scripture as the Word: The Essence of the Ultimate Reality

On the subtlest level scripture is depicted as the Word in its totality, which is the essence of the ultimate reality, particularly in its manifest form in relation to creation. The Veda is at times described in Vedic and post-Vedic mythology as the Word, *brahman,* which is the essence of Brahman, the ultimate reality, and is particularly associated with the *saguṇa* dimension of Brahman that expresses itself in creation. In this context the Veda is identified in certain post-Vedic texts with Śabdabrahman, Brahman embodied in the Word. The Torah is similarly identified with the Word of God or Name of God, an identification that is generally assumed but not expanded upon in rabbinic texts. The Torah as the Word of God or Name of God is described in certain kabbalistic texts as the total manifestation of God's essence that is revealed in and through creation and is at times directly identified with God himself.

Veda and Torah are represented as participating in the ultimate reality not only as its inner essence, but also as its form. The body of Brahman is described in certain Vedic and post-Vedic texts as constituted by the Vedic *mantras,* and in particular by the forty-eight *varṇa*-sounds of Sanskrit that compose the *mantras*. Similarly, certain kabbalists maintain that the mystical body of God is constituted by the letters of his Name (= Torah), while others claim that the very substance of the Godhead is woven with the twenty-two letters of the Hebrew alphabet that compose the Torah.

2. Scripture as Knowledge: The Creator Principle

Scripture is not only identified with the essence of the ultimate reality, it is also more specifically associated with that aspect of the divine which is responsible for bringing forth creation. On this level scripture is represented as that undifferentiated totality of knowledge which serves as the immediate source of creation. The Veda is at times identified with the creator Prajāpati or Brahmā, the demiurge principle, who is extolled as the embodiment of knowledge and Veda incarnate. The Torah is personified in certain rabbinic texts as Ḥoḵmāh, primordial wisdom, which serves as God's architect or co-worker in creation. In kabbalistic texts the Torah as Ḥoḵmāh is hypostatized as the Father, who functions as the demiurge principle in the scheme of *s^e^p̄îrôṯ*.

3. Scripture as Divine Language: The Blueprint of Creation

Scripture is also depicted as the subtle plan or blueprint of creation, its constituent sounds or letters constituting the primordial elements of the divine language from which the forms of creation are structured.

On this level scripture has differentiated from its original state of unity; the one Word has given rise to words. On the most subtle level these words are the "ideas" of all the forms of creation conceived in the mind of the creator as the ideal plan of the universe. These ideas are then uttered by the creator as vocalized words, which are then precipitated to form the manifold phenomena of creation. The Vedic *mantra*s are represented in certain Vedic and post-Vedic accounts as the primordial utterances through which the creator brings forth the universe. In post-Vedic texts this notion is articulated in the image of the Vedas as the archetypal plan of creation, which the creator recites in order to manifest the names, forms, and functions of all beings. In the parallel conception found in certain rabbinic and kabbalistic texts, the divine architect consults his blueprint, the Torah, "looking into," contemplating, and/or uttering its words in order to bring forth the phenomenal world.

This subtle blueprint, Veda or Torah, is at times represented as multidimensional, its various forms reflecting the laws and structure of the various levels of creation. While the Vedic *mantra*s together are considered to constitute the blueprint of creation in its entirety, the Ṛg-, Yajur-, and Sāma-Vedas are each correlated more specifically with the three worlds—earth, midregions, and heaven—and with their presiding deities—Agni, Vāyu, and Sūrya/Āditya—and thus represent the plan for that particular level of creation. Similarly, the conception of Torah as the blueprint of creation is extended by certain kabbalists to include the notion that there are different forms of the Torah corresponding to each of the four worlds—*'ăṣîlûṯ, bᵉrî'āh, yᵉṣîrāh,* and *ʿăśiyyāh*—and to the four *sᵉp̄îrôṯ* that are associated with each of these worlds—Ḥoḵmāh, Bînāh, Tip̄'ereṯ, and Malḵûṯ. Each of these forms of the Torah is held to constitute a plan of the corresponding world.

Another significant parallel concerns the conception of an all-encompassing sound or Name that is identified with Veda or Torah and that is the basis of all creation and the source of all language. In certain Vedic and post-Vedic texts the syllable Om is said to represent the sound embodiment of Brahman and in this sense corresponds to the Veda as Śabdabrahman. Moreover, the three constituent sounds of Om are correlated with the three Vedas and the corresponding three worlds together with their presiding deities. In certain kabbalistic schools the Tetragrammaton, YHWH, is identified with the Torah as the one great Name of God. The four letters of the Tetragrammaton are correlated with the four forms of the Torah and the four worlds together with their corresponding *sᵉp̄îrôṯ*. Understood from this perspective, the Veda as Śabdabrahman and the Torah as the Name of God represent the most fundamental and encompassing level of scripture, incorporating all other levels and containing the potentiality of all linguistic expression.

4. Scripture as Concrete Text

The primordial Word that serves as the source and blueprint of creation is represented as becoming instantiated on earth in a finite corpus of texts. Revered by their respective traditions as the concrete embodiment of the Word, these texts have been meticulously preserved and passed down from generation to generation either through oral transmission, in the case of the Vedic Saṃhitās, or in the form of a written text together with an oral tradition of interpretation, in the case of the Torah.

Levels of the Word

All four of these aspects of Veda and Torah can be correlated with different levels of the Word. As we have seen, this Word cannot be delimited to either the written word or the spoken word in the sense of a circumscribed text. The conception of scripture as written text or oral text applies only to the fourth level of scripture described above, which is the mundane dimension of scripture. The Word as embodied in Veda and Torah is also represented as having a supramundane dimension, in which the two aspects of the Word—knowledge and speech—both find expression. On the subtlest level, scripture is the Word in its undifferentiated totality—Veda as *brahman*/Śabdabrahman, Torah as the Word of God or Name of God. On the second level, the knowledge dimension of the Word manifests as the immediate source of creation—Veda as Prajāpati or Brahmā, Torah as Ḥoḵmāh. On the third level, the speech dimension of the Word is activated, and the totality of knowledge finds expression in the individualized impulses of divine language from which the realm of forms is manifested—Veda or Torah as the blueprint of creation.

Stages of Manifestation

These various levels of scripture are represented in certain strands of the traditions as progressive stages of manifestation through which the Word unfolds in creation. In this context striking structural affinities can be discerned in certain brahmanical and kabbalistic descriptions of the various stages of manifestation in the cosmogonic process. Creation is represented in these accounts as involving a two-stage process—one unmanifest and undifferentiated, the other manifest and differentiated—in which the male and female principles both participate.

(1) In the first stage, with the emergence of the desire to create, the male principle, who is identified with knowledge, implants his seed in the womb of the female principle, who is generally identified with speech. That speech with which knowledge unites in this stage is still the unexpressed, transcendent level of speech. The female principle conceives and her womb expands in preparation for infusion with the life principle. Brahmanical cosmogonies describe how the male principle, the embodiment of knowledge, implants his seed in the womb of the female principle, who is at times identified with Vāc, speech. The seed is brought to fruition in a cosmic egg, which is still lifeless at this point. Similarly, the Zohar's account of creation describes how Ḥoḵmāh, wisdom, sows his seed in the "house" that he has built, Bînāh, the Great Voice. The house, which is still uninhabited, conceives and expands in preparation for habitation.

(2) In the second stage the male principle enters the womb of the impregnated female, making it his abode, and is born from it as a child, who represents the second phase of manifestation of the male principle. The child emerges from the womb of the female and speaks. This speech, which is the second phase of the female principle, is the expressed, vocalized level of speech through which the three worlds and all animate and inanimate beings are projected into concrete manifestation. In brahmanical cosmogonies the male principle enters the egg and infuses it with life, making the egg his abode. His second manifestation is then born from the egg and proclaims through speech (= second phase of Vāc) the primordial utterances from which the three worlds—earth, midregions, and heaven—and all beings are manifested. In the Zohar's account Ḥoḵmāh encloses himself in the house that he has built, transforming it into an "inhabited house." From this inhabited house, Bînāh, is born the lower Ḥoḵmāh, Tip̄'ereṯ, who utters in vocalized speech (= Malḵûṯ, the lower Mother) a sequence of commands from which the earth, firmament, and heaven and all phenomena are brought into being.

Corresponding to this two-stage process of creation, in which the male and female principles, knowledge and speech, both participate, are two phases of scripture. (1) In the first stage scripture emerges as the undifferentiated totality of knowledge that is identified with the male principle. This stage encompasses the first two levels of scripture outlined above: scripture as the essence of the ultimate reality, and scripture as the creator principle. (2) In the second stage the wholeness of scripture/knowledge differentiates into individualized impulses of knowledge contained in the expressions of the divine language, which constitute the words that the male principle speaks when his second manifestation is born. The child speaks, and what he speaks are the words of scripture. These subtle impulses of divine language are then precipitated to form the concrete phenomena of creation. This stage corresponds to the third level of scripture as the cosmic blueprint. The various stages through which the Word unfolds in creation, as described in certain brahmanical texts and in the Zohar, are schematized in the figure on page 160.

Divergences in Conceptions of Language

While we thus find significant structural affinities among the symbol systems associated with Veda and Torah, especially as expressed in the later strata of the traditions, there are also significant differences among these formulations, which are linked to three fundamental points of divergence in the traditions' conceptions of language. (1) The brahmanical tradition gives precedence to the oral channel of language, while the rabbinic and kabbalistic traditions give primary emphasis to the written register. (2) This divergence has its corollary in a corresponding divergence in modes of perception, in which brahmanical conceptions of language and text emphasize the auditory channel and rabbinic and kabbalistic conceptions the visual channel. (3) The brahmanical tradition gives priority to the phonic dimension of the word, while the rabbinic and kabbalistic traditions emphasize the cognitive dimension. These differences become apparent when we examine more closely the language and imagery that are used to represent Veda and Torah, respectively, as the blueprint of creation. We will begin by comparing the ways in which the blueprint is depicted in passages, cited earlier, from two of the latest strata of the traditions: the Bhāgavata Purāṇa and the Zohar.

The Bhāgavata Purāṇa describes how the creator Brahmā brings forth the manifold forms of creation through reciting the words of the Vedic *mantras*.

> While he was contemplating, "How shall I bring forth the aggregate worlds as before?" the Vedas issued forth from the four mouths of the creator. . . . From his eastern and other mouths he brought forth in succession the Vedas known as Ṛg, Yajur, Sāma, and Atharva. . . .[252]

From the speech utterances of the creator, from his recitation of the Vedic words, the names, forms, and functions of all beings are spontaneously manifested.

UNFOLDMENT OF THE WORD IN CREATION

Veda	Overview of Stages	Torah
	ABSOLUTE	
Nirguṇa Brahman	Absolute as the ultimate source of creation	'Ên-Sôp̄
	↓	
	WORD	
Saguṇa Brahman	The Word as the essence of the ultimate reality in relation to creation	Keṯer
Veda as *brahman*/ Śabdabrahman	Scripture as the Word	Torah as the Word of God or Name of God
	↓	
	KNOWLEDGE	
Creator principle	Knowledge as the immediate source of creation	Ḥoḵmāh
Veda as creator principle	Scripture as creator principle	Torah as Ḥoḵmāh
Union of creator and his consort	Union of knowledge and speech	Union of Ḥoḵmāh and Bînāh
	↓	
	SPEECH	
"Second self" of creator	Second phase of male principle is born	Lower Ḥoḵmāh (Tip̄'ereṯ)
↓	↓	↓
Vocalized speech (*vāc*)	Vocalized speech	Vocalized speech (Malḵûṯ)
↓	↓	↓
Creation	Creation	Creation
Veda differentiates into Vedic *mantras*	Differentiation of scripture	Primordial Torah differentiates into Written Torah and Oral Torah
Vedas as blueprint	Scripture as the blueprint of creation	Torah as blueprint

The Zohar describes how God brings forth heaven and earth and all phenomena through "looking into," in the sense of "contemplating through seeing," the words of the Torah.

> When the Holy One resolved to create the world, He guided Himself by the Torah as by a plan. . . . He looked into the Torah, into its every creative word, and fashioned the world correspondingly. . . . God looked at His plan in this way. It is written in the Torah: "In the beginning God created the heavens and the earth"; He looked at this expression and created heaven and earth. In the Torah it is written: "Let there be light"; He looked at these words and created light; and in this manner was the whole world created.[253]

In both the Bhāgavata Purāṇa and the Zohar the creator is described as using the words of Veda or Torah in order to bring forth the manifold forms of the universe. However, in the Bhāgavata Purāṇa the primary emphasis is on the creator speaking the words of the Vedic *mantras*, which emerge from his mouths as recited sounds. In the Zohar, on the other hand, the primary emphasis is on the creator contemplating, through an act of mental and visual cognition, the words of Torah, which is depicted as the supernal counterpart of the written text preserved on earth.

Are these differences in emphasis systemically significant? Having abstracted out these images, we need to re-embed them in their larger textual and cultural matrices in order to interpret the meaning and significance of the differences they bring to light. What we discover is that the differences in the Bhāgavata Purāṇa's and Zohar's uses of the blueprint analogy are indeed systemically significant in that they are consonant with the larger symbol systems reflected in their respective textual traditions as well as in the matrix of practices associated with the Vedic Saṃhitās and the Written Torah. With respect to the textual evidence that corroborates these findings, brief mention should be made of a few salient points.

Brahmanical Texts

In the Bhāgavata Purāṇa's portrayal the Vedic *mantras* issue forth through the speech of the creator Brahmā and manifest the forms of creation. The *oral* expression of the divine language is emphasized in this image, which carries with it an implicit emphasis on the *phonic* dimension of the Vedic words apprehended through the *auditory* channel. These emphases are consonant with the representations of the Vedas found in other brahmanical texts.

(1) The image of the Vedic *mantras* as the archetypal blueprint of creation is generally associated with the speech of the creator. While the creator is at times described as seeing as well as uttering the *mantras*, he is generally depicted in Vedic and post-Vedic cosmogonies as bringing forth creation through a series of speech-acts, rather than through an act of visual or mental cognition. There is little emphasis in brahmanical texts on the creator contemplating the words of the Vedas; he simply utters the Vedic words and the corresponding forms appear.

(2) The Vedic *mantras* as the blueprint of creation are composed of the subtle impulses of the divine speech, which are generally identified with the forty-eight *varṇas* of Sanskrit. These *varṇas* are phones, the fundamental units of speech, and not letters, the fundamental units of script. Vedic and post-Vedic myths contain numerous speculations on the sound structure of the *varṇas* without reference to their concrete embodiment in script.

(3) The Sanskrit *varṇas* are depicted in Vedic and post-Vedic mythology as the primordial sounds that are the structural elements of creation. The *varṇas* combine in various configurations to form the words of the Vedic *mantras* from which concrete phenomena are structured.

(4) The sounds that structure the Vedic *mantras* are designated as *śruti,* "that which was heard" by the Vedic *ṛṣis* at the beginning of creation as the primordial rhythms reverberating forth from the Transcendent. Although the phenomenology of Vedic cognition is described in Vedic and post-Vedic texts in terms of both hearing and seeing—hence the designation *ṛṣis*, "seers"—the *ṛṣis* are celebrated primarily for their role in preserving what they heard and saw through their speech. They "recorded" the Vedic *mantras* through their speech, thereby initiating an unbroken line of oral transmission through which the Vedas would be passed down to subsequent generations.[254]

Rabbinic and Kabbalistic Texts

The Zohar's image of the Torah as the plan of creation emphasizes God contemplating through sight the words of the written text. The *written* form of the text is emphasized, in which the words of the Torah are inscribed in visible characters that God sees. The words of Torah are apprehended through the *cognitive* act of contemplation, which simultaneously involves a *visual* component. These emphases resonate with representations of the Torah found in rabbinic texts as well as in other kabbalistic texts.

(1) In rabbinic portrayals of the Torah as the plan of creation, as discussed earlier, we find two different images that correspond to the

Zohar's portrayal: Torah as the concrete plan that God "looked into" in order to create the world, or Torah as the mental plan of creation contemplated in the mind of God. The written and cognitive dimensions of the words of Torah take precedence over their phonic dimension in these images.

(2) The Torah that constitutes the blueprint of creation is composed of the twenty-two letters *('ôṯiyyôṯ)* of the Hebrew alphabet that are the fundamental elements of the divine language. In contrast to the brahmanical emphasis on the sound units of Sanskrit, rabbinic and kabbalistic speculations tend to emphasize the script units of Hebrew, focusing in particular on the shape and semantic significance of the letters and their cosmic role in creation, with relatively little emphasis on their sound value. In certain kabbalistic texts the material letters of the Hebrew script are described as gross manifestations of the subtle letters that exist in the upper worlds. These subtle letters are generally depicted as configurations of divine light, with the emphasis again on their visible form rather than on their sound. The mundane form of the Sefer Torah inscribed on parchment is said to mirror the supramundane form of the supernal Torah, which is inscribed in light. Such kabbalistic conceptions cosmologize earlier rabbinic traditions in which the Torah as the Word of God is associated with images of light and fire.

(3) The twenty-two consonants of the Hebrew alphabet that compose the Torah are depicted in certain rabbinic and kabbalistic texts as the basic structural elements that underlie and give rise to the manifold forms of creation. The kabbalists in particular elaborate on this notion, describing how the upper and lower worlds are created through different permutations and combinations of the letters of the Torah.

(4) The preexistent Torah is depicted as becoming embodied on earth in the form of a concrete written text at the time of the revelation at Mount Sinai. The phenomenology of revelation is described in both rabbinic texts and the Zohar as a synesthetic experience that simultaneously engaged the people of Israel's faculties of sight and hearing, with more emphasis generally given to the visionary aspects of the experience. According to one rabbinic tradition, the people of Israel not only heard the voice of God proclaiming the Ten Commandments, they *saw* his voice blazing forth in words of fire.[255] The Zohar extends this notion further, describing how the people of Israel saw the voices of God carved out upon the darkness as configurations of divine light that illumined the hidden mysteries of creation.[256] Moses is depicted as the supreme prophet, designated to be the scribe of God, who recorded what he saw and heard in the form of a written text, the Sefer Torah.

This brief survey of the textual evidence would appear to corroborate our initial observation concerning the three major points of divergence between the conceptions of language that underlie the symbol systems associated with Veda and Torah, respectively: (1) oral vs. written channels of language, (2) auditory vs. visual modes of perception, and (3) phonic vs. cognitive dimensions of the word. These differences are also clearly evident in the practices associated with the Vedic Saṃhitās and the Sefer Torah, as will be discussed in the following section.

Divergences in Practices

The cosmological conceptions of Veda and Torah discussed in this essay function in their respective traditions not only as pervasive and enduring textual motifs, but as paradigmatic representations that reflect and inform practices with respect to these two scriptures. The complex rules and traditions that have evolved regarding the proper methods of transmission, study, and appropriation of the Vedic Saṃhitās and the Written Torah are of particular interest in this regard, for it is here that we can most clearly see how differences in the conceptions of language underlying these symbol systems find expression in strikingly different practices. Although an exhaustive treatment of these practices is not possible within the scope of the present essay, the most significant points of distinction will be briefly highlighted.[257]

Modes of Preservation: Oral vs. Written Transmission

The most obvious difference between the two scriptural traditions lies in the basic form in which the core texts have been transmitted—whether as spoken word, in the case of the Vedic Saṃhitās, or as written word, in the case of the Sefer Torah. The primacy of the oral or written form is traditionally held in these traditions to have been determined by the form in which these texts were originally cognized or revealed.

The traditional designation for the Vedic Saṃhitās, *śruti,* points to the fundamentally oral status of the *mantra*s, which are revered as "that which was heard" by the *ṛṣi*s in the beginning of creation and which perpetually maintain their orality as "that which is heard" in the ongoing recitations of brahmin reciters in every generation. The Saṃhitās have traditionally been transmitted only through oral recitation *(paṭhana),* and there is a virtual taboo against writing down these sacred utterances since writing is regarded as a ritually polluting activity. Graham, in his recent study of the oral-aural dimensions of scripture in the history of religions, suggests that "the ancient Vedic tradition represents the paradigmatic instance of scripture as spoken, recited word."[258] The fundamentally oral nature of the Vedas, as well as of other Hindu sacred texts, has been emphasized by a number of Indologists in recent years, including J. Frits Staal and Thomas Coburn.[259]

The Vedic Saṃhitās have been recited generation after generation in strictly accurate, unaltered form, syllable for syllable, accent for accent, since perhaps as early as the second millennium B.C.E. This unbroken chain of oral transmission, known as *sampradāya,* is traditionally believed to have been initiated by the Vedic *ṛṣi*s, the ancestors of the brahmanical lineages, who originally saw and heard the primordial impulses of speech emanating forth from the Transcendent. The *ṛṣi*s did not write down their cognitions; they preserved the *mantra*s through their own speech and passed them down to their students, and in this way *śruti,* "that which was heard" by the *ṛṣi*s, has been conveyed from generation to generation through oral transmission.

Every sound and syllable of the Saṃhitās has been meticulously maintained with absolute fidelity by male brahmin reciters known as *śrotriya*s, "masters of *śruti.*" An entire body of literature known as the Vedāṅgas, or "limbs of the Veda," was developed very early in the Vedic tradition in order to safeguard the proper preservation, recitation, and ritual use of the Saṃhitās.[260] In addition, in order to ensure absolute accuracy in the recitation and transmission of the texts, a highly intricate system of mnemonic techniques is used to train each new generation of brahmin reciters. These techniques involve memorizing the text in up to eleven different modes of recitation (*pāṭha*s) that require mastering the base text forward and backward and in a number of different patterns.[261]

The need for exactitude in recitative transmission of the Saṃhitās, as well as in performance of the Vedic sacrifices in which recitation of the *mantra*s plays a central role, is rooted in an awareness of the transcendent status of the Vedas, the sounds of which are held to be the primordial rhythms that sustain the cosmos. Accurate reproduction of these primal sounds through periodic recitation and sacrificial performances is considered essential for the periodic regeneration and maintenance of the cosmic order. Conversely, any inaccuracies in either recitation or the sacrificial ritual are believed to have calamitous effects on the cosmic order and therefore require expiation *(prāyaścitta)* through various detailed procedures. The potentially destructive effect of any errors in recitation is reflected in the Pāṇinīya Śikṣā's statement that a mispronounced or wrongly used *mantra* will destroy the patron of the sacrifice *(yajamāna),* the words becoming like a thunderbolt *(vajra).*[262] In *śrauta* sacrifices the main function of the *brahman* priest is to avert such calamities through guarding against and correcting any mistakes in the *hotṛ* priest's recitation of the *ṛcs*, the *udgātṛ* priest's chanting of the *sāmans*, or the *adhvaryu* priest's performance of the sacrificial actions.

When we turn to a consideration of traditional Jewish practices, we are immediately struck by the contrasting modes of preservation and transmission that have been adopted with respect to the Sefer Torah. While the Vedic tradition is preeminently an oral tradition, the traditional designations for the Pentateuch—*tôrāh še bi-ḵṯāḇ,* "Written Torah," and Sefer Torah, "Book of the Torah"—point to its essential status as a written text. The Sefer Torah is preserved in writing, according to the traditional rabbinic understanding, because that is the form in which God revealed it to Moses at the revelation at Mount Sinai. Moses, acting as a scribe, simply recorded the words of God as they were revealed to him and, after completing the Sefer Torah, desposited it in the Ark of the Covenant.

The absolute fidelity with which the brahmanical recitative tradition has preserved the purity of every sound and syllable of the Vedic Saṃhitās is mirrored in the scrupulous precision with which the Jewish scribal tradition has preserved every jot and tittle of the Sefer Torah. The brahmin reciters of the Vedas and the scribes of the Torah assume parallel roles as copyists dedicated to reproducing verbatim the received texts of their traditions. The scribal tradition, with its detailed laws concerning the preparation of the Torah scroll, has been dedicated to copying and preserving meticulously, generation after generation, the exact text of the Sefer Torah that is believed to have been originally transmitted by God to Moses, the scribe par excellence. The act of writing a Torah scroll, far from being a ritually polluting act, is considered a holy work, undertaken for the sanctity of the Torah and for the sanctity of the divine Name. The Talmud and later legal codes therefore contain numerous laws regulating every aspect of its preparation, including the attitude and qualifications of the scribe; the types of parchment, writing instruments, and ink to be used and manner of their preparation; and the method of writing the letters and lines of the scroll. Scrupulous attention is given to preserving accurately every detail of the text. Torah scrolls that are not written in accordance with these regulations or that are found to have missing or defective letters or other flaws are rendered unfit *(pāsûl)* for liturgical use in the synagogue.

When viewed from the perspective of the Sefer Torah's status as the concrete embodiment of the divine Word, a single mistake in writing a Torah scroll is considered to have not only ritual but cosmic ramifications. Thus we find the admonition attributed to R. Ishmael when speaking to R. Meir of his work as a scribe of the Torah: "My son, be careful in your work, for your work is the work of God. If you should perhaps omit a single letter or add a single letter, you would thereby destroy the whole world."[263] Naḥmanides, in the preface to his commentary on the Torah, points out that it is the subtle structure of the Torah as a sequence of divine names that accounts for the rigorous Masoretic tradition concerning the writing of a scroll of the Torah, in which a scroll is disqualified if even a single letter is added or omitted.[264] Naḥmanides' colleagues in Gerona, Ezra b. Solomon and Azriel b. Menaḥem, cosmologized this conception even further, emphasizing the organic unity of the Torah as a perfect divine edifice hewn from the Name of God from which not a single letter or point can be eliminated without harming the entire body.[265] The *Sēp̄er ha-Yiḥûḏ* suggests the even more radical view that all of the letters of the Torah are the forms of God, and therefore a single error in the orthography disqualifies a Sefer Torah because it no longer represents the "shape of God."[266] Since the Sefer Torah is the form of God, the act of writing a Torah scroll is tantamount to "making" God himself: "Each and every one [of the people of Israel] ought to write a scroll of Torah for himself, and the occult secret [of this matter] is that he made God himself."[267]

The detailed laws and highly developed scribal arts for preparing and preserving the written text of the Sefer Torah, together with the other regulations and customs regarding the ornamentation of the Torah scroll, the public reading of the Torah, and the proper ways of reverencing the Torah scroll in synagogue worship, point to conceptions of the sacred status of the Sefer Torah as a holy book that is more than a book, for as the concrete embodiment of the living Word of God it participates in the reality of God himself and must therefore be treated accordingly.

Modes of Study: Recitation vs. Interpretation

The methods of transmission of the two scriptural traditions—as oral texts, in the case of the Vedic Saṃhitās, or as a written text, in the case of the Sefer Torah—have profound implications for the proper modes of studying the two texts. With respect to the Saṃhitās, the phonic dimension of the words and hence their phonological accuracy is emphasized, and study is through memorization and recitation as a means of maintaining the purity of every sound and syllable of the oral texts. With respect to the Sefer Torah, on the other hand, the cognitive dimension of the words and hence their semantic significance is emphasized, and study is through interpretation as a means of drawing out the manifold meanings of every word and letter of the written text.

In the brahmanical recitative tradition maintenance of the purity of the Vedic sounds is of primary importance, and in this context phonology takes precedence over semantics and the discursive meaning of the texts is all but ignored. *Śrotriyas* may be able to recite an entire Saṃhitā of the Veda by heart, but they frequently do not understand what they recite. This emphasis on memorization and recitation is reflected in the Sanskrit term for study of the Vedas, *svādhyāya,* which means going over, repeating, or reciting to oneself.

This lack of emphasis on the discursive meaning of the Vedic *mantras* is also evident in their use in Vedic sacrifices. Staal has pointed out that even though most of the *mantras* in the Saṃhitās may have a discursive meaning, when they are recited in Vedic sacrifices they are disengaged from their original context and are employed in ways that have nothing or little to do with their meaning. What is important in Vedic rituals is not the discursive meaning of the *mantras*, but rather their phonology and syntax.[268] The brahmanical preoccupation with the phonic over the cognitive dimension of the Vedic words is further illustrated by the fact that there have been so few commentaries dedicated to interpreting the discursive meaning of the *mantras*.[269]

The preoccupation in the Vedic tradition with phonology over semantics, memorization over understanding, recitation over interpretation, is linked to the view of the special status of the Vedic language as a natural language in which the sound is held to constitute its own meaning. The Pūrva-Mīmāṃsā school provides philosophical justification for the mythological portrayal of the Vedas as the cosmic blueprint by establishing that in the case of Vedic words there is an inherent connection *(autpattika sambandha)* between *śabda* and *artha,* between the word and its denotation, between the name and the form that it signifies.[270] We may term this type of meaning "constitutive meaning," in contrast to discursive meaning, for in this conception the Vedic words constitute their own meaning in that they are constitutive of the forms that they signify. In this context the periodic recitation of the Vedic *mantras* is viewed as a means of periodically regenerating the cosmos that serves to enliven and nourish the forms of creation at their base. As long as the purity of the sounds is preserved, the recitation of the *mantras* will be efficacious, irrespective of whether their discursive meaning is understood by human beings.

The method of transmission and study of the Vedic Saṃhitās stands in diametric opposition to the traditions surrounding the Sefer Torah. Whereas the oral transmission of the Saṃhitās leads to an emphasis on phonology, memorization, and recitation, the written transmission of the Sefer Torah leads to an emphasis on semantics, understanding, and interpretation. One of the basic tenets of rabbinic hermeneutics is that God did not intend for the Sefer Torah to stand on its own, but rather he intended for it to be interpreted. The very form in which the Torah scroll is written—that is, the fact that it is written only with consonants and with no vowels, no accents, and no punctuation—points to the openness of the closed text, which calls for interpretation. The text is closed in that its consonantal form is fixed and cannot be altered in any way. However, since the consonants alone are given, without the vowels, the text remains open in that it is possible to vocalize the words in a number of different ways, giving rise to a variety of possible interpretations without violating the written letter of the text. There is of course a tradition concerning the proper way to vocalize the text, but there are variations within this tradition, opening the way to multiple interpretations.

The text is closed in another sense in that it is considered to be a kind of cryptogram written in the secret language of God, which conceals as much meaning as it reveals. The style of the narrative accounts of the Sefer Torah is laconic and minimalist, full of lacunae. The legal sections of the Sefer Torah are also obscure and ambiguous in places, making it difficult to determine the precise meaning and application of certain laws. Although the written text is thus closed, both in the sense that its form is fixed and its meaning at times is concealed, the very hiddenness of the written text contains within it the need for decipherment and interpretation.

The rabbis maintain that the tradition of interpreting and deciphering the cryptogram, the written "code" of Torah, is itself God-given and derives from the original revelation at Mount Sinai. In addition to the Written Torah, God gave Moses an Oral Torah, an oral tradition of interpretation of the written text. The process of interpretation, which assumes central importance in both the rabbinic and kabbalistic traditions, is thus viewed as a direct continuation of the original revelation at Mount Sinai and as an extension of the text itself, not something separate from it. Through the process of interpretation the closed text is opened up, the potentiality of meaning contained within it in seed form is unfolded, and the text is transformed from a bounded system into an unbounded, ongoing process mediated by the sages.[271]

We thus find a quite striking divergence of emphases in the modes of preservation and study of the Vedic Saṃhitās and the Sefer Torah. In brahmanical practices with respect to the Saṃhitās, we find an emphasis on the oral form of the texts, on highly developed recitative techniques for preserving the Vedic *mantras*, and on study of the Saṃhitās through memorization and recitation as a means of maintaining the phonological accuracy of the Vedic sounds. In traditional Jewish practices with respect to the Sefer Torah, we find an emphasis on the written form of the text, on highly developed scribal arts for preserving the written text, and on study of the text through interpretation as a means of drawing out its semantic significance.

These broad contrasts are of course an oversimplification and do not convey the full range of practices that exist within each tradition. For example, Jewish traditions also include a significant oral component, as reflected not only in the importance of the Torah reading in synagogue worship, but also in the centrality in traditional Jewish life and practice of the Oral Torah. However, the differences between the traditions can be seen even in the modes of recitation adopted for the Sefer Torah and the Vedic Saṃhitās. The public reading of the Torah, which is the focal point of the synagogue liturgy, is a communal event in which the entire congregation participates, and therefore the Torah can be read only if a minyan of ten adult males is present. The text is read from the Torah scroll, rather than memorized, and primary importance is given to the discursive meaning of the recited words, with less emphasis on their sound value. If a word is read incorrectly in such a way that its meaning might be misunderstood, the word must be repeated. However, if there is a mistake in cantillation when reciting particular words, those words need not be repeated, since the primary focus is not on phonological precision but on communication of the content of the Torah's message to the congregation. With respect to the recitation of the Saṃhitās, on the other hand, the text is inscribed in the memories of the *śrotriyas* and not in a book. Moreover, as we have seen, the primary emphasis is on the proper pronunciation of the sounds of the Vedic *mantras*, with little regard for their discursive meaning. The purpose of Vedic recitation, especially in the context of *śrauta* sacrifices, is not to inspire or instruct a group of human worshipers but rather to regenerate and maintain the cosmos through accurately reproducing the primordial sounds of the *mantras*.

If we examine more closely the modes of interpreting scripture that have been adopted by each tradition, we are once again struck by the contrasts more than the similarities. With respect to the Saṃhitās, as we have seen, little emphasis is placed on interpreting the discursive meaning of the texts, in contrast to the central importance given to interpretation of the Sefer Torah. The formal schools of Vedic exegesis, Pūrva-Mīmāṃsā and Vedānta, have placed some emphasis on interpreting the Vedas, but their hermeneutical discussions center on the Brāhmaṇa and Upaniṣadic portions of the Vedas rather than on the *mantras*. Some parallels might be drawn between rabbinic hermeneutics and the hermeneutical methods of the Mīmāṃsakas, both of which are based on the assumption that their respective scriptures constitute a perfect unitary whole that is utterly devoid of errors and contradictions. However, the primary aim of Mīmāṃsaka hermeneutics is to arrive at definitive rules for the performance of *dharma*, and while this pragmatic emphasis may be comparable to that of the halakhic Midrashists, there does not appear to be any stream within the Mīmāṃsaka tradition comparable to the aggadic Midrashists, who relish the meaning of the Torah for its own sake.

Theurgic Conceptions

The designated methods of study and practice associated with Veda and Torah are represented in certain strands of their respective traditions as theurgic operations that serve the twofold function of maintaining the structures of the cosmos and of the divine realm. The exponents of the *karma-kāṇḍa*[272] within the brahmanical tradition emphasize the theurgic efficacy of Vedic sacrifice and recitation, while certain rabbinic sages and theosophical kabbalists grant a comparable power to Torah study and practice. Moreover, each tradition invokes two types of paradigms for these theurgic practices: the paradigm of creation, in which the cosmogonic activities of the creator serve as a divine prototype for human activity; and the paradigm of cognition or revelation, in which the activities of the Vedic *ṛṣis* or of the people of Israel at Mount Sinai serve as authoritative human models.

The primary image that supports the theurgic practices associated with Veda and Torah is that of the blueprint: the Veda as the archetypal plan that reflects the structures of the human order, the natural order, and the divine order; the Torah as the blueprint that reflects the structures of the human being, the cosmos, and, according to certain kabbalists, the Godhead. Each tradition designates specific practices, modeled on the activities of the creator himself, by means of which the blueprint can be activated and the structures reflected within it nourished and sustained. In such conceptions Veda and Torah represent intermediary principles that reflect and interconnect all levels of existence, serving as the means through which human beings may not only shape their own individual and collective destinies, but may directly influence the cosmos and the divine realm as well.

According to certain brahmanical conceptions, the creator brought forth and ordered the phenomenal creation through sacrifice and recitation of the Vedic *mantras*. The brahmin priests follow his example by periodically performing sacrifices and reciting the Vedic *mantras* in order to regenerate the cosmic order and to nourish and magnify the gods, including the creator himself. According to certain rabbinic conceptions, which are more fully elaborated in kabbalistic texts, God brought forth creation through "looking into" or contemplating his blueprint, the Torah, and using its laws to structure the cosmos. The rabbis and kabbalists emulate his example by "looking into" and interpreting the Torah and performing the commandments in order to maintain the cosmos and to strengthen and sustain God himself. The divine prototype in both cases points to the appropriate means through which the blueprint may be activated: while brahmanical practices emphasize reproduction of the sounds of the Vedic *mantras* through recitation, rabbinic and kabbalistic practices emphasize activation of the content of the Torah through interpretation and observance of the commandments.

A second model for these theurgic practices is provided by the modes of reception by means of which the original human recipients are said to have obtained and implemented the knowledge of Veda or Torah. The Vedic *ṛṣis* are represented in certain brahmanical texts as assisting the gods in the process of creation through cognizing and reciting the Vedic *mantras* and performing the first sacrifices on earth. The brahmin priests emulate the cosmos-producing activities of their ancestors by preserving the recitative and sacrificial traditions initiated by them. The Israelites' acceptance of the Torah at the Sinai revelation, in which they agreed to observe its commandments, is represented in certain rabbinic and kabbalistic texts as a crucial turning point that served to consolidate the creation and establish it on a firm basis. The Jewish people follow the example of their ancestors and ensure the preservation of creation by continuing to uphold the covenant through study and practice of Torah.[273]

Modes of Appropriation

The theurgic practices associated with Veda and Torah are focused on conservation and maintenance—not only maintenance of the cosmic order and of the divine realm, but maintenance of the social order as well. In this context the paradigmatic representations of Veda and Torah serve not only to authorize particular types of practice and modes of appropriation, but also to delineate the relationship of different groups within each tradition to those practices.

The exoteric modes of appropriation promulgated by the brahmanical elite—recitation and hearing of the Vedic *mantras*—are circumscribed, limited to the male members of the three higher social classes (*varṇas*). Moreover, those practices to which maximal theurgic efficacy is ascribed—performance of Vedic sacrifices and preservation of the Vedic recitative tradition—are reserved exclusively for those who claim direct blood descent from the *ṛṣis*, the brahmin priests. One means of justification for this hierarchy of practice is provided by the tripartite taxonomy of the Brāhmaṇas, which correlates the three higher *varṇas*, brahmins, *kṣatriyas*, and *vaiśyas*, with the three *vyāhṛtis* and the three worlds and thereby indirectly with the three Vedas, Ṛg-Veda, Yajur-Veda, and Sāma-Veda, respectively.[274] According to this scheme, in which the Ṛg-Veda and brahmins are ranked at the top of their respective triads, the very structure of the Veda itself, the cosmic blueprint, provides transcendent legitimation for the *varṇa* system and the hierarchy of practice perpetuated by it. No paradigm of Vedic study and practice is provided by the exponents of the *karma-kāṇḍa* and *dharma* traditions for the larger community who are excluded from the ranks of the twice-born—women, *śūdras*, and "outcastes" who are beyond the pale of the *varṇa* system. The only recourse for the exponents of popular *bhakti* traditions was to create their own texts and to assimilate them to *śruti* by deeming them the "fifth Veda" and ascribing to their verses mantric power comparable to that of the Vedic *mantras*.

The exoteric modes of appropriation promulgated by the rabbinic elite—study and practice of Torah—are, in contrast, open to all members of the Jewish community, at least in principle. Rabbinic portrayals of the Sinai revelation emphasize that all of the people of Israel—male and female, young and old—received the revelation of the Torah and agreed to accept and observe its commandments. The covenant was established with the entire Israelite community, which as a "kingdom of priests" and a "holy nation" (Exod. 19.6) was set apart from all other nations as the chosen people of God. Thus all Jews are enjoined, as part of a national eschatology, to uphold the covenant by fulfilling the commandments of Torah. Moreover, in contrast to the brahmanical prohibitions that exclude certain members of the community from hearing Vedic recitations, all members of the Jewish community are intended to participate in communal worship in the synagogue and to hear the reading of—although not necessarily to read themselves—the Sefer Torah. In principle the obligation to fulfill the commandments includes

Torah study, although in practice the domain of those who are allowed to engage in sustained study of the Torah in rabbinic academies has been carefully circumscribed by the rabbis—as indicated by the existence of such categories of the "other" as the *ᶜam hā-'āreṣ* and women. Certain practices, in particular preservation of the Written Torah and codification of the authoritative interpretations of its teachings that constitute the Oral Torah, are the exclusive province of the rabbinic elite, who as the designated heirs of Mosaic authority claim a special status within the larger Jewish community.

The theosophical kabbalists also invoke the example of Moses, emphasizing his role as the supreme prophet and mystic to whom God revealed the "secrets of the Torah" that their own traditions claim to preserve and unfold. The process of contemplating the hidden mysteries of the Torah through study is represented in the Zohar not only as a means of fathoming the cosmic blueprint and activating its theurgic power, but also as a mystical mode of appropriation that has salvific power for the individual mystic. The goal of the kabbalist exegete is not only to replicate the interpretive activities of Moses, but to attain a level of prophetic consciousness comparable to that of the supreme prophet. The purpose of Zoharic hermeneutics is to strip away the outer garments that shroud the effulgence of Torah, and, like Moses, to attain a visionary experience of its supernal manifestations as the Oral Torah and Written Torah, the Shekhinah and Tip̄'ereṯ. The hermeneutical process ultimately culminates in mystical union, in which one discovers the architect within the blueprint and becomes united with the divine reality of Torah, the bride of Israel, for all times.[275]

The exponents of the *jñāna-kāṇḍa*[276] and meditation traditions within the brahmanical tradition similarly advocate mystical modes of appropriation by means of which one may transcend the recited texts of the Vedic *mantras*, and even the level of the cosmic blueprint, in order to attain direct realization of the transcendent structure of the Veda that constitutes the very fabric of Brahman. Their goal is not to replicate the activities of the *ṛṣis* by reciting the texts preserved by them, but rather to reproduce the state of consciousness by means of which the *ṛṣis* attained their cognitions. The exponents of the *jñāna-kāṇḍa* and the theosophical kabbalists thus share a concern to cultivate a state of consciousness that will allow them to experience directly that level of Veda or Torah which is identified with the ultimate reality. However, the language that is used to describe the mystical realization of Veda is radically different from that which is used in the Zohar to describe the mystical appropriation of Torah. Veda as an aspect of

Brahman is an impersonal reality, and thus although the texts may speak of realizing the reality of Veda, they never speaking of communing with it. The Torah, on the other hand, is represented as a living aspect of a God who is intensely personal, and thus the Zohar at times makes use of marriage symbolism and erotic imagery to describe the intimacy of divine communion with the bride of Israel.

The methods that are advocated by the *jñāna-kāṇḍin*s and the Zohar as means of attaining mystical realization of Veda or Torah also diverge sharply. While the purpose of Zoharic hermeneutics may ultimately be to overcome the distinctions between the Torah and the interpreter, interpretation of the canonical text of the Sefer Torah nevertheless serves as the primary means through which this purpose is achieved. The goal is to penetrate beyond the outer garments and body of the Torah to its innermost soul, but the garments themselves serve as the starting point. The exponents of the *jñāna-kāṇḍa* and meditation traditions, on the other hand, do not use the canonical text of the Vedic *mantra*s as the starting point for their mystical techniques. They atomize the primordial language into its most fundamental units and focus on certain seed-syllables such as Om that are held to represent the most concentrated essence of the Veda. These root *mantra*s are then used as vehicles in meditation to attain that level of Veda which is identical with Brahman.[277] In Zoharic hermeneutics one penetrates increasingly subtle levels of meaning in order to transcend the interpretive process and attain a visionary experience of the light of the Godhead. In certain practices of *mantra* meditation, on the other hand, one experiences increasingly subtle levels of sound in order to transcend all sound and merge in the utter silence of Brahman.

The mystical techniques of ecstatic Kabbalah, as represented by the school of Abraham Abulafia, would appear to have more in common with brahmanical meditation traditions in that Abulafia's techniques, in contrast to Zoharic hermeneutics, involve atomization of the canonical text of the Torah into its primary elements, the letters. Moreover, the goal of mystical realization of Torah is described in Abulafia's system in impersonal terms. However, the methods through which the letters of the divine names are employed in Abulafia's techniques differ in significant ways from the methods through which *mantra*s are generally used in brahmanical meditation practices. Abulafia's practices involve writing and recitation of the letters, as well as mental contemplation of the letters. Moreover, the internalized stage of meditation on the letters of the divine names does not focus on mental repetition of the sounds of the letters, but rather entails complex cognitive exercises involving combinatory manipulations and visualization of the forms of the letters. Finally, the purpose of Abulafia's techniques is not to still the mind, but rather to activate it in preparation for the reception of the divine influx.[278]

CONCLUDING REMARKS

In the course of our analysis of representations of Veda and Torah in the brahmanical tradition and the rabbinic and kabbalistic traditions, we have delineated certain structural affinities in the symbol systems of these scriptural traditions. We have also noted a number of fundamental points of divergence in the theories of language that underlie the symbol systems, which are reflected in textual images and conceptions as well as in practices concerning the transmission, study, and appropriation of the texts. While there are significant differences among traditional representations of Veda and Torah, they nevertheless share one important feature that is essential to our understanding of the authority and role of scripture in these traditions: Veda and Torah function in their respective traditions as symbols, and although textuality represents one facet of these multivalent symbols, they are not bound by this textual referent. Veda and Torah transcend their textual boundaries through becoming identified with the Word, which is itself represented as an encompassing category that functions on every level of reality. This Word may find its consummate expression in certain texts—the Vedic *mantras* or the Sefer Torah—but at the same time it remains a limitless, open-ended category within which can be subsumed potentially all texts, teachings, and practices authorized by the religious elite. The legitimating authority of Veda and Torah in their respective traditions can thus be fully understood only with reference to their function as symbols.

As we have seen, in certain strands of these traditions the Word is represented as constitutive of the very nature of the ultimate reality, and the unfoldment of that reality in the phenomenal creation is correspondingly understood as the unfoldment of the divine language. The divine language manifested itself in the forms of creation, which are its most precipitated expressions. However, the divine language is also said to have left another record of itself in the form of a blueprint containing the primordial elements of the divine language. This blueprint is held to have been cognized by or revealed to certain privileged representatives of humanity—the Vedic *ṛṣis* or Moses and the people of Israel—and was preserved by them in the form of earthly texts, whether oral or written. Certain texts are upheld in each tradition as the core of the cognition/revelation—the oral texts of the Vedic *mantras* or the written text of the Sefer Torah—and thus it is these texts that are to be preserved with scrupulous precision by the brahmin reciters and Jewish scribal tradition, respectively. The texts of these scriptures are fixed, and not a sound or syllable, word or letter may be altered. In this context Veda and Torah would appear to be bound by their textuality, their referents limited to a circumscribed body of texts. However, that textuality is itself viewed as the concrete embodiment of the divine language and thus points beyond itself to the structures of reality that are encoded within it.

Understood in this way Veda and Torah become multidimensional symbols representing the various levels and structures of reality, with their textuality constituting only one facet of this organic network of significations. These symbols become paradigmatic for their respective traditions because they are invested with transcendent authority. Any text or teaching that wishes to legitimate its authority can do so only by assimilating itself to the authoritative symbols: Veda or Torah. If Veda and Torah were limited to their textual significations as bounded texts—the Vedic Saṃhitās and the Sefer Torah—their domain would remain closed. However, because Veda and Torah assume the status of symbols, their domain becomes open-ended and permeable, capable of absorbing a variety of texts and teachings beyond the circumscribed compass of the core texts.

The domain of the Veda as the Word (*brahman*/Śabdabrahman) and transcendent knowledge is infinite, and while brahmanical exponents might maintain that this Word found its quintessential expression in the primordial sounds of the Vedic *mantras*, it is not believed to be limited to that expression. Potentially any text or teaching can claim to be included within the purview of Veda as long as it can establish a connection between itself and the Vedic *mantras*. This may be accomplished through a variety of strategies. For example, a text might claim that its teachings derive from lost Vedic texts, or establish a genealogy that links its teachings to the Vedas. Alternatively, a text might maintain that its own teachings were part of the primordial cognitions of the *ṛṣis*, or that they derive from some comparable form of divine revelation. The Vedic *mantras*, as the core *śruti* texts, retain their authoritative status at the center of the ever-expanding domain of Veda. Whether or not their content is known or understood, their authority is acknowledged, for it is these particular texts that provide the model for all subsequent texts and teachings aspiring to the status of Veda.

The domain of the Torah as the Word of God is also potentially limitless, and while rabbinic sages might hold that the Word found its consummate expression in the Sefer Torah, it is not believed to be limited to that expression. The key to expanding the domain of Torah lies in expanding the scope of the revelation itself so that the Word of

God revealed to Moses at Mount Sinai included not only a written text, but also the oral tradition of interpreting the written text. Thus alongside the bounded written text—which comes to include not only the Pentateuch, but also the Nevi'im and Ketuvim—an open-ended category of oral teachings is established. The Oral Torah becomes a limitlessly encompassing rubric under which can be subsumed potentially all rabbinic texts and teachings. The Written Torah remains at the center as the most authoritative expression of God's Word, while the Oral Torah continually extends beyond it, occasionally paying homage to the written text of which it purports to be an interpretation.

Are such representations of scripture as a multileveled cosmological principle unique to these traditions, or could we expect to find comparable conceptions in other religious traditions as part of what Wilfred Cantwell Smith has termed the "almost common human propensity to scripturalize"?[279] I would suggest that although other traditions may have developed cosmological conceptions of scripture, the specific parallels highlighted in this study between brahmanical conceptions of Veda and rabbinic and kabbalistic conceptions of Torah are not necessarily representative of a more "universal" trend to cosmologize notions of language and text, but are rather reflective of the more fundamental structural affinities shared by these particular traditions. As suggested at the outset of this essay, the brahmanical and rabbinic traditions provide an alternative paradigm of "religious tradition" to the Christian-based model that has tended to dominate the academic study of religion. The brahmanical and rabbinic traditions constitute what we might term "embodied communities" in that their notions of tradition-identity, in contrast to the universalizing tendencies of missionary traditions such as "Christianities," are "embodied" in the particularities of ethnic-cultural categories defined in relation to a particular people (Aryans, Jews), a particular sacred language (Sanskrit, Hebrew), and a particular land (Āryāvarta, Israel).

The manner in which these traditions construct categories of language and canon is rooted in the "embodied" nature of these traditions. Indeed, one of the metaphors that is used to represent both Veda and Torah is that of the body. Veda as the Word is described in certain brahmanical texts as undergoing a series of successive embodiments, from subtle to gross, as the body of Brahman, the body of the creator principle, and the body of the cosmos, which in turn is reflected in the human body. The "corpus" of Vedic *mantras*, as the earthly manifestation of the cosmic blueprint, reflects and interconnects these various levels of reality. While the rabbinic tradition tends to emphasize the incorporeal nature of God, the Torah is nevertheless represented at times as an organic unity that is a living aspect of the divine and that serves as the blueprint that becomes instantiated in the structures of the cosmos and the human body. The body metaphor is extended in kabbalistic texts such as the Zohar, which correlates the "body" of Torah with the body of the divine anthropos, the cosmos-body, and the human body.

The Word embodied in texts—the Vedic *mantras* or the Sefer Torah—is further instantiated in the social "body" of the communities that preserve and transmit them. The brahmanical and rabbinic traditions constitute their communities in relation to authoritative texts and in turn become the embodiment of those texts. This process of embodiment occurs on a number of different levels. First, Veda and Torah, respectively, become "incarnate" in a particular social body—the Aryan community or the people of Israel—as the constitutive category that defines its *ethnic and linguistic identity* over against other peoples—the non-Aryans or the gentiles.[280] Second, the process of instantiation involves the sociocultural reproduction of a particular *social structure,* in which the hierarchical differentiation of functions within the social body is legitimated with reference to the authoritative symbol. More specifically, the "heads" of the body politic—the brahmin priests or rabbis—are celebrated as the embodiments of Veda or Torah, and they thus assume the authority to redefine the categories in accordance with the changing sociohistorical conditions of their communities. Finally, Veda and Torah are symbols that are inscribed in the bodies of their adherents through certain types of *practices* and that serve to authorize those practices as the means to activate the primordial blueprint and thereby to maintain the social, cosmic, and divine orders.[281]

The manner in which the categories of Veda and Torah are constructed thus reflects the more fundamental categories that interconnect the brahmanical and rabbinic traditions as two species of the same genus of "religious tradition": as ethnic-based communities that define their notions of tradition-identity in terms of ethnic, linguistic, and cultural categories; as "textual communities" that codify their symbol systems and practices in the form of scriptural canons; and as religions of orthopraxy that delineate their concern for "correct practice" in elaborate legal systems, sacrificial traditions, and purity codes. The essential feature that unites these various aspects is that of embodiment: embodiment in a particular ethnic community with a sacred language, social structure, and practices that are constituted in relation to the Word embodied in scripture.[282]

9

From *Dharma* to Law

Bernard S. Jackson

The few pages that follow seek merely to highlight what the comparatist may regard as the most significant aspects of Robert Lingat's theory[1] and draw attention to related discussion in other areas of legal history. Though the present writer is strongly disposed to favour Lingat's approach and its equivalents elsewhere, the arguments here presented are intended primarily to raise questions rather than provide answers. For it is indeed the function of the comparative approach to ask questions and suggest hypotheses; answers and proof can only be provided by internal evidence.

From Lingat's account many parallels with other ancient systems of law might be noted[2] but by far the most important are those which relate to the principal theme of the book, the development of the classical texts "from *dharma* to law."[3]

Study of the history of the sources of law has been affected far more than is usually realized by the commoner models of modern legal systems. Awareness of the outstanding features of the common law and civil law traditions as they have developed predisposes us to look for three principal types of legal source: statute, precedent, and doctrine. Ancient phenomena corresponding to these modern institutions are certainly to be found. But once discovered they are all too readily invested with the particular attributes of their modern counterparts. Moreover, such identifications sometimes suggest inappropriate lines for further investigation. Much effort has been misapplied in seeking to determine such questions as whether ancient "codes" are restatements of custom or reform[4] (i.e., consolidating or reforming statutes); whether they are comprehensive or merely collections of "difficult cases"[5] (i.e., codes or miscellaneous provisions acts); whether they are "official" or "private" (i.e., statute or doctrine).[6]

An extreme case of erroneous identification with a modern model was committed by the British judiciary in India. Confronted by the immense variety of Indian local custom they seized upon the famous *dharmaśāstras* (such as the "Code" of Manu), which had developed a recognizably juridical style,[7] and transformed them into statutes. Lacking a customary law which conformed to the unity of the common law they adopted the principal English alternative, statute. The error did not go unnoticed. As Sir Henry Maine wrote in 1861:

> Their (namely, "the religious oligarchies of Asia") complete monopoly of legal knowledge appears to have enabled them to put off on the world collections, not so much of the rules actually observed as of the rules which the priestly order considered proper to be observed. The Hindoo Code, called the Laws of Manu, which is certainly a Brahmin compilation, undoubtedly enshrines many genuine observances of the Hindoo race, but the opinion of the best contemporary orientalists is that it does not, as a whole, represent a set of rules ever actually administered in Hindostan. It is, in great part, an ideal picture of that which, in the view of the Brahmins, *ought* to be the law.[8]

This view is decisively reaffirmed by Lingat.

The history of research into the legal collections of the ancient Near East, and especially the Laws of Hammurabi, has followed a similar course. In this case the laws are known to have been issued by royal authority and their influence is dramatically illustrated by the discovery of copies which were written as long as a millennium after the original promulgation. In modern systems virtually the only norms issued by sovereign authority and widely copied are statutes or subordinate legislation;[9] hence the identification of the Laws of Hammurabi as such was not unnatural.

A modern statute is authoritative both in substance and in form; not only its rules but also its particular verbal formulation of those rules are binding. The practice documents of ancient Babylonia do indicate a degree of conformity to the rules laid down in the laws and from this the substantive authority of the document is often inferred.

But in no court record yet discovered is there any clear citation or quotation of the laws.[10] Of course these records do not preserve a complete account of the proceedings. Though the arguments of the parties are often briefly recorded the tablets are not verbatim transcripts. Nevertheless, Driver and Miles correctly conclude "nothing like the English verbal interpretation of statute law was practiced by the Babylonian judges . . . neither judges nor private persons in their documents seem to have regarded it as verbally binding on them."[11] It may well be significant that the one apparent quotation from the Laws of Hammurabi now extant reproduces not one or more of the laws but rather some of the epilogue's curse-formulae, and does so in the context of an international treaty, not a private dispute.[12]

Even the substantive authority of the ancient Near Eastern collections has in recent years been thrown into doubt despite the features which these documents share with modern statutes. In articles which appeared in 1960 and 1961, two of the leading scholars in the field, F. R. Kraus and J. J. Finkelstein, reached similar conclusions:[13] the Laws of Hammurabi were the product of scribal circles closely in touch with Babylonian wisdom literature and the monument was intended as a glorification of the king and a dedication to the sun-god, Shamash. Many of its provisions were ideal and in form it differed from royal documents which were known to have been intended for legal practice, notably the *mesharum*-act or edict. This view has not yet received universal acceptance[14] and a synthesis has recently been offered by Klima, to whom the laws fulfill both legislative and literary functions.[15] Lingat's analysis of the Indian material suggests a possible resolution of this difficulty.

Similar issues arise in the study of biblical law. Traditionally, in both Jewish and Christian circles the laws of the Pentateuch have been regarded as exactly what they purported to be, *lex Dei,* a view which appeared to derive considerable support from the antimonarchical passages of the biblical historical books which depicted the king as in breach of the law. The fundamentalism of the attitude provoked an equally extreme reaction: the laws really did represent the statutes of the Israelite state, though not always in their original form. Indeed, Yaron has argued that one particular biblical and ancient Near Eastern formula represents a conscious attempt to avoid a possible difficulty of statutory interpretation.[16] But there are already signs that the pendulum is beginning to swing back; the laws of the Bible, if not divine, are at least ideal.[17] The Book of Deuteronomy in particular is primarily the product of the Israelite wisdom tradition.[18] Here too a modus vivendi is suggested by the Indian material.

Scholars have arrived at these views of the Mesopotamian and biblical legal sources unaware of the parallels with ancient India. What Lingat has provided is an overall framework and explanation of the relationship of the various phenomena which may render the results already obtained in Mesopotamian and biblical law more readily comprehensible. In particular his understanding of the nature of *dharma* and its relationship to custom and royal ordinance appears to me to be capable of extension to, insofar as it is not already implied by, our present knowledge of these other systems.

Dharma is explained by Lingat as the duty to conform to what Hindus regard as the natural order of things.[19] The books of *dharma* are instructional writings designed to train men to observe that duty. *Dharma* has, per se, no constraining power except that of its own moral authority.[20] In theory its content corresponds fundamentally with that of custom, being based in the traditions and aspirations of the Hindu world, but in practice it frequently diverges. Custom is changeable and varies according to the locale but *dharma*, as revealed by the sages, is eternal, unitary (based on the dogma of consensus) and unifying.[21] It is through the instrumentality of custom and royal ordinance that *dharma* may become legally binding. Thus custom may constitute a source, an instrument and a product of *dharma*. The ideal and the actual are not, as critics of academe may care to note, unmeeting opposites; they enjoy an intimate and complex relationship. But this relationship is not inevitable. *Dharma*-enforcing custom may change, thereby retracting the legality and, according to some views the authority, of the dharmic precept concerned by a process akin to desuetude.[22]

The relationship between *dharma* and royal ordinance is also close. The early *dharmasūtras* reflect the Brahmins' earliest efforts to provide rules for the chiefs' justice and to integrate it within their already learned system for the expiation of sins.[23] The king comes to be regarded as having a *dharma* peculiar to his office, a religious duty to protect his subjects and guarantee their security;[24] his function is to support *dharma*, but *dharma* cannot prosper in disorder, so that in some circumstances the ruler may prefer to sustain custom which is contrary to it.[25] The kings frequently did patronise the dharmic scholars; it was often in their interest so to do since *dharma* possessed a unity which was administratively more convenient than diffuse custom. Indeed royal patronage assured the works of some of the commentators and digest-writers a measure of official status and consequently an enhanced legal authority.[26] A healthy symbiosis developed between the court and the dharmic scholar, one which may have fostered the later confusion of their respective roles but which in its day implied no blurring of the distinction between what we now call natural and positive law.

The progression "from *dharma* to law" is first and foremost a *literary* phenomenon. The juridical content and technique of the sacred texts increases from the *dharmasūtras* to the *dharmáśāstras.* Yet even at this latter stage the norms convey advice, not binding law.[27] The transformation of dharmic into legal precepts is a continuing aspect of the relationship between *dharma* on one hand, and custom and royal ordinance on the other; but it is neither an inevitable nor a systematic process. The use of the *dharmaśāstras* as codifications is attributable largely to the British judiciary. Yet even today the moral authority of the dharmic texts remains independent of their actual enforcement; the concept of *dharma* has not been superseded by that of positive law.

As long ago as 1882 Sir Frederick Pollock pointed out the similarity between the role originally played by the Hindu texts and that of Roman law in mediaeval Europe:[28]

> The Roman law was said to be the common law of the Empire, but its effect was always taken as modified by the custom law of the country or city. *Stadtrecht bricht Land-recht, Landrecht bricht Gemeinrecht.* Thus the main object of study was not a system of actually enforced rules, but a type assumed by actual systems as their exemplar without corresponding in detail to any of them. Under such conditions it was inevitable that positive authority should be depreciated, and the method of reasoning, even for practical purposes, from an ideal fitness of things should be exalted, so that the distinction between laws actually administered and rules elaborated by the learned as in accordance with their assumed principles was almost lost sight of.

In light of more recent discoveries it may be suggested that the similarity between the Hindu *dharma* and its counterparts in the ancient Near East is closer still, since it extends beyond the function of the norms within the context of legal systems to the very nature of the conception. The ancient Egyptians, we are told, had no word for law in general:

> The all-embracing term which applied to legal procedure and the spirit in which legal procedure was undertaken was *ma'at,* which in different context may mean: "order, right, right-dealing, rightfulness, righteousness, truth, justice." There was no

> distinction between "truth" and "justice"; both were covered by the term *ma'at.* Thus *ma'at* as "truth" involved right relations to "facts" as they were understood in a sacred society, and *ma'at* as "justice" involved right relations between the governor and those who were governed as this was understood in a sacred society. The concept of *ma'at* definitely belonged to the religious order; it was the substance upon which gods fed; it was the daily offering of the king to the gods. It was thus a spirit which properly pervaded the civil carrying out of government and justice for the ends of religion.[29]

Likewise in Old Babylonia no technical term for law existed.[30] Hammurabi proclaims in the prologue his desire to establish *kittum u mesharum,* of which the latter refers either to equity in general or, as some take it, to the process by which equity is secured by the king.[31] The former denoted the sum of the eternal and immutable truths upon which the cosmos was founded and which the laws strove to safeguard.[32] Yet the king was not himself regarded as the creator of *kittum;* rather he was divinely commissioned to formulate rules designed to implement it.[33] Indeed even Shamash himself received *kittum* from a superior source, a source recently described as "a metadivine realm . . . a transcendent primordial force upon which the gods depend," and one to which the powers of nature, fate, time, and magic, together with *kittum,* belong.[34]

The role of the king in mediating *kittum,* and the distinction between its nature and authority and that of the positive law actually administered, is aptly expressed by Greenberg: "While the ideal is cosmic and impersonal, and the gods manifest great concern for the establishment and enforcement of justice, the immediate sanction of the laws is by the authority of the king. Their formulation is his, and his too . . . is the final decision as to their applicability."[35] It is thus part of the king's function to translate *kittum* into law but this does not mean that all *kittum* will inevitably be translated into law nor that everything the king does serves this purpose. The actual origin of the truths identified with *kittum* has been located by Kraus in the Babylonian wisdom tradition. Hammurabi is described as *emqum,* a wise man, as well as *sar mesharum,* a king of justice. The appellation *emqum* is that typically used of the scribe rather than the judge. The wisdom circles which were responsible for the drafting of the laws projected the king in their own image in recognition of the authority which the king was giving to the wisdom-laws contained in the monument.[36]

In the Bible the relationship between God and Torah is differently conceived.[37] God is the author, not merely the commissioner of Torah;

it is his creation, the product of the divine, not the metadivine. The change is closely related to the biblical rejection of polytheism (which receives strong expression in Hammurabi's prologue and epilogue). Nevertheless the moral, nonlegal nature of the authority of Torah, comparable to that of *dharma* (and, one may conclude, to that of *kittum* too), is indicated by the very etymology of the word itself; for the primary meaning of the noun *torah* is "instruction, teaching"[38] rather than *nomos,* law. The wisdom orientation of Torah in content and origin is particularly clear in Deuteronomy,[39] and the relationship of scribes and king recently laid bare by Weinfeld is strikingly similar to that manifest in the first Babylonian dynasty described above.

In India custom appears to have been both a source of *dharma* and an instrument in its implementation as law. But the content of *dharma* did not *always* conform to existing custom (local customs, moreover, frequently conflicted) nor did custom *always* fall into line with *dharma*. In the ancient Near East the role of custom is more difficult to ascertain, and from some of the literature one might conclude that it played no role at all. For example, Yaron concludes from a formal analysis of the Laws of Eshnunna that "quite generally speaking, one may assume that the rules of behavior embodied in the Laws will have their origin either (i) in the activities—in various spheres—of the ruler, or (ii) in litigation (judge-made-law) . . . all sections not using *shumma awilum* reflect one form or another of 'statute' law; most of the sections using *shumma awilum,* but not all of them, reflect litigation and precedents ('common law')."[40] The influence of modern models of legal systems is virtually acknowledged in this formulation and in a number of respects it provides an incomplete picture. First, it deals only with what in a modern system are regarded as "direct" sources. Even if all the provisions introduced by *shumma awilum* originated in actual litigation where a point of law was raised, there would still be a great deal of noncontentious law presupposed. Thus for example Laws of Eshnunna 22 cannot have originated in litigation designed to set a precedent for the case in which a man distrained upon another's slave-girl despite the absence of (or, more likely, the repayment of) a debt unless the legality of such distraint where there *was* an outstanding debt was presupposed. In all probability this latter rule was customary in origin. By including Laws of Eshnunna 22 the draftsman necessarily approved not only the contentious point which may have been litigated but also the presuppositions which underlay that case.[41] Second, Yaron's argument comes close to confusing the origin of particular laws with that of the form in which they are expressed. There are indeed good reasons to conclude that the casuistic form[42] originates in the law-court.[43] But once in circulation it is readily adapted to other uses. Thus for example it is used in Babylonian omen literature[44] and later by the Roman jurists.[45] There is no reason why the author of Laws of Eshnunna may not have used the form to express customary, unlitigated rules.

The argument against customary law in the ancient Near East has been expressed more directly by Haase,[46] who poses two extreme alternatives: the one of the Justinianic (but not, following the predominant view, classical) Roman conception of customary law, which has found its way into modern legal systems and in German is denoted *Gewohnheitsrecht;* the other that of an original social order, a *Sittenrecht,* unchangeable, unwritten, undifferentiating between legal and other obligation, a minimal social order designed only to hold a rudimentary society together. Finding neither the former expressed in the sources nor the type of society presupposed by the latter, he allows only that there may have been a "nontechnical" use of custom and takes most of the extant collections as predominantly reforming documents, the one exception being the Middle Assyrian Laws which he regards as a collection of customs.

Haase thus argues on the one hand from modern, Western and on the other from "primitive," anthropological models. No stricture is hereby intended, for the historian can do no more than proceed from the known to the unknown. Unlike Roman law the Mesopotamian collections do not classify their sources of law; indeed "sources of law" (with its positivist implications) may have been a foreign concept to them. It is therefore quite legitimate to use outside models of the role of custom in constructing hypotheses. But Roman and Roman-derived models of statutes and precedents are not the only alternatives.

The Indian model has a number of advantages. It does not require us to regard codification and reform as non-combinable elements. Statements of *dharma* embodied existing custom only insofar as existing custom conformed to current notions of *dharma*. Similarly, we may suppose, the scribes of Babylonia adopted customary rules only insofar as the latter conformed to their notions of the laws which wisdom dictated. To suppose that the ideal was so totally removed from the actual as to preclude any overlap is to imply that the scribes were guided by values so different from those of the population at large as to make them a society apart. The real question is not "codification or reform" (i.e., restatement or amendment of customary law) but "How much does the ideal conform to the actual, and how much does it diverge?" Some answers are available but they point, predictably, in both directions.[47] Nor is the situation helped by the existence of a genre of "literary legal decisions," literary presentations of (ideal?) cases.[48]

The degree of conformity may well differ from document to document but conclusions about such differences would be premature.

Dharma operated also as a unifying force in the face of the multiplicity of local custom. Political circumstances in both the first Babylonian dynasty and the original Israelite monarchy were such as to create a similar need: in the former the incorporation of both Sumer and Akkad; in the latter the unification of both northern and southern elements of the former tribal amphyctiony. In the prologue to the Laws of Hammurabi there may be a reference to linguistic unification;[49] at any rate we know that the draftsman made use of both Sumerian and Akkadian models.[50] In the Bible the unification of the tribes on the basis of a single Torah is a pervasive theme.

The classical Indian texts contain a number of notions which amount to a theory of desuetude significantly different from our own.[51] Since *dharma* is not, per se, legally binding the existence or emergence of a local custom contrary to a dharmic precept creates no problem of legality; to say that custom here abrogates a religious duty is merely to misstate the fact that *dharma* and custom operate in spheres which possess no *necessary* relation to each other. The real problem of desuetude in the texts is whether the custom abrogates or suspends the religious duty (and the consequent penance for its breach). The problem receives less prominent statement in the Semitic societies. In the talmudic period we do find the maxim "custom annuls *halakhah*." Traditional Jewish interpretation gives this rule a very restricted scope of application but it has been suggested that, in some circles at least, its importance may originally have been greater.[52] Of course the concepts of Torah and *halakhah* had by talmudic times acquired the force of legality; a minimalist notion of desuetude comparable to that in modern systems of law (despite differences in the theories they proclaim)[53] is therefore to be expected. As for the earlier period, the possibility suggested by the Indian material that a general notion of law-annulling custom (as later expressed) merely reflects the non-legal authority of the Torah (as originally conceived) may merit investigation.

In considering possible equivalents to the relationship between *dharma* and royal ordinance we find ourselves on firmer ground. The royal duty to patronise the learned, described by Lingat,[54] was amply fulfilled in Old Babylonia and seventh-century Israel, as shown by Kraus[55] and Weinfeld[56] respectively. But in Babylonia we find clear evidence of the king's role vis-à-vis (positive law) ordinance as well as (natural law) *dharma*. It was common practice for the king at or near the beginning of his reign to issue a "*mesharum*-act" (often referred to as an "edict") which was principally concerned to remit certain debts and effect certain reversions of land.[57] Formally, these edicts are quite distinct from the so-called "law codes" in that they lack prologue and epilogue and are for the most part couched in a form more distinctly legislative than that of the (predominantly casuistic) "codes."[58] The reality of the economic measures contained in them is attested by contemporary documents. But in addition to the main body of the regulations, which were of temporary effect, there were also some reforms of a permanent nature, some of which it is thought were ideal or at least unenforceable.

The literary relationship of the *mesharum*-act to the "law code" in the context of any single reign was the converse of that suggested by Lingat for *dharma* and royal ordinance. In ancient Mesopotamia proclamation of a *mesharum*-act earlier in his reign was one of the achievements of which the king proudly boasted in the prologue to his "law-code," and it was the *mesharum*-act which provided some (in fact a relatively small proportion) of the code's substantive provisions. Surprisingly, some of the more ideal-sounding provisions fall into this category; price and wage regulations[59] and reversions of land. In the case of redemption *ex lege* of the person of a debtor or a member of his family upon whom the creditor has foreclosed we find that the temporary alleviation contained in Ammisaduqa's edict[60] is institutionalized in (the earlier) Laws of Eshnunna 117 which provides for automatic release after three years of service. If the argument here presented is correct the provision in Laws of Hammurabi may be viewed as a wisdom-law, a statement of what the law ought to be. But at the same time we may not overlook its close relationship to royal ordinance. Both are expressions of the same value, freedom of the debtor's person, and both derive from the same, royal source; but one represents the extent to which the court sought to implement the ideal while the other constitutes a statement of the ideal unaffected by considerations of practicality. Although in any one reign the *mesharum*-act precedes the "law code" (where both are found) it should not be concluded that *kittum* in old Babylonia was merely an idealization of positive law. The relationship between the two, as shown by the prologues and epilogues to the codes, was conceived much as that between *dharma* and royal ordinance in India: the king's *mesharum*-act was itself an implementation of *kittum*.[61]

It is the mixture of ideal and positive law together with the very incomplete correlation of the "codes" with practice documents that leads Klima to conclude that the Laws of Hammurabi are *both* legislative and literary.[62] It is form-criticism which leads Yaron to identify different sources in the Laws of Eshnunna.[63] But in both cases modern models have distorted part of the picture through the assumptions, in the one case, that official promulgations of norms deriving from a supreme authority are ipso facto intended to be binding, and in the other, that certain drafting techniques are peculiar to the parliamentary draftsman seeking to avoid possible difficulties which may arise in the course of verbal interpretation.[64]

The role of the Biblical kings in implementing Torah and the relationship between Torah and royal ordinance in biblical times is impossible to verify by evidence independent of the Bible itself; care must therefore be taken to guard against the possibility that the king's role has not been portrayed in terms of the ideal rather than the actual.[65] Nevertheless, some reliable evidence appears to be available, its plausibility reinforced by its closeness to the ancient Near Eastern practices already described. Weinfeld views 2 Samuel 8.15 as a reflection of David's *mesharum*-act;[66] more strikingly, J. Lewy has identified a biblical act of emancipation, *deror*,[67] which parallels the Edict of Ammisaduqa's automatic redemption of debt-slaves.[68] Here too, we may note, the value of freedom of the debtor's person receives institutional recognition in the Torah itself. Exodus 21.2 provides for emancipation *ex lege* after six years and it has recently been pointed out that this is conceived in Deuteronomy 15.18 as double the normal period of service, in apparent allusion to Laws of Hammurabi 117 or some rule related thereto.[69] Emancipation of debt-slaves is a fundamental aspect of the ancient Near Eastern *mesharum*-act as may be seen from the fact that in some circles the terms *andurarum* (to which the biblical *deror* is related) and *mesharum* were interchangeable.[70]

A particularly interesting aspect of the interaction of local rules, royal ordinance and wisdom-law is illustrated in the Hittite provisions concerning capital offences. A set of instructions to garrison-commanders contains the following:

> As in the various countries the control of capital offences has been exercised in the past—in whatever city they used to execute him, they shall execute him, but in whatever city they used to banish him they shall banish him.[71]

From this, Gurney correctly concludes that the law varied in different parts of the land, and we may further note that such local variation receives royal endorsement. Royal ordinance is here at one with positive law. Güterbock however suggests that this provision contradicts the homicide rules of the Hittite Laws (§§1–4), where no death penalty is to be found, and concludes that we have here evidence that the laws were not enforced uniformly throughout the empire.[72] In fact the instruction quoted by Gurney contains no reference to homicide at all. The general law on the subject is to be found in the Proclamation of Telepinus which leaves the "master of the blood" (a kinsman of the deceased) with discretion to seek blood-vengeance or not;[73] while the laws, manifestly an academic document (as may be seen from their frequent references to what the law was "formerly") govern only the case of unpremeditated homicide.[74] There is no contradiction between the royal ordinances and the laws in this instance: in substance they complement each other. But it is significant that it is the laws which, like many of their counterparts in the ancient Near East, deal with the more interesting case. Here too we may be dealing with wisdom-laws.[75]

The progression from *dharma* to law described by Lingat is a *literary* phenomenon; throughout the history of Indian law *dharma* and positive law coexisted but increasingly texts originally written as *dharma* came to be viewed, often by foreign conquerors, as legally binding. Thus stated the progression has no parallel in the ancient Near East.[76] In Jewish law however it recurs with great clarity once one accepts that our present Torah was not originally composed or compiled as a lawbook. That is not to say that every component part of the Torah was intended as a collection of wisdom-laws. Though this may well have been so in the case of Deuteronomy it is less obvious in the case of the earliest legal collection, the *Mishpatim* or Covenant Code of Exodus 21–22, which may originally have been intended as a statement of positive law if not a statute of which the wording was verbally binding. But we have seen already that in India, Old Babylonia and the Bible itself positive law may represent one source of *dharma* or wisdom-law.

The progression from *dharma* to law probably commenced within the biblical period. It is suggested by the account of the Josianic reformation[77] and later in the constitution of the post-exilic community.[78] But we may be confident that the wisdom-laws given legal authority at those times were not identical to the Torah in its present form; if form-criticism can tell us anything it must make irresistible the conclusion that the final editors of the Torah did not themselves conceive of the five books as legally binding. Nevertheless, later generations completed the process. The Hellenistic equation of Torah and *nomos* is often regarded as a significant factor in this regard.[79] From the tannaitic period, commencing with the destruction of the Second Temple in 70 C.E., the evidence is clear. Verbal interpretation, the absence of which was noted by Driver and Miles in the case of the Laws of Hammurabi, occurs on every page of the early rabbinic commentaries on the Torah and is prominent also in the Mishnah and Tosefta even though not written in the form of commentaries. Indeed this history was to be repeated in mediaeval, rabbinic law. The code of Maimonides (the *Mishneh Torah*) was the work of a private jurist which did not receive acceptance as binding *halakhah* until well after its author's death.[80] Though the issue is less clear the same has been suggested for both the Mishnah and the Talmud.[81]

We may safely conclude that the Indian model, as described by Lingat, has significant parallels in both the ancient Near East and Jewish law; moreover, the phenomena under consideration are sufficiently clear to have attracted the attention of scholars working independently in these two culture areas. It is possible (I put it no higher) that a similar model may also aid our understanding of aspects of early Roman legal history. The problem is immense and only the briefest consideration can here be given to it.

The effect of the comparative material may best be put in negative form: certain assumptions of modern historians are proved thereby not to be universally valid. Thus the writing down of a collection of norms does not necessarily mean that all or even most of those norms were intended to be enforced; the attribution of such a collection to royal authority, even if correct, does not necessarily mean that such a collection was intended for statutory interpretation in the modern sense; even drafting comparable to modern statutory drafting need not necessarily have been intended for such interpretation; the concept of law represented by modern positivism (described by Lingat as the notion of legality, as opposed to that of authority) is not necessarily the concept of law dominant in ancient societies; the later application of the notion of legality to a particular text does not necessarily mean that such a notion was originally applied to it; publication of a collection of norms does not necessarily imply that those norms have a single origin; an altered conception of the significance of a particular collection (or indeed a change in the very concept of law) need not necessarily result from spontaneous, purely internal factors; custom, royal ordinance and wisdom-laws need not necessarily operate on unconnecting planes: their relationship on the contrary may be intimate and complex; collections of wisdom-laws do not necessarily confine themselves to cases where the ideal deviates from the actual; provisions which appear to us ideal do not necessarily lack real attempts at implementation. Many of these conclusions may appear no more than statements of common sense, containing warnings against anachronisms of which the cautious scholar needs no reminder. Yet all too often such considerations go unheeded.

10

Union and Unity in Hindu Tantrism

Elizabeth Chalier-Visuvalingam
(translated from the French by Sunthar Visuvalingam)

O vision of immortal and supreme ambrosia, resplendent with conscious light streaming from the absolute Reality, be my refuge. Through it art Thou worshipped by those who know the secret (science). Having purified the "foundation" (ādhāra-dharā) *by sprinkling it with the rapturous savor of Self-Consciousness, and mentally offering all objects presenting themselves (to the senses, as if they were) flowers exhaling an innate scent, (dipping them first in) the nectar of bliss overflowing the impeccable libation-vessel* (argha-pātra) *of my heart, I worship Thee night and day, O God united to the Goddess, in this House of* deva-sadana, *my Body.*

Abhinavagupta, *Tantrāloka*, 26.63–64, 29.176
(adapted from Silburn's translation, *Kuṇḍalinī*, p. 204)

The fundamental preoccupation of Hinduism is to put an end to the infernal cycle of rebirths *(samsāra)* and thus to attain deliverance *(mokṣa)*.[1] The Hindu ideal aims at fusion with the totality *(brahman)*, which abolishes all individuality *(ātman)*. In this regard, the different systems of Hindu philosophy seem to rally around this idea expressed in the Paramahaṃsa Upaniṣad: "I know the Unity; my soul is no longer separate but united to the cosmic soul; this is indeed the supreme union (junction)—no more 'me' nor 'you' for him (= the liberated), the very universe has disappeared."[2] Under the influence of Advaita Vedānta, unity in the Hindu tradition has been generally understood in opposition to the world of multiplicity, of illusion *(māyā),* of bodily incarnation, which must necessarily be rejected in order to unite oneself with the Absolute. Within such a perspective, it is difficult to understand how any concrete union, presupposing as it does the (at least initial) dualism of the sexes, could lead to salvation. Sexual union is after all based on the identification with the ephemeral flux of the body and the desire for its other, whereas unity is precisely the negation of the Other. In the Vedic myth, it is indeed through the desire for the Other that the One becomes many. The valorization of symbols of sexual union and the universalization of their sacrificial notation in the Brahmanical ritual functioned within a public "polytheistic" context where any aim of unity is not at all apparent. It is only in the later doctrines of Tantrism that ritualized sexual union is systematically sanctified within a nondualistic perspective, precisely as a means to individual liberation. For here unity is understood rather as the absence of oppositions between *mokṣa* and *samsāra,* an ineffable state including both transcendence and immanence that the Trika philosophical system—more widely called "Kashmir Śaivism"—designates by the term *anuttara.*

Inclusive Unity in the Trika System[3]

The Trika[4] is a doctrinal synthesis which constitutes, among other things, the sophisticated self-representation of a radical Tantric outlook within and through the high discourse of classical Brahmanism itself. Though the doctrinal bases were already laid down by the beginning of the ninth century C.E., its highly refined philosophical superstructure called the "Doctrine of Recognition" *(Pratyabhijñā)* found its fullest and most powerful formulation in the extensive work of its dominating figure, Abhinavagupta (tenth–eleventh century), who insists on going "beyond dualism and nondualism." Unlike the "exclusive" nondualism of Śaṅkara's Advaita Vedānta which simply rejects all dualism, the Trika perspective seeks to encompass the rich diversity of manifestation within the nondual principle at its diversity of manifestation within the nondual principle at its heart. The fundamental difference consists in the apprehension of activity as illusion *(māyā)* for Śaṅkara and as reality for Abhinavagupta. For the latter, the Absolute is characterized by the totality of two powers *(śakti),* that of knowledge *(jñāna)* and that of activity *(kriyā).* The sort of ideological split that occurred within the Veda-based orthodoxy between the ritualists (Mīmāṃsakas), who espoused action in this world to the detriment of knowledge, and the Vedāntins who could affirm such liberating knowledge only by negating action, is not only reconciled in practice but also resolved in theory by the Trika. Ritual confers insight and stabilizes the degrees of self-realization, just as knowledge vivifies and empowers the outer activity in turn. Hence the affirmation of a supreme nondualism *(parādvaita)* that goes "beyond both dualism and nondualism" makes good sense from the soteriological point of view.

The Trika distinguishes between two modes or rather logically successive states of spiritual realization, which have been translated by borrowing the terms "ascending" (*saṅkoca:* "retraction") and "descending" (*vikāsa:* "expansion") realization respectively.

> During the ascending realization, Consciousness isolates itself from all objectivity (including body, mind, etc.) until it transcends the latter through a process assimilated to a gradual "self-purification." . . . But the process attains completion only when Consciousness "re-descends" to assimilate the entire objective world to itself, a "universalization" culminating in the state of Anuttara, impossible to describe in terms of *saṅkoca* and *vikāsa,* understood as constituting the ultimate essence of Bhairava. This claim is typically inserted in the midst of arguments justifying the non-observance of the distinction pure/impure or edible/prohibited (food) and so on. The logic behind this equation becomes clear when we consider the definition of purity: whatever is (experienced as) distinct from Consciousness is impure, whereas whatever is (experienced as) identical with Consciousness is pure. Both terms of the opposition are therefore relevant only with respect to that preliminary, though better known, process of the ascending realization. For the Kaula adept intent on universalizing his Consciousness by re-descending to and assimilating the lowest and most impure aspects of objective manifestation, it is the pure/impure distinction itself that is considered the ultimate impurity to be transcended. It is in attempting the dangerous process of totalization that the adept often commits deliberate transgressions to shatter the rules and limitations that had earlier propped up both his worldly life and spiritual disciplines.[5]

The category of the impure, which is externally imposed by tradition, thus reveals itself to be ultimately dependent on a dialectic of interdiction and transgression correlated to the two modes of spiritual realization.

Whereas those techniques aiming at an ascending realization and the religio-philosophical currents based on them advocate turning away from the world of ordinary sensory experience to attain an ultimate reality that is transcendent, the techniques of the descent insist that it is possible to "recognize" this transcendent reality as simultaneously immanent, even glorifying itself, in the everyday world of sensory experiences. Not falling a prey to it by recognizing one's inner transcendence, it is possible to continue living in the world, enjoying it as a manifestation of the Divine. Thus the unity which the individual seeks to attain by ascending towards God is presupposed by and encompassed within a larger movement whereby God Himself redescends to reappropriate his creation through the medium of the adept who has surrendered his limited individuality to the supreme Consciousness. Functioning both as the means to and the expression of transcendence in the midst of worldly experience, transgression, by dissolving the final barriers which preserve the profane from the sacred, raises the experience of unity to a second order. It is the reconciliation of deliverance *(mokṣa)* and sensual enjoyment *(bhoga)* that permits the supreme valorization of the body in the "descending" Tantric perspective. Abhinavagupta, the living incarnation of Bhairava, attributes his highest metaphysical realization to his initiation into the technique of the "Kula-Sacrifice" *(kulayāga)* consisting primarily in the exceptional use of meat and wine in order to reinforce the bliss of incestuous sexual union.

Tantric Physiology and the Unification of Consciousness

Chapter twenty-nine of the *Tantrāloka,* which describes the *kulayāga*—the most esoteric ritual of union for the attainment of unity—is extremely difficult to understand because of Abhinavagupta's deliberately obscure style (*Tantrāloka* 29.169). Lilian Silburn's pioneering work, the lifework of a scholar and practitioner of the Trika, has proved invaluable in clearing many difficulties and I am indebted to her translation, notes, and explanations.[6] In order to understand the process of unification during sex, the following ternary structure must be especially kept in mind: *iḍá, piṅgalā* and *suṣumnā.* This detailed Tantric physiology goes back to the Upaniṣads, where the body is traversed by innumerable canals *(nāḍī)* among which these three play the dominant role (table 1).

Through the mutual friction and neutralization of the opposed solar and lunar breaths *(prāṇa/apāna),* fire is produced in the form of the ascending udāna which devours all duality, just as the twin Vedic

Table 1. Symbolic Correspondences of the *Nādīs*

Name	Place	River	Color	Light	Sex	Breath
iḍā	left	Gaṅgā	yellow	moon	female	*apāna*
piṅgalā	right	Yamunā	red	sun	male	*prāna*
suṣumnā	center	Sarasvatī	diamond	fire	neuter	*udāna*

churn-sticks were consumed in the spark of the sacrificial fire they kindled. The fusion of these three breaths, viz. *apāna, prāṇa,* and *udāna* also symbolizes the unity of desire, knowledge, and action in the Trika. The ascent of *udāna* through the median canal *(suṣumnā)* corresponds to the elevation of the *kuṇḍalinī,* the sexual energy in the form of a coiled serpent at the base of the spine. In Sanskrit, "this term has an exact synonym in the compound *bhogavatī; bhoga* is at the same time curvature, coiling up (especially of the serpent) and everything that pertains to sense experience, notably enjoyment."[7] Sensuality and, more particularly, sexuality is thus inherent in the conception and functioning of *kuṇḍalinī.* The spiritual exercises based on the tantric physiology should allow the *kuṇḍalinī* to take the way of the *suṣumnā* to reach the *dvādaśānta,* place of meeting with the Absolute and where the perfect union of Śiva and his Śakti is realized.

Unlike the later texts of *haṭhayoga* which describe the cakras as seven stationary centers visualized in elaborate detail with varying numbers of petals corresponding to the letters of the alphabet, etc., the Śaivas of the Kashmir experienced them rather as whirling many-spoked wheels serving as nodal points for energy exchanges between various parts of the body and the median channel.[8] These wheels, which in the ordinary person exist rather in the form of coagulated "knots" *(granthi)* obstructing the free circulation of conscious energy, are moreover only five in number. The "root support" *(mūlādhāra)* at the base of the spine is represented by a downward pointing *(adhovaktra)* triangle *(trikoṇa),* for the sexual energies are normally dissipated downwards. It is the seat of the dormant *kuṇḍalinī* coiled around the germinal point *(bindu)* representing Śiva and the essence of virility. The intimate relation of this center with the sexual and reproductive functions is underlined through other names like the "base of generation" *(janmādhāra)* and "place of the womb" *(yonisthāna).* When the adept successfully inverts this triangle so that the opening at its apex is directed upwards, virile energy is instead drawn into the median channel through an opening called *meḍhrakanda* "bulb (at the base) of the penis." The second wheel at the navel *(nābhi)* with ten spokes is at the junction of ten principal pathways *(nāḍrī).* The wheel of the heart *(hṛdaya),* where the breaths are understood to fuse, is especially privileged by Abhinavagupta as a seat of awakening for the *kuṇḍalinī.* Insofar as it reflects the fusion of the opposing triangles at the two extremities of the median channel, it can even be considered the primary center, infusing all the rest with its overflowing essence *(rasa).* Above the fourth wheel situated in the neck *(kaṇṭha)* is the fifth located between the eyebrows *(bhrūmadhya),* which is the "confluence of the triple current" *(triveṇhī)* of the vital breaths. In the ordinary person, this upward pointing triangle is still not effectively linked to the topmost wheel at the "orifice of Brahma" *(brahmarandhra),* which is located on the crown of the skull at the "end of twelve fingers' breadth" *(dvādaśānta)* away from it. The experience of the latter corresponds to the height of the ascent when the Self is realized in a state of meditative absorption *(samādhi).* However, the supreme *dvādaśānta* is above the body at the "end of twelve fingers' breadth" from the *brahmarandhra* itself, and corresponds to the experience of Śiva in the entire universe at the culmination of the descending realization. This eternally present "thousand-rayed" *(sahasrāra)* wheel of innumerable energies, a fusion of light *(bindu)* and sound-vibration *(nāda),* is the very nature of things. Likened to the orb of the full moon shedding ambrosia, it contains the trident representing the united triple *(trika)* energy of will (desire), knowledge, and activity that gives the Trika doctrine its name.

The aim of the practice is to retract the dispersed psychophysical energies back into the "point" *(bindu)* at the center of each wheel before directing their flow upwards so that the wheels are threaded by the median channel piercing through their centers. Ultimately, there is only a unique *bindu* on account of the fusion of all the wheels. The upturning of the inverted triangle (female) at the *mūlādhāra* results in its elevation through the flow of *kuṇḍalini* to the point between the eyebrows, where it unites with the upper triangle (male) to form the six-pointed *(ṣatkoṇa)* "Seal of Solomon" at the *brahmarandhra.* This coincidence of Śiva and Śakti so that they share a common *bindu* symbolizes the highest experience of unity possible in the body. Most pertinent is that the interaction or "friction" of these two "lotuses" leading to their fusion is conceived as a mode of sexual union that may be facilitated by, synchronized with, and wholly assimilated to an external copulation, which is precisely what happens during the *kula yāga.* The inner union of the triangles, which restores the original unity of the opposed—masculine and feminine—principles, is represented in Hinduism in the figure of the *ardhanārīśvara* or androgyne.[9]

The paradoxical "transmission" of the realization of the unity of Consciousness from the teacher to the aspiring disciple hence takes the form of an intermediate unity involving the temporary compenetration of the two at the level of their corresponding *cakras.*[10] The initiation *(dīkṣā)* of the pupil consists in the systematic "piercing" of one or more of his wheels by the teacher in order to infuse him with his own energy and momentarily raise him to the same level. It is almost a fusion of bodies resembling the Upaniṣadic sacrifice called *sampratti* wherein the son lay on the dying father—limb on corresponding limb—in order to receive the latter's breaths and sense-faculties. Though all the six modes of "initiation by piercing" *(vedhadīkṣā)* require that the teacher renew his unity with the Absolute Consciousness before uniting the disciple's limited consciousness with his own, the raising of the *kuṇḍalinī* in some of them has a particularly marked sexual component. In the mode called "piercing through virile potency" *(binduvedha),* the guru concentrates his seminal energy in his heart so as to intensify it before focusing it outwards through the *bindu* in the middle of his eyebrows. The disciple likewise receives it through the middle of the eyebrows where the guru attempts to retain it, failing which it is deposited in the heart or in the root-bulb in respective order. On reaching the latter sex-center, the breath is transformed into a seminal flow that permeates the bodies of both partners before rising to the *brahmarandhra.*

Similarly, the next two initiations (*śākta* and *bhujaṅga*) are described as different modes, gradual or instantaneous, whereby the teacher unites the female "energy" *(śakti)* at the base of his spine with the male "possessor of energy" *(śaktimat = śiva)* at the *brahmarandhra,* in order to reproduce the same inner union within the disciple. It is certainly no mere coincidence that the details of the *vedhadīkṣā* are discussed in the twenty-ninth chapter of the *Tantrāloka* (29.236–53) consecrated primarily to the exposition of the kulayāga. The secret of unity through sexual union was transmitted by preference to female disciples *(yoginī)* who subsequently initiated other males. It may be expected that some forms of "penetration," especially those with a marked inward sexual dimension, were combined in some way or other with the practice of copulation itself. This is perhaps implied in Abhinava's declaration that "by means of the couple of man and woman and without resorting to vows, to yoga . . . the *guru,* ever evoking the original sacrifice (i.e., the *kulayāga),* engages therein, and lays on the female body and on his own body, science and efficacy respectively. He meditates on the lotus (woman) in the form of the moon (knowable), and on himself in the form of the sun (knowledge).

Then he intimately merges together these two sanctuaries made up of science *(vidyā)* and efficacy (mantra)" (*Tantrāloka* 29.166–8).

Whereas the modes of ascending realization underlying the other philosophical systems denounce the (limited) ego-function *(ahaṃkāra)* as the supreme obstacle to the realization of unity, the descending perspective of the Trika rather recommends the universalization of the "I-Subject" as the highest mode of unity.[11] This totalization of Self is condensed into the word "I" *(aham)* by transforming it into a sacred formula (mantra) comprising the first (*a*) and the last *(ha)*—hence all the—letters of the Sanskrit alphabet, which merge into the single point *(bindu)* representing the nasalized *ṃ (a-ha-m).* Since the letters (*varṇa* or *mātṛkā*) of the alphabet correspond to specific energies of the wheels, the realization of "total I-ness" *(pūrṇāhaṃtā)* corresponds on the "physiological" level to the union of the male and female triangles around the unique *bindu.* Thus even the highest metaphysical realization of the universal "I-ness" is not without implications of unity at the level of the (subtle) body and vice versa. There is always a latent sexual dimension even in the case of transmission from male guru to male disciple and this is because the realization of the total "I" already implies a spiritualized sexual union within the teacher himself. The "libido" of consciousness functions—like electricity—only through its inherent tendency to polarization represented by the male and the female. The privileged mode of realizing its essential nondifferen-tiation is thus precisely through sexual union.

The Vocabulary of Union and Unity in the Trika

It is pertinent to note here that some of the terms used to denote various aspects of unification with the supreme Principle are derived from the sphere of conjugal relations or have at least unmistakable erotic connotations.[12] Perhaps partly under the influence of the "intentional" *(sandhā-)* or "twilight" *(sandhyā-)* language *(bhāṣā)* of the Tantrics, terms referring to sexual practices or states are given a highly refined but innocuous epistemological or theosophical content. Thus even the term *kula,* which Abhinavagupta charges with the most diverse meanings (*Tantrāloka,* 29.4–6), could literally mean "clan" or (extended) "family" and hence the sexual rite that goes by that name could have simply served to underline their incestuous or "endogamic" character. The term *āveśa* derives from the root *viś-* "enter into," it is often translated by "possession" which is understood in the Trika context as identification with the state of Bhairava *(bhairavāveśa).* This does not obviate its external manifestation in the form of a palpitating trance, as evidenced by its characterization through words meaning "trembling" *(kampa),* "swirling" *(ghūrṇi),* "fainting," and so on. In the Kaula context *(kulāveśa),* the term refers more specifically to the absorption in the divine energy brought about through sexual union. The term *melāpa,* which is defined as the perfect unity that dissolves the dichotomy between subject and object, also refers more concretely to the ritualized practice of group sex. The term *sāmarasya* designates the "homogeneity" of the undifferentiated Consciousness, in this context the "equalization" (from *sama-,* "equal") of its "flow" (from *rasa,* "sap") in and especially between the opposite sexes during the their union. On a more concrete level, it is applied even to the "fusion" of male and female reproductive substances. From here we easily arrive at the term especially used by the tradition to designate union: *yāmala,* whose primary meaning is "twin." It is remarkable that it is this term that has been retained to translate the union of Śiva and Śakti, and there are entire compendia which go under the name (Brahma-, Rudra-, etc.) *Yāmala,* which is also the denomination of an entire subcurrent of Tantrism, where the feminine element begins to take the upper hand. At a deeper level, the union *between* the sexes is merely the means to reproduce their divine unity *within* each partner, and thus the figure of the twins oscillates between that of the "sexed couple" and the androgyne.[13] In the Tantric rites of union, the woman hence plays an indispensable—and sometimes even the dominant—role: the feminine and the masculine are fundamental symbols of reality, and Tantrism abolishes this duality in order to accede to unity through union.

Kulayāga: Paradigm of Union and Unity in Hinduism

Though the divine "energy" *(śakti)* which is intrinsic to Consciousness may be realized through various techniques, the method of the *kulayāga* insists on the difficulty, if not impossibility, of realizing unity in all its plenitude without resorting to physical union with an external woman, technically called *dūtī* (*Tantrāloka* 29.96). The dynamic flow of Consciousness during the sex act is expressed in terms of the interaction between the secondary wheels *(anucakra)*—in this context, particularly the five sense-faculties and the mind that coordinates them—and the main wheel *(mukhyacakra)* which refers to the sex organs, the heart, and ultimately to the supreme Consciousness (*Tantrāloka* 29.106–15). This extraordinary usage is based on the unification of these centers at the height of the sexual union. The partners begin with mutual stimulation of their secondary wheels in a congenial atmosphere, heightened through the use of food, incense, flowers, etc. pleasing to the senses, and thus engage in worship of the main wheel. The external and internal sensations of kissing, etc., take the place of the delicious "food" offered to the deity in normal worship. Due to the introverted attitude, the satiated senses feed their energies into the sex center, which expands only to merge into the wheel of Consciousness. The movement thus corresponds to an "ascending" realization, a retraction into the quiescent Self using the sensuous experience itself as a support. Thereby a first degree of unity is achieved through the absorption of the secondary wheels into the central wheel of Consciousness.

Paradoxically, this spiritualization renders the union far more delightful and satisfying than ordinary sex, wherein (the energies and experiences of) the secondary centers remain distinct, neither vibrating nor satiated, precisely because their unification is hindered by the false identification with the body in the form of egoistic feelings of "I" and "you." As the climax of union is approached, a reverse process takes place whereby the plenitude of the main wheel of Consciousness overflows through the sex center back into the secondary centers, infusing them with its own virile energy *(vīrya).* A second degree of unity is attained, corresponding to the "descending" realization, whereby the central wheel of Consciousness in turn expands outwards *(vikāsa)* to appropriate the functioning of the senses and their respective contents, namely, the multiplicity of external objects. This indescribable condition of bliss is designated by the term "the mouth of the *yoginī*" *(yoginīvaktra),* which refers to the unity of the sex center with the other two primary *cakras* of the heart and the *brahmarandhra.* Hence it is also designated as the "heart of the *yoginī*" *(yoginīhṛdaya),* the "middle center" *(madhyacakra),* and so on. These verbal equations underline the fact that, under these specific conditions, the physical experience culminates in an emotional plenitude wherein the heart, vitalized by the influx of sexual energy, expands to envelope both the organ of generation below and the supreme seat of Consciousness *(brahmarandhra)* above. In a profound sense, the heart thus mediates in a total experience, where the sexual union seems to take place at the *brahmarandhra* within the supreme Consciousness, and conversely this realization of the unity of Consciousness seems to take place within the experience of sexual union. It is this mediation of the heart that explains the use of the same term rasa to refer to the "flow" of Consciousness, to the sexual "fluid," and to the emotional "essence" of the aesthetic experience. And it is the unification of the sex center with the supreme Consciousness that underlies Abhinavagupta's universalization of the aesthetic experience beyond the world of the theater.

The experience of unity through sexual union is such that it informs both the means and the final condition attained. On the one hand, the duality of the partners—of the enjoyer and the enjoyed—tends to dissolve into a unitary experience of bliss and, on the other hand, the absolute Consciousness reveals itself to be a polarity best represented as a sexed couple (Śiva-Śakti). This bi-unity is revealed especially in the indescribable fusion—wherein all differentiation is dissolved—of the quiescent transcendent *(śānta)* and the emergent immanent *(udita)* poles of the supreme Consciousness (*Tantrāloka* 29.115–20, 126–27). The supreme secret of the *kula* is neither quiescent nor emergent but the ground of these two alternating and co-existing movements. It is simultaneously and equally experienced by both the sexes, with the only difference that the emergent aspect is shared through the union of the organs by the partners intent on enjoying each other, whereas the quiescent aspect is experienced independently and inwardly by each partner. Those intent on final emancipation concentrate exclusively on the latter dimension, whereas those seeking the lordship of creative (magical) powers and longevity particularly cultivate the former aspect. The real emission *(visarga)* which culminates the union is not external but internal, and the extraordinary concentration of energies produced by the sexual friction is released primarily into Consciousness to fill it with a universalizing quasi-androgynous bliss *(sāmarasya)*. At the heart of the *kula* is the unitive friction (*sanghaṭṭa*) of the two flows—external *(udita)* and internal *(śānta)*—of emission which somehow replicates the union of the external couple within each partner. This then is the ultimate significance of the term *yāmala* (twin) applied not only to the union of the sexed couple *(mithuna)* but also and especially to each partner as a fusion *(sāmarasya)* of Śiva and Śakti: there could be no better symbol of the identity of the couple and of the polarization of the One than the figure of the (identical) twin(s).

In the case of the discriminating gnostic endowed with the required purity of heart, and who can therefore dispense with the ritual preliminaries and supports, this alternation of contraction and expansion corresponds to the equalizing technique of the *kramamudrā* which, like the *bhairavīmudrā,* is a technique that is generally practiced quite independently of any rites of sexual union. However, unlike the *bhairavīmudrā,* which grasps the inner and the outer simultaneously in a single immobile perception, the "sequential posture" *(kramamudrā)* is a dynamic movement where Consciousness repeatedly flows inwards and outwards so as to dissolve the barriers that hinder the experience of transcendence in the midst of worldly experience. The two stages of ascent towards quiescence and descent towards emergence are more sharply distinguished by Abhinavagupta, when he recapitulates the technique of the *kulayāga* for the benefit of those whose discrimination is not so mature (*Tantrāloka* 29.129–39). The latter ritualists are enjoined to worship the divinities of the wheels beginning with the outermost: Gaṇeśa with his attendants, the couple of *kula* teachers, the three goddesses of the Trika at the points of the trident, etc. These are to be worshipped, while in a sexually aroused *(udita)* state, as residing in the "main wheel" of the *yoginī* and in the aspirant's own body. During the ascending stage, the aspirant repeatedly focuses his heart-consciousness on the quiescent aspect (the "internal emission") and thus establishes himself in the state of the transcendent Śiva. Like an ocean unruffled by waves, this static mode of bliss *(nirānanda)* is characterized rather by the immobilization of the host of divine energies in the sex center which remain suspended in the void. Likewise, the secondary wheels of sight, etc., which depend on the energies of the main wheel, are also immersed in this tranquil bliss and lose their individual natures. However, it must not be forgotten that this "ascending" mode is being effected within, and is conditioned by, the highly sensuous context of sexual union. Though immobilized in turn and (temporarily) desisting from their respective pleasures, the senses nevertheless continue to crave for their corresponding forms of enjoyment but now as instruments of the supreme Consciousness. And though they next rush out to exuberate in the midst of external impressions overflowing with the sap of their own individual flavors, whatever moments of satisfaction (of the sex center) derived thereby are now experienced as offerings to the supreme Self. All these delightful streams of sense impressions flow into the already stabilized main wheel to infuse it with a tremendous stir of virile energy *(vīryavikṣobha)*. With this vehement (sexual) effervescence of the hitherto unruffled reservoir of Consciousness, the Lord of the wheel(s) too expands impetuously towards the external world. Though this "redescent" clearly presupposes the ascent, the end result is the saem fusion of the two poles that characterized the experience of the accomplished adept almost from the beginning. Hence, Abhinava again distinguishes the three modes of emission *(visarga)*: creative or emergent identified with Śakti and the *kunda* ("womb"), resorptive or quiescent identified with Śiva and the *liṅga* ("phallus"), and the supreme or unitive *(snaghaṭṭa)* identified with their indescribable union *(melaka)*.

The unity achieved through union is simultaneously realized on three correlated levels which are experientially and symbolically superposed so as to seal it with the essence of the supreme posture *(khecarīmudrā, Tantrāloka* 29.150–54). The friction *(saṅghaṭṭa)* within the median channel of the sun and the moon representing all the pairs of dualities—from the most material ovum/sperm to the most abstract knowledge/known level—results in the production of Fire representing both the (supreme) knower and the resulting conception. This unitive friction serves to equate the external union between the male and the female (organs) with the friction between the lower inverted triangle at the *mūlādhāra* and the upper upright triangle, which is precisely what awakens the *kuṇḍalinī* in the median channel and ultimately leads to their total fusion above. Since the stem of the median channel is also visualized as inseparably linked to the sex organs—as it indeed is in the esoteric experience—there results a symbolic identification of the male and female united through the phallus with the sexually polarized triangular lotuses strung on and united through the median channel. It is no doubt here, in the reciprocal "sexualization" of the median channel and the "spiritualization" of the coital exchange—that the mythical identity of the *axis mundi* with the *liṅga* has its true rationale.[14] The germ which sprouts in the womb from the union of the male and the female is hence simultaneously fertilized by the spiritual seed descending the median channel from the union on high represented by the seal of Solomon. The *yoginībhū* is thus primarily the fiery consciousness born of the union *(yāmala)* internal to each partner and is only secondarily the new physical sheath that sprouts from the external sexual union. In fact, the term *yoginībhū* refers primarily to this indescribable condition and only secondarily to the child that may or may not issue from it. Through this *khecarīmudrā,* naturally arising from the coalescence of moon, sun and fire, the adept becomes rooted in the transcendental "fourth" *(turya)* state and inwardly engages in the instantaneous sequence of creation, etc. The idea seems to be implied that the process of "creating an embryo" is being initiated at that supreme level where the adept has appropriated the Lord's function of universal creation, etc.

Though the Kaula texts are generally written from the male point of view which characterizes the larger culture and though Abhinava himself elsewhere often describes the male as the enjoyer *(bhoktṛ)* and the woman as the enjoyed *(bhogya),* it is nevertheless emphasized in this context that there is no difference between the experience *(śāntodita)* of the two sexes. Which is precisely why it is called "twin" *(yāmala)* with respect to either and both of the partners. When the distinction is made, it is on the contrary in favor of the woman (*Tantrāloka* 29.121–29), who alone is capable of nurturing the creative germ not only in the biological but also in the spiritual sense. Though the female physiology may be relatively less adapted to the ascetic or "ascending" modes of realization, it surrenders far more readily to the spontaneous expansion of the median channel that defines the "descending" mode of the sexual union. Hence, like Śivānandanātha, the founder of the Krama school, the guru imparts the secret doctrine *(kulārtha)* to the *dūtī* as the true depositary of the experience, who in turn initiates male disciples. The (temporary) unity of consciousness between guru and disciple during the "initiations through piercing" *(vedhadīkṣā)* is probably achieved here through the medium of sexual union. The mainstay of the esoteric tradition is the "mouth of the *yoginī*" understood not only as the supreme wheel of Consciousness but also as its physiological basis, the mouth of the vagina. The transmission of salvific knowledge "from mouth to mouth," that is, orally and hence secretly, acquires in this context the additional quasi-literal meaning of the transfer of the combined male and female reproductive substance *(kuṇḍagolaka)* to the mouth of the male and vice versa, before it is deposited in an external "libation vessel" (*arghapātra;* see also *Tantrāloka* 29.22). The idea is that the semen and the ovum emitted are highly purified, infused with the spiritual condition of the partners, and that their ingestion has quasi-medical results resulting in the rejuvenation of the body. The real elixir of immortality, of which the *kuṇḍagolaka* is as it were the tangible concentrate, is thus the "substance of the Kaula experience" (*kulārtha* has both meanings). By the same logic, the embryo resulting from such a union has in reality been conceived within the womb of Consciousness *(yoginīvaktra)* and has the nature of Śiva even before its birth (*Tantrāloka* 29.162–63). Though this theme is not explicitly developed by Abhinavagupta, it is pertinent to ask whether it is not in some sense implied that the partners—particularly the male adept—are themselves reborn and rejuvenated in and through this universal womb. Would it not be in this sense rather that Abhinavagupta's own claim to being a *yoginībhū* ought to be taken?

The principle of the "redescent" shatters the barrier between the sacred and the profane, it obliterates the distinction between (ritual) means and (physiological) side effects. The arduous exercises practised in order to attain unity now manifest instead as spontaneous expressions of the Kaula state, or are otherwise effortlessly integrated in their essential nature into the experience of union (*Tantrāloka* 29.142–61). Having mastered this art of awakening, bringing to rest and penetrating *(samāveśa),* as applied to the ascending and descending current in the median channel, and (from there) to the remaining 72,000 channels, the wheels, junctions, and joints, (the adept identified with) Śiva fuses the parcelled elements of consciousness diffused throughout the body into a vibrant undifferentiated unity. The state of Bhairava characterized by "unitive emission" *(saṅghaṭṭa)* thus permeates the entire organism, and the unity of Consciousness is experienced within the body. The alternating solar and lunar breaths, which the *yogin* otherwise strives assiduously to neutralize, easily give way to the experience of the supreme Subject in the median channel, when the adept focuses his attention thereon during this total immersion in the quiescent-cum-emergent Kaula state. Mantra is no longer the separate repetition of sacred syllables but the absorption in the spontaneous resonance of Self-awareness which arises from the fusion of the triple flow of emission. By focusing one's personal mantra onto this original vibration underlying all sound, the adept understands the emergence of (all) mantra, assimilates their potency *(vīrya),* and applies them with least effort (even for material ends). The effects aimed at by 300,000 recitations *(japa)* of the mantra divided between the quiescent, emergent and unitive states, are naturally achieved by simply focusing on the (silent) reverberation *(nāda)* during the convergence of the secondary wheels into the central wheel of Consciousness. Similarly, when the couple is immersed in the quintessential *khecarīmudrā* described above, even their experience of mutual kisses, fondling, play, laughter, etc., is endowed with all the eight increasingly subtle stages of sound that internally constitute the (potency of) mantra. By entering the eightfold wheel of this *mudrā*—which is deployed in the to-and-fro movement of the breath, in the intellect, in hearing, sight, in the mere contact of both the sexual organs, in their actual union, at the *dvādasānta,* and finally in the twin *(yāmala = sāntodita)* state of union comprising all this—in order to utter the spontaneous *japa,* the adept attains the state of the eight Bhairavas presiding over these stages. The indistinct cry *(śītkāra)* arising spontaneously in the heart of the beloved to emerge from her lips at the climax of the union, is itself the privileged vehicle of ultimate appeasement for the adept who hears it, just as the agitation subsides, at the center of both wheels (Śiva and Śakti, as forming the single *yoginīvaktra*). Through it he realizes the omnipenetration *(vyāpti)* of the mantra—composed of light, sound, and touch—the supreme eightfold Bhairava in the form of sound *(nāda).* The commentator adds that this Bhairavian "octave" is designated by the neuter gender because it arises from the state of complete homogeneity *(sāmarasya)* between Śiva and Śakti. Through the *kulayāga,* the essence of all the spiritual techniques—mantra, *mudrā, kuṇḍalinīyoga,* etc.—has been distilled into the single experience of sexual orgasm proper to an androgynous twin.

The whole *kulayāga* may thus be recapitulated through the various meanings of the term kula: "the Lord's energy *(śakti),* efficacy *(sāmarthya),* elevation *(ūrdhvatā),* freedom *(svātantrya),* vitality *(ojas),* efficience *(vīrya),* embryo *(piṇḍa),* consciousness *(samvit),* and body *(śarīraka)*" (*Tantrāloka* 29.4), all of which elements are integral to the rite. The unity of Consciousness is experienced within the body itself, which accounts for the term *kula* meaning both "body" and "Consciousness." So in addition to the abstract metaphysical meanings provided by the commentator, Jayaratha, we may risk indicating some of the more concrete connotations related particularly to the body. *Śakti* designates of course the *dūtī* identified with the Goddess, and *urdhvatā* the "ascent" of the *kuṇḍalinī* corresponding to the "erection" of the phallus. *Vīrya* is the inherent vitality of Consciousness and more concretely the semen. *Piṇḍa* not only refers to the experience of the universe as a compact, homogeneous "mass" but literally means "embryo" which could simultaneously refer to the fusion of reproductive substances and to the spiritual "birth from the *yoginī*." The compenetration *(samāveśa)* which results in the "sexualization" of the supreme Consciousness and the "divinization" of the body is perhaps best summed up in Abhinava's closing declaration that "the body itself is the supreme *liṅga,* the auspicious Śiva comprising all the elements, the dwelling of the (primary) wheel of divine energies, and the abode of the highest worship *(pūjā).* It is indeed the chief *maṇḍala* composed of the triple trident, the lotuses, the wheels, and the etheric void.[15] It is there that the circles of divinities should be unceasingly worshipped, both externally and internally. With full awareness of their respective mantras, let them appropriate the manifold sap of bliss issuing therefrom (from the principal wheel in the form of the body), through the process of creation and absorption (through the emergent and quiescent modes). Sovereign over the wheel of Consciousness, which is suddenly awakened through this contact, he attains the supreme abode by satiating all the gods (the divine energies within the body). May he satisfy them externally through objects pleasing to the heart and internally through appropriate acts of self-awareness" (*Tantrāloka* 29.171–75). If he were reincarnated in our own times to aesthetically relive this ultimate Kaula experience of Unity, one wonders whether Abhinavagupta would have at all hesitated to reformulate it in quasi-materialistic terms.

Alexis Sanderson has argued that the Kaula current is in fact a domesticated version of a more radical cremation-ground culture,[16] and the adoption of the Kāpālika-Bhairava—with all his gruesome imagery—as its highest metaphysical principle is perhaps the most telling indication of this. What is striking nevertheless is the scrupulous retention of this symbolic universe through visualization, substitutions, semantic equations, and so on. In their radical versions, these sex rites were practised in the cremation grounds and could even make use of corpses. In Abhinava's description, however, the whole imagery is internalized, through a play on the word *citi* which means both funeral pyre and (the supreme) consciousness:

> Behold within the body itself that *citi,* resplendent like the Fire at the end of Time, wherein everything is dissolved and all the elements are consumed. This cremation ground in the form of the void is the most terrible playground, the resort of the *yoginīs* and the perfected ones *(siddha),* where all forms are disintegrated. The chains of obscurity are dispelled by the circle of its own (fiery) rays (the sense-organs) to reveal only the (supreme) state of bliss, free of all mentation (*vikalpa* = doubts). Having entered this receptacle of all the gods, this cremation ground of consciousness, so terrible with its innumerable funeral pyres *(citi)* strewn all around, who indeed would not attain perfection (through performing the *kulayāga*)? (*Tantrāloka* 29.182–85).

It is not merely a question of using images borrowed from the cremation ground to depict the destruction *(samhāra)* aspect of unity with the supreme Consciousness, for the ritual of cremation itself merely exteriorizes an initiatic process. In the holy city of Benares, which is the "great cremation ground" *(mahāśmaśāna)* of the Hindu universe, where the pious go to perform the funeral rites of their relatives and to await their own death, the ritual is modelled on both the Vedic fire-sacrifice and the Tantric physiology underlying the process of liberation. Sexual union with the deceased is optionally prescribed for the wife in certain Brahmanical funerary texts.[17] Though necessarily downplayed in the domesticated and aestheticized setting of the Trika, it would seem that the all-consuming bliss of the *kulayāga* was nevertheless experienced as a mode of inner death, a dimension which is central to the Vedic *dīkṣā.* The confirmation of this is to be found not only in the designation of the *suṣumnā* and, by extension, of the awakened *kuṇḍalinī,* as *śmaśāna* but also in the symbols of death and the real animal sacrifices associated with concretizations of the *axis mundi* whether it be the Vedic *yūpa,* the posts representing Potu Rāju in South India, or the Newar New Year poles which are identified with the *liṅga.* The *suṣumnā* is nevertheless said to devour death, for the initiatic death—even when it presupposes the loss of individual identity—is the means of attaining a mode of immortality. The sacrificial death has been symbolically equated with sexual union through the frequent practice of inserting the right foot of the male victim into its own mouth in conjunction with the marriage of the post to the Goddess. This makes sense only if we consider the union as taking place within the androgynized animal at the level of its head, that is, with its mouth representing the *yoginīvaktra.*

The impurity of death which infests the cremation ground and transforms it into the very image of hell for the classical brahmin, so obsessed with ritual purity, is perhaps the most vivid spatialization of transgression in the Hindu imagination. The union of the *kulayāga* is indeed an experience of transgression in every sense of the term (*Tantrāloka* 29.10–17). On the concrete level this takes the form of violating the prohibitions that define the Brahmanical ideal of orthodox Hinduism. Abhinavagupta indeed begins by affirming that to the intelligent are prescribed those disgusting substances like meat, alcohol, and those of sexual origin, which are forbidden in the traditional religious treatises. The first two Ms—meat *(māṃsa)* and wine *(madya)*—serve primarily as aphrodisiacs in facilitating and reinforcing the bliss of the third M, sexual union *(maithuna).* The experience of union is concretized in the fusion of male and female reproductive substances, the primary offering (*argha = kuṇḍagolaka)* to which are added (twelve) other secret substances selected specifically on account of their impurity. Though this is not explicit in the description given in the *Tantrāloka,*[18] it is well known that in the radical forms of Tantric union the woman was expected to be menstruating and her blood was ingested with the other reproductive substances. This transformation the impurest of substances into the "elixir of immortality" is not peculiar to India, for Lévi-Strauss has demonstrated that honey (or maple syrup) is likewise used as a metaphor for menstrual blood in Amerindian mythology, where its relation to "fire" parallels that of Soma in the Indian tradition.

Moreover, the choice of the woman *(dūtī)* is determined regardless of beauty, caste, age, birth, etc., and solely in terms of her capacity to identify with the adept (*Tantrāloka* 29.99–103). In the radical forms of the Tantric union, this often implied a predilection for untouchable women drawn even from the castes related to the cremation ground rituals. The breaking of caste-barriers through the joint participation of Brahmins and untouchables is merely the systematic application of the valorization of impurity in a dialectic of transgression. However, the "domesticated" tradition which Abhinava himself inherited from his

Kaula teacher, Śambhunātha, is in a sense even more radical in that it enjoins the choice of women related through direct familial ties—mother, daughter, and sister—or through second-degree ties—grandmother, granddaughter, and aunts, nieces, etc. The *dūtī* could herself be the "mother" in the sense of teacher, "daughter" in the sense of disciple, or a "sister" initiated by the same teacher. Here however, spiritual affinity between the male and female adept is reinforced by worldly—genetic—affinity, and the Kaula "secret society" becomes a "family" *(kula)* tradition in the literal sense of the term.

The wife is expressly excluded from the sacrifice because of worldly attachment to her. Though this is interpreted in terms of desire for mere sexual enjoyment *(riramsā)* by the commentator, it is clear that "attachment" here rather refers to the adulteration of pure sexual desire *(kāma)* in her case by other worldly concerns that restrict the experience of union to a carnal level.[19] As for next-of-kin who are normally forbidden precisely because of worldly overproximity, breaking the incest-barrier may be understood, on the contrary, as the most effective means of raising the sex-experience to a transcendental level. So central is transgression to the *kulayāga,* that Abhinava affirms that those who perform this sacrifice without the sources of bliss, the three Ms, will simply go to a horrible hell. More significant than the violation of fundamental Brahmanical taboos, however, is Abhinava's systematic redefinition of principles like *brahman* in terms of transgression (*Tantrāloka* 29.97–100). Thus a *brahmacārin* is no longer one who is chaste, but one who literally "walks the (path of) *brahman*" by incorporating the supreme bliss of *brahman* within his own body in its concrete forms of wine, meat, and especially (the substance of) sexual intercourse. The choice of the brahmanicide Bhairava as the ultimate symbol of the indescribable Anuttara underlines that the experience of the sacred, as revealed through the *kulayāga,* is transgressive at its very core. Bhairava's appropriation of the fifth and central head of Brahmā suggests, however, that even the experience of Brahman through the *kulayāga* is ultimately derived from the Vedic sacrifice.

Sexual Union as Sacrifice: Between Veda and Tantra

The *kulayāga* presents itself as a "sacrifice" *(yāga)* more precisely designated by the term *yajña.*[20]

> The order of the world rests on the sacrifice *(yajña)* and more generally on the rites of which the sacrifice is the supreme

form and the model. . . . The very structure of the sacrifice is such that the sacrificer is necessarily an individual, just as it was an individual and, for good reason, the primordial sacrificer when he performed the sacrifice amounting to the creation of the world. In this primordial sacrifice, of course, the oblatory matter can only be the sacrificer's own body because nothing else exists.[21]

Now the essence of the *kulayāga* resides in the fact that the oblatory matter is the body of the participants, often reduced to the form of seed, which is offered into the fire of Consciousness. Moreover, this rite of union is an act of creation not only on the physiological but especially at the most fundamental level of participating in cosmic creation. There thus seems to be an "incontestable filiation"[22] between the Vedic and the Tantric sacrifice. The latter consciously models itself on the former by borrowing and elaborating its metaphors and even applying them quite literally. Sexual union *(maithuna)* is already considered to be a sacrifice in the Vedic current, for it is known that the act of creation is represented as a coupling. "In the Vedic sacrifice, the presence of the wife of the sacrificer is in general indispensable, for the destiny of the couple is inextricably intertwined."[23] Women "cannot by themselves fulfill the role of *yajamāna* [sacrificer] but it is also true that the sacrificer is supposed to have his wife beside him in order to perform most of the rites and the sacrificer is the couple formed by the husband and the wife *(dampati)*."[24] The Kaula justification for the necessity of the female partner *(dūtī)* is in this respect most significant: "Just as the *brahman*'s wife takes part in the Vedic sacrifice, so too does the *dūtī* participate in the *kulayāga*" (commentary on *Tantrāloka* 29.96).

Despite her vital presence for the efficacy of the Vedic ritual, the role of the woman is, however, passive and wholly subordinate. Union in this public context is reduced to a profusion of metaphors, extended even to pairs of inanimate and abstract entities. The aim of the Vedic *mithuna* is ostensibly "procreation" in the sense of abundance and prosperity, both in this and the other world, which would distinguish it from the Tantric *maithuna,* which has procreation as an aim only in the rare cases of the *yoginībhū.* In the *kulayāga,* it is no longer a question of a simple presence but of an active participation. The woman is identified with the Goddess as a direct consequence of the conception of the divinity as Śiva-Śakti.

If, in most of the cases the Absolute in his ultimate form remains the *Puruṣa* in whom everything—including his femi-

> nine energy or Śakti—is reabsorbed, the god of the manifested cosmos can only be united to this Śakti in a permanent and happy union. The divine is a couple analogous to the human couple, and inversely, the man or the woman can approach him only by attempting to reproduce in themselves the original couple. . . . The formula is to be taken literally. This signifies, among other things, that sexual union between man and woman can only be one of the means employed in order to reproduce in oneself this permanent union consubstantial to the divine.[25]

In the Tantric context, it is rather Śiva-Śakti who represent the ultimate form of the Absolute; and even within the bi-unity of the divine couple, the dynamic Śakti may be elevated above the prostrate corpse of the passive Śiva.

Despite this glaring contrast between the concrete roles of the woman in the classical Brahmanical sacrifice and the later Tantric *kulayāga,* what is truly striking is the facility with which the sexual symbolism of the former has lent itself to literal application by the Tantric adept.

> The union is a ceremony, comprising many preliminary purifications, symbolical homologizations, and prayers—just as in the performance of the Vedic ritual. The woman is first transfigured; she becomes the consecrated place where the sacrifice is performed: "Her lap is a sacrificial altar; her hairs, the sacrificial grass; her skin, the soma-press. The two lips of the vulva are the fire in the middle [of the vulva (Bṛhad-Āraṇyaka Upaniṣad 6.4.3)]. . . . The identification of the sacrificial fire with the female sexual organ is confirmed by the magical charm cast on the wife's lover: 'You have made a libation in my fire,' etc. [ibid. 6.4.12].[26]

The Vedic altar *(vedi)* in which the sacrificial fire is kindled is assimilated to the vulva, and the sacrificial post *(yūpa)* on its edge—half within and half without—is likewise not without phallic notations, so much so that one would be justified in following Biardeau in seeing in the later aniconic form of Śiva as the *liṅga*-in-the-*yoni* no more than a subsequent transposition of the Vedic motifs.[27] Moreover, the "female" ring *(caṣāla),* fitted around the "male" knob at the summit of the *yūpa* at the time of its erection, strangely recalls the sexual union at the *brahmarandhra* or *dvādaśānta;* for it is only the length of the *yūpa* till the *caṣāla* that is measured to the height of the sacrificer. Even the tripling of the altars recalls the different but correlated meanings of the "mouth of the *yoginī*" in the *kulayāga*. This raises the question as to whether the Tantric reworking is a willful misreading of the Vedic paradigms in favor of a preconceived ideology or rather the systematic exegesis of a hidden dimension already latent in the original sacrifice. We may even go on to explore the extent to which the Vedic structures may in turn shed light on certain aspects of sexual union that remain obscure in the exegesis of the Tantrics themselves, an exegesis which is on the whole focused on a metaphysical understanding of the unity thereby achieved.

In fact, the archaic strata of Vedic ritual must have given more explicit and pronounced expression to sexual (and violent) elements, vestiges of which still remain even after its reorganization into its purified classical form. Thus in the *Mahāvrata,* for example, there was an obligatory and public ritual copulation between a Brahmin student and a prostitute. In the imperial Aśvamedha, the chief queen was supposed to copulate under a tent with the (dead) sacrificial horse which represented the royal sacrificer himself in a symbolically "incestuous" context. Surprisingly, one of the central and most persistent mythological motifs built into the Vedic sacrifice is that of incest, which characterized Prajāpati as the mythical sacrificer, as the victim offered in his place and also as the sacrifice itself. Already at a very early period, there had been sacrifices like the Gosava, where it was obligatory for the sacrificer to subsequently commit various forms of incest in order to fulfill his vows. The mythical incest of Prajāpati however seems to function at a primarily symbolic level, and is connected rather with the inner state of the sacrificer who, on being consecrated *(dīkṣita),* regressed into an impure, deathly, prenatal condition. The underlying idea is that the sacrificer is in some way being reborn from the womb of his own wife, which also accounts for her indispensable ritual presence in the classical sacrifice, where they form an indissociable couple. Nevertheless, Prajāpati characteristically mates not with his mother but with his virgin daughter, a crime which is inherited by his successor, the Brahmā of the Purāṇas, and which is also the pretext for the latter's (sacrificial) beheading by Bhairava. This "irrational" identification of the mother and the virgin within a transgressive context is a constant in the later Hindu universe, and suggests that it is not so much any concrete sexual union—incestuous or otherwise—but rather the symbolic reality and the inwardly lived experience encoded in it, that is the prime focus of the ritual.

The relation between sexual union as conceived in the paradigmatic but outmoded public drama of the Brahmanical sacrifice and the wholly internalized and transgressive *kulayāga* may be clarified by recognizing the manner in which their respective meanings overlap in the mythico-ritual structures that determine the regular worship of the ordinary Hindu. Though the devotee acknowledges the ultimate desirability of liberation, which is actively sought for by the Tantric adept, his immediate intent is nevertheless still the assurance of his worldly welfare in the Vedic sense. The pilgrimage to the chaste, vegetarian goddess Vaiṣṇo Devī in northwestern India is undertaken as a pious vow normally presupposing the purity of the pilgrims, who arduously ascend the mountain in order to offer her coconuts and other materials of worship at her cave-shrine at the summit. Yet the founding myth which structures its successive stations and its actual content is based on the attempt of Bhairava to rape the virgin Goddess when she refused him the meat and wine he had demanded of her during an "adoration of the virgin" *(kumārīpūjā).* At the end of his pursuit, she emerged from her cave to punish him with decapitation before according the repentant demon-devotee the privilege of being worshipped immediately after her by the pilgrims. The pious devotee, who has no deliberate intention of following Bhairava's example, nevertheless retraces the entire itinerary, which includes penetrating into her womb-cave midway up the mountain, before symbolically offering up his own head in the form of coconut wrapped in blood-red cloth. Despite his subordinated role, Bhairava functions as a sort of divine consort to the Goddess, and the pilgrim's symbolic violation of her womb is charged with all the transgressive notations of the *kulayāga.* The Goddess reveals herself in the paradoxical figure of the Virgin-Mother and the devotee's violation of the virgin is at the same time an initiatic death and a return to the maternal womb. After all, the *kumārīpūjā* and the *kulayāga* are ritual elaborations of complementary roles accorded to the feminine within the Tantric ideology, and the purity of the virgin and the breaking of the incest-barrier are but the two extreme poles of a single dialectic of transgression. In the final analysis, the blood-thirsty Goddess and her victim Bhairava constitute a single symbolic entity, for it was Vaiṣṇo-Devī herself who first hid in the cave like an embryo in her own womb. Despite variations due to doctrinal context, social milieu and regional history, it could be shown that this paradigm of the preclassical Brahmanical sacrifice has still a pan-Indian application, especially at the symbolic level.[28] The traditional insistence that Abhinavagupta ended his terrestrial life by disappearing into the cave of Bhairava would suggest that the above scenario is relevant to a fuller understanding of what it really means to be "born of the *yoginī.*" The wearing of (generally red) female attire by the male partner in order to reinforce his identity with the Goddess, also reflects in its own way the androgynous fusion of the embryo with the maternal womb. From this symbolic perspective, the *kulayāga* would remain "incestuous" even if implemented in a mitigated form with the wife assuming the role of *dūtī.* Even the function of "fertility" generally attributed to (the role of sexual elements and sexual symbolism in) the sacrificial rituals of archaic cultures may well reveal itself to be ultimately the exteriorization of the inner rebirth and rejuvenation obtained through such esoteric techniques.

The Vedic roots of the *kulayāga* are to be found in the birth of the Brahmin priests Vasiṣṭha and Agastya from the common seed of the dual divinity Mitra-Varuṇa which was shed into a pot, so much so that one of their frequent appellations is "born from a pot" *(kumbhayoni).* In the later mythology, the spirit of Vasiṣṭha enters into the body shared by Mitra-Varuṇa, and then into the body of the celestial courtesan Urvaśī as well, when this dual divinity unites with her on the seashore. Later Mitra and Varuṇa split into separate bodies, and whereas Mitra unites with the consenting nymph, Varuṇa looks on lustfully and simultaneously sheds his seed into a pot. The seed of Mitra, oozing out from Urvaśī's womb onto the earth, is mixed with Varuṇa's seed already in the pot, and it is from the common seed in the "surrogate" womb that Vasiṣṭha and his twin, Agastya, are born. Already in the obscure Ṛgvedic hymn, both Vasiṣṭha and Agastya are said to emerge from the pot as the sons of Mitra-Varuṇa *(maitrāvaruṇi).* This doubling of the womb by the pot makes sense if Mitra corresponds to the "emergent" *(udita)* aspect of the emission, which is common to the male-female couple, and Varuṇa corresponds to the "quiescent" emission into the inner (pot-) womb (of consciousness) related to the base of the spine. The mixing of the seed would then express the idea that Agastya and Vasiṣṭha—who duplicate the polarization of the twin divinity—were born from that union of both emissions which later characterizes the *kulayāga.* Vasiṣṭha's penetration into the body of Urvaśī during the coupling further suggests that Varuṇa, who is himself represented by the pot and whose element is the (subterranean) waters, constitutes the feminine dimension of the twin divinity. Vasiṣṭha in fact embodies the ideal of the Vedic priest and his lineage was most sought after for the role of royal chaplain *(purohita)* even in later India. The duality of Mitra-Varuṇa is inherent in the later divinity, Brahmā, the latter being—like the closely related god, Bṛhaspati—no more than the mythical projection of the *brahman* officiant and *purohita.* The androgynous dimension of the *brahman,* already present in the Ṛgvedic material, finds expression later in the female aspect and even maternity of Brahmā,[29] which is retained especially in the pot-belly of the elephant-headed god Gaṇeśa, whom the Hindus traditionally identify with Bṛhaspati. The Vedic sacrificer, whatever be his caste, was reborn, after his consecration *(dīkṣā)*, as a *brahman* from the womb of the *brahman* officiant, and the guru is likewise said to bear his disciple in the womb during the process of initiation. The *purohitas* are credited with a significant role in the formulation of the emerging Tantric systems and Kaula lore brings Vasiṣṭha specifically into relation with orgiastic sexual practices which he is supposed to have "discovered" in Buddhist Tibet. The Vedic antecedents hence likewise suggest that the eugenics of the *yoginībhū* is ultimately the transposition of an inner embryogony of taking the place of the Mother (-Goddess) in order to give birth to oneself.

Bhairava-Consciousness and the All-Devouring Fire

Though this requires a separate study that would provisionally bracket aside the specific philosophical doctrines and the theistic context in which the *kulayāga* is inscribed and the specific social and ritual context in which the Vedic sacrifice was earlier practiced, a privileged key in establishing this continuity would be Fire *(agni)* both in its domesticated and in its terrible form. Fire is universally used as a metaphor for the sexual appetite *(kāmāgni)* insofar as it "burns" and "consumes" and through the intensity of its light it also serves as a metaphor for (degrees of) Consciousness. The metaphor of "friction" *(sanghaṭṭa)* between the solar and the lunar breaths to kindle consciousness in the form of the knowing subject *(pramātā)*, is itself directly borrowed from the churning of fire from the "sexual union" of two pieces *(araṇī)* of wood, male and female, in the brahminical ritual.[30] The "incestuous" character of this union is best underlined by the ritual stipulation that the male rod should be made of an aśvattha tree which was growing out of a *śamī* tree, from which the hollow female part should be made. The *aśvattha* is called "born from the *śamī*" *(śamīgarbha)* not only because the latter is its "mother" but also because, through a play on the root *śam-*, it is "appeased in the womb" or has "a pacified womb" *(śāntayoni)*. This would correspond to the "tranquil" *(śamī)* and "emergent" *(aśvattha)* poles of the Fire of Consciousness during the Kaula experience of sexual union. Yet, both *aśvattha* and *śamī* are considered forms of fire, so much so that the child devours the parents at birth only because the parents themselves are born of Fire. The frequent option of having both male and female parts made from *aśvattha* (born-of-the-*śamī*) alone, would suggest, first, that the maternal "incest" is primarily symbolic and, more importantly, that the male and the female again form a couple of twins *(yāmala).* The difficulty of deciding unilaterally in favor of a single option for the female *araṇī* would again suggest that through sexual union the partners *(aśvattha),* particularly the male, are in fact being reborn from the womb of Fire *(śamī).* "To pacify" *(śam-)* is, moreover, a euphemism for "to kill" (as in *śāmitṛ,* the Vedic executioner), and all these ideas come together in the later Hindu representations of the divinized male victim, the "Buffalo-King" Potu Rāju, by a (hence androgynous) pole made of *śamī* wood beneath a pippal *(aśvattha)* tree located at the center of the South Indian village.

It is the staff of the first Agnihotrin, planted at the confluence of two rivers, that sprouted to become the Varuṇa-tree now within the compound of the temple to Agni at Patan. And from its wood is sculpted the Mitra-Varuṇa emerging from a pot, like the *purohita* Vasiṣṭha, in order to incarnate the priest himself. Popularly represented by a pot (-womb), even at the confluence of three rivers, *(Ṭikka)* Bhairava (at the southern limit of the Katmandu valley) is also the terrible fire that devours the dualism of the vital breaths to ascend through the spinal column *(suṣumnā).* Already during the Licchavi period, which saw the efflorescence of Vedic ideology in tribal Nepal, the enlightened king Amśuvarman offered human flesh into the fire for Bhairava. It is thus by prolonging the embryonic dimension of Varuṇa through a properly Tantric modality, that this Agnihotra installed by the king Śivadeva, himself assimilated to a Bhairava of Assam, has been able to integrate this supreme god of the Kāpālika adepts of the Soma doctrine *(somasiddhānta).* In the final analysis, the ease with which the image of the Brahmanical sacrificer merges with that of the Tantric adept, obliges us to ask whether Vedic religion was not founded from the beginning on such esoteric practices aiming at the expansion of the fire of consciousness. Abhinava repeatedly internalizes the Vedic "fire-sacrifice" *(agnihotra)* as the external paradigm for the techniques of maintaining an intensified Consciousness such as those employed in the *kulayāga.*[31] The Brahmin householder had to offer oblations of "semen" in the form of milk and clarified butter into the sacrificial fire *(āhavanīya)* mornings and evenings to nourish the gods. In Chāndogya Upaniṣad V.19–24, it is already internalized as an offering to the Self as the universal Fire *(vaiśvānara).* In the transgressive context of the *kulayāga,* this universalization assumes the form of the all-devouring Bhairava-consciousness to which Abhinava attributes his highest spiritual realization.

> Once it has been sufficiently kindled, Fire, instead of being snuffed out, purifies in the very process of consuming whatever impurities it comes into contact with. Whereas only pure offerings are made in the brahminical sacrificial fire, the Trika technique of *haṭhapāka* "cooking, burning or digesting (the world) by force" aims at offering the entire objective universe into the blazing gastric Fire of one's own Bhairava-Consciousness so that it is transformed into undifferentiated ambrosia to be relished till satiation. In the *vidūṣaka* [clown of the classical Indian theater], this totalization is symbolized by his gluttonous, all-devouring appetite, the dramatic transposition of the mythical Fire that in the Purāṇic cosmogonies destroys the world at the end of each cycle and whose imagery has been borrowed in the above technique. His rounded sweet-meats *(modaka)* likewise represent the Vedic *soma-amṛta* (ambrosia), which would seem to ultimately refer to the supremely blissful state—often induced by sexual techniques—of Consciousness, which moreover is believed in the Trika to have a rejuvenating influence on the psycho-physical system as a side-effect.[32]

In the Mahābhārata, the god Agni indeed assumes the form of a gluttonous Brahmin to consume the Khāṇḍava (= "sweetmeat") forest in the context of Arjuna-and-Kṛṣṇa's dalliance with the innumerable women of the harem. Lévi-Strauss has moreover demonstrated that, in Amerindian mythology, the all-devouring forest-fire, often ignited through the friction of two fire-sticks, is symbolically equated to incest.

The total immersion in the expansive sexual joy of the *kulayāga* is used as a vehicle for the universalization of Consciousness, and it is the symbolism of Fire that permits the merging of these two levels of experience. If the Vedic motifs and patterns lend themselves so easily to their subsequent Tantric exploitation to communicate an inner lived experience, it is not at all unreasonable to suppose that the Brahmanical sacrifice—though elaborated to satisfy other, primarily socio-cosmic, concerns—was from the beginning rooted in such an experience. In such a context, unity would have referred not so much to the abolition of all difference between the sacrificer and a personal god or a metaphysical Absolute, but rather to the totalization of the sacrificer's self or "vital breath" *(ātman)* through a realization of its symbolic correspondences with a mythico-ritual universe. A systematic analysis of the content, structure and organization of these enigmatic correspondences could well reveal this universe to be already the coded projection and hypostatization *(brahman)* of a unified state of consciousness proper to the Vedic "shaman" *(ṛṣi)*. This is indeed implied in Abhinavagupta's "etymology" (*Tantrāloka* 29.164–66) of the "primordial" sacrifice *(ādiyāga)* as not only conferring the "essence" of the sacrifice but as constituting the "original" *(ādi)* sacrifice. The original meaning of *brahman,* now identified with *kula,* was (ritual) enigma and resolving the enigma was universally equated with committing an incest. Of course, Tantric and Vedic ritual are worlds apart, but Abhinava insists (*Tantrāloka* 29.5–9) that the *kulayāga* does not require the outer paraphernalia like the sacrificial circle *(maṇḍala),* fire-pit *(kuṇḍa),* purificatory gestures *(nyāsa),* baths, etc., though one may opt to include them at will. In fact, the sacrifice may resort to six different supports: (1) the external world, (2) a woman *(śakti),* (3) the body, (4) union between a couple *(yāmala),* (5) the flow of breath (in the median channel), and finally (6) thought itself. According to Abhinavagupta, (the essence of) the *kulayāga* belongs to the adept freed from all doubts, who sees the whole universe as Kula (*Tantrāloka* 29.5–6), that is, as constituted of the union of Śiva and Śakti (Jayaratha's commentary), just as the Vedic ritual saw the whole (sacrificial) universe in terms of the mithuna of pairs of objects. The *kulayāga* is whatever the Tantric "hero" does—mentally, verbally, and physically—in order to establish himself permanently in such a mode of Consciousness, for this sacrifice is ultimately nothing but "knowledge and the knowable." Transgressive sexual union may have been the indispensable external setting wherein all the above modes and faculties were once effectively integrated, but the ultimate realization of Unity procured by the original sacrifice could just as well become the normal condition of humanity with no other material supports than the body and consciousness itself.

11

Union and Unity in the Kabbala

Charles Mopsik
(translated from the French by Sunthar Visuvalingam)

The Proclamation of the Divine Unity and the Male/Female Couple

It would be difficult to find anything more conclusive than the oft-repeated Jewish declaration of faith, the proclamation of the divine unity: "Hear Israel, YHVH our God, YHVH is one" (Deuteronomy 6.4). The latter, according to the kabbalists, relates to the union of masculine and feminine entities. It is man's duty to realize this union for, according to the Jewish esotericists, the role of man is to perfect the divine unity through his action whose theurgic bearing is constantly underlined. Unlike a magician who operates from a distance and thus acts from without, man functions here quite evidently as a mediator within the very heart of the divine world. Through the ritual or the appropriate words, it is ultimately God himself who realizes his own unity in the human act of unification. In man and through his mediation, God performs the rite of his own unification. Man is thus not invested with a power over a God who would be external to him. It is because the divine passes through him, because he is a phase of emanation or stage of existence, that he is capable of acting as God, of consolidating his unity, in reuniting the male and female poles. Some illustrations will suffice to give an idea of the meaning of this union according to the kabbalists. The first is a text of R. Moses de Léon, Castilian theologian of the thirteenth century, to whom we owe at least a part of the literature of the Zohar: "The secret of the Shema Israel: the Bride returns to her Bridegroom in order that they unite in a real unity."[1]

It is interesting to note that numerous kabbalists, including R. Moses de Léon (and the Zohar), have detailed the *kavanot,* intentions that must be kept in mind while enunciating the *Shema;* these have the aim of affirming the unity that underlies the totality of the ten *sefirot* which, as R. Isaac of Acco explains, "are all united in the En Sof (the Infinite)."[2] But it is clear that this unity of the *sefirot* can be epitomized in the union of masculine and feminine. R. Joseph of Hamadan clearly equates the divine unity with the reunion of the male and female poles:

> For this reason we are in exile: because the holy King is not embracing the Queen, being in a back-to-back position. When the House of the sanctuary was standing, when the holy King and the Queen were embracing face to face, their face was turned towards the West, because the body of the holy King was united to the Queen. That is why R. Eliezer says: When the Temple was standing, the Holy One, blessed be his name, was One; now, it may be said, at the present time, he is not One, as it is said: "YHVH will be king over the whole earth, on that day YHVH will be one and his name one" (Zachariah 14.9). See how many secrets of secrets are hidden in this verse, for the sacred Body is called YHVH, whereas the Small Face, the Queen, bears the name of Lord (Adonay). If the sacred Body has its face turned towards the East and shows the back to the Queen, the "moon" suffers damage, that is why it is written "will be" [one] in the future, when the face of each will turn towards the other and the sacred Body will unite with the Queen, glorifying and uniting in the splendor of the Queen like a flame in the embers, he will be One, as it is written: "Hear Israel, YHVH is our God, YHVH is One" (Deut. 6.4). Blessed be the name of the glory of his royalty forever.[3]

The evocation of the words of R. Eliezer refers to the Midrash on Lamentations 3 *in fine,* where it is written: "R. Eliezer says: When then will the name of those be eliminated from the world, and when will astrolatry and its worshippers be eradicated from the world and the Holy blessed-be-he be unique in the world? Thus it is written: 'YHVH will be king over the whole earth and his name one' (Zacchariah 14.9)." The divine unity is conceived as the union of the King and the Queen, but this union is not a nontemporal constant, for it is related to history.

The cause of Israel's exile is none other than the back-to-back position or disunity of the male and female aspects of the divine. In the same way, the eschatological vision of the Redemption depends on the suprahistorical event of the reunion of these masculine and feminine dimensions when they turn to face each other again. In the Indian domain, it is never a question of a collective, and even less national, utility of the acts of unification realized by the mystics.

The place, both terrestrial and celestial, where this union was accomplished was the Temple of Jerusalem, in which the embrace of the cherubim signified both the union of Israel and its God and the union within the God's divinity of the male and female aspects. The Talmudic story which underlies this conception is found in Yoma 54b: "When the Israelites accomplished the pilgrimage, [the priests] withdrew the curtain and showed them the cherubim embracing each other. They told them: See, your love before God is like the love of the male and the female." In another passage of the Talmud (Baba Bathra 99a), the position of the cherubim with regard to each other depends on the conduct of Israel: their faces are turned towards each other if Israel accomplishes the will of God; otherwise their heads are turned away. These old stories are the framework on which R. Joseph of Hamadan embroiders his theosophical and hiero-historical canvas. While this kabbalist is apparently not troubled by making the unity of God historically relative, conceiving it as related to human becoming at the risk of seriously endangering his transcendence, other kabbalists—very few it is true—have adopted a more prudent procedure. Thus, the author of the *Tikkunei ha-Zohar* carefully distinguishes what he calls the "associative (relational) one" from the "one without a second":

> As to the Cause beyond all causes, there is no second to which it could refer, it is unique, anterior to all, without associate. It is with regard to it that it is written: "See now that I am he, and that there is no Elohim with me" (Deut. 32:39), from whom he may take counsel, having neither second nor associate, not entering into the numerical series. There exists a "one" which is associative like the male and the female, of which it is said: "For he called them one" (Isaiah 51:2). Whereas He is one beyond number, without associate[4].

This work takes over an expression of philosophical origin, the "Cause of all causes," in order to designate the *Ein-Sof* as the transcendental God, as opposed to the associative one of the male and the female which characterizes the unity of the *sefirot* standing in couples. Beyond the sefirotic world, which for our author is the realm of the divinity's action, is found the One without a second, which is not constituted by the union of two entities, masculine and feminine. This is of a wholly different kind. In a passage of this work preserved in the *Tikkunim Hadashim,* the Shekhinah is described as that through which all the *sefirot,* and even the Cause of all causes, may be known:

> Intelligent ones *(maskilim)* are those who have the intelligence which allows them to know the Master of the world, the Cause of all causes, from within the *Shekhinah.* . . . On the side of the ten *sefirot* she is a limit . . . but on the side of the Cause of all causes above which there is nothing, she has no limit nor boundary on that side, no power is above her nor outside of her, she has neither dimension nor measure. Moreover, on the side of the central Column she has an associate and a companion, like male and female, she is the *Dalet* and her associate is the *Aḥ* (brother), together they are *Ehad* (One), whereas on the side of the Cause of all causes she is One without association.[5]

For the author of these lines, the Shekhinah is the mirror in which the totality of the divine world shows through. In fact, she is identified in turn with each of the superior entities, including God in his transcendence. At this level she is neutral and loses all character of differentiation; not only is she no longer united with a masculine partner, but her femininity is totally dissolved. The "philosophical" option of the *Tikkunei ha-Zohar* obliges its author as it were to return to more common theological considerations. No doubt even other kabbalists had perceived the danger inherent in a conception of the One as a union of two—moreover, sexually differentiated—terms but, unlike the author of the *Tikkunei ha-Zohar,* they have chosen to maintain this interiority of the One haunted by the couple against wind and tide. A kabbalist like R. Moses de Léon, whose "dualistic" interpretation of the Shema we have just cited, forcefully affirms in the same work:

"God is one and unique, without any change . . . and although the *sefirot* are upright and straight mirrors, they are one without any separation."[6] The conjuration of dualism or of the "materializing" understanding of the entities of emanation is a common enough practice which is found in the introduction of numerous kabbalistic works, whose authors rid themselves in this way of anxiety and all scruples in order to go on and elaborate without hindrance their conception of the plural One. As this idea of the divine unity clashed starkly with so many theological prejudices, of which our kabbalists were perfectly aware, we are impressed with their courage in affirming their conceptions, going against the canons of their epoch as they did. A good example is that of the anonymous author of the book entitled precisely *Sefer ha-Yihud* (Book of Unity), written towards the end of the thirteenth century. His conception of the divine Unity and of its proclamation is presented in a very interesting manner. He declares that "the veritable Yihud is neither affirmative nor negative," meaning it is neither an apophatic nor a kataphatic theology, which would be capable of giving meaning to the divine unity. The signification of the latter "is very very profound and it is esoteric in the Torah: the veritable Yihud consists in knitting the One in such a way that no cut nor separation appears in the heart of man at the moment of uniting."[7]

It is not possible to translate the latter expression simply by the habitual "attestation of divine unity," as one would do in the context of the exoteric Yihud. For our kabbalist, the veritable Yihud, the esoteric Union, may be accomplished in three ways: through the study of the Book, through the observance of the commandments and finally through the ritual reading of the Shema morning and evening. The three modalities are detailed as follows. Study consists in joining the written Torah to the oral Torah—the Bible with its traditional commentary—and these two Torahs are a reflection *(dugma)* of the Double-Face. The written Torah reflects the masculine face, the *sefirah Tiferet,* whereas the oral Torah reflects the feminine face, the *sefirah Malkhut:* "The one has need of the other and the form of the two is Man."[8] Thus he "who studies the two Torahs by uniting them together makes them Two Faces,"[9] constituting the sefirotic structure in the image of the Man on high. The accomplishment of the commandments consists likewise in reuniting *Tiferet* and *Malkhut,* and our author illustrates his propositions by explaining the theosophical significance and the theurgic function of wearing the *tefilin.* Finally, the third form of the Yihud is the classic reading of the Shema, which aims at uniting the "two cherubim," *Tiferet* and *Malkhut.*

It seems that the order in which the explanation of the three varieties of Yihud is given indicates an order of preference or of value: the Yihud "realized" through study is first in importance whereas that which is effectuated through the ritual prayer occupies the last place. In every case it has of course to do with the same Yihud, of the same union of masculine and feminine dimensions through three different means. But as the kabbalists say, it is in the "heart of the man" who undertakes what must be called a unification that the latter manifests. This idea is comparable to that of the esoteric *tawhīd* in Sufi and Ismailian Islam, which Henri Corbin describes in opposition to the exoteric *tawhīd:* "The theological *tawhīd* poses and presupposes God as being ever and already in being, *Ens supremum.* Now, the word *tawhīd* is a causative; it means to make one, to cause to become one, to unify."[10]

In fact, in Hebrew also, the word *yihud* is a causative. The clearly theurgic meaning attributed to it by the kabbalists should not make us forget what the anonymous author of the *Sefer ha-Yihud* recalls from the beginning: the success of the act of unification through which the one comes into being depends on the unity of its emanations realized in the "heart of man." As attested by the following examples, it is not the position of "retreat" of the author of the *Tikkunei ha-Zohar* which subsequently prevailed. R. Moses Cordovero, who elaborates a detailed commentary on the recitation of the Shema, summarizes the meaning upon which the worshipper must meditate as he enunciates the word "One": "The *Malkhut* unites with *Tiferet*."[11] R. Mattathias Delacrout, a Polish kabbalist of the sixteenth century, affirms in the same vein: "The reading of the Shema relates to the secret of the union [effectuated] with the mouth and the concentration of the heart, for one reunites the young Bride with the young Groom, as also his best men, by saying: 'YHVH our God, YHVH is one.' "[12] A Moroccan kabbalist of the sixteenth century, R. Joseph Ibn Teboul, who was one of the disciples of R. Isaac Louria, further specifies: "Such is the secret of the unification of the Shema Israel: unite the Bridegroom and the Bride. . . . [W]hen one unites them, the Bridegroom gives the consecrations *(qiddushin)* to the Bride. . . . This is indeed 'sanctifying the Name': consecrate [in marriage] the *Malkhut* called 'name.' "[13]

Still among the successors of Isaac Luria must be mentioned R. Israel Saroug who describes at length the accompanying procedure of the recitation of the Shema with diverse meditations which begin in this way:

> Secret of the Union of the recitation of the Shema: first one must meditate in order to ready the *Zaïr Anpin* (the Male) and his Female, to adorn her so as to raise them higher so that they are the coupling feminine waters Father and Mother, by devoting our soul to the sanctification of the Name when we meditate on the One . . . In this way: by [pronouncing] the word "Hear" the name of seventy [letters] must be meditated upon; explanation: the *Malkhut* is a point and we construct it as the secret of a configuration . . . by [pronouncing] the word One, the rising of the *Zaïr Anpin* and of his Female, who have been adorned at the same time that we devote our soul to the sanctification of the Name, must be meditated upon . . . and when they mount they become the feminine waters for the coupling

> of the Father and the Mother. This coupling consists in meditating on the embrace of YHVH and of "I will be."[14] (Commentary attributed to R. Israel Saroug, published in *Tefillah le-Moshe,* commentary on the prayer of R. Moses Cordovero, Prezmysl, 1891, 69b–70a, 70b).

In the Lurianic doctrine, the "feminine waters" designate the action exercised by a lower level on a higher level. Through uniting and preparing *Tiferet* and *Malkhut* (the Male and the Female), we allow them to rise and rejoin *Hokhmah* and *Binah* (Father and Mother), and thereby to contribute to their coupling. The recitation of the Shema acts in view of the union not only of the inferior sefirotic couple constituted by *Tiferet* and *Malkhut,* but also in order to conjoin *Hokhmah* and *Binah,* at the summit of the sefirotic structure. It is thus not a question of attesting the divine Unity, but of contributing thereto by uniting through the rite its male and female components.

The Ancient Sources

This esoteric conception of the divine unity is not an invention of R. Moses de Leon and it comes from earlier sources. In an ancient tradition reported by R. Eleazer of Worms, which Moshe Idel cites and analyzes in his *Kabbalah: New Perspectives,*[15] the Creator and the Shekhinah are depicted as husband and wife, and the prayers of Israel are perceived as means for raising this Shekhinah to its divine husband. It may be supposed that a similar goal was attributed to the proclamation of the Unity. Besides, an author contemporary to the first kabbalists but who had no relations with them, R. Elhanan ben Yakar of London, also conceives the divine unity as the union of two entities, as he indicates in his commentary on the creation of the world:

> After the completion of the whole work of creation, when the day of Sabbath came, the Breath of the living God placed his Shekhinah on the Glory, then the Breath and the Glory united together, and they did not separate so that YHVH could be One, as the body and the soul of life [are united] in man, then the two names YHVH and Elohim found their harmony, when the whole work was finished with the consecration of the day of Sabbath.[16]

In order to understand this passage correctly, it must first be considered as an exegesis of Genesis 2.4, where for the first time in the narrative God is designated by two juxtaposed names, YHVH

Elohim—a peculiarity that has since long attracted the attention of rabbinical commentators. The latter observe that this double denomination intervenes during the announcement of the completion of creation: "Elohim blessed the seventh day and sanctified it, for therein he rested from all the work that Elohim had created by making it; such was the genesis of heaven and earth when they were created, on the day when YHVH Elohim made the earth and heaven" (Gen. 2.3–4). Thus in the midrash Genesis Rabbah, an anonymous master comments: "He mentions a complete Name with regard to a complete world" (13.3). Now each of these names corresponds, according to the ancient tradition (see already Genesis Rabbah 12.15), to a divine attribute: YHVH corresponds to the attribute of Mercy *(midat ha-rahamim),* Elohim to the attribute of Judgement *(midat ha-din).* The mention of these two linked names in the verse thus signifies the union of two divine aspects in a kind of *coincidentia oppositorum.* The divinity manifests itself in its plenitude when the creative action comes to an end and the sabbath begins. In the text cited earlier of R. Elhanan, these names designate two degrees of manifestation called Breath of the living God and Glory. When their union is realized, "YHVH is one." The divine unity is a union of two of these powers—in this case the divine Breath and the Glory.

But no explicit mention is made of the masculine and feminine dimensions, even if it may always be considered that since the divine names YHVH and Elohim refer to two attributes, they are for this very reason capable of being apprehended as masculine and feminine principles. A grammatical element can confirm this supposition. The Hebrew verb translated as "found their harmony" in the phrase, "The two names YHVH and Elohim found their harmony," is *nit'omemyu.* This verb is formed from the substantive *te'om,* which signifies "twin." The meaning of the proposition cited earlier is that these two divine names become united like twins. A couple formed by twins connotes the figure of the ideal male-female couple in rabbinical literature. In this way the expression "my perfect" *(tamati)* in the Song of Songs, which qualifies the beloved woman should be read *"teyumati,"* that is, "my twin," according to the midrash Cantique Rabbah (5.2). Each of the children of Jacob had his own twin for a companion, according to *Pirkei of Rabbi Eliezer* (chap. 36).

The text of R. Elhanan ben Yakar may be compared to an interesting development which we owe to the kabbalist Joseph Gikatila (thirteenth century), who writes, after having cited the sentence of Genesis Rabbah:

> When the work of the commencement was finished, [the Scripture] begins to mention YHVH Elohim with regard to the plenitude of the world. Know and believe that the secret of the [divine] Unity in its entirety is the secret of YHVH Elohim, and the sign thereof is: "Hear Israel YHVH our God, YHVH is one" (Deut. 6.4). It is in this way that you should know that wherever you find in the Torah YHVH Elohim, which is the complete Name, all things found in the [biblical] section where YHVH Elohim is mentioned, have been accomplished by all the attributes in their totality, by the attribute of judgment and the attribute of mercy . . . everything in full perfection, with mercy and judgment . . . As a function of this principle the Torah has said: "The Rock, perfect is its action" (Deut. 32.4), of which the explanation is: the Rock which decrees the verdict does not act with violence, does not decide the sentence with cruelty, but "perfect is its action," for the word "perfect" *(tamim)* is the secret of two things, it is as if he had said: "twins" *(teumim),* but it is a polite way of saying for two things on high the expression *tamim* (perfect) and for two things below the expression *teumim* (twins) . . . below twins, on high perfect, because below they appear as two things, a thing and its contrary, as the advocate and the prosecutor, but on high everything is in a single direction, the advocate and the prosecutor have the same finality.[17]

The divine unity is presented as the union of its two attributes, perceived as contrary poles forming a couple of twins which constitute "on high" a perfect unity and which coincide and converge despite their apparent opposition in the lower world. The two attributes, which are also two divine names, are manifested for the first time in their plenitude at the close of the narrative of creation. It is their reunion which is the object of the ritual recitation of the Shema. The divine bi-unity is seen through the two opposed attributes which coincide in God himself, and this representation, which depends on very ancient Jewish conceptions, forms a general framework where the motif of the divine unity conceived as the union of masculine and feminine dimensions fits in quite naturally. In fact, the conception of the unity of the male and female principles must not be seen as a late kabbalistic elaboration from the couple of the divine attributes; on the contrary, the motif of the union of attributes merely translates a substratum of primitive thought into a more theological language. As

Mircea Eliade says, "all the attributes coexist in the divinity, and one should expect to see, in a more or less manifest form, that the two sexes likewise coincide therein. The divine androgyny is none other than the archaic formula of the divine bi-unity: mythical and religious thought, even before expressing this concept of divine bi-unity in metaphysical *(esse—non esse)* or theological (manifested—nonmanifested) terms, has begun to express it in biological terms (bisexuality)." In the hands of the kabbalists, the rabbinical and other theological material will regress to the primordial, symbolical stage; the more abstract constructions will be reduced to the first degree of religious thought. This operation is all the more surprising in that it integrates notions taken over from philosophy—albeit from a Neoplatonism that is already disposed to this return to mythical roots.

The first properly kabbalistic explanation of the reading of the Shema has been transmitted to us by R. Acher ben Saul of Lunel, a Provençal rabbi of the twelfth century, in his *Sefer ha-Minhagot:* "One recites the Shema Israel. Explanation: each of the Israelites says to himself and his neighbor: Accept that 'YHVH our God,' who is the glory resting on the cherubim, 'YHVH is one,' it is the supreme Crown. . . . Some say that this refers to the *Tiferet Israel,* therein is a great secret."[19]

It is clear that it is the recognition of the unity of two entities which is considered to be the aim and the significance of the proclamation of the Shema. It is not impossible that the "glory resting on the cherubim" here designates a feminine entity, whereas the Crown—or more surely *Tiferet*—refers to a masculine dimension.

The proclamation of the Shema is followed by a formula which must be enunciated in a low voice. An *aggadah* of the Talmud (Pessahim 56a) has been interpreted by the kabbalists as expressing the sorrow of the Shekhinah: she saw that the Israelites proclaimed the unity of the Bridegroom and mentioned her only in an allusive manner, that is through the letter *Dalet* of the word *Ehad* (One)—a letter signifying, moreover, "indigence." The version given by R. Isaac ben Jacob Hacohen is perhaps the oldest. But there exist numerous more or less similar versions in the same tradition: R. Josua Ibn Chouaib[20] and R. Isaac d'Acco[21] have taken up and reworked the story of the episode; the same is true with Rabbenu Behaye, whose analysis is worth examining:

> Because Moses has not explicitly evoked the dimension of the *Malkhut,* and although allusion is made to her in the letter *Dalet,* [the sages] have told a strong parable: "A daughter of the king sniffed the odor of a spicy dish. If she declared this it would be a shame on her, if she did not say it she would suffer

> for it. What did her servants do? They brought it to her discreetly *(behachaï)*" (Pessahim 56a). . . . Clarification of the parable: the daughter of the king who sniffed the spicy dish is the Shekhinah which feels the praise of the tribes and the unity they proclaim of the great Name, if she had pronounced through her mouth the following praise: just as He is unique, She also is unique, that would have been shameful for her; if she had not said it, She would have suffered when Her own glory would not have been united to His own Glory, it is in this way that the Israelites who are the servants of the Shekhinah came to say "Blessed is the name of the glory of his royalty" discreetly, which is the lower unity.[22]

The first part of the formulation of the Unity pronounced aloud corresponds to the union on high, that of the upper *sefirot,* the second part said in a low voice (except on Yom Kippur) corresponds to the lower union, where the feminine dimension is evoked in full. These examples attest that the divine Unity has been apprehended as the plenitude of the union of at least two entities, of which one is masculine, the other feminine.

Copulation as a Mystical Experience

We have devoted a separate study to this important question in relation to a brief epistle which we owe to the Spanish Kabbala of the thirteenth century, the *Lettre sur la sainteté,* which partly deals with rites of union and procreation. One of the first kabbalists, R. Yehuda ben Yakar, who composed a vast commentary on prayer and benedictions, already gives conjugal copulation the status of a symbolic imitation of the relation between the divine Bridegroom and the Community of Israel. He mentions this with regard to the benediction to be recited before coitus—a ritual coitus—a practice described in the book *Halakhot G'dolot* (at the beginning of "The rules on the marriage contracts"), but fallen into disuse and rejected by a majority of ruling authorities. Here is a version of the text in question:

> There are newlyweds who say the following benediction before coitus: "[Blessed art thou Lord our God, king of the world], who has planted a walnut-tree in the garden of Eden," as a function [of the verse] "I have descended into the garden of the walnut-tree" (Song of Songs 6.11), said by the Holy One, blessed-be-he, the Bridegroom, to Israel, the Bride, and for many reasons the new bride has been compared to the walnut-tree.[23]

This first trace of the importance given by kabbalists to coupling as a ritual act is indicative of their perception of its symbolic significance. Many writings go into great detail on this question; we will only partially cite here a piece that is particularly rich and exhaustive in order to demonstrate how kabbalistic conceptions of the sexual union on high were transformed into meditational motifs which were to be dwelt upon during sexual intercourse. In the text we are about to read—from a work of Rabbi Moses Cordovero (1522–1570)—the bodies of the partners, down to each limb and organ, represent a parallel structure constituting the different attributes of the divine world of emanation:

> On the subject of the meditation in the course of the [sexual] act, it should be known that the male comprises 248 organs, so too in [the *sefirah*] *Tiferet* is the secret of the 248 organs on high. They comprise the first three *[sefirot]* at the level of the head, and as many aspects *(behinot)* as the number of organs. The same at the level of the arms, [which represent the *sefirot*] *Hessed* and *Gevurah* and as many aspects as the number of organs. And in the trunk: *Tiferet* and as many aspects as the number of organs. So too in [the *sefirot*] *Netsah, Hod, Yessod* [which correspond] to the sides, to the foundation [i.e., the penis] and to the feet, in which the organs are as many aspects. This is the case likewise of the secret of the female: she has 248 organs. . . . When the male and the female below conjoin, they meditate on the liaison and the union of the Male and the Female on high: 248 [organs] joined to 248 [organs], as really the attachment of flesh to flesh. One will thus meditate on the secret of the superior union. Here is its mystery and the meditation required with regard to it: first one will wash one's hands at midnight or during the hours that follow and will purify one's consciousness and void the spirit of all evil thought; one could also meditate on the repenting of one's faults and prolong one's prayer according to one's force. Then [the man] will gladden his wife with speech relating to the commitment [of sexual union], at the same time he will bring his awareness closer to the sacred. He will conduct his meditation to the best, according to his force. Then he will undertake to meditate on the secret of the embrace: he is at the level of [the *sefirah*] *Tiferet,* she is at the level of [the *selfirah*] *Malkhut;* the man will thus embrace the head of the woman with his left arm which he will place beneath, meditating on the mystery of

the *[sefirah] Gevurah* taking hold of the *[sefirah] Malkhut,* in the joyful mode in view of coupling and not in the mode of rigor *(din).* Then with his right he will embrace the head from above, in order to include love in the right and the left. After which he will meditate on the union of the four faces, the two faces [of the face] of the female with the two faces [of the face] of the male, which are the four letters [of the divine name] YHVH. The four arms are the four wings which are the name *Adonay* [Lord] and allude to the union *(yihud)* of the name YAHDONHY [the letters YHVH interlaced with the letters ADONY]. He will bear in mind that the secret of the head against the head [implies] that the first three *sefirot* which are in him [unite] with the first three *sefirot* which are in her [*Keter, Hokhmah, Binah* of the Male reunite with their homologue in the Female]. He will think that the arms, which are the *[sefirot] Hessed* and *Gevurah* which are in him [unite with the *sefirot*] *Hessed* and *Gevurah* [that is, the arms] which are in her. He [will then be aware] that body in body, that is to say the six extremities [the six lower *sefirot* which are in him rejoin] the six extremities [which are in her], that the two thighs, i.e. [the *sefirot*] *Netsah* and *Hod,* the penis, i.e. [the *sefirah*] *Yessod,* [rejoin] the two thighs which are in her. The secret of the Alliance is [the letter] *Yod* which links the secret of [the letter] *Dalet* (d) [to the word] *Ehad* (One), that is to say of the Brother *(aḥ)* with the Sister *(ahot),* which gives *Ehad* (One), and the trunk of the *Yod* found in [the letter] *Dalet* links the Brother *(aḥ)*—the nine upper *sefirot*—to [the *sefirah*] *Malkhut* [the Sister]. It is in this way that the man will cause *Yessod* to penetrate into the heart of the domain of *Dalet,* in order to complete it, for [the woman] does not possess the sign of the alliance. The male completes her and this member is half included in her and half included in him: male and female unite in such a manner that in the *Shiur Koma* which is in him there are ten *[sefirot]* and in that which is in her there are ten. This is the secret of: "Ten, ten, the bowl, following the *shekel* of the sanctuary" (Num. 7.86). The ten belonging to her are oriented from below upwards in the field of the reparation *(tikkun)* of the body, and the ten belonging to him are orientated from on high downwards in the field of the reparation of the body. He will meditate, during the seven kisses, on the secret of the union of the breaths, which constitute the interiority of the *sefirot.* . . . The seven kisses are the seven *sefirot* which link and unite to the first three *[sefirot],* for they form the mouth of the head, i.e. the *[sefirah] Malkhut,* which is in the first three *[sefirot].* Then he will meditate on the union of the eyes and the nose, those of one in those of the other. In his movement [of penetration] the man will meditate on the secret of the phase during which the *[sefirah] Yessod* gathers the semen and the light from the *[sefirah] Hokhmah* on high, it is on the latter that he will meditate with all his awareness in order that the *Hokhmah* sheds itself from the brain of the *Arikh [Anpin]* to the brain of the *Zeir [Anpin],* and from there towards the *[sefirah] Binah,* in accordance with the secret of the head ornaments, and from there, through the central column [the *sefirah Tiferet*], towards the two eggs of the male [the *sefirot Netsah* and *Hod*], which cook and prepare [the luminous semen] then give it to [the *sefirah*] *Yessod,* through which it passes and emerges from the secret of the Yod of the [divine] Name, the *[sefirah Hokhmah]* being the *Yod* of the name YHVH, in the direction of the *Yod* of the name *Adonay,* which is a drop including the ten *[sefirot].* This happens at the moment of the donation of the drop coming from him to her, namely: "a tenth part of an ephah of fine flour" (Lev. 5.11), without any waste, and it is "kneaded in oil" (Lev. 2.5) in conformity with the secret of the "crushing" (Ex. 29.40 etc.) effectuated by the *Yessod,* as we have explained in regard to the movement [of penetration]. Then [the drop] is shed in the *[sefirah] Malkhut.*[24]

The first part of the text poses a general principle: the totality of the organs of the human body, numbered at 248 by the old aggadic tradition, corresponds, in detail, to the components of the structure of the divinity. Two *sefirot, Tiferet* and *Malkhut,* are considered to be containing in themselves the totality of the *sefirot.* The couple formed by them encompasses the rest of the *sefirot* as if the latter were only parts within a whole comprising two poles, one of them corresponding to the masculine partner of the human couple, the other to the feminine partner. Each member of the body of one or the other corresponds to a sefirotic element present in the *sefirah Tiferet* (for the male) and in the *sefirah Malkhut* (for the female). The reunion of each particular organ with its homologue in the partner's body during sexual union theurgically assures the reunion of their superior parallels. The conjugal relation follows a progression in the course of which the union becomes more and more complete, in close correspondence with the hierarchy of the union between the diverse divine members composing the *sefirot Tiferet* and *Malkhut.* The body of the man and that of the woman are explicitly considered to be like a *Shiur Koma,* ancient expression deriving from the mysticism of the Palaces (first centuries of the Common Era), where it designated the measure of the stature of the divine body (or of the divine glory). The structure of the body of the man is the same as the structure of the *sefirah Tiferet,* similarly for the body of the woman with regard to the *sefirah Malkhut.* The right arm, to take an example, corresponds to the *sefirah Hessed* (goodness), *sefirah* which is here only an element, an organ of the *sefirah Tiferet,* taken as an entire sefirotic system: a *Shiur Koma.* It is the same with the members of the woman with respect to the *sefirah Malkhut,* which is here likewise a complete sefirotic structure, except for a spiritual organ: the *sefirah Yessod,* which corresponds to the penis. The latter is lacking in the feminine *Shiur Koma:* the sexual relation aims at fulfilling this lack. The penis engaged in the vagina is partly in the man, partly in the woman. The same is true of the *Yessod* at the higher level, partly in *Tiferet,* partly in *Malkhut.* In this way, conjugal union is a way of sharing the phallus. A good part of the text is devoted to the meditations that the partners ought engage during the amorous sports: each corporeal gesture should be imaginarily ascribed to the relations between the organs constituting the *sefirot.* The final act, ejaculation, symbolizes (in the strongest sense of the word) the passage of the seminal light, the divine influx, from the point of the *sefirah Yessod,* identified with the letter *Yod,* the Thought or *Hokhmah* on high, into the *sefirah Malkhut.* The tension which precedes the ejaculation should also be redacted or redirected to the initial passage of the spiritual semen from the brain of *Arikh Anpin,* or Long-Face (that is to say the *sefirah Keter*), to *Zeir Anpin,* the Small-Face (which corresponds, still following the terminology of the Zohar to which this text refers, to the *sefirah Tiferet*). More exactly, R. Moses Cordovero expressly indicates that it is the meditation accompanying sexual tension, which, when conducted in the correct order and brought into relation with the divine superior structures, brings about the shedding of seminal light—the influx of emanation—from the summit of the organism to its base, the *sefirah Malkhut.* The luminous drop shed in this way contains a particle of the spiritual substance issuing from the totality of the sefirotic body and holding within itself all the aspects of the divine being. The same applies to the seed of the parents, which is their concentrated essence.

It goes without saying that a part of the process of spermatogenesis described here depends on the conceptions of antique medicine.

But it is difficult to escape from the feeling of déjà vu when this text is compared to certain Tantric writings, in particular those transcribed and commented upon by Mircea Eliade.[25] Of course, the cultural and ethical horizon is extremely different, but very many structural homologies remain intriguing. It is not within our intentions here to try and interpret them, but it was necessary at least to point them out.

It seems to me that the most significant difference between the Tantric and the kabbalistic orientations of sexual union is in the direction given to the movement of the semen. In both traditions, the semen constitutes a luminous energy, or more precisely, in the words of Tara Michael, "the semen *(bindu)* produced in the genital organs, at the level of the *mūlādhāra-cakra,* is only a gross materialized form of the causal *bindu* or creative energy present in the superior centers of the head."[26] For the kabbalists, however, the aim is to concentrate this semen from the brain and all the organs of the body in order to propel it with the greatest force and determination towards the female partner, so as realize a perfect union, which would be the active symbol of the union of the male and female *sefirot* (*Tiferet* and *Malkhut*). For the Hindu Tantrics, on the contrary,

> the aim is to reduce this gross form of semen to its original subtle form, to reconvert it into nectar, by drawing it in the ascending movement towards the summit of the skull, which is represented by the path of re-ascent, the *suṣamnā.* If the *yogin* has not been able, through the *khecarī-mudrā,* to immobilize the virile energy at the highest level. In the cerebral centers, he must be capable of making this accumulated energy in the form of semen re-ascend through the *vajrolī-mudrā.* . . . Even if he is married or unites ritually with a companion in the Tantric way, the *yogin* must never let his semen escape. "The fall of the sperm is death; life is the retention of sperm" (Śiva-Saṃhitā, IV, 88).[27]

Hence the application of a special practice, called *vajrolī-mudrā,* which permits the reabsorption by the penis of the sperm which has been allowed to escape.

The fusion of the masculine and feminine essence must be achieved within the body of the *yogin* and not outside, in the female womb, and "through this conjunction of opposed elements is accomplished the task of yoga which is the neutralization of the web of dualities."[28] Instead of the tension of corporeal and spiritual energies of the kabbalist which are oriented by him towards procreation—not only physical procreation but also the procreation or the attraction of a sanctified soul—the Tantric sexual union aims, thanks to a self-mastery, at the reintegration "of the feminine principle in the masculine principle, a reintegration culminating in an experience of beatitude, of 'union without end,' which is unknown at the level of the senses."[29] No doubt, this radical difference in the orientation of the coupling depends on the differing worldviews. Not only with respect to the conception of the passage of time from which the *yogin* fundamentally seeks to liberate himself, whereas the kabbalist experiences time as a meaningfully oriented process, polarized by a redemptive end which is more or less near. But also with regard to their respective notions of accomplishment: for the Tantric, what is essential is the movement from below to above which permits the return to the initial state of nonseparation; for the kabbalist the essential consists in best assuring the descent of the superior light and its implantation in an inferior place such that the latter is only the receptacle necessary for the flow, within which the holy union is realized. This feminine receptacle is a vase of light, the power of reception which was never absolutely separated from the power of emission. Between the Masculine and the Feminine, there can be alienation, distance, dissociation, which can take on the traits of a separation or of an exile. But it is never a question of a substantial or ontological separation. However far the kabbalists may have gone in the affirmation of a fission in the One, of a disjunction between its structuring Masculine and the Feminine poles, never does this fission assume the form of an essential or substantial separation. It always concerns an internal exile, a divorce where the two terms move apart and are disjoined within a continuum which has its source beyond being and which is occupied and totally filled by a tension towards a redemptive future. It is this same tension which is the primary focus in the mystical ceremony of coupling described in the text of R. Moses Cordovero.

Nevertheless, Tantricism also proposes a conception of union which brings it closer in a way to the kabbalistic vision. When the plenitude of the yogic state is realized, when the breaths stirred into motion dissolve in the uncreated Source—the formless Absolute—the state of *samādhi* is achieved. The re-ascent of these subtle energies within the body of the *yogin* amounts to a re-ascent of the Śakti, the feminine power of Śiva: "Kuṇḍalinī Śakti is brought back to Śiva in the thousand-petalled lotus, the place of identity; the primordial Woman is reunited with the primordial Man, Power with Consciousness, the universe of duality is reabsorbed, and the original Unity is restored."[30] And to reproduce an ancient Hindu text: "This wife entering the royal path, resting at intervals in the sacred sites, embraces the supreme

Husband and releases the flow of nectar" flooding the microcosm, the body of the *yogin*.[31] The exercises of Tantric yoga seek to imitate the model of the integral union of the god Śiva and his feminine power, called Śakti, somewhat in the manner in which, among the kabbalists, the conjugal union aims at imitating the superior model of the union of the *sefirot Tiferet* and *Malkhut*. However, the place and support of this union is in the former case the mystic's body itself, whereas in the latter case this place is the very *relation* itself and not the body or the mind of the man or of the woman, but their bonding, the in-between where they meet, a place that properly belongs neither to one nor to the other. Neither matter nor substance, but where both find their original unity which is also their final unity, not a unity of reabsorption, but a unity of expansion, the result of the inner tension towards exteriority which is metamorphosed into a supplement, into an increase of interiority. A triumphant interiority which brings about the revelation or the turning back of exteriority, which manifests its pre-ontological proximity. One feature specific to the Kabbala is to consider the feminine receptacle as already united in advance with the emitting masculine organ, for the one is destined for the other through a bond—the *qiddushin* or marital sacraments—which transmutes exteriority by realizing the exclusivity of the consecration of a wife. It is thus wholly essential, for the kabbalist, that the mystical rites of coupling be accomplished by a legitimate couple (who are besides not necessarily a legal couple though they tend to be taken as such), for it is the condition sine qua non for the emergence of the place of union, a place which transcends the body and the soul of either and which is situated at their point of intersection: their own private beyond, an extremity bordering on a nonexistent through which is established and passes a certain flux issuing from the Infinite.

For Cordovero, if the totality of the commandments of the Torah refer to the union of the *sefirot*, only human coupling, the first prescription enunciated in Genesis, is its perfect symbol.[32] For this reason, ritual meditations are attached to it, which render life and physical love sacred. However, these spiritual practices enter into the framework of ordinary conjugal relations, unlike the Tantric rituals, which are exceptional and extraconjugal. If the masculine and feminine *sefirot* are called Brother and Sister, they have that status because at the level of the divine world their union is not an incest; but there is no question of imitating the superior model at the human level, contrary to certain Tantric conceptions which recommend this during the sacred *mithuna*. Finally, for our kabbalist, in the case where a man finds himself without his wife, on the evening of the sabbath which is the most propitious moment for mating, "he must accomplish this union through speech."[33] In other words, he should enunciate the kabbalistic text which describes its modalities. Speech can thus substitute for the concrete sexual act, and even be its exact replica. This affirmation will serve us as a conclusion: even if it finds support in the physical reality of the conjugal act, the union is accomplished essentially at the symbolic level.

But it must never be forgotten that the kabbalists, though they belong to a small elite circle, only give a larger significance to the current practice accomplished by all in accordance with the religious prescriptions. They do not claim to inaugurate a new practice, but to provide the ultimate meaning or the fundamental truth of the ordinary rituals. The kabbalist is one who has understood the inner essence of the religious commandments; in general, he has not innovated in this regard. He has learnt to know the true and precise significance of the laws and their hidden meaning, thus giving a renewed force and a fullness, which is both more conscious and more determinate, to the practices which were already his own since his childhood.

We must also ask ourselves if, beyond the divergent verbal formulations, the meaning of unity and of the One has something in common in the two traditions. For the kabbalist, unity has its center in the history of his people and depends very largely on this history. It is a unity linked to a collective memory, whose cosmic significance is the result of the projection onto the external world of its subjective perception by a consciousness. Tantrism confronts us with the reverse of this process. Unity is first of all perceived as belonging to cosmic reality, and it is only subsequently interiorized by consciousness. It is without history in the true sense. It remains unrelated to any human drama lived through as the starting point of a collectivity and its norms. The carefully thought out conceptions of the kabbalists and the tantricists perhaps differ not so much in their intellectual options but in their modes of life and the specific directives imposed by the nature of their respective societies. It seems to me impossible, both in principle and in practice, to ignore or suspend the social and anthropological differences in order to somehow set free the concepts which could be compared. A religious concept is tied, like the skin to the flesh, to the concrete conditions of its expression. But this is not to say that their similarities are only a mirage. There is no universal logic of religion that would preside, beneath all the particular historical forms, over the development of systems of belief and of practice. There is a human fact, a human genetics, which gives all men a language, a body and identical physical needs. Starting from here, all kinds of religious elaborations and human responses may be discerned, classified and, of course, compared. The universality of a particular conception or response is only the product of the researcher's point of view and his own presuppositions. It is never an objective fact that may be discovered within the human nature being explored. Hence, there is no science of religions which is not first of all a science of inner consciousness, to begin with, that of the researcher himself. It is simply astounding that one's consciousness could interest one's neighbor and that the examination of one's modes of thought, when confronted with the conceptions of a religion under study, is capable of enriching parallel reflections and work. To compare is a constant endeavor of reflexive thought. Between systems of thought, there can only be a living dialogue of knowing subjects; it is never a matter of an entomologist comparing the wings of butterflies.

The principal aim of a study like this should be a kind of language of translation which would permit the passage from one conceptual idiom to another. In this, the comparative scholar is only the precursor of a dialogue—for which he would have prepared the vocabulary and assured the syntax—between the religious consciousness of interlocutors in search of a common language. On this score, a long way—whose stumbling blocks should not be minimized—remains to be travelled between Jerusalem and Benares. But already the approaches brought together in this volume and our own contribution reveal the possibility of a common trajectory that responds to human questions which are often the same despite the geographical distance and differing conditions of existence.

12

Rabbi Abraham Isaac Kook and Sri Aurobindo: Towards a Comparison

Margaret Chatterjee

There is a passage in Rabbi Kook's *Lights of Holiness*[1] which provides some encouragement for the exploration ventured in the following pages. Kook writes: "The doctrine of evolution that is presently gaining acceptance in the world has a greater affinity with the secret teachings of the Cabbalah than all other philosophies. . . . Existence is destined to reach a point when the whole will assimilate the good in all its constituted particulars . . . towards this objective one needs to be sensitized spiritually to seek God on a higher plane." Kook was a kabbalist of modern times (1865–1935) who was born in Latvia and later became Rabbi of Jaffa and then Chief Rabbi in Jerusalem.

He was influenced by Lurianic Kabbalah and Hasidism and also by modern thought. Evidence of the latter can be found in his analysis of the changed consciousness of modern man: a sense of the larger human society which extends beyond frontiers, the impact of scientific knowledge, and the idea of evolution as a concept not only applicable to the biological realm but to culture as a whole. He was familiar with Bergson's thought but disagreed with the notion of an undirected élan vital, believing as he did that the main thrust of the evolutionary impulse was man's yearning for God. From 1885 to 1895, he was Rabbi in the town of Zoimel and spent nights studying with Solomon Eliashov of Shavli, who was learned in the doctrine of emanation and through whom he became familiar with the views of Rabbi Elijah Gaon of Vilna. Another probable influence is that of the Hasidic mystic Shneur Zalman of Liadi, who founded the Lubavitch/Chabad tradition.[2] Rabbi Shneur Zalman presented Kabbalah in Hasidic dress. Most notably, he elucidated the concept of the *beinoni,* the average man, who although falling short of the heights attained by the *ẓaddik* could yet resist evil through enlisting his spiritual powers, and so rise to higher and higher degrees of perfection. In the Lithuanian Yeshivot of Kook's day, the *musar* culture of the Mitnaggedim still prevailed. Kook's thinking shares with this culture its moral fervor and its concern with discovering a form of education that would be in tune with both tradition and the needs of the times. He was able to put some of this into practice after he settled in Jerusalem, where he set up a Yeshivah known as Merkaz ha-Rav. Here he experimented with an integrated program of education in which mystic insight and practical activities were both encouraged. What was especially remarkable was the way in which he was able to combine a strong identification with the Zionist movement with a commitment to a universalistic horizon of human society, finding in nationality a necessary stage in the progress of man towards that horizon, but never losing sight of the ultimate goal.

Sri Aurobindo (1872–1950) was Kook's contemporary. Born in Calcutta, he had a brilliant career as a classics scholar at Cambridge. On his return to India, he took up Sanskrit studies in earnest and became proficient in them. It is worth noting that whereas Rabbi Kook had Hebrew as his mother tongue, indeed it was the very lifeblood of his thought, Aurobindo started to acquire Sanskrit only in his twenties, and always preferred to write in English. In 1902 he became engaged in extensive political work, including political writing. He became the principal of Bengal National College as soon as it opened. He met Bal Gangadhar Tilak but found his own sympathies were with the extremists and not with the moderates. The years 1907 and 1908 were critical for him. Arrested on the charge of sedition in 1907, he was acquitted only to be arrested again the following year. He had already succeeded in splitting the Congress Party by a speech he made at the Surat Session. On his release Sri Aurobindo moved to Pondicherry, then a French colony, and spent the rest of his life in the ashram he founded there, devoting his time to education, meditation, and a wide range of writings.

These are but the barest outlines of a life which successively combined scholarship, political activism, educational experimentation, and a rigorous spiritual ascesis. Sri Aurobindo could have echoed the following remark by Kook: "Ours is a wonderful generation. . . . It consists of opposites, darkness and light exist in confusion."[3] Like Kook, he was spurred on by the vision of a common goal for humanity, yet he had a deep local allegiance. Both men had faith that science could be used for the good of humanity in spite of its catastrophic potential.

This ties in with the relation that both had with their respective traditions. A section of the Hasidim held back from commitment to Zionism on the grounds that, since all things are in God's hands, the "end" cannot be hastened by human agency. The life of obedience to Divine law, waiting and listening, is enjoined at all times. A different kind of "determinism" had been "read off" from the karma theory by many Hindus. But both Kook and Sri Aurobindo discovered within their own traditions an activist strand which needed strengthening and which could become a lifeline for their own peoples. Both saw this as something quite distinct from secularist/materialist/atheist tendencies which were surfacing, especially among the young, in their respective societies. They were equally critical of these tendencies.

From the perspective of the comparative study of religion, Kook and Sri Aurobindo are linked by their confidence in a process of cosmic evolution believed to be taking place in nature, with the goal of divine perfection. This itself can be a theme for a more detailed study. Such a study would take into account how each develop the mystic strain in their respective traditions, while bearing in mind that the content of religious experience, whether mystic or otherwise, is itself shaped by tradition, including concepts and practices seen in a historical perspective.

I should now confess that I am encouraged to pursue the comparison of these two thinkers from entirely diverse cultural and religious backgrounds by an increasing interest in what I have myself termed "spiritual landscape," but whose configurations I have yet to properly determine.[4] The usual distinction between the inner side of religion, including, inter alia, beliefs, hopes and fears, and the outer side, dealing with observances, does not really take into account what I have in mind. The very phenomena of physical landscapes form a starting point—for example, the landscapes of Mount Sinai and of the Himalayas, the *dybukkim* of desert places, and all that is to be feared in the dense forests of Aryavarta. The unmistakeable topography of biblical literature or the Vedas is like a well-known terrain in which one can walk on familiar paths. The trees, the climate, the wind, sun, rocks—all are deeply engraved in religious consciousness. We know *where* we are. But the "spiritual landscape," needless to say, contains far more than this. It is a plenum in which what is usually classified into "inner" and "outer" lives moves and has its being. Suffused by the numinous, and relatively free from the categories of the intellect, it must not be confused with *Weltanschauung,* with which it shares only the mark of association with lived experience. We do not *inhabit* a worldview. But we inhabit a spiritual landscape. And here the word landscape serves us ill, perhaps, if all it suggests is what can be gazed upon. But I think it suggests more. I further suggest that the spiritual landscapes to be found portrayed, even further, witnessed to in the writings of Rabbi Kook and Sri Aurobindo have such striking similarities of topography that this in itself is an invitation to comparison. I need to crave the reader's indulgence, however, for the following reason. Exploring this topography, even in an introductory manner (and I cannot claim more than this) involves biography, ontology, cosmology, ethics, and much else besides, all of which deserve detailed treatment of their own. What I seek to do is to invite fuller exploration of two spiritual landscapes which stand out in importance in the human world of religious experience.

Both Kook and Sri Aurobindo owe much to religious *lore,* as distinct from *theology,* tied up as the latter term is with Christian theology, and for which no precise counterparts can properly be said to exist in other traditions. In drawing on the Kabbalah, Kook delved into a mystic world of esoteric wisdom whose symbolism recalls primeval archetypes. Some of these archetypes are no doubt common to Hellenistic and Persian religion and still more to the fringe phenomena connected with various gnostic sects. Both Kook and Sri Aurobindo manifest in their writings, and especially in their poetry, an apocalyptic vision which may or may not have had as one of its main inspirations the powerful darkness/light archetypes of ancient Persia. Influence apart, and this must always remain a matter of speculation, what is far more important is the way in which religious imagination throws up rich configurations in diverse cultural matrices, and how this provides a dynamism which the merely conceptual is less able to provide. Our focus, then, is not on an exigetical method but on richly peopled universes of "expression" which seem to well up from sources within the psyche, giving birth to cosmo-poetic visions, and finding a characteristic shape thanks to the traditions within which they are situated. There is one major difference to bear in mind, however: the fact that kabbalistic thought, including its later manifestations, never fails to have an anchor in the Torah. The Torah provides a strong pedalnote against which the rest is counterpoint. Is there anything analogous in Sri Aurobindo's way of thinking? An answer to this must now be ventured.

Sri Aurobindo's intellectual biography is idiosyncratic in that he discovered his own cultural roots well after his entry into Western thought. While he was a student of classics at Cambridge, he came across the philosophy of Heraclitus and admired the way he sought to reconcile reason with an essential dynamism in the cosmos. The idea of knowledge as the key to freedom, as he understood it both in Indian and Greek thought, struck him as inadequate. Heraclitus' metaphysic of Becoming attracted him greatly, and his semipoetical style, packed with riddles and paradoxes, seemed to him eminently appropriate for describing a world in a constant state of flux. About this time he became convinced that a cyclical view of time was inimical to a dynamic conception of reality, and although he found an "onwards and upwards" concept of progress too symplistic, he discovered further possibility was available, that of an upwards and downwards movement, whose root-metaphor may well have been derived from fire, but whose inner verity he had already discovered for himself in the life of the spirit. His main criticism of Heraclitus was that his metaphysic seemed singularly lacking in *ānanda*. Traditional Indian thought, he felt, however, was wanting in that it failed to bridge the gap between *sacchidānanda* and the phenomenal world. He began to suspect that the dichotomy between spirit and matter, the *paramārthika* and the *vyavahārika,* might be a false one. The *jīvanmukta* must surely be able to make an impression on the world and not just survive in it.

As for the Indian classics, the cosmology of the Vedas and its poetry strongly echoed in his own consciousness and he quoted approvingly these lines from the Ṛg Veda:

> O, Flame, thou goest to the ocean of Heaven, towards the gods; thou makest to meet together the godheads of the planes, the waters that are in the realm of light above the sun and the waters that abide below.[5]

The Vedic language of ascent centered around three ideas: the flame metaphor, inseparable from the image of Agni as messenger of the gods, to whom offering must be made at the beginning of each ritual; the ladder metaphor, and, thirdly, the allusion to climbing from peak to peak which goes along with the Himalayan cluster of images. The last of these, the Himalayan reference, is explicit in the quotation given above where poetry chimes in with sound geology, the cloud formations of the heights being the source of the water systems of the plains. Tied in with this is a parallel reference to planes of consciousness which, likewise, have their degrees of ascent. That Sri Aurobindo should have himself translated part of the Vedas under the title *Hymns to the Mystic Fire* witnesses to the impression they made on him. This finds fullest expression in his poetry.

But the Vedas are not the only inspiration for Sri Aurobindo's thought. The Brahman-Ātman equation of the Upanishads offered a very different image—that of the motionless stillness of illumination. How could this be reconciled with the dynamism of Kali, the Divine Mother, the deity which, as a Bengali, he was disposed to find most dear? In Sri Aurobindo's thinking, the way opened out through understanding Brahman as a fount of *creativity,* a divine power which blazes forth in myriad ways, which can also be intuited as the Śakti at work in all things. One of the most interesting questions that arises in this connection is whether Sri Aurobindo regarded this luminosity as *svayaṃprakāsā,* self-luminosity, or as the source of the illumination of all else. I suspect that, on balance, he sidesteps the Upanishadic and Platonic ways of dealing with this by shifting to the "inner light" reckoned to be effected by *pūrṇayoga,* the on-all-fronts ascesis which is all-integrating. If this interpretation is on the right track (and it may not be, for the gnomic style of Sri Aurobindo is not easy to unpack), Śakti à la Sri Aurobindo lacks the transcendence of Shekhinah, and if Kali is a vibrant presence, as she surely is for him, it embraces, as it "immanently" must, the demonic no less than the *sāttvika.* This would be consonant with the *rudrarūpa* presented in the *viśvarūpadarśanaṃ* of the Gīta, the divine presence seen in the form of *tremendum.* Śakti for Aurobindo would then remain the effulgence that was *beyond* good and evil. This fits in with the Tantrikas' understanding of Śakti, which to my mind misses entirely the dynamism of *goodness.* To go into this would take us beyond our immediate concern, crucial though I believe it to be if metaphysical and religious truth is to have any bearing on the world of man. Suffice it to say that there is another matter wherein Sri Aurobindo borrowed from the Tantrikas: the linking of consciousness with the "topography" of the body. This fitted in with his own understanding of yoga in progressive stages and his determination not to "leave the body behind" but somehow to transform it, all human endowments bearing seeds of self-transcendence.

A further clue leading to Sri Aurobindo's line of thought is found in his reaction to the Saṃkhya system, according to which the entire cosmic process is geared to the telos of human liberation. Sri Aurobindo regards evolution not in terms of becoming more and more saintly but in terms of becoming more and more *conscious.* Man has a pivotal place in the ascent from matter to life and from life to higher awareness. As evolution advances there is both a deepening of inwardness within man and an increasing capacity of man to act as a conscious spearhead of the cosmic evolutionary process. Pari passu, his efforts are met by the descent of the Divine, the matching of *sādhanā* by the infusion of divine power. At this point the influence of Mahayana Buddhism becomes evident—commitment to the goal of *sampatti* in the place of individual *mukti,* and the tapping of all man's powers in the interest of a "perfected community."

So far it seems as if the single pedal-note which we were seeking, a potential parallel in Sri Aurobindo to what the Torah is for Abraham Kook, remains elusive. Sri Aurobindo's thought-system draws on various philosophical roots, even though, in intent, it may seem to soar beyond philosophy. This must be said even if, in terms of strict usage, it might be proper to regard him as a sage rather than as a philosopher. His followers regard him not only as a sage, however, but as a prophet-seer, and those, whether from within India or outside, who seek to identify "contemporary Indian philosophers" often include his name. There is no doubt that many philosophical questions are raised by Sri Aurobindo's writings, including matters such as the nature of yoga, the structure and levels of consciousness, and the leverage and direction of the evolutionary process. Rather than try to situate Rabbi Kook vis-à-vis philosophical kabbalists or prophetic Kabbalah, something which I am not competent to do, I would only venture to say that an interfusion of philosophical and religious elements fits more easily within Hinduism than it can ever do within Jewish thought. The latter has historically found it necessary to demarcate itself from a wide spectrum of philosophical outlooks ranging from Hellenism to Enlightenment rationalism and beyond. It may at first seem as if the Vedas are for Sri Aurobindo what the Torah is for Kook. But this comparison is not suggestive since there is nothing in the Vedas, especially the Ṛg Veda (the part that Sri Aurobindo admired and from which he made translations), comparable to the *mitzvot* which for the kabbalist are not only compelling, but have the power to reintegrate a fragmented world.

Speaking in Delhi some years ago, Rabbi Ben Zion Bokser presented Kook as essentially a mystic and moralist, one who understands morality in terms of redressing wrongs. The speculative impulse in Sri Aurobindo is certainly much stronger than the moral temperament, although his contemporary interpreter, Sisirkumar Ghose,[6] sees him as an apostle of the social validity of mysticism, a modern mystic who relies on the ability of a transformed consciousness to change the world. Rabbi Kook's strong moral orientation was derived from his halakhic upbringing and his immersion in rabbinic decision-making. Hunting for something parallel in Sri Aurobindo, one needs to turn not to anything he may have said on the Dharmaśāstras but to his *Essays on the Gīta,*[7] which contain much on his conception of dharma.

Early on in the *Essays*[8] he writes that the master conceptions of the Gīta are "God or the Eternal and spirituality or the God-state." To paraphrase, the outer sense of *dharma* is the observance of social law, but the inner sense is the law of religious and spiritual life. Dharma in the full sense holds together our inner and outer activities. The way to liberation and perfection lies through "increasing impersonality." The "Godseeker" begins with established social and religious rule in the community and "lifts it up by imbuing it with the Brahmic consciousness." The problem is that Sri Aurobindo regards ethics as obtaining at the "lower level of ego-consciousness." If this is so and the ego rests on an illusion, so must ethics. It so happens that Sri Aurobindo was not in tune with the atheist activist interpretations of the Gīta of some of his contemporaries, nor did he agree with Swami Vivekananda's identification of duty with noninjury. The core of Sri Aurobindo's *pūrṇayoga* is neither devotion nor works, each of which requires a genuine "other," but a staged ascent of consciousness aimed at the divinisation of all that is.

This, it seems to me, would provide warrant enough for saying that we cannot find in the Gīta, any more than we can find in the Vedas, an analogue for Kook's Torah for Sri Aurobindo. It might also be pertinent to note that Sri Aurobindo's experience in jail convinced him that yoga and social and political activity were incompatible. He abandoned the struggle for national independence on his release from prison and moved to Pondicherry in 1910. The rest of his life was devoted to scholarly and poetic writings and the administration of the ashram was gradually delegated to others. I mention this because his life span shows a sharp divide between the outer and inner activities mentioned earlier as being integrated in his conception of dharma.

I venture one further comment. In inheriting the halakhic spirit, Kook inherited a way of thinking at the heart of which was the covenant relationship. Thanks to this relationship, the tradition of Israel never has to strain to find a link between man and God or between man and man or man and nature. There is nothing parallel to this *Ur*-relationship in the diverse Indian traditions which Sri Aurobindo's thinking strived to synthesize. The Puruṣasūkta recounts a mythical self-sacrificial event but it is weakly injunctive vis-à-vis what can be supposed to bring about *lokasaṃgraha.* It evokes and perhaps even describes, but it does not *address.* It is because of the covenant that it makes sense to speak of the *ẓaddik* as a Living Torah. It would not make sense to speak of the *pūrṇayogin* as a living Veda, nor has anyone done so.

If all this would seem to set an unbridgeable distance between the two thinkers, I should make it clear that this was not my intention. The distinctive topography of the two spiritual landscapes needed to be sketched first. In what remains we shall encounter some striking similarities of terrain.

The most complex but rich starting point in both thinkers is the way in which the Divine is envisaged. In the famous "Speech of Elijah,"[9] the way in which *Ein-Sof* escapes all conceptual nets is put like this: "Elijah began his discourse saying: Thou are He who is exalted above all exalted ones, mysterious above all mysteries. Thought cannot grasp thee at all!" This amounts to a fundamental critique of all attribute/name language with reference to the Divine One. Some would say that even a word like "exalted" would need to be qualified by the term *kibyakhol,* in order to guard against literality. Kook's comment on this whole area of discourse is profound:[10]

> Faith chiefly involves the conception of God's greatness so that whatever the heart conceives is as nought compared with that which it is fitting to conceive, and this, in turn, is nought compared to the Reality. All the divine names, whether in Hebrew or in other languages, convey no more than a faint spark of the hidden light for which the soul longs and which it gives the name "God." Every definition of the divine leads to denial and all attempts at defining the divine are spiritual idolatry. Even the definition of divine intellect and will and even the divine itself and even the name "God" are definitions and lead to denial unless they are qualified by the higher knowledge that these are but the light of sparks flashing from that which is above definition. . . . [If] it is a natural thing for all creatures to be submissive to the divine, for all particular being to be as nought before Being in general, how much more before the source of all general being? In this there is nothing of pain or repression but only delight and strength, majesty and inner power. . . . When the central point of the recognition of the divine is weak the divine Existence is thought of as no more than a tyrannical force from which there is no escape and before which one must be humbled. One who approaches the service of God in this empty situation, when the lower fear of God is torn from its source in the higher fear through the dark

> conception of the divine, arrived at as a result of lack of intelligence and of *Torah,* gradually loses the illumination of his world.

If concepts can be a source of idolatry, so can "unbridled imagination," he goes on to say. Paradoxically, but surely truly, the "higher knowledge" is an awareness of limitation, for "sparks" are not light in themselves. Mention of "the service of God" is highly significant. The injunction is to walk in His way. In other words, Torah is integral to illumination, and this illumination is of "His world." What follows is of utmost importance: "The majesty of God cannot then be revealed in the soul."

But what, then, are the sparks to which there is such frequent reference in Kook's writings, and with which we shall shortly parallel several passages in Sri Aurobindo's works? Kook conceives *Ru'ah ha-Kodesh* as a dynamic flow of grace from the Divine Pleroma to the souls of men. The two currents in creation are *hitpashtut,* the current of expansion which flows from God downwards, and *histalkut,* the current of unification through which *or hozer,* the sparks or reflected light, ascend towards their source. This is the unifying movement of "the sparks of holiness." Kabbalists have argued over the centuries as to the manner of the emanation of the *sefirot* from *Ein-Sof,* the relation of what is hidden to what is manifested, the appropriateness of "creation" language, the meaning of light-symbolism, what questions may or may not be legitimately asked and much else besides. The idea of an overflow on account of plenitude (cf. Ps. 23.5) when applied to *Ein-Sof* would account intelligibly for a dispersion of sparks of light throughout the universe, thanks to the breaking of the vessels, and no less to an "ingathering" prefigured by the Psalmist, "Return to me, you children of men" (Ps. 90.3). The upwards/downwards symbolism chimes in with Merkabah mysticism, the "natural" archetype of flames[11] rising and falling, if not even with the heights of Sinai, the terrain that surrounds it and the ascending/descending experience of Moses in this connection (cf. Alfred de Vigny's poem, "Moïse"). Rabbi Bokser finds in Kook, Teilhard de Chardin, and Sri Aurobindo a common concept of cosmic evolution where nature advances towards divine perfection. But as mentioned earlier, for Kook there is no *return* without Torah and penitence.[12] In cleaving to His ways, the divine *sefirot,* we identify ourselves with the divine purpose, the channels through which God works. Kook finds in diversity the presence of divine design and challenge and speaks of:

> the spatial separation of plants, which serves as an aid to their growth, enabling them to suck up [from the earth] their needed sustenance. Thus will each one develop to its fullness, and the distinctive characteristics of each will be formed in all its [sic] particularities. . . . The proper unity results only from the separation. One begins by separation and concludes by unification.[13]

Neither Kook nor Sri Aurobindo commit themselves to pantheism[14] per se. Unification is not the same as blanket unity.

There is another interesting overtone in Kook's writings. Following the Zohar's tripartite distinction of the soul into *nefesh, ru'ah,* and *neshamah,* with the divine spark identified with the last of these, Kook refers to the "cages" of substance and of spirit in his poem "Expanses, Expanses." This indicates the possibility of ascending beyond *ru'ah,* going beyond the ability to distinguish between good and evil to the firm disposition (thanks to the Torah) to do the good.

This point throws light on how Kook understands the link between mysticism and morality. If *neshamah* is "a part of God alone," the connection between mystic intuition and goodness is thereby elucidated. The higher the ascent in mystic knowledge, the greater the sense of what is to be *done*[15] and the greater the possibility of achieving a *tikkun.* Once more we can see how, through cleaving to Torah, kabbalistic thought was able to distinguish itself from gnosticism, close though it often came to that cluster of traditions. The ascent of mystic knowledge is not to be seen in cognitive terms so much as in an insight that we are "bidden to love."[16] In spite of the "impediment to speech" and the "impediment to hearing," man is called to a fruition of powers which stem from his rootedness in the Infinite. Even the smallest insight into the Infinite is at once the dawning of all love for all creation and the recognition of the demand to restore what has been fragmented, to bring together separated realms, to reunite the remnant, to bring about the return of the sparks to the divine fire.

We turn next to the treatment of the "spark" metaphor in Aurobindo's work. It bears the imprint of both Heraclitus and the Vedas. The "concealed soul-spark" has "the task of meeting and striving with the forces of the universe."[17] Like Heraclitus, Sri Aurobindo found, in strife and conflict, processes that were inherent in nature. The additional element for him was given in his analysis in terms of *guṇas,* the traits of inertia, activity, and illumination which we find tangled up in all matter.[18] This soul-spark, he explains elsewhere, is divine: "There dwells the little spark of the Divine which supports this obscure mass of our nature and around it grows the psychic being, the formed soul or the real man within us."[19]

He also refers to the spark as growing: "The psychic being is the spark growing into a Fire, evolving with the growth of the consciousness."[20] That the spark is not only in man is clarified in this passage: "This spark of Divinity is there in all terrestrial living being from the earth's highest to its lowest creatures."[21] He also says that the soul or spark is present before vitality and mind start developing.

The theme is continued in the rich imagery of his poems, from which here are a few examples. Continuing the theme of the last quotation, he writes in "The Hidden Plan":[22]

Even in the stone and the beast the godhead lurks
    A bright Persona of eternity.
It shall burst out from the limit traced by Mind
    And make a witness of the prescient heart;
It shall reveal even in the inert blind
    Nature, long veiled in each inconscient part,
Fulfilling the occult magnificent plan,
The world-wide and immortal spirit in man.

As it happens, the idea of the real as "veiled" is also a familiar one in kabbalistic thought.

Sri Aurobindo used another set of images in "Musa Sanctus":[23]

O Word, concealed in the upper fire,
    Thou who hast lingered through centuries,
Descend from thy rapt white desire,
    Plunging through gold eternities
Break the seals of Matter's sleep,
    Break the trance of the unseen height
O Muse of the Silence, the wideness make
    In the unplumbed stillness that hears thy voice.

This is a poem of prayer and invocation which has many overtones, recalling the Vedic mystic fire, *logos* and *vāk,* along with echoes of Romantic poetry, especially Shelley. Sri Aurobindo is also herein giving the poet a special role in mediating between the "upper fire" and sleeping matter below.

Another poem, "Rose of God," combines invocation of the higher realm with prayers rising from below:[24]

Rose of God, vermillion stain on the sapphires of heaven,
Rose of bliss, fire-sweet, seven tinged with the ecstasies seven!

Leap up in our heart of humanhood, O miracle, O flame
Passion-flower of the Nameless, bud of the mystical Name.

I have an idea that the language used here would be familiar to any kabbalist. Sri Aurobindo wrote in English, and is given to a lushness of expression which he derived from some of the Romantic poets. But the symbolism of bud and flower, light, height and depth, precious stones, time and eternity, belong to a visionary landscape that can be found in more than one tradition.

The symbol of the flight of a mystic bird follows naturally from the idea of winged inspiration and this, along with fire, comes into his poem, "The Bird of Fire":[25]

Gold-white wings a throb in the vastness, the bird of flame
went glimmering over a sunfire curve to the haze of the
west . . .
Rich and red is thy breast, O bird, like blood of a soul climbing
the hard crag-teeth world
One strange leap of thy mystic stress breaking the barriers of
mind and life, arrives at its luminous term thy flight;

Many strands are woven into Sri Aurobindo's mystic consciousness. In keeping with his own tradition, he conceives of the ultimate heights in terms of bliss, *ānanda.* And yet in *Savitri,* which is his major poetic work, he strikes what is almost a note of warning:[26]

He who would save the race must share its pain;
This he shall know who obeys the grandiose urge.

The epic poem presages a new life for man:[27]

The spirit shall look through Matter's gaze
And Matter shall reveal the Spirit's face
The mighty Mother shall take birth in Time
And God be born into the human clay
In forms made ready by your human lives.

Savitri tells her husband:[28]

Let us go through this new world that is the same.
For it is given back, but it is known,
A playing ground and dwelling-house of God
Who hides himself in bird and beast and man,
Sweetly to find himself again by love,
By oneness.

It is in *Savitri* that the theme of love becomes most explicit in Sri Aurobindo's writings:[29]

> Love must not cease to live upon the earth;
> For love is the bright link twixt earth and heaven,
> Love is the far Transcendent's angel here,
> Love is man's lien on the Absolute.

The theme of *Savitri* is the theme of restoration, the conquest of death by love. When Savitri is asked how the miracle has come about, she replies:[30]

> To feel love and oneness is to live
> And this the magic of our golden change
> Is all the truth I know or seek.

This is also Sri Aurobindo's rejoinder to the Keatsian identification of truth and beauty.

What are we to make of such apocalyptic language? At times there is almost a messianic note in his writing. Eclectic as he undoubtedly is, there are constant resonances from diverse traditions, so that in spite of the overall Indianness of his way of describing the mystic ascent, especially in his assumption of the crowning experience of *ānanda,* at times he reaches out to something like universality. However this may be, at least we can say that this was his intention. In terms of spiritual landscape Sri Aurobindo offers for our exploration a many-levelled, many-dimensional world. At times we seem to break loose from the moorings of nature, but the intent again is most surely a return to "Nature's ways" with a transformed understanding.

Sri Aurobindo resorted to the poetic form of expression more often than Kook, and yet the corpus of Kook's poetry must not be ignored if we are to enter more fully into his thought. The style of the two poets is very different, even allowing for the difference in language. Sri Aurobindo, as was seen earlier, owes a lot to Vedic hymns and to Romantic poetry. At times he seeks to attain the conciseness of mantra. But, on the whole, effusiveness and profusion of imagery prevail. Kook's work, as we would expect, is full of rabbinic, kabbalistic, and Hasidic allusions. But his poetic gifts break through all frameworks, just as the unbounded light exceeds the sparks which are its residue. Rather than use an abundance of words he reveals a sense that words are inadequate to express his yearning passion for God and the intimations of the grandeur of the Infinite that are vouchsafed to him. His religious lyricism reveals an intense love of all creation and a longing for the renewal of Zion. At times, like Sri Aurobindo, he feels immersed in a sea of light and longs to press on, even beyond "the exalted and the ethereal." A few passages may serve to give an inkling into his mind and also draw attention to some striking resemblances to the Sri Aurobindo quotations above. The poem "When I Want to Speak" describes the meeting between the descending stream of light and the ascent of what in Sri Aurobindo is the "soul-flame":

> The ascending stream from my mortal self
> Joins the descending stream from the source of my soul,
> And seeds of light
> Fill the world, my whole being.[31]

The promise of a new life and a new world is prefigured in "The Whispers of Existence":

> And a generation will yet arise
> And sing to beauty and to life
> And draw delight unending
> From the dew of heaven . . .
> And from the delight of song and life's beauty
> A holy light will abound.
> And all existence will whisper,
> My beloved, I am permitted to you.[32]

And in "I Am Filled with Love for God" he writes:

> In every life pulse,
> In all existence,
> There is a spark, a spark of a spark,
> Faint and fainter than faint.
> The inner light,
> The light of God supreme,
> Builds and establishes,
> Assembles what is scattered,
> Reflects worlds without end,
> Orders and binds together.[33]

Perhaps the noblest statement of all comes in his longer poem called "Expanses, Expanses." A sense of the inadequacy of all conceptual formulations breaks out from him in the cry, "I thirst for truth, not for a conception of truth." And then comes the agony that goes along with mystic insight, the need to articulate, to share, and yet the knowledge that words act as a veil before the face of God and obscure vision:

> I am bound to the world,
> All creatures, all people are my friends,

> Many parts of my soul
> Are intertwined with them,
> But how can I share with them my light?
> Whatever I say
> Only covers my vision,
> Dulls my light.
> Great is my pain and great my anguish,
> O, my God, my God, be a help in my trouble,
> I shall declare before the multitude
> My fragments of Your truth, O my God.[34]

The theme of expansion is a very important one in Kook's thinking. He writes:

> The individual identity continues to expand, it becomes part of the general being of the people in a very real fusion, and from there it is absorbed in the general existence of the whole world. As part of universal existence it finds its happiness in divine splendor, in its great strength, its light and its delight, a richness of life that sends forth the flow of eternal being.[35]

But we have to see next how this fits in with both the kabbalistic conception of *sefirot* and, more specifically with Kook's understanding of evolution. The *sefirot* are heuristic postulations which are regarded, by later kabbalistic cosmologists, as emanations of the *Ein Sof.* From the fourteenth century onwards detailed diagrams of the *sefirot* are depicted in the form of a tree. In the *Sefer Bahir* the tree begins growing when it is watered by the waters of Wisdom, and it therefore appears virtually as an upturned tree. While there is a great deal of literature of a more speculative kind on the *sefirot* and in which the sequence and nature of the various emanations are discussed in detail, there is another approach which takes its departure from the fact that the Zohar is basically a Midrash on the Torah and it is this approach which is followed by Rabbi Kook. It is the light of the commandments which provides the link between the root of the soul in the individual and the grandeur of the infinite. The *sefirot* seen from one perspective stem from the Divine. From the human perspective they are channels of communication between man and God, and the return of the sparks to the fire provides the leading metaphor for this. To cleave to the attributes of God, the divine *sefirot,* is to cleave unto His ways.

Now there are at least two reasons why, in spite of kabbalistic influence on this thought, Kook avoids detailed discussion of the *sefirot,* and even expressly denies that they are needed. The first is that unlike Sri Aurobindo, Kook is not a speculative thinker, but a deeply spiritual man drawing strength and inspiration from his own tradition, and inclined above all to go back to its roots, in this case the Torah, and find therein endless sources of nourishment. Unlike the thought of Aurobindo, there is nothing syncretic or eclectic about his thinking. His inspiration is sustained by the *halakhah* and centuries of Jewish deliberation on ethical problems. This is why when he comes to speak of evolution he writes:

> Evolution sheds light on all the ways of God. All existence evolves and ascends, as this may be discerned in some of its parts. . . . It ascends toward the heights of the absolute good. . . . And everything aspires, longs, yearns, according to a pattern that is adorned with holiness and girded with beauty. . . . The light of your own presence, O lord, our God, is imprinted on the law that governs life.[36]

The spur of evolution, then, is the nisus of man's yearning for God, a striving to identify with the Divine rhythm. The whole of creation takes part in this movement of aspiration, and yet, through his many powers, man has a special place—and, more especially, through his knowledge of the Torah. There is no limit to the heights to which one can aspire, but it is necessary to begin at the beginning with a sound body and sound mind.[37] As for the path of ascent, this is not a matter of steady progress. He writes:

> Nothing remains the same; everything blooms, everything ascends, everything steadily increases in light and truth. The enlightened spirit does not become discouraged even when he discerns that the line of ascendence is circuitous including both advance and decline, a forward movement but also fierce retreats, for even the retreats abound in the potential of future progress.[38]

The path involves an embracing of "divine ideals" and these are elucidated as "pure morality and a heroism for higher things."[39] He sometimes uses the expressions "the higher Torah" and "the higher moral Torah."[40] This may be compared with Rabbi Menahem Nahum of Chernobyl's call to such a study of Torah which will reveal the hidden light through which the path to God can be found.[41]

Kook's understanding of penitence is very important in this regard. *The Lights of Penitence*[42] speaks of the power of the smallest act of penitence to aid the spiritual ascent not only of the individual but of the community. Morality is described as the "central direction of the will of existence" and therefore penitence "is, in essence, an effort to return to one's original status, to the source of life and higher being in their fullness." When Kook says, "existence, in its overall character, is sinless," and that "sin appears only in the goals of particular human beings," the goal of evolution and man's role in it is made clear. Divine energy guides creation to its goal. The whole of nature is rising towards the messianic consummation of godliness. I. Epstein writes:[43]

> This conception led Rabbi Kook to his belief in the inevitability of human progress. In every generation there is to be found a number of men who strive whole-heartedly towards the divine good in the world and thereby raise even the weaker members of the race to a higher level. Moreover, there is still another factor which contributes to progress—the deeds and thoughts of the great men of the past. The good which these men acquired during their lives does not disappear after their deaths. They add to the sum total of the spiritual, moral and intellectual, and influence the lives of later generations.

While this brings out the role of the outstanding individual who in Kook's view combines the fervor of the *ḥasid* with the uprightness of the *ẓaddik,* Kook, in tune with Rabbi Sheur Zalman's concept of the *beinoni,* believed that the ordinary man was capable of a life of "mending the fragments," enlisting his spiritual faculties so that they ignite through Divine power. That is to say, both great and small play their part in the work of evolution, and the word "work" may be significant here: for although from one angle the divine purpose for His creation is all-compelling, it is given to every man to undergo a process of "refinement" or "cleansing," increasing love by degrees, beginning with love of Torah and of all creation. What Kook is suggesting here includes but goes beyond *mitzvot,* enjoining an increase of vision in accordance with the lights of holiness, a vision which issues in knowledge of what is to be done. Another way of putting this is to say that man is called to be *eved Adonai,* God's servant.

Kook sometimes uses organic language:[44] "On reaching full maturity, the human spirit aspires to rise above every manner of conflict and opposition, and a person then recognized all expression of the spiritual life as an organic whole."[45] But whereas the organic idea in philosophical literature has often gone along with a submerging of personality, Kook lays stress on the development of each "spark," the elevation of each so that he can become a blessing. When he writes of a blossoming of spiritual powers, an intertwining of branches and a deepening of roots, this not only has deep echoes as far as the doctrine of the *sefirot* is concerned, but foreshadows a messianic "bringing together" which recalls the prophet Isaiah and which for Rabbi Kook provides the key motif of a new life and a new world to come.

We now turn to the preceding themes in the context of their analogues in Sri Aurobindo's writings, that is to say, the treatment of evolution, its leverage and goal, how human perfection is to be attained, and the role of special individuals in bringing about a transformed world. Apology must be given in advance for a very abbreviated treatment of what is in fact a very large syllabus of issues which Sri Aurobindo discussed over a period of many decades and whose elaboration is particularly complex by reason of his synthesis of elements of diverse historical origin.

Perhaps the chief clues to be followed up in Sri Aurobindo's treatment of the Absolute are his desire to avoid the *Advaitin māyāvāda* and, no less, Saṃkhya dualism, to emphasize the dynamic nature of the real, and to highlight the crucial role of the human individual in bringing about an ascent of consciousness in the direction of bliss. In terms of his relation to Indian philosophical treatments of the real, it is important to note that he does not put Brahman beyond the sphere of becoming and that he cuts through the *nirguṇa/saguṇa* distinction by speaking of the Divine as "the one transcendent Conscious Being and the All-person of whom all conscious beings are the selves and the personalities; for He is the highest Self and the universal indwelling Presence."[46]

If we next ask how everything began, Sri Aurobindo's answer is found in the idea of *līlā* or divine play, traditionally interpreted as an expression of joy. At times he indicates that even a game suggests an object to be accomplished. But theology does not fit very easily in an emanationist account of creation, and Sri Aurobindo's most frequent references are to the spontaneity of the creative process, regarding this as being quite compatible with the "working out of a truth inherent in being," or the self-expression of *sacchidānanda.* The spirit (for this word can also be used) manifests itself in a certain sequence, the descending order being Supermind, overmind, mind proper, life, and matter. Supermind indicates the ability of the Divine to actualize its potentiality, and the subsequent stages of manifestation are described in terms of involution of consciousness, an immanence which provides the nisus of the evolutionary movement. The bottom level, so to say, is matter, which Sri Aurobindo describes in his long poem *Savitri* as "the fire burning on bare stone."[47] Another way of putting this is to say that matter contains those sparks which are the furthest removed from the divine fire. He also uses the terms "Inconscience" and "vast occult

Intelligence" to refer to this. It would not be possible to account for life and mind at all, Sri Aurobindo thinks, were the higher not already involuted in the lower.

What he does here is to take sides in a very longstanding debate about causality in Indian philosophical systems. Evolution is explained as an "inverse action" of involution. At each stage on the way up, evolution works through a triple process of widening, heightening, and integrating. Widening can be elucidated as expansion and complexity of organization. The heightening aspect concerns incresing degrees of consciousness as we advance in the evolutionary scale. As the higher stages emerge, the lower manifestations are not left behind but are caught up and transformed. I venture this example. Dancing does not cancel the law of gravity but transfigures it in the course of graceful movement. (Sri Aurobindo's departure from Advaita Vedanta shows itself here too. For Sankara, higher awareness cancels out the lower, for example, it is not possible to be both awake and asleep.)

The evolutionary process comes to a crucial point with the emergence of man, for in *jīvātma* the spark of the Divine is imbued with the capacity to move from the obscurity of half-light to a larger clarity. The journey is a long climb from mind to higher mind, illumined mind, intuitive mind, and overmind. All this is envisaged in language which recalls the Buddhist treatment of the *lokas* no less than several occultist descriptions early in this century of planes of being or consciousness, multiple worlds and the like.

The relation of the ontological to the psychological account needs to be borne in mind. The ontological presentation in Sri Aurobindo's work is propelled by both mystical insight and mythopoetic creativity. The psychological description gives us his conception of *pūrṇayoga,* an integral ascesis which is Sri Aurobindo's answer to the traditional distinction between alternative yogic paths, and also his rejoinder to traditional accounts of *mukti* which is considered a liberation *from* nature. When he goes so far as to say that "all life is yoga," he has in mind the integrating processes at work in the natural world, albeit operating unconsciously. Sri Aurobindo writes:

> The method we have to pursue, then, is to put our whole conscious being into relation and contact with the Divine and to call Him in to transform our entire being into His, so that in a sense God Himself, the real Person in us, becomes the Śadhaka of the Sādhanā[48] as well as the Master of Yoga by whom the lower personality is used as the centre of a divine transfiguration and the instrument of its own perfection.[49]

The language of ingathering is used in the following: "Yoga . . . is a gathering up and concentration of the movements dispersed and loosely combined in the lower evolution."[50]

The goal of yoga is a certain kind of transformation which Sri Aurobindo distinguishes from conversion, purification, and enlightenment. He describes it as a "bringing down of the Divine consciousness" into the mind, heart and body, so as to remove the veil which our present consciousness sets up between us and the divine, and so as to remove the mixture of *guṇas* which otherwise prevails at the natural level. In this connection he says that the three *guṇas* became transformed: *sattva* becomes *jyoti* (light), *rajas* becomes *tapas* (intense power), and *tamas* becomes *śama* (divine quietness). Sri Aurobindo also refers to the "triple transformation," psychic, spiritual, and supramental. Psychic transformation is the awakening of the psyche so that the light emanating from the "ever pure flame" of the divinity in us illuminates out total being. Spiritual illumination is a further expansion which intensifies the awareness of *sacchidānanda*. Supramental transformation occurs when spiritual ascent is matched by the descent of the supermind, bringing about what Indian philosophers usually describe as "realization." Sri Aurobindo, however, speaks of "gnostic being." Such a being would be completely "divinized." And now he draws on the *bodhisattva* idea. The gnostic being or superman seeks to bring about Divine life on earth. The gnostic consciousness may show itself in many different ways, so Sri Aurobindo is not committing himself to any simple form of monism or pantheism here. This is borne out by his various statements regarding the nature of a transformed collective life. These span a considerable number of years, beginning from his early nationalist writings.

In 1905, he wrote: "We need a nucleus of men in whom the *Shakti* is developed to its uttermost extent, in whom it fills every corner of the personality and overflows to fertilize the earth. These, having the fire of *Bhavani* in their hearts and brains, will go forth and carry the flame to every nook and cranny of our land."[51] At this period in his life he was considerably under the influence of Bankim Chandra Chatterjee. This is evident in the following: "No artificial or ceremonial ways of preparing the soul can approach in effectiveness the spiritual process of merging one's hopes, desires, and one's very life in a wider individuality such as that of one's nation."[52] This statement can be paralleled by Rabbi Kook's whole corpus of writings on Eretz Yisrael and its necessary link with a religious renaissance. After 1909 Sri Aurobindo became less and less a prophet of nationalism and far more a lover of humanity. In 1922 he could write "the true basis of work and life is the spiritual."[53] And in *The Human Cycle* he wrote that the "enemy of all real religion is human egoism, the egoism of the individual, the egoism of class and nation."[54] It was in the same work that he spoke of "great men" who combine *yugadharma* (the spirit of the time) with *swadharma* and called them "swallowers of formulas."[55] He further says that "the human mind needs to think, feel, enjoy, expand; expansion is its very nature." If this is so, human allegiance must always go beyond frontiers. Just as the human mind in its deeper reaches has no demarcations,[56] there is a parallel overflowing of boundaries and outreach of human sympathies within the family of man, something which the "elevation of consciousness encourages and helps to foster." "A deeper brotherhood, a yet unfound law of love is the only sure foundation possible for a perfect social evolution no other can replace."[57] These are some of the trends of thought which reveal Sri Aurobindo's faith in the basic goodness of human nature and in the ultimate evolution of one world.

Any emanationist philosophy, however, faces problems with the existence of evil, and we may turn to this next, pulling round the discussion to the comparative perspective with which we began. Both Judaism and Hinduism are free from any doctrine of original sin. For Sri Aurobindo evil is rooted in materiality, or more properly, in its insentience. Insofar as this has an important role in the evolutionary process it seems as if evil is virtually given a transitional status by him. Another problem is the way his view seems to underplay the central horror of our times, and possibly of all times: the inhumanity of man to man, something which cannot easily be ascribed to "materiality."

However, there is a striking similarity between the *kelippot,* the shards or shell of which the Kabbalah speaks, and the concept of *kośas* or sheaths which Sri Aurobindo takes over from classical Indian thought. The "breaking of the vessels" in Lurianic Kabbalah arises from the spilling over of light. There is a certain order in the emergence of the *kelippot* and likewise a prescribed method for bringing about *tikkun* or restoration. The Saṃkhya-Yoga tradition, much of which Sri Aurobindo inherited, likewise looked at evolution in a strictly sequential manner. Sri Aurobindo's own form of yoga could be described as a method for mending what had become fragmented (cf. the recurring theme of integrality), whether this be human consciousness, society or world.[58] He refers to imperfection as "a privilege and promise, for it opens out to us an immense vista of self-developing and self-exceeding."[59] There is also the following passage about pain: "Is it not so that in nature pain is a possibility which has to be exhausted and man has been selected as the instrument to bring it into existence, in a limited space, for a limited time, and work it out of the cosmos?"[60] While this recognizes the human responsibility for both the existence and the removal of suffering, from a Jain perspective (which, as far as I know, was not incorporated into Sri Aurobindo's worldview) it totally leaves out of account suffering in the animal kingdom.

Turning to Kook, we find in his writings an interesting departure from the Zohar and the discussion of the problem of evil in Lurianic Kabbalah.[61] Kook sees evil as the product of a kind of *avidya,* of not seeing the unity of things, of being led astray by partiality of vision (the last of these is very Jaina in spirit). Rotenstreich says that for Kook, "the defects that exist are not in the world but in ourselves and in our faulty vision, our limited comprehension."[62] Bergman maintains that Kook's view of the function of evil was "to push evolution ahead until men will realize that the distinction between good and evil is unreal. . . . Evil exists only in man's limited view of reality. For God, there is no evil."[63] For Kook, darkness will be overcome by light, evil by love.

In spite of the poverty of the historic situation in their day, and despite the fact that full-fledged nationhood had yet to come into flower for either of their countries, both Kook and Sri Aurobindo had an immense faith in the potential of man, a firm conviction that goodness and truth would prevail. Both were strangely confident in the future. While in Kook's thinking this was deeply grounded in the messianic idea, there was nothing similar for Sri Aurobindo to draw on in his own tradition. Hindus look to a mythical *past* glory, that of Ramārājya, rather than to a future "utopia." Aurobindo's mystic insight, however, enabled him to interpret a sense of the "dawn" in terms of the time which was to come and for which preparation must be made now. This is why he can echo Kook's intuition that nothing is to be foregone; everything is to be illumined. Vision may be dim, the divine spark may be encrusted over with shells, with *upādhis,* but a *mārga* is indicated. There is the promise of prophets, seers, and sages, the promise that the divine will descend to gather up the fragments and ignite the fading embers in a blaze of light, the promise of an apotheosis which has ever been the summit of human aspiration.

What tentative conclusion can emerge from the diverse discussions of the preceding pages? Kook carried the kabbalistic tradition into modern times, and transformed it by witnessing to the imperative that stems from a Beyond that is ever-present here and now. Sri Aurobindo synthesized several traditions which in the course of time had competed with each other. Each had in his mind and heart an *Ur*-community,[64] but wanted his message to travel beyond its bounds. In each we find a religious imagination rich in vision; each is blessed with outstanding spiritual gifts. Each discovered that ascent is circuitous, but that man is met halfway; man is both seeker and sought. We discovered a striking similarity of spiritual landscape and also no less striking differences. Jewish religious insight must always find the terminus in *devekut,* a turning to God, a cleaving which precludes identity. To speak of the divine as He who wears light as a garment is to suggest a *Deus absconditus,* more like the Being proclaimed by the Upanishads than the more metaphysically resonant "He who is" proclaimed by the prophets. Both Kook and Sri Aurobindo *celebrate* light and in so doing touch a common base in response to one of those powerful archetypes available to all people at all times in history. It might be mentioned that another of their contemporaries, Rabindranath Tagore, incorporates a prayer for "more light" into more than one of his poems. The upturned tree, whether of the Kabbalah or the Upanishads, suggests a nourishment stemming from heaven, or, more inwardly, a blossoming which nothing external can account for. Even though in both thinkers the mythopoetic religious consciousness branches out richly in manifold directions there is still a considerable distance between an orientation towards goodness and love, harmony raised to holiness, and one whose *fons et origo* is *ānanda.* We seem to traverse oceans and continents in order to pass from one to the other.

For this reason, I close with the following words of Rabbi Nahman of Bratslav:

> Two men who live in different places, or even in different generations, may still converse. For one may raise a question, and the other who is far away in time or space may make a comment or ask a question that answers it. So they converse, but no one knows it save the Lord, who hears and records and brings together all the words of men, as it is written: "They who serve the Lord speak to one another, and the Lord hears them and records their words in His book" (Mal. 3.16).[65]

Contributors

HANANYA GOODMAN is Director of the International Association for the Study of Jewish Mysticism and Editor of *Kabbalah: A Journal of Jewish Mysticism and Spirituality.*

ELIZABETH CHALIER-VISUVALINGAM received her Ph.D. from the University of Paris–X and has tuaght Sanskrit and Indian Studies at Harvard and Budapest University.

MARGARET CHATTERJEE was Professor of Philosophy at Delhi University, and then Director, Indian Institute of Advanced Study, Simla. She teaches at Westminister College, Oxford.

WENDY DONIGER is Professor at the Divinity School, University of Chicago.

DAVID FLUSSER is Professor of Jewish History at the Hebrew University of Jerusalem.

BARBARA HOLDREGE is Associate Professor of Religious Studies at the University of California, Santa Barbara.

DENNIS HUDSON is Professor of Religion at Smith College.

BERNARD JACKSON is Professor of Law, University of Kent at Canterbury.

CHARLES MOPSIK is Chargé de Recherche at the National Center for Scientific Research in Paris and Director of the Collection "Les Dix Paroles" published by Editions Verdier.

CHAIM RABIN is Professor of Biblical Studies and Hebrew Language at the Hebrew University of Jerusalem.

FRANCIS SCHMIDT is Director of Religious Studies at the École Pratique des Hautes Études, Section des Sciences Religieuses at Sorbonne, Paris.

DAVID SHULMAN is Professor of Indian Studies at the Hebrew University of Jerusalem.

SHALVA WEIL is Senior Lecturer at the School of Education, Hebrew University of Jerusalem.

Notes

Notes to Chapter 1

1. Letter dated 19 April 1976. Now in English translation as "Shekhinah: The Feminine Element in Divinity" in *On the Mystical Shape of the Godhead* (New York: Schocken Books, 1991), 140–96; see especially 194ff. Scholem's personal copy of Friedrich Otto Schrader's *Introduction to the Pancaratra and the Ahirbudhnya Samhita* (Adyar, 1916), at the Scholem Library at the Hebrew University contains marginal notes in which he makes comparisons with kabbalistic motifs. For example, on page 55, Schrader writes: "The Pancaratra teaches a chain, as it were, of emanations; each emanation, except the first, originating from an anterior emanation; and thus the favourite image of the process has with the Pancaratrins become that of one flame proceeding from another flame." Scholem notes: *madlik nir mi'nir-nir,* "light one light from the other." On page 25 Schrader discusses an idea that parallels the Kabbalistic conception of *zimzum,* the divine withdrawal that allows creation to exist: "He, by sacrificing Himself, actually became the whole world." On page 32 Schrader discusses six *guṇas* as instruments of pure creation, a notion that parallels the Kabbalistic doctrine of the *sefirot.*
2. Wilhelm Halbfass, *India and Europe: An Essay in Understanding* (Albany: SUNY Press, 1988); Raymond Schwab, *The Oriental Renaissance: Europe's Rediscovery of India and the East, 1680–1880,* translated by Gene Patterson-Black and Victor Reinking with a foreword by Edward W. Said (New York: Columbia University Press, 1984); Donald F. Lach, *Asia in the Making of Europe* (Chicago: University of Chicago Press, 1965, 1977); Catherine Weinberger-Thomas, *L'Inde et l'imaginaire,* Collection Purusartha 11 (Paris: Editions de L'Ecole des Hautes Etudes en Sciences Sociales, 1988). See also: Bernard Lewis, Edmund Leites, and Margaret Case, "As Others See Us: Mutual Perceptions, East and West," *Comparative Civilizations Review* 13 (Fall 1985) and 14 (Spring 1986); Rudolf Wittkower, "Marvels of the East: A Study in the History of Monsters," *Journal of the Warburg and Courtauld Institutes* 5 (1942): 159–97; Stephen Jay Greenblatt, *Marvelous Possessions:*

The Wonder of the New World (Chicago: University of Chicago Press, 1991); Jacques Le Goff, "Medieval West and the Indian Ocean," in *Time, Work and Culture in the Middle Ages* (Chicago: University of Chicago Press, 1980), 189–204.

3. La Crequiniere, *The Agreement of the Customs of the East-Indians with those of the Jews, and other Ancient People* (London, 1705). (Translated from the French edition published in Brussels, 1704).
4. For the historical context of Le Crequinere, see Frank E. Manuel's *The Eighteenth Century Confronts the Gods* (Cambridge, MA: Harvard University Press, 1959), 17ff.
5. See Giancarlo Carabelli's *Tolandiana: materiali bibliografici per lo studio dell'opera e della fortuna di John Toland (1670–1722)* (Florence: La nuova Italia, 1976), 114. I am endebted to Robert E. Sullivan for this source.
6. Voltaire's Correspondence, LXVII, 255–56, cited in P. J. Marshall's *The British Discovery of Hinduism in the Eighteenth Century* (Cambridge: Cambridge University Press, 1970), 24, 33. See also the earlier source of this idea in Guillaume Postel, where the link between Abraham and Brahman is made; see William J. Bouwsma's *Concordia Mundi: The Career and Thought of Guillaume Postel (1510–81)* (Cambridge, MA: Harvard University Press, 1957), 61, where the source for Postel's connection between Abraham and the Brahmans is drawn directly from his studies of the Zohar. Compare the commentary of the Zohar I: 100b and 133b on Genesis 25.6. The Zohar follows Talmud Sanhedrin 91a, where the initial idea appears that Abraham's teachings were sent to the East where they were then transformed into impure spiritual forms. Also, see Shlomo Pines, "*Jāhiliyya* and *'Ilm*," *Jerusalem Studies in Arabic and Islam* 13 (1990): 175–94, where another possible source for these ideas may be found in the fourth century *Recognitions.* For further material on Postel's Jewish studies, see: Salo Wittmayer Baron, *A Social and Religious History of the Jews* (New York: Columbia University Press, 1969), 403–4; Leon Poliakov, *The Aryan Myth,* translated by Edmund Howard (New York: Basic Books, 1974), 186, where in discussing Kant's comparisons of Abraham and Brahma, he cites Guillaume Postel as an earlier source for this comparison. Poliakov's study is recommended for a history of Aryan and Semitic comparisons. I would like to thank Oliver W. Holmes for encouraging me to pursue the history of the Abraham/Brahma motif.
7. Antonin Debidour, "L'Indianisme de Voltaire," *Revue de litérature comparée* 4 (1924): 26–40; D. S. Hawley, "L'Inde de Voltaire," *Studies on Voltaire and the Eighteenth Century* 120 (1974): 139–78; Catherine Weinberger-Thomas, "Les mystères du Veda. Spéculations sur le texte sacré des anciens brames au Siècle des Lumières." *Puruṣārtha* 7 (1983): 177–231.
8. Joseph Priestley, *A Comparison of the Institutions of Moses with those of the Hindoos and other Ancient Nations* (Northumberland, PA, 1799). For historical context, see P. J. Marshall's *The British Discovery of Hinduism,* 34–37, 43; W. Halbfass, *India and Europe,* 421. For Priestley's sources, see

Dale Riepe, *Philosophy of India and Its Impact on American Thought* (Springfield, IL: Charles Thomas, 1970), 16.

9. See Shmuel Ettinger. "Jews and Judaism as Seen by the English Deists of the Eighteenth Century," *Zion* 29 (1964): 182–206. (Hebrew)
10. Karl Theodor Johannsen, *Die Kosmogonischen Antichten der Inder und Hebraer* (Altona, 1833).
11. F. A. Korn, *Braminen und Rabbinen oder: Indien das Stamland der Hebraer und ihrer Fabeln* (Meissen, 1836). Fifteen years before Theodor Benfey, Korn suggested the Indian origins of Jewish legends and compares a variety of myths. For other examples, see Luitpold Wallach, "The Parable of the Blind and the Lame: A Study in Comparative Literature," *Journal of Biblical Literature* 62 (1943): 333–39; Joseph Jacobs, "Aesop's Fables among the Jews," in *The Jewish Encyclopedia,* vol. 1 (New York: Funk and Wagnalls, 1901–1906), 221ff; Alexander Haggerty Krappe, "An Indian Tale in the *Midrash Tanchum,*" *Jubilee Congress of the Folk-Lore Society: Papers and Transactions* (London: William Glaisher, 1930) 277–83. For sources of possible early historical intercourse between Jews and Indians, see Walter Schmitthenner, "Rome and India: Aspects of Universal History during the Principate," *Journal of Roman Studies* 69 (1979): 90–106.
12. Louis Jacolliot, *Bible in India: Hindoo Origin of Hebrew and Revelation* (New York: Carleton Publishers, 1870); François Jean-Marie Laouenan, *Du brahmanisme et de ses rapports avec le judaisme et le christianisme,* vol. 1 (Paris: Challamel, 1884); Maurice Fluegel, *Philosophy, and Vedanta: Comparative Metaphysics and Ethics, Rationalism and Mysticism, of the Jews, the Hindus and Most of the Historic Nations, as Links and Developments of One Chain of Universal Philosophy* (Baltimore: Sun Printing Office, 1902). The theosophical speculations of Madame Blavatsky and the outgrowth of the academic comparativist side of the perennial philosophy movement, which included René Guenon, Carl Jung, Ananda K. Coomaraswamy, Mircea Eliade, and Joseph Campbell, sought to synthesize traditional mythologies for the purpose of promoting universal consciousness. To that end, only Coomaraswamy made conscientious and positive comparisons of Jewish and Indian concepts and texts. See Roger Lipsey (ed.), *Coomaraswamy* (Princeton: Princeton University Press, 1977).
13. Henri Hubert and Marcel Mauss, "Essai sur la Nature et la Fonction du Sacrifice," *L'Année Sociologique* 2 (1898): 29–138; English version: *Sacrifice, Its Nature and Function,* translated by W. D. Halls (Chicago: University of Chicago Press, 1964), 7. Compare Olivier Herrenschmidt's contrast between biblical "symbolic sacrifice" and Brahmanical "effective sacrifice" in his "Sacrifice: Symbolic or Effective?," in *Between Belief and Transgression: Structuralist Essays in Religion, History, and Myth,* edited by Michel Izard and Pierre Smith (Chicago: University of Chicago Press, 1982), 24–42.

Compare Sylvain Lévi's *La doctrine du sacrifice dans le Brahmanas* (Paris, 1898; reprint Presses Universitaires de France, 1966). For studies dealing directly with comparisons of Christian and Hindu sacrifice, see Joe Thachil, *The Vedic and the Christian Concept of Sacrifice* (Kerala, India: Pontifical Institute of Theology and Philosophy, 1985); Francis Clooney, "Sacrifice and its Spiritualization in the Christian and Hindu Traditions: A Study in Comparative Theology," *Harvard Theological Review* 78 (1985): 3–4, 361–80; W. F. Albright and P. E. Dupont, "A Parallel between Indic and Babylonian Sacrificial Ritual," *Journal of the American Oriental Society* 54 (1934): 107–28; Karl-Heinz Golzio, *Der Tempel im Elten Mesopotamien und Seine Parallelen in Indien* (Leiden: E. J. Brill, 1983).

For an interdisciplinary approach, see Irene Winter, "Ritual Treatment of Images in the Ancient Near East: Art History and Ethnoarchaeology," a paper delivered at the College Art Association session on interdisciplinary approaches to the art of the ancient Near East, 1990 (thanks to Professor Richard Davis for this). See also Alf Hiltebeitel, "Rama and Gilgamesh: The Sacrifice of the Water Buffalo and the Bull of Heaven," *History of Religions* 19 (February 1980): 187–223.

Mention should also be made of comparative studies of purity and impurity. See J. Duncan M. Derrett's unpublished paper "Ritual Immersion in Hinduism and Judaism" (1988); Richard Holt Davis, "The Uses of Purity in Medhatithi's Manubhasya," unpublished master's thesis, University of Toronto, 1978. Compare also A. Kevin Reinhart, "Impurity/No Danger" *History of Religions* 30 (August 1990): 1–24; David P. Wright, *The Disposal of Impurity: Elimination Rites in the Bible and in the Hittite and Mesopotamian Literature* (Atlanta: Scholars Press, 1987), 105–11.

14. James Darmesteter, "David et Rama," *Revue des Etudes Juives* 2–3 (1881); Sylvain Levi, "Problemes Indo-Hebraiques," *Revue des Etudes Juives* 82 (1926): 45–54.
15. Maurice Bloomfield, "Joseph and Potiphar in Hindu Fiction," *Transactions and Proceedings of the American Philological Association* 54 (1923): 141–67; cf. John D. Yohannan, *Joseph and Potiphar's Wife in World Literature: An Anthology of the Story of the Chaste Youth and the Lustful Stepmother* (New York: New Directions Books, 1968), 1–9.
16. Walter Ruben, "Bible and Purana," *Indian Studies: Past and Present* 7 (1966): 137–51, 337–48.
17. Michael David Futterman, "Judaism, Hinduism and Theodicy: A Comparative Study of the Judaic and Hindu Treatment of the Problem of Evil" Ph.D. dissertation, New York University, 1977.
18. Daniel Friedland Polish, "The Flood Myth in the Traditions of Israel and India," Ph.D. dissertation in the Study of Religion, Harvard University, 1974. See also Alan Dundes, *The Flood Myth* (Berkeley: University of California Press, 1988).
19. Barbara A. Holdrege, *Veda and Torah: Transcending the Textuality of Scripture* (Albany, NY: SUNY Press, forthcoming).
20. Carlos A. Ayarragaray, *La Justicia en la Biblia y el Talmud (Con un Commentario a la Ley de Manu, por Alberto Lopez Camps)* (Buenos

Aires: Libreria Juridica, 1948); Eugene Combs and Kenneth Post, *The Foundations of Political Order in Genesis and the Chandogya Upanishad* (Lewiston, NY: E. Mellen Press, 1987). Comparative biblical and Indian mythology can be found in the footnotes of Theodor H. Gaster's *Myth, Legend, and Custom in the Old Testament* (New York: Harper and Row, 1969); and Dan Ben Amos, "Hebrew Parallels to Indian Folktales," *Journal of the Assam Research Society* 15 (1963): 37–45. Yehezkel Kaufmann *Toldot ha-Emunah ha-Israelit* (Tel Aviv: Bialik Institute-Dvir, 1937), 331–50) compares the monotheistic idea of early Israel with that of the Indians. For a critique of comparative biblical approaches, see Shemaryahu Talmon, "The 'Comparative Method' in Biblical Interpretation—Principles and Problems," in *Essential Papers on Israel and the Ancient Near East,* edited by Frederick E. Greenspahn (New York: New York University Press, 1991), 381–419. For comparative linguistics, see Saul Levin, "In What Sense Was Hebrew a Primeval Language?," *General Linguistics* 29 (1989): 221–27; idem, *The Indo-European and Semitic Languages* (Albany, NY: SUNY Press, 1971). Levin is developing a systematic comparative grammar of Semitic and Indo-European. Levin has observed, along with others, the double tradition of sacred texts, the oral and written, in Hebrew and Sanskrit traditions. Cf. Jean Canteins, *Phonèmes et Archetypes* (Paris: G.-P. Maisonneuve et Larose, 1972).

See also Norman W. Brown, *The Indian and Christian Miracles of Walking on Water* (Chicago/London: Open Court, 1928); D. J. A. Clines, "In Search of the Indian Job," *Vetus Testamentum* 33 (1983): 398–418; Cristiano Grottanelli, "The King's Grace and the Helpless Woman: A Comparative Study of the Stories of Ruth, Charila, Sita," *History of Religions* 22 (August 1982): 1–24; Jacob Yuroh Teshima, "Self-Extinction in Zen and Hasidism," in *Zen and Hasidism: The Similarities between Two Spiritual Disciplines,* edited by H. Heifetz (Wheaton: Theosophical Publishing House, 1978); Jacob Yuroh Teshima, "The Problem of 'Strange Thoughts' and Its Treatment," in *Perspectives on Jews and Judaism: Essays in Honor of Wolfe Kelman,* edited by Arthur A. Chiel (New York: Rabbinical Assembly, 1978), 421–42, and "Self-Extinction in Zen and Hasidism," ibid., 108–17; W. Kirfel, "Indische Parallelen zum Alten Testament," *Saeculum* 7 (1956): 369–84; Arnold Kunst, "An Overlooked Type of Inference," *Bulletin of the School of Oriental and African Studies* 10 (1942): 976–91; Judith Ann Linzer, "Jewish Identity and Eastern Religions: A Phenomenological Investigation," Ph.D. dissertation, United States International University, 1984; Joseph P. Schultz, "The Concept of Illusion in Vedanta and Kabbalah," *Judaism and the Gentile Faiths* (East Brunswick, NJ: Associated University Presses, 1981) 70–100; Jacob N. Shimmel and Satyaraja Dasa Adhikari [Steven Rosen], *Om Shalom Judaism and Krishna Consciousness* (Brooklyn: Folk Books, 1990). Rosen edits and publishes the *Journal of Vaiṣṇava Studies.* The late Deirdre Green wrote a paper on "Kundalini Yoga and Kabbalistic Meditation" to be published in a forthcoming issue of *Avaloka: A Journal of Traditional Religion and Culture.*

21. Shlomo Pines, "A Doctrine of the Brahmans (Barahima) according to Al-Qasim b. Ibrahim and Saadia Gaon," *Jerusalem Studies in Arabic and Islam (JSAI)* 2 (1980): 220–33; and Sarah Stroumsa, "The Barahima in Early Kalam," *JSAI* 6 (1985): 229–41.
22. Moses Maimonides, *The Guide of the Perplexed,* translated and introduction by Shlomo Pines (Chicago: University of Chicago Press, 1963), 515, 516, 519, 581. See S. D. Goitein, "Moses Maimonides, Man of Action: A Revision of the Master's Biography in the Light of the Genizah Documents," in *Hommage à George Vajda,* edited by G. Nahon and C. Touati (Louvain: Deiters, 1950), 162–63; S. D. Goitein, "From the Mediterranean to India," *Speculum* 29 (April 1954): 181–97. Goitein found Jews engaged in extensive trade with India in the medieval period, and his students are in the process of preparing Goitein's "India Book," which documents this trade. On Maimonides' attitude to non-Jews and Hindus, see David Novak, *The Image of the Non-Jew in Judaism* (Lewiston, NY: Edwin Mellen Press, 1983), 141.
23. See note 61 below.
24. See Gershom Scholem, *On the Kabbalah and Its Symbolism* (New York: Schocken, 1969), 183–84.
25. See Isaac Abravanel's commentary on Noah.
26. Manasseh ben Israel, *Nishmat Hayyim* (Amsterdam, 1652), section 4, chapter 21. He draws on Abravanel.
27. Shalem Shabazi, a seventeenth-century Yemenite kabbalist, cites India as the source of his knowledge of sand geomancy, to be found in his commentary on *parshat shoftim,* Deuteronomy 16.18–21.9.
28. Moses Mendelssohn, *Jerusalem,* translated by Allan Arkush, introduction and commentary by Alexander Altmann (Hanover, NH: Brandeis University Press, 1983), 114–15, 225. See W. Halbfass, *India and Europe,* 61. For a closer examination, see Arnold Eisen, "Divine Legislation as 'Ceremonial Script': Mendelssohn on the Commandments," *Association of Jewish Studies Review* 15 (Fall 1990): 239–67.
29. David ben ibn Abi Zimra (sixteenth century) responsa on the Jews of India in Alexander Marx, "Contributions à l'histoire des Juifs de Cochin," *Revue des Etudes Juives* 89 (1930): 293–304; Jacob ben Sheshet, cited by David R. Blumenthal, "Religion and the Religious Intellectuals: The Case of Judaism in Medieval Times" in Jacob Neusner, ed., *Take Judaism, for example* (Chicago: U. of Chicago Press) 1983) 127. Yehezkiel Landau responsum of 1778, cited by Louis Jacobs, *Theology in the Responsa* (London: Routledge and Kegan Paul, 1975); Solomon Eliashov, *Leshem Shevo ve-Ahlamah* (Petrokov, 1912), drush 3, section 21, part 2; Yehudah Moshe F'taya, *Sefer Minhat Yehudah* (1933; reprinted Jerusalem: Chazon F'taya), 40; Zvi Yehuda haKohen Kook, "Responsa on Indian meditation," 10 Adar 5739 (1978). Jerusalem. For Menachem M. Schneerson on transcendental meditation, see *Lubavitch News Service,* Brooklyn, NY, press release of 20 August 1979. Matityahu Glazerson, *From Hinduism to Judaism* (Jerusalem: Himelsein, Glazerson, 1984). Contrast this with one of Schneerson's

students, Zalman Schachter, who led a *saṭsaṅga* at the Kripalu center in Massachusetts on 12 August 1992.

30. Hegel wrote in 1824: "The Jewish God [is], just like Brahma, imageless and supersensible, but a supersensible that is a mere abstraction of thought, which does not yet have within it the plenitude that makes it spirit." G. W. F. Hegel, *Lectures on the Philosophy of Religion* (Berkeley: University of California Press, 1984), 331. See extensive discussions on Hegel in Halbfass, *India and Europe;* M. Hulin, *Hegel et l'Orient* (Paris: Vrin, 1979).
31. Moses Hess, *Rome and Jerusalem* (1862, German edition), translated by Meyer Waxman (New York: Bloch Publishing, 1945), 208–11. For a discussion, see Shlomo Avineri, *Moses Hess, Prophet of Communism and Zionism* (New York: New York University Press, 1985), 171–239.
32. Shlomo Pines, "Islam according to the *Star of Redemption,*" *Bar Ilan Annual* 22–23 (1987): 303–14. (Hebrew)
33. Maurice Friedman, "Martin Buber and Asia," *Philosophy East and West* 26 (October 1976): 411–26; see also Buber's foreword to *Bagawadgita: Shirat ha-Mevorakh,* translated into Hebrew by Immanuel Olsvanger (Jerusalem: Mossad Bialik); Paul Mendes-Flohr, "Fin-de-Siecle Orientalism, the *Ostjuden* and the Aesthetics of Jewish Self-Affirmation," in *Studies in Contemporary Jewry,* vol. 1, edited by Jonathan Frankel (Bloomington: Indiana University Press, 1984), 96–139. Compare Buber to Elie Wiesel, who "went to India for a few months. There I studied in an ashram; I studied the Vedas. I was preparing a dissertation, a comparative study of asceticism—Jewish, Buddhist, and Christian" *Against Silence: The Voice and Vision of Elie Wiesel* (New York: Holocaust Library, 1984), vol. 3, p. 218.
34. See below, note 54.
35. For example, David Shulman and Moshe Idel taught a seminar on Indian and Jewish approaches to language at Hebrew University in the fall of 1992. Sessions dedicated to Judaism and Hinduism were held at the annual meetings of the American Academy of Religion in 1992 and 1993. At Emory, Professors Daird Blumenthal and Paul Cartright, have co-taught an introduction to religion course structured around Jewish and Hindu sources.
36. Wendy Doniger O'Flaherty, *Other Peoples' Myths* (New York: Macmillan, 1988).
37. The idea for this section came to me while listening to Alan Slifka speak at the Yale Hillel Alumni Forum, 1 June 1991. I thank him for his insights.
38. Anson Laytner, *Arguing with God: A Jewish Tradition* (Northvale, NJ: Jason Aronson, 1990). Laytner is also editor of the Sino-Judaic Institute Newsletter.
39. Adin Steinsaltz, *The Talmud: The Steinsaltz Edition—A Reference Guide* (New York: Random House, 1989).
40. Moshe Idel, *Kabbalah: New Perspectives* (New Haven, Yale University Press, 1988), 247, 267; *Language, Torah, and Hermeneutics in Abraham Abulafia* (Albany: SUNY Press, 1989).
41. Samuel C. Heilman, *The People of the Book: Drama, Fellowship, and Religion* (Chicago: University of Chicago Press, 1983).

42. Deborah Schiffrin, "Jewish Argument as Sociability," *Language in Society* 13 (1984): 311–35.
43. William Novak and Moshe Waldoks, *Big Book of Jewish Humor* (New York: Harper and Row, 1981). Waldoks has taken a leading role in Jewish-Tibetan dialogues. See note 55 below.
44. Edmond Jabes, *The Book of Questions* (Middletown, CT: Wesleyan University Press, 1976). See also Edmond Jabes, *The Sin of the Book,* edited by Eric Gould (Lincoln: University of Nebraska Press, 1985); Susan A. Handelman, *Slayers of Moses: The Emergence of Rabbinic Interpretation in Modern Literary Theory* (Albany: SUNY Press, 1982); Jose Faur, *Golden Doves with Silver Dots: Semiotics and Textuality in Rabbinic Tradition* (Bloomington: Indiana University Press, 1986); *Midrash and Literature,* edited by Geoffrey H. Hartman and Sanford Budick (New Haven: Yale University Press, 1986); Harold Coward, *Derrida and Indian Philosophy* (Albany: SUNY Press, 1990).
45. See Michel Meyer, *Questions and Questioning* (Berlin and New York: Walter de Gruyter, 1988); Karl Popper, *Conjectures and Refutations: The Growth of Scientific Knowledge* (New York: Basic Books, 1963); Hans-Dieter Bastian, *Theologie der Frage* (Munich: Chr. Kaiser Verlag, 1970); Gemma Corradi Fiumara, *The Other Side of Language: A Philosophy of Listening,* translated by Charles Lambert (London and New York: Routledge, 1990). See theme issue on "Questions" in *Parabola: The Magazine of Myth and Tradition* 13 (Fall 1988).
46. George Steiner, "Our Homeland, the Text," *Salmagundi* 66 (Winter-Spring 1985): 7–8.
47. George Steiner, "Some 'Meta-Rabbis,' " in *Next Year in Jerusalem: Jews in the Twentieth Century,* edited by Douglas Villiers (London: Harrap, 1976), 64–75.
48. I owe this insight of "law as nurturing" to Edmund Leites in a discussion we had on Foucault and Judaism. The emphasis of the culture of questions is on the pursuit of cross-cultural resonances and the affirmation of life. We suggest this approach as a possible counterpoint to the orientalist debate provoked by Edward Said's *Orientalism.* We would argue that his orientalism derives from a philosophically unexamined assessment of the relationship between cultural truth and the coercive definition and delimitation of others. The culture of questions, in contrast, emphasizes the ability of two cultures, such as the Hindu and Jewish, to engage in free discourse from within the Orient itself, and therefore face each other from a position of greater moral, existential, and ontological equality. For an example of this approach, see Julia Alexis Kushigian, "Three Versions of Orientalism in Contemporary Latin American Literature: Sarduy, Borges and Paz," Ph.D. thesis, Yale University, 1984. See also Jonathan Z. Smith, "Differential Equations: On Constructing the 'Other,' " Thirteenth Annual University Lecture in Religion, Arizona State University, 5 March 1992.
49. E. Bevan and C. J. Singer (eds), *Legacy of Israel* (London: Oxford, 1927), 173–314; George Steiner, *After Babel: Aspects of Language and Transla-*

tion (Oxford: Oxford University Press, 1975); Ben-Ami Scharfstein, "Cultures, Contexts, and Comparisons," in Ben-Ami Scharfstein, Ilai Alon, Slomo Biderman, Dan Daor, Yoel Hoffmann, *Philosophy East/Philosophy West: A Critical Comparison of Indian, Chinese, Islamic, and European Philosophy* (New York: Oxford University Press, 1978), 9–47.

50. This orientation is not limited to Indology, but can be found in the works of Jewish scholars working in Asian studies. Consider Vera Schwartz, "Mingled Voices: On Writing My Father's Memoirs," *Columbia: A Magazine of Poetry and Prose* (Fall 1991): 120–37; or David G. Goodman, *Toboshi* [My Escapology] (Tokyo: Shobunsha, 1976), which deals with the impact of Jewish hermeneutics and values on the way in which Japanese culture is approached. Joseph Levenson's work is also influenced by a Jewish sense of history.
51. Peter Berger, *The Heretical Imperative* (Garden City, NY: Doubleday, 1979). The pattern continues in Peter Berger, *The Other Side of God* (Garden City, NY, Doubleday, 1981), 7–8. For a critique, see Michael L. Morgan, "Judaism and the Heretical Imperative," *Religious Studies* 17 (1981): 109–20. Cf. Stanley J. Samartha, "Can Mount Sinai and River Ganga Meet?," *Tantur Year Book* (1975/76): 99–120.
52. Berger, *Heretical Imperative,* 159.
53. Ibid., 167.
54. The Christian-Buddhist-Hindu discussions tend to focus on (1) ontological questions concerning transcendence, being, and absolute nondualism; (2) existential concerns regarding charismatic figures, enlightened beings, and divine incarnations (for example, Christ and Buddha, saints, saviors, avatars, and gurus); (3) epistemological questions concerning such issues as interiority, spiritual embodiment, and the ritual-aesthetic power embedded in material objects; and (4) the ethical implications of traditions such as monasticism, asceticism, celibacy, and meditation. Alternative themes for the study of Jewish-Hindu comparative civilization might include an examination of legal traditions, the intermingling of nationalism and religion, the role of sacred time and space, pilgrimage festivals, ritual meaning and behavior, the relationship between center and diaspora, karma and holocaust, exile and continuity, purity and impurity, family and the communal self, personal transformation and the devotional life, ethical obligations, and comparative hermeneutics traditions.

    For the image of Christianity in Hindu thought, see K. R. Sundararajan, "The Hindu Models of Interreligious Dialogue," *Journal of Ecumenical Studies* 23 (Spring 1986): 239–50; Richard Fox Young, *Resistant Hinduism: Sanskrit Sources on Anti-Christian Apologetics in Early Nineteenth-Century India,* ed. G. Oberhammer (Leiden: E. J. Brill, 1981). See also George Chemparathy, *Bible et Veda: Comme Parole de Dieu* (Louvain: Centre d'Histoire des Religions, 1981); Arvind Sharma, "Selected Bibliography" [on contemporary Hindu-Christian dialogue], in *Religious Issues and Interreligious Dialogues,* edited by Charles Wei-hsun Fu and Gerhard E. Spiegler (Westport: Greenwood Press, 1989), 497–509;

Harold Coward (ed.), *Modern Indian Responses to Religious Pluralism* (Albany: SUNY Press, 1987).

On Christian dialogue with Hinduism and Buddhism, see Ernst Benz and Minoru Nambara, *Das Christentum und die Nicht-Christlichen Hochreligionen: Begegnung und auseinandersetzung eine internationale bibliographie* (Leiden: E. J. Brill, 1960); Seiichi Yagi and Leonard Swidler, *A Bridge to Buddhist Christian Dialogue* (Mahwah: Paulist Press, 1990); G. W. Houston, *The Cross and the Lotus: Christianity and Buddhism in Dialogue* (Delhi: Motilal Banarsidass, 1985); Donald S. Lopez and Steven C. Rockefeller, *The Christ and the Bodhisattva* (Albany: SUNY Press, 1987); R. Panikkar, *The Unknown Christ of Hinduism* (London: Darton, Longman and Todd, 1964); Paul O Ingram and Frederick J. Streng, *Buddhist-Christian Dialogue* (Honolulu: University of Hawaii Press, 1986); *Buddhist-Christian Studies,* East-West Religions Project, University of Hawaii; Joseph Spae, *Buddhist-Christian Empathy* (Chicago Institute of Theology and Culture, 1980). See also Eric Sharpe, "Neo-Hindu Images of Christianity," *Neo-Hindu Views of Christianity,* ed. Arvind Sharma (Leiden: E. J. Brill, 1988), 1–15.

55. The expulsion and dispersion of a religious people from its homeland is an experience shared by Jews and Tibetan Buddhists. In contrast, Hindus have remained at home for millennia, except for the self-exiled. Praiseworthy dialogue has begun between Jewish leaders and the Dalai Lama. See Nathan Katz, "The Dalai Lama and the 'Jewish Secret,' " *Jerusalem Post,* 23, 30 April, 7 May 1991; Ari Goldman, "Dalai Lama Meets Jews of 4 Branches," *New York Times,* 26 September 1989; Rodger Kamenetz, "Searching for Lost Angels," *Baltimore Jewish Times,* 30 November 1990. Rodger Kamenetz, *The Jew in the Lotus: A Poet's Re-Discovery of Jewish Identity in Buddhist India* (San Francisco: Harper, 1944). The encounter of Jews with the Dalai Lama focused on giving him advice from one diaspora people to another and on the comparison of techniques of spirituality, including ritual and mystical conceptions and practices. Nathan Katz, "The Jewish Secret and the Dalai Lama: A Dharamsala Diary," *Conservative Judaism* 43 (Summer 1991): 33–45. On 16–18 August 1991 a conference on "Jewish Diasporas in China: Comparative and Historical Perspectives" was held at Harvard and on 12–13 September 1992, the Jewish-Buddhist Conference, held in Barre, Massachusetts, was sponsored by the Barre Center for Buddhist Studies, the Jewish Community of Amherst, and the Nathan Cummings Foundation. The Sino-Judaic Institute, Menlo Park, California, publishes *Points East,* which reviews current interest and scholarship in Jewish East/West relations.

56. Hayim Greenberg, "The Universalism of the Jewish People," in *The Inner Eye* (New York: Jewish Frontier Association, 1953), 26: "The Jews of antiquity were scarcely aware of the great civilizations of the Far East (China, India); even had they known them well, who can tell how they would have reacted?" (Compare Franz Rosenzweig, *Star of Redemption* (Boston: Beacon Press, 1972), 35ff: "It is not by coincidence that revelation, once it

started on its way into the world, took the road to the West, not to the East. The living 'gods of Greece' were worthier opponents of the living God than the phantoms of the Asiatic Orient."

57. Abraham Joshua Heschel, *God in Search of Man* (New York: Harper and Row, 1966), 15. Arvind Sharma, "Hindu-Jewish Dialogue and the Thought of Abraham Heschel" in *No Religion is an Island: Abraham Joshua Heschel and Interreligious Dialogue* edited by Harold Kasimow and Byron L. Sherwin (Maryknoll, NY: Orbis, 1991) 163–174. Harold Kasimov, "The Jewish Tradition and the Bhagavadgita," *Journal of Dharma* 8: 3 (July/September 1983) 296–310.

58. For an extended discussion of these issues, see Shalva Weil, "Bene Israel Indian Jews in Lod, Israel: A Study of the Persistence of Ethnicity and Ethnic Identity," Ph.D. thesis, University of Sussex, 1977; Shirley Berry Isenberg, *India's Bene Israel: A Comprehensive Inquiry and Sourcebook* (Bombay and Berkley: Popular Prakashan and Judah Magnes Museum, 1988), especially, pp. 98–147 on caste and life-cycle parallels with the Hindu; and J. Bruce Long, "Mahashivaratri: The Saiva Festival of Repentence," in *Religious Festivals in South India and Sri Lanka,* edited by Guy Welbon and Glenn Yocum (Delhi: Manohar, 1982).

    For information on the Jews of India, see Nathan Katz, "An Annotated Bibliography about Indian Jewry," 1991 (available from author, Dept. Religious Studies, University of South Florida, Tampa, Florida); *India and Israel* [Journal], Bombay, 1948–53; Joan G. Roland, *Jews in British India: Identity in a Colonial Era* (Hanover and London: Published for Brandeis University Press by University Press of New England, 1989); Thomas A. Timberg, *Jews in India* (New Delhi: Vikas, 1986). The official recognition of Israel by India in early 1992 ought to have a significant impact on the frequency and quality of dialogue between the two nations. See Monroe Rosenthal and M. S. Solow, "India and Israel—A Common Affinity," *Midstream,* August/September 1991, pp. 23–26. Beginning in 1993, Zubin Mehta and Shalva Weil Chaired the Israel-India Cultural Association.

59. Nathan Katz and Ellen S. Goldberg, "The Ritual Enactments of the Cochin Jews: The Powers of Purity and Nobility," in *Ritual and Power,* edited by Barbara A. Holdrege, *Journal of Ritual Studies* 4 (Summer 1990): 199–238, esp. 200–1. See also their "Asceticism and Caste in the Passover Observances of the Cochin Jews," *Journal of the American Academy of Religion* 57 (Spring 1989): 53–82. Nathan Katz and Ellen S. Goldberg, *The Last Jews of Cochin: Jewish Identity in Hindu India* (Columbia: University of South Carolina Press, 1993).

60. Steven Katz, "Language, Epistemology, and Mysticism," in *Mysticism and Philosophical Analysis,* edited by S. T. Katz (New York: Oxford, 1978), 22–74. In contrast, see Robert K. C. Forman, *The Problem of Pure Consciousness: Mysticism and Philosophy* (New York: Oxford University Press, 1990; Charles Elliott Vernoff "Hinduism, Judaism and the Theoretical Definition of Mysticism," unpublished paper, 1988. See comments of Stanley Jeyaraja Tambiah in his *Magic, Science, Religion, and the Scope of*

Rationality (Cambridge: Cambridge University Press, 1990). These same issues arise in anthropology. See Richard A. Shweder, "Anthropology's Romantic Rebellion against the Enlightenment, or There's More to Thinking than Reason and Evidence," *Culture Theory,* edited by Shweder and Robert A. LeVine (Cambridge: Cambridge University Press, 1984), 27–66. Especially stimulating is the discussion on "frameswitching." See also Fitz John Porter Poole, "Metaphors and Maps: Towards Comparison in the Anthropology of Religion," *Journal of the American Academy of Religion* 54: 411–57; Howard Eilberg-Schwartz, *The Savage in Judaism: An Anthropology of Israelite Religion and Ancient Judaism* (Bloomington: Indiana University Press, 1990).

61. For an example of resonance in Judaism, see Abraham Ibn Ezra's twelfth-century *Commentary on the Torah,* where he cites what he believes to be contemporary Indian practices which resonate with those present in the Torah. He sought to validate an understanding of the text by highlighting the likely reality of the phenomena from a comparative perspective. See also Moritz Steinschneider, "Ist Ibn Esra im Indien gewesen?," in *Gesammelte Schriften,* edited by Heinrich Malter and Alexander Marx (Berlin: M. Poppelauer, 1925), 498–502. Compare the statements of a contemporary Orthodox rabbinic scholar, Aaron Lichtenstein: "The explicit systematic discussions of Gentile thinkers often reveal for us the hidden wealth implicit in our own writings" (*Gesher* 1 [June 1963]: 11). My thoughts on cultural resonance and the value of questions in developing openness to others is similar to Stephen Greenblatt's succinct formulation: "By resonance I mean the power of the object displayed to reach out beyond its formal boundaries to a larger world, to evoke in the viewer the complex, dynamic cultural forces from which it has emerged and for which as metaphor or more simply as metonymy it may be taken by a viewer to stand. By wonder I mean the power of the object displayed to stop the viewer in his tracks, to convey an arresting sense of uniqueness, to evoke an exalted attention." Stephen Greenblatt, *Learning to Curse: Essays in Early Modern Culture* (London: Routledge, 1990) 170.

Notes to Chapter 2

1. Hananya Goodman tells me that Sylvain Lévi wrote in 1927 (cited on p. 208 of *L'Alliance Israelite Universelle et la Renaissance Juive Contemporaine,* 1965): "Juif et indianiste bouddhisant, je cumule dans cet ordre-la."
2. This discussion stems from a part of my book, *Other Peoples' Myths: The Cave of Echoes* (New York: Macmillan, 1988).
3. One that has in fact been well discussed by Daniel Gold in *Comprehending the Guru: Toward a Grammar of Religious Perception* (Atlanta, 1988), and by Judy Linzer in her 1984 dissertation "Jewish Identity and Eastern Religions: A Phenomenological Investigation," *Dissertation Abstracts International,* vol. 45, No. 08, 1985.

4. Heinrich Zimmer, *Myths and Symbols in Indian Art and Civilization* (New York, 1946), 219–21, citing Martin Buber's *Die Chassidischen Bucher* (Hellerau, 1928), 532–33.
5. Zimmer, *Myths and Symbols,* 219.
6. Charles H. Long, "The Dreams of Professor Campbell: Joseph Campbell's *The Mythic Image,*" in *Religious Studies Review* 6 (October, 1980): 261–71.
7. Robert Jungk, *Heller als tausend Sonnen: Das Schicksal der Atomforscher* (Bern, 1956), 211; English translation: *Brighter than a Thousand Suns: The Moral and Political History of the Atomic Scientists,* translated by James Cleugh (London, 1958), 202.
8. Presented at the Brooklyn Academy of Music during October, November, and December 1987. Mimi Kramer wrote in the *New Yorker* (2 November 1987): "Peter Brook [is] not really interested in the conflict between the Pandavas and the Kauravas at all; he's interested in the threat of nuclear war. The warring factions in his 'Mahabharata' are *almost explicitly* likened to two rival superpowers" (p. 147). I have added the emphasis; "almost explicitly" reflects the implicit power of the myth to force us to draw personal analogies.
9. Wendy Doniger O'Flaherty, *The Origins of Evil in Hindu Mythology* (Berkeley, 1976), especially chap. 6, "The Birth of Death." It was Dennis O'Flaherty who pointed out to me the relevance of my work on death to my experience of death.
10. William Sax nicely translates *prasāda* as "edible grace."

Notes to Chapter 3

1. M. Wheller, *Cambridge History of India,* supplementary volume (Cambridge, 1960), 90–95. For other references, see note 18 below.
2. See references ibid., 218, note 4.
3. Cf. Manfred Mayrhofer, *Die Indo-Arier im alten Vorderasien* (Wiesbaden, 1966). For a contrary view, see Annelies Kammenhuber, *Die Arier im Vorderen Orient* (Heidelberg, 1968).
4. Mayrhofer, *Kurzgefaßtes etymologisches Wörterbuch des Altendischen,* vol. 4 (Heidelberg, 1956), 597; R. T. O'Callaghan, "New Light on the Maryannu as 'Chariot-Warrior,' " *Jahrbuch für kleinasiatische Forschung* 1 (1951): 309–24.
5. The Hurrians were a non-Semitic and non-Indo-European people, who ruled in the fifteenth century B.C.E. over Mitanni, north of Mesopotamia. For their language, see Frederick William Bush, *A Grammar of the Hurrian Language* (Ann Arbor, 1964).
6. In Sanskrit, *arya-* means "hospitable nobleman"; cf. Mayrhofer, *Kurzgefaßtes etymologisches Wörterbuch,* vol. 1, 52.
7. Cf. Rabin, *Sefer Shmuel Yeivin* (Jerusalem, 1970), 462–97 (Hebrew).
8. J. Charpentier, "Zur arischen Wortkunde," *Zeitschrift für vergleichende Sprachforschung* 43 (1910): 168.
9. Paul A. de Lagarde, *Gesammelte Abhandlungen* (Leipsig, 1866), 163 (microfiche, American Theological Library Assn.).

10. A. Alt, "Die Herrenschicht von Ugarit," *Zeitschrift des deutschen Palästina-Vereins* 45 (1942): 144–64.
11. *Jaarbericht Ex Oriente Lux* 18 (1964): 339–44. The connection had already been suggested by J. Scheftelowitz, *Zeitschrift für vergleichende Sprachforschung* 38 (1905): 272; H. Kronasser, *Die Sprache* 4 (1958): 127; and Mayrhofer, "Der hentige Forschungsstand zu den indoiranischen Sprachresten in Vorderasien," *Zeitschrift der Deutschen Morgenländischen Gesellschaft* 111 (1961): 454.
12. These words, as well as those mentioned before, are discussed in detail (in Hebrew) in *Sefer Shmuel Yeivin* (cf. above, note 7).
13. *Shilapadikaram,* by Ilango Adigal. The subsequent text is combined from the translations of V. R. Ramachandra Dikshitar (Oxford, 1939), 110, and of A. Daniélou (London 1965), 18.
14. Cf. Mayrhofer *Kurzgefaßtes etymologisches Wörterbuch,* vol. 1, 527; vol. 3, 56. In the first reference, he points out that other Sanskrit words for "water" were borrowed from Dravidian languages. *Tarshish* is translated "sea' in Isaiah 2.16 by the Aramaic Targum, the Septuagint, and Saadiah Gaon; in Isaiah 23.10 by Targum and Saadiah; in Ezekiel 1.16 by the Vulgate. See also S. B. Hoenig, *Jewish Quarterly Review* 69 (1978/9): 181–82, where he connects the word with the Greek *thalassēs,* "of the sea."
15. Cf. Mayrhofer, *Kurzgefaßtes etymologisches Wörterbuch,* vol. 1, 90.
16. The *el-* in Greek *elephās* could be a prefix marking large animals; cf. Julius Pokorny, *Indogermanisches etymologisches Wörterbuch* (Bern, 1959), 303.
17. The meaning given to *tukkī* in Modern Hebrew, "parrot," is due to the Turkish *toti.*
18. The *Jātaka,* edited by E. B. Cowell (Cambridge 1957), vol. 3, 83–84; also edited by V. Fausboell, vol. 3 (London, 1963) 126–128. Cf. C. Rabin, "The Song of Songs and Tamil Poetry," *Sciences Réligieuses* 3 (1973/4): 205–6.
19. Cf. Song of Songs 7.12–14. A number of such poems are translated in Naladai R. Balakrishna Mudaliar, *Golden Anthology of Ancient Tamil Literature* (Madras, 1959/60). A few extracts are quoted in Rabin (see note 18), 211–12.
20. See, however, the tannaitic debate in Mishna *Yaddayim* 3.5 (in the translation of H. Danby [Oxford, 1938] 781–82).
21. Mayrhofer, *Kurzgefaßtes etymologisches Wörterbuch,* vol. 3, 282.
22. Jules Bloch, *Structure grammaticale des langues dravidiennes* (Paris, 1946), 16. This particular form is not listed by T. Burrow and M. B. Emeneau, *A Dravidian Etymological Dictionary* (Oxford, 1966), item no. 4306, p. 358, but they give *wanjī* and *vanjī* the same meaning in other languages.
23. For details, cf. Rabin, "Rice in the Bible," *Journal of Semitic Studies* 9 (Spring 1966): 2–9.
24. H. Blank, *Dictionary of Iraqi Arabic,* 148.

Notes to Chapter 4

1. Genesis Rabbah 39.1 (edited by Albeck, 365); English from *Midrash Rabbah,* vol. 1, translated by H. Freedman (London and Bournemouth, 1951), 313. At

the end of the first sentence of the quotation, I have substituted the phrase "lighted" for Freedman's translation, "in flames." See also E. E. Urbach, *The Sages: Their Concepts and Beliefs* (Jerusalem, 1979), vol. 1, 30–31.

2. L. Ginzberg, *The Legends of the Jews* (Philadelphia, 1947), vol. 1, 189, and vol. 5, 210 n. 16; see below for a discussion of its sources.
3. The legend resembles the argument in the Wisdom of Solomon 13.1–9. See on this passage D. Winston, *The Wisdom of Solomon* (New York, 1979), 248–57.
4. Genesis Rabbah 33.11 (to Gen. 11.28), edited by Albeck, 363–65. See also the parallel in *Midrash ha-Gadol* (to Gen. 15.7), edited by M. Margulies, 252, and see the note there.
5. In that context, the legend was adapted to the new framework and changed into a dialogue between Nimrod and Abraham. It becomes clear that the legend is an addition when one compares the text of Genesis Rabbah with Seder Eliahu Rabbah, chap. 6, edited by M. Friedmann (Vienna, 1904), 27, and see the note there. The story is narrated there without the whole legend, and only the worship of fire is mentioned, because it belongs to the story. See also the appendix to Seder Eliahu Zuta, 47–49.
6. See the preceding note and Ginzberg, *Legends,* vol. 5, 210 n. 16; A. Jellinek, *Bet ha-Midrasch* (Jerusalem, 1938), vol. 1, 26, and vol. 2, 118; *Yasher,* edited by L. Goldschmidt (Berlin, 1923), 28. The most important evidence is, it seems, *Midrash ha-Gadol* (to Gen. 12.1), 210–11. The source of the whole passage was discovered in the Genizah of Cairo and published by Jacob Mann, *The Bible as Read and Preached in the Old Synagogue* (Cincinnati, 1940), vol. 1, 49. The legend is also cited by Maimonides, *Mishneh Torah, Hil, Avodah Zarah* 1.3. Cf. also Joseph ibn Kaspi, "Guide to Knowledge," chap. 7 (1332 C.E.), quoted in *Hebrew Ethical Wills,* edited by Israel Abrahams (Philadelphia, 1926), 142–43.
7. There are now two important translations of the Apocalypse of Abraham: by R. Rubinkiewicz, in *The Old Testament Apocrypha,* edited by J. H. Charlesworth (New York, 1983), vol. 1; and Belkis Philonenko-Sayar, "Die Apokalypse Abraham," in *Jüdische Scriften aus hellenistisch-römischer Zeit* (Gütersioh, 1982), vol. 5, chap. 7 (see also there an important list of parallels).
8. See above, note 1.
9. See Gen. Rabbah 95.3 (to Gen. 15.28), 1189, and ibid., chap. 61, beginning (to Gen. 25.1), 657–58. See also W. Bacher, *Die Agada der Tannaiten,* vol. 2 (Strasbourg, 1890; reprinted 1966), 115, and note 2 there; Ginzberg, *Legends,* vol. 5, 225 n. 100. There is also a rabbinic legend that Abraham studied in the academy of Shem and Eber; see Ginzberg, *Legends,* vol. 5, n. 132, 225 n. 102.
10. Wilhelm Rudolph, "Der Wettstreit der Leibwächter des Darius 3. Esr. 3, 1–5, 6," *Zietschrift für die Altest amentliche Wissenschaft (ZAW)* 61 (1945–48): 176–90.
11. *Panchatantra* 3.9. We used the English translation by Fr. Edgerton (Delhi: Hindu Pocket Books, 1973), 127–28. A variant of the short story is a Latin

fable written by Odo of Cherington (first half of the thirteenth century C.E.): *De mure qui voluit matrimonium contrahere* (On the mouse who wanted to marry). The text and the German translation appear in H. C. Schnur, *Lateinische Fabeln des Mittelalters* (Munich, 1979), no. 63, pp. 290–93. See also Perry, ed., *Babrius and Phaedrus* (London, 1975), 547 (no. 619). Cf. Jean de La Fontaine, *Fables* 9.7.

12. T. Benfry, *Panschatantra* (Berlin, 1859; reprinted 1962), vol. 1, 376–77; see Ginzberg, *Legends,* vol. 5, 210 n. 16.
13. Aesopus 50 and Babrius 32. See *Corpus Fabularum Aesopicarum,* edited by A. Hausrath and H. Hunger (Leipzig, 1920), vol. 1, 69–70; Perry, ed., *Babruis and Phaedrus,* 44–47.
14. For this study, I have used the English translation from Sanskrit by R. E. Hume, *The Thirteen Principal Upanishads* (Oxford, 1931; reprinted Madras, 1954). See also Heinrich Zimmer, *Philosophies of India* (New York, 1956).
15. Zimmer, *Philosophies of India,* 334.
16. Ibid., 343–45.
17. See especially: Bṛhad-Āraṇyaka Upanishad II.1.1–8 (Hume, *Thirteen Principal Upanishads,* 92–94); II.5.15 (ibid., 104); III.6 (ibid., 113–14); IV.3.1–6 (ibid., 133); Taittiriya Upanishad II.18 (ibid., 288–89); Kaushitaki Upanishad I.3 (ibid., 304); Kaṭha Upanishad V.15 (ibid., 358); Muṇḍaka Upanishad II.2.10 (ibid., 373); Maitri Upanishad VI.35 (ibid., 448–50).
18. Bṛhad-Āraṇyaka Upanishad IV.4.13 (ibid., 142).
19. Śvetasvatara Upanishad VI.14 (ibid., 404).
20. Kaṭha Upanishad V.15 (ibid., 358); Muṇḍaka Upanishad II.2.10 (ibid., 373); Śvetasvatara Upanishad VI.14 (ibid., 410).
21. Taittiriya Upanishad II.8 (ibid., 288); Kaṭha Upanishad VI.3 (ibid., 358).
22. For the most important of these, see above note 16.
23. Bṛihad-Āraṇyaka Upanishad IV.3.1–6 (Hume, *Thirteen Principal Upanishads,* 133).
24. Idem. I.4.6 (53).
25. The way in which Abraham demonstrated the stupidity of idolatry very much resembles the proofs offered by Daniel in the legend of Bel and the Dragon in the additions to Daniel.
26. This does not exclude the possibility that the cycle of legends about Abraham as a whole was conceived later. As we have seen, it existed already in the early Maccabaean period because it is attested to in the Book of Jubilees.
27. St. John Damascene, *Barlaam and Ioasaph* VII.49–50 (London: Loeb, 1967), 86–89. See B. Altaner and A. Stuiber, *Patrologie* (Freiburg: Herder, 1966), 529–30.
28. O. S. Wintermute, "Jubilees," in *The Old Testament Pseudopigrapha,* edited by J. H. Charlesworth, vol. 2, 81. (Garden City, NY: Doubleday, 1983–1985) Brad Young called my attention to the close relationship between the text in Jubilees and the mishnah cited in the following note.
29. M. Berakhot 2.2, 2.5; see also *Midrash ha-Gadol* on Deut. 6.4, edited by S. Fisch (Jerusalem, 1972), 127–28, and the note there.

30. Sifre on Deuteronomy edited by Saul Horovitz and Louis Finkelstein. (New York: Jewish Theological Seminary of America, 1969), 354–55.

Notes to Chapter 5

1. J. Filliozat, *Les relations extérierues de l'Inde,* vol. 1 (Pondicherry: Institut Français d'Indologie, 1956), 1–30.
2. A Dupont-Sommer, "Une nouvelle inscription araméenne d'Asoka trouvée dans la vallée du Laghman (Afghanistan)," *Comptes rendus des séances de l'Académie des Inscriptions et Belles-Lettres* (May 1970), 9–11.
3. Cf. ibid.; A. Dupont-Sommer, "Essénisme et Bouddhisme," *Comptes rendus des séances de l'Académie des Inscriptions et Belles-Lettres* (April 1981), 698–715; M. Philonenko, "Un écho de la prédication d'Asoka dans l'Epître de Jacques," in *Ex orbe religionum: Studia Geo Widengren,* vol. 1 (1972); R. Stehly, "Une citation des Upanishads dans Joseph et Aséneth," *Revue d'Histoire et de Philosophie religieuses* 55 (1975): 209–13.
4. F. Hartog, "Les Grecs égyptologues," *Annales E.S.C.* 5 (1986): 953.
5. If, in fact, we must attribute a *History of India* to this Philostratus. The text of Josephus is uncertain on this point: "Philostratos en tais (Indikaîs kai) Phoinikaîs historiais." Jacoby (*Die Fragmente der griechischen Historiker,* III, C2 (Leiden: Brill, 1958), 801–2 n. 789) cites this single reference to Philostratus under the heading of historians of Phoenicia and not of India.
6. On the different versions of the conversation between Alexander and the ten gymnosophists, attested to notably by Plutarch, *Life of Alexander* 64.1–2, cf. A. J. Festugière, "Trois rencontres entre la Grèce et l'Inde," *Revue de l'Histoire des Religions* 125 (1943): 33–40. On the Jewish tradition, see L. Wallach, "Alexander the Great and the Indian Gymnosophists in Hebrew Tradition," *American Academy for Jewish Research* 11 (1941): 47–83.
7. This name is found as both Mandanis and Dandamis; here I stick to the first spelling. On Calanus and Mandanis in Greek tradition, see G. C. Hansen, "Alexander und die Brahmanen," *Klio* 43–45 (1965): 351–80. The Cynical nature of these traditions was emphasized by V. Martin ("Un recueil de diatribes cyniques. Pap. Genev. inv. 271," *Museum Helveticum* 16 [1959]: 77–115) and P. Photiades ("Les diatribes cyniques de papyrus de Genève 271, leurs traditions et élaborations successives," *Museum Helveticum* 16 [1959]: 116–39) on the occasion of the publication of a papyrus dating from the second century C.E. containing a *Dialogue between Alexander and Dandamis.*
8. The fragments of Megasthenes on India are collected in Jacoby, *Die Fragmente,* 603–39.
9. P. Vidal-Naquet, "Flavius Arrien entre deux mondes," afterword to *Arrien, Histoire d'Alexandre: L'anabase d'Alexandre le Grand,* translated by P. Savinel (Paris: Minuit, 1984), 331, 343.

10. On Calanus as the image of the renegade, see the *Alexander* of Pseudo-Callisthenes, version A, III.11–13.
11. M. Petit, *Quod omnis probus liber sit: Introduction, texte, traduction et notes,* vol. 28 of *Les oeuvres de Philon d'Alexandrie* (Paris: Cerf, 1974), 25–28.
12. Translated by F. H. Colson (Loeb Classical Library). Or, "our deeds are swift and our words are short; but they have power, securing for us blessedness and freedom" (Loeb note ad loc., based on Ambrose's paraphrase). For various conjectures as to the correct text here, see Petit, *Quod omnis probus liber sit,* 214–15 n. 2. See also J. André and J. Filliozat, *L'Inde vue de Rome: Textes latins de l'Antiquité relatifs à l'Inde* (Paris: Belles-Lettres, 1973), 210–11.
13. As is suggested by part of the Greek tradition; see especially Diodorus Siculus XVII.107.3; Strabo, *Geography* XV.1.68; Plutarch, *Life of Alexander* 69.6; Arrian, *Anabasis* VII.3.1.
14. M. Stern, *Greek and Latin Authors on Jews and Judaism,* 2 vols. (Jerusalem: Israel Academy of Sciences and Humanities, 1976–80), 45–46.
15. H. Lewy, "Aristotle and the Jewish Sage according to Clearchus of Soles," *The Harvard Theological Review* 31 (1938): 205–35.
16. L. Robert, "Les inscriptions," in *Fouilles d'Aī Khanoum,* vol. 1, edited by P. Bernard (Paris: Klincksieck, 1973), 225–37. The name *Calanoi*—a plural derived from Calanos—points to a misunderstanding: this is why J. Filliozat ("Le valeur des connaissances gréco-romaines sur l'Inde," *Journal des Savants,* April–June 1981, 117–18) believes that when Clearchus wrote his *Dialogue on Dreams* he had not yet been to Bactria.
17. Cf. J. Bidez and F. Cumont, *Les Mages hellénisés* (Paris: Belles-Lettres, 1973), vol. 1, 18–19.
18. M. Hengel, *Judaism and Hellenism: Studies in Their Encounter in Palestine during the Early Hellenistic Period* (London: SCM Press, 1974), vol. 1, 255–61; A. Momgliano, *Alien Wisdom* (Cambridge: Cambridge University Press, 1976), 95–208; J. Mélèze-Modrzejewshi, "Sur l'antisémitisme païen," in *Pour Léon Poliakov: La racisme, mythes et sciences,* edited by M. Olender (Brussels: Editions Complexe, 1981), 418–25.
19. On the problem of Josephus' treason in becoming a Roman citizen, cf. P. Vidal-Naquet, "Flavius Josèphe et Masada," *Revue historique* 260 (1978): 3–21; reprinted in idem, *Les Juifs, la mémoire et le présent* (Paris: Maspero, 1981).
20. Cf. especially *War of the Jews* III.354, V.367. V. Nikiprowetzky ("La mort d'Eléazer fils de Jaïre et les courants apologétiques dans le *De Bello Judaico* de Flavius Josèphe," in *Hommage à André Dupont-Sommer* [Paris: Maisonneuve, 1971], 481–86) believes that Josephus is here borrowing a theme of Roman propaganda.
21. H. C. Cavallin ("Lebven nach dem Tode im Spätjudentum und im frühen Christentum. I. Spätjudentum," in *Aufsteig und Niedergang der römanischen Welt,* II, 19.1 [Berlin: de Gruyer, 1979], 308–10)—who provides a bibliography—relates Eleazar's speech on the immortality of the soul with Pharisaic doctrine.

22. Cf. W. Morel, "Eine Rede bei Josephus (Bell. Iud. VII 341 sqq.)," *Rheinisches Museum für Philologie,* N.F. 75 (1926): 106–10. See especially *Phaedo* 64c, 67a, 81a, 84b, 107c, 114b.
23. Feldman ("Masada: A Critique of Recent Scholarship," in *Christianity, Judaism and other Greco-Roman Cults: Studies for Morton Smith at Sixty,* edited by J. Neusner, vol. 3 [Leiden: Brill, 1975], 231) notes that Joseph Klausner, in a Hebrew article that I was unable to consult ("The Beginning and End of the Heroes of Masada," in *Ke-she-ummah nilhemet 'al herutah* [When a Nation Fights for Its Freedom] [Tel Aviv, 1952[8]], 189–214), wanted to see the Essene doctrine on the immortality of the soul in this passage of Eleazar's speech. Yadin's discovery at Masada of a fragment identical with the *Angelic Liturgy* of Cave IV at Qumran poses the problem of the relations between the Essenses and the Sicarii. The fragment was published by C. Newsom and Y. Yadin ("The Masada Fragment of the Qumran Songs of the Sabbath," *Israel Exploration Journal* 34 (1984): 77–88). Yadin (*Masada: Herod's Fortress and the Zealots' Last Stand* [Jerusalem: Steimatzky's, 1966]; *Masada: La dernière citadelle d'Israël* [Jerusalem: Steimatzky's, 1966], 173–74) suggested that some Essenes may have joined the ranks of the insurgents and sought refuge at Masada.
24. For the mystique of fire, which for Eleazar's companions have the value of purification and holocaust, cf. Nikiprowetzky, "La mort d'Eléazar," 470–71 n. 2. In this incendiary context, the self-immolation of the Indian sages takes on additional meaning.
25. According to Filliozat ("La mort volontaire par le feu et la tradition bouddhique indienne," *Journal asiatique* 251 [1963]: 48 n. 32), *Khega* in Sanskrit means "ascended to heaven." Zarmanochegas would then be the name that his companions gave him after his death on the pyre, and would mean "*sraman* who has ascended to heaven."
26. P. Vidal-Naquet, "Flavius Josèphe et Masada," 20–21; idem, *Les Juifs,* 70–72.
27. W. Morel ("Eine Rede bei Josephus," 106–14) has drawn attention to the parallel between the passage on the self-immolation of Indian sages (*War of the Jews* VII.352–56) and a passage in Porphyry's *De abstinentia* (IV.18.1), generally considered to be part of a quotation from Bardesanus (Porphyry, *De abstinentia* IV.17.2–18, 1; quoted by Jacoby, *Die Fragmente,* 645–47 n. 719. According to Morel, Bardesanus (died 222) and Josephus could have borrowed from a common source: Megasthenes. This hypothesis was taken over recently by M. Stern (*Greek and Latin Authors on Jews and Judaism,* vol. 2, 424 n. 5). For G. C. Hansen, on the other hand ("Ein verkanntes Iosephos-Zitat bei Porphyrios," *Klio* 48 [1967]: 199–200), the quotation from Bardesanus ends at *De abstinentia* IV.17.5. According to him, in the following passage on the self-immolation of the Indian sages, Porphyry is directly quoting from the text of Eleazar's second speech (*War of the Jews* VII.352–56). Porphyry was in fact familiar with the *War of the Jews,* which he had previously quoted with regard to the Essenes' practice of abstinence (*War of the Jews* II.119–61, quoted in *De*

abstinentia IV.11–14; cf. Stern, *Greek and Latin Authors on Jews and Judaism,* vol. 2, 435–43). Moreover, asserts Hansen, Josephus' source could not have been Megasthenes, because according to the latter the gymnosophists condemned self-immolation (cf. Strabo, *Geography* XV.1.68). In my opinion, Josephus and Bardesanus may have borrowed independently from a common Greek source. It should be noted that Porphyry was in the habit of explicitly mentioning his sources, and does not indicate that the passage on self-immolation was borrowed from Josephus. Thus, in contrast to Hansen's suggestion, the continuation could very well be part of the citation from Bardesanus. But it seems difficult to identify this common source as Megasthenes. In addition to Hansen's argument to this effect, there is another: Megasthenes' note on the Brahmins and *sramans* (quoted by Strabo, *Geography* XV.1.59–60; cf. Jacoby, *Die Fragmente,* 636–38), whose overall structure is similar to that of Bardesanus' text, makes no mention of suicide by self-immolation. In conclusion, I deem it possible that Josephus is here citing a Greek historian of India; unfortunately, the source remains unidentified.

28. On this ambiguity in Philo, cf. *De Abrahamo* 182–83. Certain afflicted spirits refused to see Abraham's willingness to sacrifice his son as an admirable and truly unique action. Others, they said, among the Greeks or the barbarians, had made similar sacrifices. Thus "again they point out that in India the gymnosophists even now when the long incurable disease of old age begins to take hold of them, even before they are completely in its clutches, make up a funeral pile and burn themselves on it, though they might possibly last out many years more. And the womenfolk when the husband die before them have been known to hasten rejoicing to share their pyre, and allow themselves to be burned alive with the corpses of the men. These women might reasonably, no doubt, be praised for their courage, so great and more than great is their contempt for death, and the breathless eagerness with which they rush to it as though it were immortality. Why, then, they ask, should we praise Abraham, as though the deed which he undertook was unprecedented, when private individuals and whole nations do it when occasion calls?"

29. This article was originally published in *Puruṣārtha* 11 (1988): *L'Inde et l'imaginaire* 9–31, edited by C. Weinberger-Thomas.

Notes to Chapter 6

1. The seventy-two page edition used here reads as follows: *Caivatuṣaṇaparikāram,* Yāḻppāṇam Caivapprakācacamācīyaravarkaḷ kattiya rūpamākac ceytatai, Yāḻppāṇattu-Nallūr Catācivappiḷḷaiyavarkaḷ anumatiyiṉpēril Ceṉṉai Intujaṉapūṣaṇi Pattirātipar Tirumayilai Vi. Cuntaramutaliyārāl Ceṉṉapaṭṭaṇam Victory Jubilee Accukkuṭattiṟ patippikkappaṭṭatu. Virōti varuṣam, Paṅkuni mācam, 1890. [In English translation: *The Abolition of the Abuse of Śaivism,* written in prose by Members of the Splendor of Saivism Society of Jaffna; published, with the

permission of Sadasiva Pillai of Nallur, Jaffna, by the editor of the Madras Hindu Jana Bhusani, Vi. Sundara Mutaliyar of Tirumayilai; and printed at the Victory Jubilee Press in Madras in the year Viroti and the month Pankuni, 1890].

2. I am indebted to my colleagues Bruce Dahlberg and Howie Adelman for critical readings of a draft of this essay. I am also indebted to Smith College for its continuing support of the research of which this study is a part, and to the Fulbright Program for archival research in Madras in 1983–84 relating to Ārumuga Nāvalar.
3. Ārumuga Nāvalar studied the Authorized or King James version of the Christian Bible of 1611. I have consulted here the Revised Standard Version of 1952 *(The Holy Bible: Containing the Old and New Testaments* [New York: Thomas Nelson and Sons]), and the Tamil translation of 1966 *(Paḷaiya Eṟpāṭum Putiya Eṟpāṭum ataṅkiya Paricutta Vetākamam* [Bangalore and Colombo: The Bible Society]). All biblical passages cited here are my summaries or paraphrases of his summaries and paraphrases, not quotations or translations.
4. For Ārumuga Nāvalar's early life as a Śaiva reformer and apologist, see D. Dennis Hudson, "Arumuga Navalar and Hindu Renaissance Among the Tamils," in *Religious Controversy in British-India: Dialogues in South Asian Languages,* edited by Kenneth Jones (Albany, NY: SUNY Press, 1992), 27–51; 246–55; "Winning Souls for Siva: Arumuga Navalar's Transmission of the Saiva Religion," *A Sacred Thread: Modern Transmissions of Hindu Traditions in India and Abroad,* ed. Raymond Brady Williams (Chambersburg, PA: Anima Press, 1992), 23–51; and "Tamil Hindu Responses to Protestants: The Nineteenth Century Literati in Jaffna and Tinnevelly," in *Indigenous Responses to Western Christianity,* edited by Steven Kaplan (forth-coming).
5. Ārumuga Nāvalar (known at the time as Ārumuga Piḷḷai) signed his letter "The son of a Śaiva desiring good doctrine" *(Caiva Kumāran Naṉmatarapēṭcan).* It appeared with an English translation in the *Supplement to the Utayatārakai—Morning Star* 32. (26 January 1843), 21–23. The editors' lengthy reply appears in *Utayatārakai—Morning Star* 3.3–6 (1843).
6. To allow maximum recognition of the technical terms used in this essay, Tamil words that are also Sanskrit words will be given in their Sanskrit form. Thus *catcamayam* is rendered as *satsamaya, Caiva* as *Śaiva, catti* as *śakti,* etc.
7. The table of contents of the main part of the booklet reads as follows: (1) The Lord *(Pati);* (2) The holy place *(Punyasthāla);* (3) The temple *(Ālaya);* (4) The linga *(Liṅga);* (5) The consecration *(Abhiṣeka);* (6) The food offering *(Naivedya);* (7) Incense *(Dūpatīpa);* (8) Lights *(Tīpa);* (9) Instrumental music *(Vādya);* (10) Auspicious time *(Punyakāla);* (11) The Śiva *ācārya* *(Śivācārya);* (12) Bodily purity *(Śarīraśuddhi);* (13) Uncleanness *(Asauca);* (14) The endowment *(Nibandhadravya);* Discussion (Viveśana) (15) The marks of Siva *(Śivacihna);* (16) Visualizations, etc. *(Dhyānāti);* (17) Prostrations, etc. *(Namaskārāti);* (18) The Śiva Purāṇa *(Śivapurāṇa);* (19) Holy

bathing places *(Puṇyatīrtha);* (20) The gift of gold *(Svarnadāna);* (21) The gift of food *(Annadāna);* (22) Asceticism *(Tapas);* Discussion *(Viveena).*

8. He adds from the New Testament: And Jesus said the King will say, "as you did it to one of the least of these my brethren, you did it to me." (Matthew 25.40).
9. The word *puṇya* is used variously to denote purity, merit, holiness, and auspiciousness. Describing an act, it denotes a meritorious act as opposed to a sinful act *(pāpa).*
10. Here Nāvalar cites the holy mountain mentioned in 2 Peter 1.18.
11. Nāvalar adds passages from the New Testament describing Jerusalem as the place men ought to worship (John 4.20), as the holy city (Matthew 4.5), and as the city of the great king (Matthew 5.35).
12. *Ācārya,* used for "priest" by Nāvalar, is a word I have kept in English to suggest Nāvalar's sense of familiarity with the biblical cultus. He uses it throughout to refer both to Śaiva and to Aaronic and Levitical priests, indicating that he viewed their level of learning and function as analogous.
13. He provides a fifth parallel from Revelations 8.3–5: In John's vision of the seven seals opened by the Lamb, after the seventh seal was opened, an angel with a golden censer burned incense at the altar standing before the throne of God, mingling its rising smoke with the prayers of the saints. He then filled the censer with fire from the altar and threw it on the earth, producing thunder, loud noises, lightning, and an earthquake.
14. The five Seers *(ṛṣi)* are Kauśika, Kāśyapa, Bhāradvāja, Gautama, and Agastya, born from the five faces of Sadāśiva, the partially differentiated mode of the Transcendent Being that mediates between the unmanifest *Śivam-śakti* and the fully manifest Śiva and Pārvati.
15. Nāvalar cites here Matthew chapter 10, where Jesus told his disciples, Whoever receives you receives me, and he who receives me receives him who sent me. Whoever gives to one of these little ones a cup of cold water to drink because he is my disciple will not lose his reward. And, the chapter relates, Jesus gave them the authority to heal diseases and to cast out demons.
16. Here Nāvalar cites two examples from the New Testament, Matthew 8.4 and 2.11: Jesus told the leper he had healed to go to the priest and offer the gift that Moses had commanded as a proof to the people; and, the three wise men worshipped the baby Jesus, offering him gifts of gold, frankincense, and myrrh.
17. He lists as texts for "everlasting statute": Genesis 17.7, 12–13; Exodus 12.14, 17; 28.43; 29.9; 28.42; 30.8, 10, 21, 31; 31.13, 16; 40.15; Leviticus 3.17; 6.22; 7.33, 35; 10.11, 15; 16.29, 31, 34; 17.7; 22.3; 23.14, 21, 41; 24.3, 8, 9; Numbers 10.8; 18.11, 19, 23; 19.20; 28.6.
18. Here Nāvalar cites: Acts of the Apostles 18.18–21; 21.26; and 16.3.
19. Citing Paul's letters to the Hebrews and to the Romans.
20. *Aṭimai* literally means slave or property and is commonly used to mean devotee. I have retained "slave" to specify the devotee who, as Nāvalar describes him, is more than ordinary. Such slaves of Śiva are the subjects

of the twelfth-century Tamil Śaiva hagiography, *Periya Purāṇam,* "The Purāṇa of the Great [Slaves of Śiva]" or "The Great Purāṇa [of the Slaves of Śiva]." See D. Dennis Hudson, "Violent and Fanatical Devotion among the Nāyaṉārs: A Study in the *Periya Purāṇam* of Cēkkiḻār," in *Criminal Gods and Demon Devotees: Essays on the Guardians of Popular Hinduism,* edited by Alf Hiltebeitel (Albany, NY: SUNY Press, 1989), 373–404.

21. Nāvalar cites Hebrews 9.13: If the blood of goats and bulls and the ashes of a heifer purify the flesh, how much more shall the blood of Christ purify the conscience from dead works.
22. Here he cites Revelation 9.4: Locusts with the power of scorpions were told to harm only those people who do not have the seal of God on their foreheads.
23. The same critique can be made of the four parallels he cites from the New Testament: Colossians 3.16; 1 Thessalonians 5.17; Romans 15.11; and Matthew 6.
24. See Heinrich Zimmer, *Artistic Form and Yoga in the Sacred Images of India,* translated and edited by Gerald Chapple and James B. Lawson with J. Michael McKnight (Princeton: Princeton University Press, 1984).
25. Nāvalar cites two parallels from the New Testament: The wise men fell down and worshipped the child with Mary (Matthew 2.11); and all the angels fell on their faces before the throne of God and worshipped (Revelation 7.11–12).
26. He cites one parallel from two places in the New Testament: Paul ordered that his letter be read to all the brethren (1 Thessalonians 5.27 and Colossians 4.16).
27. He cites one parallel from the New Testament: The pool of Bethzatha near the Sheep Gate in Jerusalem where the invalid, blind, lame, and others bathed in the waters while they were troubled in order to be healed (John 5). Nāvalar notes also that Christians use a bath in water to remove all ignorance from their initiates and to infuse them with knowledge.
28. Responding to the missionary's objection that in the case of Naaman, in the case of the sick at the pool of Bethzatha, and in the case of baptism it is not the water but the power in the water that effects the cleansing, Nāvalar cites Peter's statement in Acts of the Apostles 2.38: Receive baptism in the name of Jesus Christ for the forgiveness of sin and you will receive the gift of the Holy Spirit. That is the same conjunction of water and divine power, he suggests, that is found in the Śaiva understanding of holy bathing places.
29. Nāvalar cites eleven parallel statements from the New Testament: Hebrews 13.16; Romans 12.13; 2 Corinthians 9.6–7 and 9.12; Matthew 5.42; 1 John 3.17–18; Luke 6.38, 18.22, and 19.8–9; Acts of the Apostles 10.4; and Luke 12.33.
30. Nāvalar cites four passages from the New Testament: Matthew 10.42; Matthew 25.34–46; Luke 3.11; and Luke 14.13.
31. All his citations are from the New Testament: 1 Corinthians 7.1, 12, 33, and 40; Matthew 19.10–12, 23–24, and 29; Luke 14.26 and 33; and Matthew 6.24.
32. Nāvalar cites three parallels from the New Testament. Two refer to the cutting of hair as part of a vow (Acts of the Apostles 18.18 and 21.24) and one refers to wearing sackcloth and sitting in ashes (Luke 10.12–13).

33. He cites three parallels from the New Testament: Colossians 2.23; Romans 13.14; and Matthew 6.16.
34. Nāvalar's New Testament parallels are five. For continuous thought of God, he cites Matthew 6.6; Luke 11.5–10, and Luke 18.7. For the ascetic life focused on God he cites John the Baptist in Matthew 3.1 and 4, and in Matthew 11.7–11.
35. In support, he cites from the New Testament James 2.14–26, Matthew 7.21, and James 1.22.
36. Nāvalar consistently uses *mukti* to refer to the goal conferred on souls by Śiva and *mokṣa* to refer to the goal conferred by Jehovah. He uses *mokṣa* in the sense of "heaven," meaning perhaps the lesser emancipation known as *patamukti* from which the soul returns to birth and death.
37. Nāvalar cites Matthew 27.44 and Luke 23.42–43.
38. Here Nāvalar cites Luke 7.36–48.
39. The mantra, in the proper context, functions as a sacrament. See Gerhard Oberhammer, "The Use of Mantra in Yogic Meditation: The Testimony of the *Pāśupata*," and Ludo Rocher, "Mantras in the *Śivapurāṇa*," in *Mantra,* edited by Harvey P. Alper (Albany, NY: SUNY Press, 1989), 177–223.
40. To show parallels in the Christian scriptures to the concept of holy things and holy times, he cites Jesus' instruction to eat bread and drink wine as his body and blood in Matthew 26.26–28, and the missionary's own celebration of the Last Supper. As parallels to the holiness of God's name, he cites Mark 9.38 and Luke 9.49, where unbelievers cast demons out in Jesus name. As a parallel to the holiness of things worn, he cites Mark 5.25–29, where a woman who touches Jesus' garment is healed of a flow of blood.
41. He cites two parallels from the New Testament: Acts of the Apostles 5.15–16, where the sick and possessed are healed by the mere touch of Peter's shadow, and 19.12, where the sick and possessed are healed by handkerchiefs and aprons that had touched the body of Paul.
42. First he addresses the practice of the anonymous missionary who takes Śaiva texts out of context and tries to use them to prove the inherent irrationality of the Śaiva system. Then he addresses the missionary's observation that even after performing meritorious acts according to the Śaiva scriptures, people often continue being sinful. His response is to point out the same thing among the Christians and to vent his own view of their inconsistencies.
43. As a New Testament parallel, he cites Matthew 12.31, where Jesus says that unlike other sings, the blasphemy against the Spirit will not be forgiven.
44. He cites also Matthew 1.20 and 19.28, Revelations 14.1–4, and Luke 15.
45. He also cites Matthew 11.24, Luke 12.47–48.
46. Moreover, he adds, Jesus' disciples taught orally and sent letters. It does not seem that they gave their scriptures to others to study either.
47. For example, Leviticus 1–10.
48. See David Novak, *The Image of the Non-Jew in Judaism: An Historical and Constructive Study of the Noahide Laws* (New York and Toronto: The Edwin Mellen Press, 1983), especially chapter ten.

Notes to Chapter 7

My thoughts on this subject have been enriched by the comments of Shlomo Deshen, Chris Fuller, Hananya Goodman, Don Handelman, and David Shulman.

1. C. J. Fuller, "The Hindu Pantheon and the Legitimation of Hierarchy," *Man* 23 (1988): 18–39.
2. According to H. G. Reissner, in 1837 the total Jewish population of the Indian subcontinent was 6,951, of whom 5,255 were Bene Israel; in 1941 the total Jewish population was 22,480, of whom 14,800 were Bene Israel ("Indian Jewish Statistics, 1837–1941," *Jewish Social Studies* 12 [1950]: 349–65).
3. Today, a single *Shanwār telī* remains in the Konkan.
4. S. Weil, *From Cochin to the Land of Israel* (Jerusalem: Kumu Berina, 1984) (in Hebrew).
5. S. Weil, "Symmetry between Christians and Jews in India: The Cnanite Christians and the Cochin Jews of Kerala," *Contributions to Indian Sociology* 16 (1982): 175–96.
6. This contention is my interpretation. The Bene Israel certainly acknowledge the Hinduistic influences on their religion and view themselves as occupying a particular place in Indian society, but they do not formulate the argument in the same way.
7. Fieldwork among the Bene Israel in Israel was carried out between 1972 and 1975. Subsequent field visits to the Bene Israel in India were made in 1978 and 1980. Extensive historical material on the Bene Israel in India has been analyzed by this author throughout this decade.
8. The Jewish calendar is lunar. The month of Tishri falls around September.
9. Rev. J. Wilson, "Abstract of an Account of the Bene Israel of Bombay," *The Oriental Christian Spectator* 11 (1840): 23–36.
10. S. B. Isenberg, *India's Bene Israel* (Bombay: Popular Prakashan, 1988), 22.
11. The first Bene Israel synagogue, Sha'ar Rahamim or "Gate of Mercy Synagogue," was founded in Bombay in 1796.
12. Isenberg, *India's Bene Israel,* 221.
13. *Mahzor (Prayer Service) for the Day of Atonement* (New York: Hebrew Publishing Co., 1928) (in Hebrew with English translation), 216.
14. It is noteworthy that the oral Torah was unknown to the Bene Israel until they aligned themselves with world Jewry.
15. *Mahzor,* 225.
16. Ibid., 284.
17. Ibid., 285.
18. S. Deshen, "The Kol Nidre Enigma: An Anthropological View of the Day of Atonement Liturgy," *Ethnology* 18 (1979): 121–33.
19. Ibid., 304.
20. Rabbi Solomon Abraham Adret, known as the RashBa (1235–1310), was strongly opposed to the custom on the grounds that it was similar to the biblical atonement rites and therefore a heathen superstition. It was also

opposed by Nachmanides, known as the Ramban (1194–1270), and Joseph Caro (1488–1575, the compiler of the oral Torah), who called it a "stupid custom" (*Encyclopaedia Judaica,* 1971).

21. Some Jewish communities substitute money for the fowl while reciting the same prayer and excluding the word "fowl."
22. A. Beteille, "Individualism and Equality," *Current Anthropology* 27 (1986): 132.
23. Dumont, "A Modified View of Our Origins: The Christian Beginnings of Modern Individualism," *Contributions to Indian Sociology* N.S. 17 (1983): 1–26.
24. Dumont, *Homo Hierarchius* (London: Paladin, 1972).
25. Beteille, "Individualism and Equality," see note 22 above.
26. Cf. A. Van Gennep, *The Rites of Passage* (London: Routledge & Kegan Paul, 1960; originally published 1908).
27. D. Pocock, *Mind, Body and Wealth* (Oxford: Basil Blackwell, 1973), 91.
28. L. Babb, "Destiny and Responsibility: Karma in Popular Hinduism," in *Karma,* edited by C. Keyes and V. Daniel (Berkeley: University of California Press, 1983), 165.
29. A. L. Basham, *The Wonder That Was India* (New York: Grove Press, 1977; originally published 1954), 239.
30. C. J. Fuller, "Hinduism and Scriptural Authority in Modern Indian Law," *Comparative Studies in Society and Tradition* 30 (1988): 243.
31. Basham, *The Wonder That Was India,* 336.
32. Deshen, "The Kol Nidre Enigma," 124.
33. Of course, there are means of achieving relative purity while retaining one's caste status, but I am attempting the difficult task of pinpointing major differences in central doctrines.
34. Deshen, "The Kol Nidre Enigma," 126.
35. V. W. Turner, *The Ritual Process* (Chicago: University of Chicago Press, 1969).
36. H. S. Kehimkar, *The History of the Bene Israel of India* (Tel Aviv: Dayag, 1937; originally published 1897), 173.
37. *Ne'ilah* was originally recited on all public fast days (*Encyclopaedia Judaica,* 1971, 943–44).
38. On Yom Kippur, the literal closing of the Temple gates was associated with the symbolic closing of the heavenly gates, which remained open until sunset (*Encyclopaedia Judaica,* 943–44).
39. J. Sapir, *Even Sapir* (Lyck, 1866) (in Hebrew).
40. Solomon Reinemann, *Solomon's Travels in India, Burma and China,* edited by Wolff Schur (Vienna: Georg Breg, 1884) (in Hebrew).
41. "Bene Israels," in "Population," *Bombay Gazetteer* (Poona), 1885, p. 514.
42. Kehimkar, *The History of the Bene Israel,* 173.
43. "Bene Israels," *Bombay Gazetteer,* 514.
44. Kehimkar, quoted in H. J. Lord, *Jews in India and the Far East* (Kohalpur: Mission Press, 1907), 35n. Kehimkar's 1892 book was a precursor to his longer book *(The History of the Bene Israel in India)* and is mentioned also by Immanuel Olswanger in the preface to the 1937 edition of the 1897 book.

45. Kehimkar, *The History of the Bene Israel,* 18.
46. Ibid., 172.
47. Ibid., 173.
48. Deshen claims that the consensus of research is that *kaparot* are a carryover from the biblical offering of the scapegoat (Leviticus 17.2) practiced in the Temple until 70 C.E. ("The Kol Nidre Enigma," 130). However, the rite only appears in the writings of the *gaonim* for the first time in the eighth century C.E. (*Encyclopaedia Judaica,* 1971).
49. Kehimkar, *The History of the Bene Israel,* 173.
50. R. E. Enthoven, *Folklore of the Konkan* (New Delhi: Cosmo, 1976; originally published 1915).
51. S. Weil, "The Persistence of Ethnicity and Ethnic Identity among Bene Israel Indian Jews in Lod, Israel," D. Phil. diss., 1977.
52. Ibid.
53. Different parts of the Yom Kippur liturgy (for instance, particular prayers in the Musaf service) are attributed greater importance by other Jewish communities, especially in Western Europe and the United States.
54. I have isolated similar ritual mechanisms in a very different context ("The Language and Ritual of Socialization: Birthday Parties in a Kindergarten Context," *Man* N.S. 21 (1986): 329–41).
55. Cf. J. Heesterman, *The Inner Conflict of Tradition* (Chicago: University of Chicago Press, 1985).
56. D. Shulman, *The King and the Clown in South Indian Myth and Poetry* (Princeton: Princeton University Press, 1985).
57. "Bene Israels," *Bombay Gazetteer,* 514. Kehimkar rejects this theory, although he says "some ignoramuses" might have thrown grains of rice or showed coins to the moon "in imitation of local usage, but it cannot be said that it has been practised generally" (*The History of the Bene Israel,* 176).
58. S. Weil, "The Persistence of Ethnicity and Ethnic Identity among Bene Israel Indian Jews in Lod, Israel," D. Phil. diss., 1977.
59. Dumont, *Homo Hierarchicus,* 258.
60. S. Weil, "The Influence of Caste Ideology in Israel," in *Educational and Cultural Transition: The Case of Immigrant Youth,* edited by M. Gottesman (Jerusalem: Magnes, 1988).

Notes to Chapter 8

Abbreviations: **I. Indological Sources** *AB*—Aitareya Brāhmaṇa; *Artha* S.—Artha-Śāstra; *AV*—Atharva-Veda Saṃhitā; *BAU*—Bṛhadāraṇyaka Upaniṣad; *BP*—Bhāgavata Purāṇa; *CU*—Chāndogya Upaniṣad; *JB*—Jaiminīya Brāhmaṇa; *JUB*—Jaiminīya Upaniṣad Brāhmaṇa; *KB*—Kauṣītaki Brāhmaṇa; *KP*—Kūrma Purāṇa; *KU*—Kauṣītaki Upaniṣad; *LP*—Liṅga Purāṇa; *Maitri*—Maitri Upaniṣad; *Mark.*—Mārkaṇḍeya Purāṇa; *Mbh.*—Mahābhārata; *MP*—Matsya Purāṇa; *MS*—Manu-Smṛti; *MU*—Muṇḍaka Upaniṣad; *PB*—Pañcaviṃśa

Brāhmaṇa; *Praśna*—Praśna Upaniṣad; *Ram.*—Rāmāyaṇa; *RV*—Ṛg-Veda Saṃhitā; *Sadv. B.*—Ṣaḍviṃśa Brāhmaṇa; *SB*—Śatapatha Brāhmaṇa; *Skanda*—Skanda Purāṇa; *SP*—Śiva Purāṇa; *SU*—Śvetāśvatara Upaniṣad; *TB*—Taittirīya Brāhmaṇa; *TS*—Taittirīya Saṃhitā; *TU*—Taittirīya Upaniṣad; *VP*—Viṣṇu Purāṇa.

II. Judaic Sources *'Ab.*—'Āḇôṯ; *Ber.*—Bᵉrāḵôṯ; *Deut. R.*—Deuteronomy Rabbāh; *ᶜErub.*—ᶜÊrûḇîn; *Esth. R.*—Esther Rabbāh; *Exod. R.*—Exodus Rabbāh; *Gen. R.*—Genesis Rabbāh; *Ḥag.*—Ḥăḡîḡāh; *Lev. R.*—Leviticus Rabbāh; *Mak.*—Makkôṯ; *Meg.*—Mᵉḡillāh; *Mek.*—Mᵉḵîltā' dᵉ-R. Ishmael; *Men.*—Mᵉnāḥôṯ; *Mos.*—De Vita Mosis (Philo); *Ned.*—Nᵉḏārîm; *Op.*—De Opificio Mundi (Philo); *Pes.*—Pᵉsāḥîm; *Pes. K.*—Pᵉsîqtā' dᵉ-R. Kahana; *Pes. R.*—Pᵉsîqtā' Rabbāṯî; *PRE*—Pirqê dᵉ-R. Eliezer; *Qid.*—Qîddûšîn; *RH*—Rō'š ha-Šānāh; *Šab.*—Šabbāṯ; *Sanh.*—Sanheḏrîn; *Šeb.*—Šᵉḇûᶜôṯ; *Sip̄rê Deut.*—Sip̄rê on Deuteronomy; *Sip̄rê Num.*—Sip̄rê on Numbers; *Song R.*—Song of Songs Rabbāh; *Sot.*—Sôṭāh; *Taan.*—Taᶜănîṯ; *Tanḥ.*—Tanḥûmā'; *Zeb.*—Zᵉḇāḥîm

1. Jacob Neusner in particular has challenged the notion of a single "Judaism" and has emphasized instead the plurality of "Judaisms" or "Judaic systems" that have developed in the course of Jewish history. See his *Death and Birth of Judaism: The Impact of Christianity, Secularism, and the Holocaust on Jewish Faith* (New York: Basic Books, 1987), esp. 3–29.
2. This term derives from Brian Stock, *The Implications of Literacy: Written Language and Models of Interpretation in the Eleventh and Twelfth Centuries* (Princeton: Princeton University Press, 1983).
3. The significance of the systematic comparison of "Hinduisms" and "Judaisms" as the basis for constructing alternative paradigms of "religious tradition" has been emphasized by Paul Morris in a series of personal communications with me. Morris has stressed in particular the heuristic value of positing two discrete models—missionary traditions (Christianities, Islams, Buddhisms) and nonmissionary traditions (Hinduisms, Judaisms)—in order to elucidate the notion of "religious tradition." See Paul Morris, "The Discourse of Traditions: 'Judaisms' and 'Hinduisms' " (Paper delivered at the Annual Meeting of the American Academy of Religion, San Francisco, 1992).
4. The essays in the present volume delineate a number of historical connections and cross-cultural resonances among "Judaisms" and "Hinduisms." This collection of essays represents one of the first efforts by a group of scholars of Judaica and Indology to explore the affinities among these traditions. See also the illuminating studies by Nathan Katz and Ellen S. Goldberg of the Jewish community in Cochin, India, in their *The Last Jews of Cochin: Jewish Identity in Hindu India* (Columbia, SC: University of South Carolina Press, 1993); idem, "The Ritual Enactments of the Cochin Jews: The Powers of Purity and Nobility," in *Ritual and Power,* edited by Barbara A. Holdrege, *Journal of Ritual Studies* 4, no. 2 (1990): 199–238.
5. The Manu-Smṛti, for example, maintains that all traditions and philosophies that are not derived from the Veda are worthless and untrue *(anṛta)* and produce no reward after death. See MS XII.95–96; cf. MS II.10–11.

6. See Sanh. X.1, which declares that one who denies *tôrāh min ha-šāmayim,* "the Torah is from heaven," has no share in the world to come.
7. The studies of Smith and Graham have inspired the recent volume *Rethinking Scripture: Essays from a Comparative Perspective,* edited by Miriam Levering (Albany: SUNY Press, 1989), which contains essays by Smith and Graham and a number of other scholars, who discuss their different approaches to rethinking the category of scripture as a general religious phenomenon in the comparative history of religions. Among other relevant essays by Smith, see "Is the Qur'an the Word of God?," chapter 2 of his *Questions of Religious Truth* (New York: Charles Scribner's Sons, 1967), 39–62; "Some Similarities and Some Differences Between Christianity and Islam," chapter 13 of his *On Understanding Islam: Selected Studies,* Religion and Reason 19 (The Hague: Mouton, 1981), 233–46; and "The True Meaning of Scripture: An Empirical Historian's Nonreductionist Interpretation of the Qur'an," *International Journal of Middle Eastern Studies* 11, no. 4 (1980): 487–505. For Smith's extended reflections on the category of scripture, see his recently published book, *What is Scripture? A Comparative Approach* (Minneapolis: Fortress Press, 1994). Among Graham's works on scripture, see his *Beyond the Written Word: Oral Aspects of Scripture in the History of Religion* (Cambridge: Cambridge University Press, 1987), and "Scripture," *The Encyclopedia of Religion,* edited by Mircea Eliade et al. (New York: Macmillan, 1987), s.v.
8. The term *Wirkungsgeschichte* is used by Hans-Georg Gadamer to describe the tradition of successive interpretations in the history of a text that implicitly influences each new interpretation of a text. See Hans-Georg Gadamer, *Wahrheit und Methode: Grundzüge einer philosophischen Hermeneutik,* 3rd ed. (Tübingen: J. C. B. Mohr [Paul Siebeck], 1972), esp. 283–90. In the present context the term *Wirkungsgeschichte* is being used in a broader sense to include the text's role as scripture in the ongoing life of a particular religious community.
9. Graham, *Beyond the Written Word.*
10. Jonathan Z. Smith, "Sacred Persistence: Toward a Redescription of Canon," chapter 3 of his *Imagining Religion: From Babylon to Jonestown* (Chicago and London: University of Chicago Press, 1982), 52.
11. Ibid., 48.
12. The earliest references to the Veda(s) in Vedic texts generally focus on the triad *ṛcs, yajuses,* and *sāmans,* which are designated as the "threefold knowledge" *(trayī vidyā)* or "threefold Veda" *(traya veda).* This emphasis on the "threefold knowledge" of the §g-Veda, Yajur-Veda, and Sāma-Veda suggests that it took some time before the *atharvans* of the Atharva-Veda were accorded an equivalent status as forming part of the "four Vedas" *(catur veda).*
13. The term *mantra* is used in the present context to refer to the *ṛcs, yajuses, sāmans,* and *atharvans* collected in the four Saṃhitās, as distinct from the Brāhmaṇa and Upaniṣadic portions of the Veda. It should be noted, however, that although the terms *mantra* and Saṃhitā are often used interchangeably,

they are not entirely synonymous, as the Taittirīya Saṃhitā (Black Yajur-Veda) contains in addition to *mantras* some Brāhmaṇa material discussing the sacrificial ceremonies.

14. In making a distinction between "Vedic texts" and "post-Vedic texts," modern Western scholars generally adopt, on philological as well as historical grounds, this broader definition of Veda as including the Saṃhitās, Brāhmaṇas, Āraṇyakas, and Upaniṣads.
15. See Mbh. I.57.74; Mbh. XII.327.18; Ram. I.1.77; BP I.4.20; BP III.12.39; Skanda V.3.1.18; Artha S. I.3.1–2. The Bhāgavata Purāṇa (I.4.20), for example, declares that "the four Vedas, known as Ṛg, Yajur, Sāma, and Atharva, were separated out [from the one Veda], and the Itihāsa-Purāṇa is called the fifth Veda *(pañcamo veda).*" As early as the Upaniṣads we find the notion that the Itihāsa and Purāṇa are "the fifth" among sacred brahmanical texts and sciences, although they are not explicitly referred to as the "fifth Veda." See CU VII.1.2,4; CU VII.2.1; CU VII.7.1, which enumerate "the Ṛg-Veda, the Yajur-Veda, the Sāma-Veda, the Atharvaṇa as the fourth *(caturtha),* Itihāsa-Purāṇa as the fifth *(pañcama)*. . . . "
16. See n. 13.
17. Many of the later Upaniṣads are highly sectarian, and thus this phenomenon represents one of the strategies used by sectarian movements to legitimate their own texts through granting them the nominal status of *śruti.*
18. See Thomas Coburn's illuminating discussion of the relationship between *śruti* and *smṛti* in Hindu conceptions of scripture in " 'Scripture' in India: Towards a Typology of the Word in Hindu Life," *Journal of the American Academy of Religion* 52, no. 3 (1984): 435–59; reprinted in *Rethinking Scripture,* edited by Levering, 102–28.
19. See, for example, Louis Renou and Jean Filliozat, *L'Inde classique. Manuel des études indiennes,* vol. 1 (Paris: Payot, 1947–1949), 381, 270; Sarvepalli Radhakrishnan and Charles A. Moore, eds., *A Source Book in Indian Philosophy* (Princeton: Princeton University Press, 1957), xix; R. N. Dandekar, "Dharma, The First End of Man," in *Sources of Indian Tradition,* edited by Wm. Theodore de Bary et al. (New York: Columbia University Press, 1958), 217; Jan Gonda, *Die Religionen Indiens,* vol. 1, *Veda und älterer Hinduismus,* Die Religionen der Menschheit, vol. 11 (Stuttgart: W. Kohlhammer, 1960), 107; A. L. Basham, *The Wonder That Was India: A Survey of the History and Culture of the Indian Sub-continent Before the Coming of the Muslims,* 3rd rev. ed. (London: Sidgwick and Jackson, 1967), 112–13; Oscar Botto, "Letterature antiche dell'India," in *Storia delle Letterature d'Oriente,* edited by Oscar Botto, vol. 3 (Milan: Casa Editrice Dr. Francesco Vallardi, Società Editrice Libraria, 1969), 294. For a discussion and critique of such characterizations of *śruti* and *smṛti* as a distinction between "revelation" and "tradition," see Sheldon Pollock, " 'Tradition' as 'Revelation': *Śruti, Smṛti,* and the Sanskrit Discourse of Power," in *Lex et Litterae: Essays on Ancient Indian Law and Literature in Honour of Oscar Botto,* edited by Siegfried Lienhard and Irma Piovano (Turin: CESMEO, forthcoming). Pollock's views will be discussed below.

20. In opposition to the view of the Mīmāṃsakas and Vedāntins that the Vedas are eternal and *apauruṣeya,* the exponents of the Nyāya, Vaiśeṣika, and Yoga schools use a variety of arguments to establish that the Vedas Are noneternal *(anitya)* and *pauruṣeya,* created by the personal agency of Īśvara.
21. See Pollock, " 'Tradition' as 'Revelation' "; idem, "From Discourse of Ritual to Discourse of Power in Sanskrit Culture," in *Ritual and Power,* edited by Holdrege, *Journal of Ritual Studies* 4, no. 2 (1990): 322–28.
22. See, for example, RV VIII.59.6. The *ṛṣis'* cognitions are at times described in the Ṛg-Veda as synesthetic experiences that involved both hearing and seeing.
23. Among contemporary Hindus this position is articulated, for example, by the philosopher-yogi Śrī Aurobindo Ghose (1872–1950): "The Rishi was not the individual composer of the hymn, but the seer (*draṣṭā*) of an eternal truth and an impersonal knowledge. The language of Veda itself is *śruti,* a rhythm not composed by the intellect but heard, a divine Word that came vibrating out of the Infinite to the inner audience of the man who had previously made himself fit for the impersonal knowledge." Aurobindo Ghose, *On the Veda* (Pondicherry: Sri Aurobindo Ashram Press, 1956), 11.
24. J. Muir has collected together numerous passages from Vedic and post-Vedic texts regarding the origin and cosmological status of the Veda, although apart from brief introductory statements he does not attempt to analyze and interpret the significance of and interrelationship among these texts. J. Muir, comp. and trans., *Original Sanskrit Texts on the Origin and History of the People of India, Their Religion and Institutions,* vol. 3, *The Vedas: Opinions of Their Authors and of Later Indian Writers on Their Origin, Inspiration, and Authority,* 2d rev. ed. (1874; reprint, Amsterdam: Oriental Press, 1967). I am particularly indebted to Muir for bringing to light a number of important passages that are pertinent to my analysis of cosmological conceptions of Veda.
25. A number of these modes of assimilation are discussed by Pollock in "From Discourse of Ritual to Discourse of Power in Sanskrit Culture," 332.
26. See Brian K. Smith, *Reflections on Resemblance, Ritual, and Religion* (New York and Oxford: Oxford University Press, 1989), 3–29, esp. 20–29.
27. Ibid., 26, 13–14.
28. J. Gonda, *Change and Continuity in Indian Religion,* Disputationes Rheno-Trajectinae, vol. 9 (The Hague: Mouton, 1965), 7. For statements by other Indologists concerning the authority of the Veda as the decisive criterion of Hindu orthodoxy, see Smith, *Reflections on Resemblance, Ritual, and Religion,* 18, n. 45.
29. See N. Subbu Reddiar, "The Nālāyiram as Drāvida Veda," chapter 26 of his *Religion and Philosophy of Nālāyira Divya Prabandham with Special Reference to Nammāḷvār* (Tirupati: Sri Venkateswara University, 1977), 680–93.
30. For a discussion of the "vedacization" of the *Rāmcaritmānas,* and of *Mānas* recitation rituals in particular, see Philip Lutgendorf, "The Power

of Sacred Story: *Rāmāyaṇa* Recitation in Contemporary North India," in *Ritual and Power,* edited by Holdrege, *Journal of Ritual Studies* 4, no. 2 (1990): 115–47. See also Lutgendorf's *The Life of a Text: Performing the Rāmcaritmānas of Tulsidas* (Berkeley: University of California Press, 1991).

31. See A. K. Ramanujan, trans., *Speaking of Śiva* (Harmondsworth, Middlesex, England: Penguin Books, 1973), 19–55.
32. Abhinavagupta (tenth century C.E.), the most famous exponent of Kashmir Śaivism, asserts, "[T]he wise *sādhaka* [tantric practitioner] must not choose the word of the Veda as the ultimate authority because it is full of impurities and produces meager, unstable, and limited results. Rather, the *sādhaka* should elect the Śaivite scriptures as his source. Moreover, that which according to the Veda produces sin leads, according to the left-handed doctrine, promptly to perfection. The entire Vedic teaching is in fact tightly held in the grip of *māyā* (delusional power)." *Tantrāloka* 37. 10–12; cf. 15.595–99. Cited in Paul E. Muller-Ortega, "The Power of the Secret Ritual: Theoretical Formulations from the Tantra," in *Ritual and Power,* edited by Holdrege, *Journal of Ritual Studies* 4, no. 2 (1990): 49.
33. J. C. Heesterman, "Veda and Dharma," in *The Concept of Duty in South Asia,* edited by Wendy Doniger O'Flaherty and J. Duncan M. Derrett (New Delhi: Vikas, 1978), 92–93.
34. See, for example, Brian K. Smith's remark:

> The great paradox of Hinduism . . . is that although the religion is inextricably tied to the legitimizing authority of the Veda, in post-Vedic times the subject matter of the Veda was and is largely unknown by those who define themselves in relation to it. Its contents (almost entirely concerning the meaning and performance of sacrificial rituals that Hindus do not perform) are at best reworked (being, for example, reconstituted into ritual formulas or mantras for use in Hindu ceremonies), and [in] many cases appear to be totally irrelevant for Hindu doctrine and practice.

Smith, *Reflections on Resemblance, Ritual, and Religion,* 20. Paul Younger has similarly noted that "in spite of the acknowledgment of its authority, the content of the *Veda* does not seem to be used very directly in guiding the later development of the Religious Tradition." Paul Younger, *Introduction to Indian Religious Thought* (Philadelphia: Westminster Press, 1972), 71.

35. Louis Renou, *The Destiny of the Veda in India,* translated by Dev Raj Chanana (Delhi: Motilal Banarsidass, 1965), 2, 1. Renou's study provides a useful survey of the different attitudes, beliefs, and practices that the major texts, philosophical schools, and sects of the Indian tradition have adopted with respect to the Veda in the course of its history. J. L. Mehta has challenged some of Renou's perspectives on the "destiny of the Veda" and suggests that the Veda may possess an inherent potency, or *svadhā,* that has enabled it to create its own destiny in spite of the perils of history. J. L. Mehta, "The Hindu Tradition: The Vedic Root," in *The World's*

Religious Traditions: Current Perspectives in Religious Studies. Essays in Honour of Wilfred Cantwell Smith, edited by Frank Whaling (Edinburgh: T. and T. Clark, 1984), 33–54. See also Wilhelm Halbfass's discussion of the role and "destiny" of the Veda in traditional Hindu self-understanding in his *Tradition and Reflection: Explorations in Indian Thought* (Albany: SUNY Press, 1991), esp. 1–22.

36. Pollock, "From Discourse of Ritual to Discourse of Power in Sanskrit Culture," 332. See also Robert Lingat's suggestion that "in reality, it seems that when a Hindu affirms that *dharma* rests entirely upon the Veda, the word Veda does not mean in that connection the Vedic texts, but rather the totality of Knowledge, the sum of all understanding, of all religious and moral truths." Robert Lingat, *The Classical Law of India,* translated by J. Duncan M. Derrett (Berkeley: University of California Press, 1973), 8.
37. While Smith views the authority of the Veda as pivotal to his definition of Hinduism, he declines from including "the orthodox claim that the Veda is a body of transcendent and super- or extra-human knowledge" as part of his definition, for "from the standpoint of the academic and humanistic study of religion, the Veda, like all other canonical literatures, was entirely composed [by] human beings." Smith, *Reflections on Resemblance, Ritual, and Religion,* 19. I would of course agree with Smith that as scholars of religion we are not ourselves in a position to adopt the traditional brahmanical view of the Veda as transcendent knowledge. I would nevertheless argue that the authority that the Veda holds in the brahmanical tradition—if not in all Hindu traditions—is directly predicated on its status as transcendent knowledge. If the Veda were stripped of that status, it would thereby lose its legitimating function as a *transcendent* source of authority.
38. J. Frits Staal's studies of Vedic recitation and ritual have provided important insights into the oral-aural character of the Vedas, in which priority is given to phonology and syntax over semantics. See particularly his *Nambudiri Veda Recitation,* Disputationes Rheno-Trajectinae, vol. 5 (The Hague: Mouton, 1961); idem, "The Concept of Scripture in the Indian Tradition," in *Sikh Studies: Comparative Perspectives on a Changing Tradition,* edited by Mark Juergensmeyer and N. Gerald Barrier, Berkeley Religious Series (Berkeley: Graduate Theological Union, 1979), 121–24. For a more recent formulation of Staal's theories, see his *Rules Without Meaning: Ritual, Mantras and the Human Sciences* (New York: Peter Lang, 1989), esp. 191–311.
39. It should be noted, however, that there are a variety of opinions concerning the origin and meaning of the root *yrh.* For a discussion of the scholarly debate one may refer to Michael Fishbane's article "Torah" in *Encyclopedia Miqrā'îṯ* (Jerusalem: Mosad Bialik, 1962–1988), s.v.
40. For a discussion of rabbinic conceptions of Written Torah and Oral Torah, see Ephraim E. Urbach, "The Written Law and the Oral Law," chapter 12 of his *The Sages: Their Concepts and Beliefs,* vol. 1, translated by Israel Abrahams, 2nd rev. ed. (Jerusalem: Magnes Press, Hebrew University, 1979), 286–314.

41. Jacob Neusner, *The Ecology of Religion: From Writing to Religion in the Study of Judaism* (Nashville: Abingdon Press, 1989), 240. For a brief discussion of the complex of meanings ascribed to the term Torah in various rabbinic texts, see ibid., 240–49, 109–12, 120–23. For a more extended discussion, see Neusner's *Torah: From Scroll to Symbol in Formative Judaism* (Philadelphia: Fortress Press, 1985).
42. Elliot Wolfson, in discussing the personification of the Torah as a feminine figure in rabbinic and kabbalistic texts, argues that in rabbinic sources such characterizations are generally intended metaphorically and do not imply a mythical or mystical conception of the Torah as the divine feminine.

> In [rabbinic texts] . . . it is clear that the feminine images were originally meant figuratively and are thus almost always expressed within a parabolic context as literary metaphors. I do not mean to suggest that the Torah was not personified by the rabbis; indeed, for the rabbis the Torah did assume a personality of its own, culminating in the conception of the Torah as the preexistent entity that served as the instrument with which God created the world. Nevertheless in the rabbinic writings the female images of the Torah are for the most part metaphorical in their nuance.

It is significant that Wolfson singles out the conception of the Torah as the instrument of creation as the culminating expression of the rabbis' personification of the Torah, implying that conceptions such as these might not be intended simply as a literary metaphor. Elliot Wolfson, "Female Imaging of the Torah: From Literary Metaphor to Religious Symbol," in *From Ancient Israel to Modern Judaism: Intellect in Quest of Understanding. Essays in Honor of Marvin Fox,* edited by Jacob Neusner, Ernest S. Frerichs, and Nahum M. Sarna, vol. 2 (Atlanta: Scholars Press, 1989), 272–73.

43. See Abraham Joshua Heschel, *Tôrāh min ha-Šāmayim bā-'Aspaqlaryāh šel ha-Dôrôṯ,* 2 vols. (London and New York: Soncino Press, 1962, 1965).
44. Ḥag. II.1. Cf. the Gemara on this Mishnah, Ḥag. 11b–16a.
45. Gershom Scholem has emphasized the continuity between the speculations of these mystically oriented rabbinic circles and the Merkabah speculations of the Hêḵālôṯ texts. See, for example, his *Major Trends in Jewish Mysticism,* 3rd rev. ed. (1954; reprint, New York: Schocken Books, 1961), 40–43; *Jewish Gnosticism, Merkabah Mysticism, and Talmudic Tradition,* 2nd ed. (New York: Jewish Theological Seminary of America, 1965). See also Ithamar Gruenwald, *Apocalyptic and Merkavah Mysticism,* Arbeiten zur Geschichte des antiken Judentums und des Urchristentums, vol. 14 (Leiden: E. J. Brill, 1980); idem, *From Apocalypticism to Gnosticism: Studies in Apocalypticism, Merkavah Mysticism and Gnosticism,* Beiträge zur Erforschung des Alten Testaments und des antiken Judentums, vol. 14 (Frankfurt: Peter Lang, 1988); Ira Chernus, *Mysticism in Rabbinic Judaism: Studies in the History of Midrash* (Berlin and New York: Walter de Gruyter, 1982). Since the publication of Peter Schäfer's *Synopse zur Hekhalot-Literatur,* Texte und Studien zum Antiken Judentum, vol. 2

(Tübingen: J. C. B. Mohr [Paul Siebeck], 1981), the views of Scholem and his followers concerning the primary focus of Hêkālôṯ speculations and their connection with rabbinic *maʿăśēh merkāḇāh* have been challenged by scholars such as Schäfer and David Halperin. See Peter Schäfer, *Gershom Scholem Reconsidered: The Aim and Purpose of Early Jewish Mysticism.* The Twelfth Sacks Lecture (Oxford: Oxford Centre for Postgraduate Hebrew Studies, 1986); idem, "Engel und Menschen in der Hekhalot-Literatur," *Kairos,* n.s., 22, nos. 3–4 (1980): 201–25. Both essays are reprinted, along with other essays by Schäfer, in his *Hekhalot-Studien,* Texte und Studien zum Antiken Judentum, vol. 19 (Tübingen: J. C. B. Mohr [Paul Siebeck], 1988). See also David J. Halperin, *The Faces of the Chariot: Early Jewish Responses to Ezekiel's Vision* (Tübingen: J. C. B. Mohr [Paul Siebeck], 1988); idem, *The Merkabah in Rabbinic Literature,* American Oriental Series, vol. 62 (New Haven: American Oriental Society, 1980).

46. For an extended discussion of kabbalistic conceptions of Torah and language, see Gershom Scholem's groundbreaking essay, "The Meaning of the Torah in Jewish Mysticism," chapter 2 of his *On the Kabbalah and Its Symbolism,* translated by Ralph Manheim (New York: Schocken Books, 1965), 32–86, and his two-part article, "The Name of God and the Linguistic Theory of the Kabbala," *Diogenes* no. 79 (1972): 59–80 (Part 1); no. 80 (1972): 164–94 (Part 2). Among Moshe Idel's numerous studies, see in particular his "Tᵉp̄îsaṯ ha-Tôrāh bᵉ-Sip̄rûṯ ha-Hêḵālôṯ wᵉ-Gilgûlêhā ba-Qabbālāh," *Jerusalem Studies in Jewish Thought* 1 (1981): 23–84, as well as his more recent studies, "Infinities of Torah in Kabbalah," in *Midrash and Literature,* edited by Geoffrey H. Hartman and Sanford Budick (New Haven and London: Yale University Press, 1986), 141–57; "Reification of Language in Jewish Mysticism," in *Mysticism and Language,* edited by Steven T. Katz (New York: Oxford University Press, 1992), 42–79; and *Language, Torah, and Hermeneutics in Abraham Abulafia,* translated by Menahem Kallus (Albany: SUNY Press, 1989). Among Elliot Wolfson's studies, mention should be made of his "Female Imaging of the Torah: From Literary Metaphor to Religious Symbol," cited earlier; "The Hermeneutics of Visionary Experience: Revelation and Interpretation in the *Zohar,*" *Religion* 18 (1988): 311–45; "The Anthropomorphic and Symbolic Image of the Letters in the Zohar" [in Hebrew], in *Proceedings of the Third International Conference on the History of Jewish Mysticism: The Age of the Zohar,* edited by Joseph Dan, *Jerusalem Studies in Jewish Thought* 8 (1989): 147–81; "Letter Symbolism and *Merkavah* Imagery in the *Zohar,*" in *ʿAlei Shefer: Studies in the Literature of Jewish Thought,* edited by Moshe Ḥallamish (Ramat-Gan: Bar-Ilan University Press, 1990), 195–236; and "Erasing the Erasure/ Gender and the Writing of God's Body in Kabbalistic Symbolism," in his *Along the Path: Studies in Kabbalistic Hermeneutics, Myth, and Symbolism* (Albany: SUNY Press, forthcoming). See also Isaiah Tishby's discussion of Zoharic conceptions of the Torah in his *The Wisdom of the Zohar: An Anthology of Texts,* vol.

3, translated by David Goldstein (Oxford: Oxford University Press, 1989), 1077–154. For an extended analysis of the role of language in Jewish mystical traditions, see Elias Lipiner, *The Metaphysics of the Hebrew Alphabet* [in Hebrew] (Jerusalem: Magnes Press, Hebrew University, 1989).

47. While this aspect of Veda is generally designated as "knowledge," as the etymology of the term itself suggests, the corresponding aspect of Torah is generally designated as Ḥoḵmāh, "wisdom." In the analysis that follows I will use the term "knowledge" to encompass both conceptions.

48. Even though the term "blueprint" is obviously a modern designation for which no literal equivalent can be found in Sanskrit or Hebrew, I have nevertheless chosen to use the term at times when discussing images of the Veda or Torah as the plan of creation in order to connote the plan's association with the architect of creation.

49. The brahmanical tradition's focus on oral transmission as the most appropriate vehicle for the Vedic *mantras* has its counterpart in an emphasis on the auditory mode of perception, just as the rabbinic and kabbalistic traditions' focus on written transmission of the Sefer Torah results in a corresponding emphasis on the visual channel. The brahmanical emphasis on the oral-aural over the written-visual dimensions of language and of Veda is linked to the essentially aniconic orientation of the Vedic tradition, in which *śrauta* rituals are traditionally performed in a temporary sacrificial enclosure, constructed for the purpose of the particular sacrifice, without iconic representations of deities. It is only with the advent of popular *bhakti* traditions in post-Vedic "Hinduism" that we find a shift to iconic forms of worship, with the introduction of temples and *pūjā* ceremonies centered on offerings to images of the gods. In the post-Vedic period the gods become "incarnated" in images, and certain sacred texts, such as the epics and Purāṇas, become embodied in written form and are themselves at times revered as visible icons of the divine. It is important to emphasize, however, that this represents a departure from the Vedic model, which gives priority to the oral-aural over the written-visual. The converse is true of rabbinic and kabbalistic conceptions of language and of Torah. While the rabbinic tradition is generally characterized as "aniconic" in that it eschews the use of images and other visual representations of the divine, certain rabbinic conceptions, which are further developed in kabbalistic texts, point to an almost iconic veneration of the Sefer Torah as the visible presence of the Word of God. As we embark on this comparative analysis, then, we must temporarily hold in abeyance the opposition "iconic 'Hinduism' vs. aniconic 'Judaism' " as inappropriate and misleading for certain strands of the brahmanical and Jewish traditions that we will be investigating.

50. See Barbara A. Holdrege, *Veda and Torah: Transcending the Textuality of Scripture* (Albany: SUNY Press, 1994).

51. The first phase of my analysis, as presented in my extended study, *Veda and Torah,* is tradition specific and involves analyzing the network of symbols associated with Veda and Torah separately, within the context of

each individual tradition. I call this phase "history of interpretations" in that my analyses are undertaken within a diachronic framework and involve tracing the history of certain representations of Veda and Torah, respectively, through the core texts of each tradition's formative development. The history with which I am concerned in this phase is not *Entstehungsgeschichte,* a history of origins and cause-effect relations, but rather *Wirkungsgeschichte,* a history of effects, understood as the tradition of successive interpretations of particular symbolic complexes associated with Veda and Torah. A useful model for this phase of my analysis is stratigraphy in geology. Stratigraphy involves examining and classifying the properties of individual strata and cross-correlating the different strata in order to discern regular patterns and recurrences of species as well as evolutionary changes in species from stratum to stratum. Similarly, the historical phase of my longer study is concerned with examining the symbolic complexes found in the core strata of texts in each tradition and cross-correlating the various strata in order to discern structural continuities as well as transformations from layer to layer. In this context I am particularly concerned with analyzing documentary contexts and the ways in which certain symbolic complexes are reshaped and reformulated in different textual environments in accordance with the epistemological framework of each stratum or genre of texts. The analysis also attempts to illuminate the ways in which these differences in textual perspective may reflect competing or shifting sectional interests based on changing sociohistorical factors.

52. For a more detailed analysis, including a consideration of methodological issues and full documentation of relevant references, see Holdrege, *Veda and Torah.*
53. While the present essay focuses primarily on mythological material, my longer study also includes a consideration of philosophical speculations concerning the status and authority of the Veda found in the Darśanas, with particular emphasis on Pūrva-Mīmāṃsā and Advaita Vedānta.
54. These dates encompass the principal Upaniṣads that were composed in the Vedic period, which ends ca. 200 B.C.E.
55. My extended study also includes a consideration of the antecedents of the concept of primordial wisdom/Torah in pre-rabbinic literature, with particular emphasis on Proverbs 8.22–31, the wisdom books of the Apocrypha (Wisdom of Ben Sira, Baruch 3.9–4.4, and Wisdom of Solomon), and the Alexandrian Jewish philosophers Aristobulus and Philo.
56. My analyses have focused on those Tannaitic Midrashim for which we have complete manuscripts: Mᵉḵîlṯā' dᵉ-R. Ishmael, Sip̄rā', Sip̄rê on Numbers, and Sip̄rê on Deuteronomy.
57. Classical Amoraic Midrashim include Genesis Rabbāh, Leviticus Rabbāh, Pᵉsîqtā' dᵉ-R. Kahana, Lamentations Rabbāh, Esther Rabbāh I, Song of Songs Rabbāh, and Ruth Rabbāh.
58. My analyses of post-Talmudic Midrashim have focused on Pᵉsîqtā' Rabbāṯî (ca. seventh century C.E.); Tanḥûmā' Yᵉlammᵉḏēnû Midrashim (ca.

ninth century C.E.), which include various editions of the Tanḥûmā', Exodus Rabbāh II, Numbers Rabbāh II, and Deuteronomy Rabbāh; and Pirqê d[e]-R. Eliezer (ca. eighth century C.E.).

59. The exponents of ecstatic Kabbalah, particularly as represented by the school of Abraham Abulafia, developed conceptions of Torah and language that are distinctly different from those elaborated by the theosophical kabbalists. For an exposition of Abulafia's views, see Idel, *Language, Torah, and Hermeneutics in Abraham Abulafia.*
60. See, for example, AV IV.1; AV X.2.25; AV X.7.32–34,36; AV X.8.1; cf. AV X.8.37–38. For discussions of the term *brahman,* see Paul Thieme, "Bráhman," *Zeitschrift der Deutschen Morgenländischen Gesellschaft* 102 [n.s., 27] (1952): 91–129; J. Gonda, *Notes on Bráhman* (Utrecht: J. L. Beyers, 1950). On specifically Vedic usages of the term, see also Louis Renou and Liliane Silburn, "Sur la notion de *bráhman,*" *Journal Asiatique* 237 (1949): 7–46.
61. Each of the Upaniṣads depicts Brahman-Ātman from its own particular perspective, in which different aspects of Brahman-Ātman's nature are emphasized. For example, the Bṛhadāraṇyaka Upaniṣad, while acknowledging the two aspects of Brahman, formed and formless (see BAU II.3.1), tends to emphasize the formless, transcendent aspect of Brahman-Ātman, which is *neti, neti* ("not this, not that"), completely devoid of qualities, and while dwelling in all things is at the same time other than all things. See BAU III.6–8; BAU III.9.26. The Chāndogya Upaniṣad, on the other hand, emphasizes the immanence of Brahman-Ātman, providing a series of definitions in which Brahman-Ātman is progressively identified with various psychical faculties (speech, mind, thought, and so on) as well as with various objective phenomena (water, heat, ether, and so on) and is ultimately proclaimed to be "this all" *(idam sarvam).* See CU VII.1–26.
62. The term Śabdabrahman occurs for the first time in the Maitri Upaniṣad, which distinguishes two forms of Brahman—Word *(śabda)* and non-Word *(aśabda)*—although no explicit reference is made to the Veda in this context. Maitri VI.22–23 identifies Śabdabrahman with the sacred syllable Om, which is described as the most concentrated essence of the Veda in Vedic and post-Vedic cosmogonies.
63. Cf. AV X.7.14.
64. The Brāhmaṇas, as the sacrificial manuals attached to the Saṃhitās, give priority in their cosmogonies to the creator Prajāpati, who is identified with the sacrifice. They are therefore primarily concerned to clarify the relationship of the Veda to Prajāpati and his consort Vāc, speech, and give little emphasis to the Veda's relationship to *brahman*/Brahman. Upaniṣadic speculations, on the other hand, focus on the ultimate reality, Brahman-Ātman, that is the source not only of creation but of the creator himself, and therefore the relationship of the Veda to Brahman-Ātman becomes a paramount concern.
65. TU II.3.
66. KU I.7.

67. See, for example, Mbh. XII.330.32–34; XII.271.27; XIII.135.27; XIII.143.34; XIV.53.8. See also VI.31.17 [Bhagavad-Gītā].
68. Mbh. XII.330.32–34.
69. See, for example, Mbh. XIII.15.30,34; XII, App. I, no. 28, 262–265,291; XIII.17.88–89; cf. XIII.85.4–6.
70. VP VI.4.42.
71. VP III.3.22; VP I.22.81.
72. VP III.3.29–30.
73. VP I.22.81–83. See also VP II.11.7–11, which describes the threefold Veda—*ṛcs, yajuses,* and *sāmans*—as the body *(aṅga)* of Viṣṇu and as identical with his supreme energy *(śakti)* that abides within the sun and is responsible for the preservation of the universe. Cf. Mark. 102.15–16,20–22; Mark. 103.6; Mark. 104.28.
74. The Purāṇas particularly extol Viṣṇu-Nārāyaṇa as the incarnation of Veda when he assumes the form of a boar *(varāha)* at the beginning of the Vārāha Kalpa in order to rescue the earth that lies submerged beneath the waters. See, for example, KP I.6.15; VP I.4.9,21–25,32–34; BP III.13.34–44 (esp. vv. 34,41,44); MP 248.67–73. Cf. Mark. 47.3–9 (esp. v. 8), which depicts the creator Brahmā, not Viṣṇu, as Nārāyaṇa, who assumes the form of a boar composed of the Vedas in order to save the earth.
75. MP 164.20.
76. MP 167.12.
77. See, for example, SP Rudra. II.15.46,52,64. The Śaiva sections of the Kūrma Purāṇa similarly celebrate Śiva as that eternal, unmanifest Brahman whose Self is knowledge *(jñānātman, vidyātman)* and who as the secret essence of the Veda *(veda-rahasya)* is the embodiment of the very self of Veda *(vedātma-mūrti).* See KP II.3.6,20; KP I.10.46–47,68.
78. SP Rudra. I.8.1–53.
79. RV X.90.9.
80. JUB I.46.1.
81. See, for example, SB X.4.2.26; SB X.3.1.1; SB VI.2.1.30; AB II.18; PB XIII.11.18; TB III.3.9.11; cf. SB XII.1.4.1–3; SB XII.6.1.1; KB VI.15. For the identification of the threefold Veda with Prajāpati's counterpart, the sacrifice, see SB I.1.4.3; SB V.5.5.10; SB III.1.1.12; JB I.358.
82. TB III.3.2.1; TB III.3.8.9.
83. See, for example, AB V.32; KB VI.10; TB II.3.10.1; SB VI.1.1.8–10; SB X.6.5.5 [= BAU I.2.5]; SB XI.5.8.1–3; JB I.68–69; JB I.357; PB VII.8.8–13; Sadv. B. I.5.7; JUB III.15.4–7; JUB I.23.1–5.
84. JB I.68–69; cf. PB VI.1.6–11. These passages build on earlier conceptions found in the Saṃhitās, in particular the Puruṣa-Sūkta and TS VII.1.1.4–6.
85. Relevant passages will be discussed below.
86. MU II.1.4,6.
87. MU II.1.4,9,10.
88. CU I.7.5.
89. Mbh. III.186.6; III.194.11; XII.327.46; I.1.30.
90. Mbh. XII.175.15.

91. Mbh. III.194.12.
92. Mbh. XII.203.8,14,18, for example, describes Viṣṇu as the ultimate source of the Vedas, which Brahmā then acquires. See also XII.200.33 with n. 545*; XII.181.2; XII.314.46; XII.327.30; XII.335.25; XII.160.21.
93. VP IV.1.4.
94. KP I.2.26.
95. KP I.4.39.
96. KP I.9.19.
97. BP III.11.34; BP III.12.48.
98. BP III.8.15; BP III.9.43; cf. BP II.6.34.
99. BP III.12.1; BP III.13.6.
100. BP III.12.34–35,37–39,44–47. Cf. SP Rudra. I.8.1–53, mentioned above, which describes Śiva as Śabdabrahman, whose body is composed of the Sanskrit *varṇas*.
101. RV I.164.45 indicates that this earthly dimension constitutes only one quarter of the total reality of Vāc: "Vāc is measured in four quarters. Those *brāhmaṇas* whose thoughts are inspired know them. Three [quarters], hidden in secret, do not issue forth. The fourth [quarter] of Vāc is what human beings speak." The Ṛg-Veda contains two hymns that are devoted entirely to Vāc: Ṛg-Veda X.125, a hymn of self-praise by and to the goddess Vāc, and Ṛg-Veda X.71, which focuses more on the manifest dimensions of Vāc in human language.

For discussions of the role of Vāc in the Ṛg-Veda, see W. Norman Brown, "The Creative Role of the Goddess Vāc in the Rig Veda," in *Pratidānam: Indian, Iranian and Indo-European Studies Presented to Franciscus Bernardus Jacobus Kuiper on His Sixtieth Birthday,* edited by J. C. Heesterman, G. H. Schokker, and V. I. Subramoniam, Janua linguarum, Series maior, 34 (The Hague and Paris: Mouton, 1968), 393–97; reprinted in W. Norman Brown, *India and Indology: Selected Articles,* edited by Rosane Rocher (Delhi: Motilal Banarsidass, 1978), 75–78; Frits Staal, "Ṛgveda 10.71 on the Origin of Language," in *Revelation in Indian Thought: A Festschrift in Honour of Professor T. R. V. Murti,* edited by Harold Coward and Krishna Sivaraman (Emeryville, Calif.: Dharma Publishing, 1977), 3–14; Laurie L. Patton, "Hymn to Vāc: Myth or Philosophy?" in *Myth and Philosophy,* edited by Frank Reynolds and David Tracy (Albany: SUNY Press, 1990), 183–213. See also Vidya Niwas Misra, "*Vāk* Legends in the *Brāhmaṇa* Literature," in *Proceedings of the Twenty-Sixth International Congress of Orientalists, New Delhi, January 4–10, 1964,* vol. 3, pt. 1 (Poona: Bhandarkar Oriental Research Institute, 1969), 109–18; Carl Anders Scharbau, *Die Idee der Schöpfung in der vedischen Literatur. Eine religionsgeschichtliche Untersuchung über den frühindischen Theismus,* Veröffentlichungen des orientalischen Seminars der Universität Tübingen, no. 5 (Stuttgart: W. Kohlhammer, 1932), 123–31, 135–38; Bénard Essers, "Vāc: Het Woord als Godsgestalte en als Godgeleerdheid in de Veda, in het bijzonder in de Ṛgveda-Saṃhitā en in de Atharvaveda-Saṃhitā" (Ph.D. diss., Groningen, Netherlands, 1952);

André Padoux, "Early Speculations about the Significance and the Powers of the Word," chapter 1 of his *Vāc: The Concept of the Word in Selected Hindu Tantras,* translated by Jacques Gontier (Albany: SUNY Press, 1990), 1–29.

102. See, for example, RV X.125.5; RV X.71.3,4.
103. See, for example, SB VI.1.1.8–10. As will be discussed on pp. 134–35, these two levels of Vāc are correlated with the two different stages in the process of creation that are described in several accounts in the Brāhmaṇas.
104. SB VI.5.3.4; SB X.5.1.2,5; cf. AB V.33; PB X.4.6,9.
105. See, for example, TB II.8.8.5. Cf. PB VII.8.8–13, in which Prajāpati creates the *pṛṣṭha sāman*s out of the womb *(yoni)* of the *gāyatrī* meter. In post-Vedic texts Gāyatrī is hypostatized as a feminine principle who is identified with Vāc and is the consort of the creator. Like Vāc, Gāyatrī is called in post-Vedic texts the "Mother of the Vedas." See n. 120.
106. See, for example, SB V.5.5.12; SB IV.6.7.1–3; cf. SB IV.5.8.4.
107. Relevant passages will be discussed below on pp. 130–31.
108. Cf. JUB I.1.3–5; Sadv. B. I.5.7. See also SB II.1.4.11–13, which describes how Prajāpati's utterance of the three *vyāhṛti*s generates not only the three worlds, but also the three powers that are the essence of the three higher social classes (*varṇa*s)—*brahman* (→brahmins), *kṣatra* (→*kṣatriya*s), and *viś* (→*vaiśya*s)—as well as the self *(ātman),* human beings, and animals.
109. See, for example, AB II.16; PB VII.5.1; JB I.116; JB I.117; JB I.128; JB I.148; JB I.160.
110. See, for example, AB IV.23; KB V.3; KB XII.8; PB IV.1.4; PB VI.1.1; PB VI.3.9; PB XVIII.7.1.
111. See, for example, AB V.32; KB VI.10.
112. PB VI.9.15; cf. JB I.94. The verse cited from the Ṛg-Veda (IX.62.1) reads:

    ete asṛgram indavas tiraḥ pavitram āśavaḥ |
    viśvāny abhi saubhagā ||

    "These swift Soma drops have been poured out through the filter for the sake of all blessings."

    In PB VII.5.1 Prajāpati is described as bringing forth beings by means of the *āmahīyava sāman,* while in JB I.104 he generates beings through chanting the words of the *bahiṣpavamāna stotra.* See also AB II.33, which depicts Prajāpati as the *hotṛ* priest who brings forth all beings through a series of twelve utterances, which are identified with the twelve lines of the *nivid* ("proclamation"), a prose formulary that is inserted at specified points in the recitation of certain Ṛg-Vedic hymns of praise (*śastra*s).
113. MU II.1.4.
114. BAU II.4.11; cf. BAU I.3.20–22; BAU I.6.1.
115. BAU IV.1.2; CU VII.2.1–2.
116. The term *tapas* has been left untranslated since it is difficult to find a single word or phrase that can satisfactorily convey the complex of

meanings encompassed by the term. The term literally means "heat," and in the present context particularly refers to the internal heat generated through meditation and various types of ascetic practices, by means of which one accumulates spiritual and creative power.

117. Maitri VI.6.
118. BAU I.2.4–5. This passage also forms part of the Śatapatha Brāhmaṇa (X.6.5.4–5).
119. BAU III.8.9.
120. Sarasvatī is celebrated as the Mother of the Vedas in Mbh. XII.326.52. Gāyatrī/Sāvitrī is designated in a similar manner in Mbh. VI, App. I, no. 1, 24. In VI, App. I, no. 1, 23–24, which forms part of a hymn to the goddess Durgā, Durgā is celebrated "as Sarasvatī, as Sāvitrī, the Mother of the Vedas," indicating perhaps a direct correlation between Sarasvatī and Sāvitrī, although in the epic the two goddesses are generally depicted as distinct goddesses.
121. See, for example, Mbh. XII.327.94.
122. Mbh. VI.63.5.
123. See, for example, Mbh. XII.326.7–8; XII.327.81; cf. XII.335.50.
124. Mbh. XII.8533 (Calcutta ed.). Sanskrit text cited in Muir, *Original Sanskrit Texts,* vol. 3, 16. Cf. the critical edition, XII.224.55 with n. 671*, which reads *nityā* in place of *vidyā.*
125. The latter part of this passage is cited below on p. 133.
126. See, for example, MP 3.30–44; MP 171.21–24.
127. MP 4.7,10.
128. See, for example, BP III.12.26.
129. See, for example, VP I.5.52–55; Mark. 48.31–34; KP I.7.54–57; LP I.70.243–46; SP Vāyavīya. I.12.58–62; cf. Mark 102.1–6; Mark. 45.20; BP III.12.34–35,37–40; MP 3.4.
130. BP III.12.34,37.
131. See, for example, SB VIII.7.4.5.
132. The three *vyāhṛtis* are at times directly identified with the three Vedas. See, for example, JUB II.9.7; JUB III.18.4. However, they are more often described as their essences. See AB V.32; KB VI.10–11; SB XI.5.8.1–4; Sadv. B. I.5.7–10; JB I.357–58; JB I.363–64; JUB I.1.2–5; JUB I.23.6; JUB III.15.8–9.
133. See, for example, SB XI.1.6.3, cited earlier on p. 127. See also JUB I.1.3–5; Sadv. B. I.5.7.
134. See, for example, SB II.1.4.11–13.
135. AB V.32; KB VI.10; SB XI.5.8.1–4; JB I.357; JUB I.1.1–7; JUB III.15.4–9; JUB I.23.1–8; cf. SB IV.6.7.1–2; SB XII.3.4.7–10; Sadv. B. I.5.7–10; Sadv. B. V.1.2; JB I.363–64.
136. See, for example, AB V.32.
137. See, for example, SB XII.3.4.7–10; cf. JB I.249. These correlations build upon those established earlier in the Puruṣa-Sūkta. See RV X.90.13.
138. While the *ṛc* is consistently identified with speech, the *sāman* is at times identified with the mind, as well as with the breath *(prāṇa).* The *yajus* is also sometimes correlated with the mind. See, for example, JB I.326; JUB I.53.2;

JUB I.9.2; JUB III.34.1; JUB I.25.8–10; JUB I.57.7–8. The *sāman* and the *yajus* are thus associated with both mind and breath, which are intimately related in the speculations of the Brāhmaṇas. See, for example, SB VII.5.2.6, which describes the mind as the first of the *prāṇas* and identical with all the *prāṇas*.

139. SB X.4.2.21–22.
140. It is perhaps in this sense that SB IV.6.7.1–2 establishes a direct identity between the three Vedas and the three worlds, declaring that the *ṛcs* are the earth, the *yajuses* are the midregions, and the *sāmans* are the heavens, for the sounds of each Veda are held to reveal the underlying structure of the corresponding world. Cf. Sadv. B. I.5.7–10; Sadv. B. V.1.2.
141. See, for example, CU IV.17.1–3; CU II.23.2–3; CU I.3.7; CU III.15.5–7; BAU I.5.4–5; Maitri VI.5. TU I.5 provides one of the rare variants of this set of correspondences, in which the *sāmans*, rather than the *yajuses*, are associated with the utterance *bhuvaḥ,* the midregions, and Vāyu. The correlations with the faculties of speech, breath, and the eye are not mentioned in these Upaniṣadic passages.
142. See, for example, CU IV.17.1–3; CU II.23.2–3; cf. BAU I.5.1–13.
143. Maitri VI.5.
144. TU I.5. This "3 + 1" structure is evident elsewhere in the Upaniṣads. See, for example, the Māṇḍūkya Upaniṣad's discussion of the three states of consciousness—waking, dreaming, and deep sleep—to which a fourth *(caturtha),* transcendent state of consciousness is added, which is designated in the Bṛhadāraṇyaka Upaniṣad (V.14.3–4,6–7) as *turīya* and in the Maitri Upaniṣad (VI.19; VII.11) as *turya.* One of the most well known examples of this "3 + 1" structure is the addition of *mokṣa* to the *trivarga—kāma, artha,* and *dharma*—as the fourth end of human life *(puruṣārtha).* See Troy Organ, "Three into Four in Hinduism," *Ohio Journal of Religious Studies* 1, no. 2 (1973): 7–13.
145. For a discussion of relevant passages in post-Vedic texts, see Holdrege, *Veda and Torah,* chapter 1, "Purāṇas."
146. MS I.28–30.
147. MS XII.94,99; MS I.23.
148. MS I.21.
149. MS XII.97–99.
150. See, for example, Mbh. XII.224.55 with n. 671*–XII.224.56 with n. 672*; XII.335.30,66.
151. See, for example, Mbh. XII.327.84; XII.326.57–58; XII.224.56 with n. 672*.
152. Mbh. XII.224.56 with n. 672*.
153. VP I.5.62–63. This same passage appears with slight variations in Mark. 48.42–43; KP I.7.64–65; LP I.70.257–59; SP Vāyavīya. I.12.67–69.
154. See, for example, VP I.5.44–45,42–43.
155. F. B. J. Kuiper, "Cosmogony and Conception: A Query," *History of Religions* 10, no. 2 (1970): 91–138.
156. For an analysis of passages from the Brāhmaṇas illustrating this two-phase process of creation, see Holdrege, *Veda and Torah,* chapter 1, "Brāhmaṇas."

157. For a discussion of relevant passages from the Manu-Smṛti, Mahābhārata, and Purāṇas, see Holdrege, *Veda and Torah,* chapter 1, "Veda and Creation in Post-Vedic Mythology."
158. See, for example, Sip̄rê Num. §112; Gen. R. XXVIII.4; Gen. R. I.10; Song R. V.11, §4; Pes. K. Suppl. 3.2; Sanh. 99a; Šeb. 13a; Ber. 22a; Taan. 4a; Taan. 7a; Šab. 88b; Sanh. 34a; Pes. R. 8.5; Pes. R. 33.10; Pes. R. 21.21; Exod. R. XXXVI.3.
159. Gen. R. XXVIII.4; Gen. R. I.10; Song R. V.11, §4; Pes. R. 21.21.
160. Gen. R. XXVIII.4. Cf. Gen. R. I.10, variants of which appear in Song R. V.11, §4; Pes. R. 21.21. Song R. IV.4, §9 declares that God foreshortened the thousand generations in order to bring the people of Israel the Torah. Song R. IV.4, §1 designates Moses as he "who came for a thousand generations." Ḥag. 13b–14a mentions the 974 generations that remained uncreated. See also Gen. R. I.4; Gen. R. XXI.9; Lev. R. IX.3; Lev. R. XXIII.3; Pes. K. 12.24; Pes. 118a; Pes. R. 5.3, which mention the tradition that the Torah was revealed after twenty-six generations.
161. Šab. 88b; Zeb. 116a. Psalm 105.8 is not mentioned as a proof text in this context.
162. See Ephraim E. Urbach, ed., "Śerîḏê Tanḥûmā' Yelammeḏēnû," *Qōḇeṣ 'al Yāḏ* 6 (16), pt. 1 (1966): 20. This Midrash is cited below on pp. 143–44.
163. See pp. 146–48.
164. See, for example, Lev. R. III.7; Song R. I.3, §1; Song R. VIII.11, §2; Ber. 6a; Ber. 21a; Ber. 11b; Šab. 88b–89a; Šab. 115b–116a; Mak. 11a; Deut. R. VII.3; Deut. R. VIII.2; Pes. R. 25.3.
165. For a detailed analysis of the various ways in which the *sep̄îrôṯ* have been interpreted in kabbalistic texts, see Moshe Idel, *Kabbalah: New Perspectives* (New Haven: Yale University Press, 1988), 136–53.
166. These ten words will be discussed below on pp. 147–48.
167. See Moses b. Naḥman (Naḥmanides), *Pêrûšê ha-Tôrāh,* edited by Ḥayyim Dov (Charles B.) Chavel, vol. 1 (Jerusalem: Mosad ha-Rav Kook, 1959), 6–7. For a translation of this passage, see *Ramban (Nachmanides), Commentary on the Torah,* vol. 1, translated by Charles B. Chavel (New York: Shilo Publishing House, 1971), 13–15.
168. See, for example, Ezra b. Solomon, Commentary on the Talmudic 'Aggāḏôṯ, Vatican MS Cod. Hebr. 294, f. 34a; MS Leiden, Warner 32, f. 23a; Azriel, *Pêrûš hā-'Aggāḏôṯ,* edited by Isaiah Tishby (Jerusalem: Mekize Nirdamim, Mosad ha-Rav Kook, 1945), 37–38, 76. See also Jacob b. Sheshet, *Sēp̄er hā-'Ĕmûnāh we-ha-Biṭṭāḥôn,* in *Kiṯḇê Rabbênû Mosheh b. Naḥman,* edited by Ḥayyim Dov (Charles B.) Chavel, vol. 2 (Jerusalem: Mosad ha-Rav Kook, 1963), 353–448, esp. chap. 19 [ascribed erroneously to Naḥmanides]. See Scholem's discussion in "The Meaning of the Torah in Jewish Mysticism," 39, 44–45.
169. Zohar II.90b; II.124a; II.87a; II.161b; III.13b; III.35b,36a; III.73a; III.80b; III.113a; III.298b.
170. Zohar II.60b; cf. II.60a.
171. Zohar II.86a.

172. The Hebrew term *dāḇār* itself conveys the double meaning of "word" and "thing," for in ancient conceptions found throughout the Near East the name participates in the reality and essence of what is named.

173. MS Jerusalem, 8° 597, f. 21b. Cited in Scholem, "The Meaning of the Torah in Jewish Mysticism," 44. Gikatilla's work is contained in this manuscript under the name of Isaac b. Farḥi or Peraḥia. Menaḥem Recanati (ca. 1300 C.E.) similarly ascribes to the kabbalists the notion that God and the Torah are one: "The Torah is not outside Him, and He is not something outside the Torah. Therefore the kabbalists say that the Holy One, blessed be He, *is* the Torah." Menaḥem Recanati, *Ṭaʿămê ha-Miṣwôṯ*, edited by S. Lieberman (London: Makhon Otzar ha-Ḥokhmah, 1962), f. 2a. For a discussion of passages in other kabbalistic texts that emphasize the identity of the Torah with the Name of God, and ultimately with God himself, see Idel, "Tᵉp̄îsaṯ ha-Tôrāh bᵉ-Sip̄rûṯ ha-Hêḵālôṯ wᵉ-Gilgûlêḥā ba-Qabbālāh", 49–84; idem, *Kabbalah*, 244–47.

174. Cf. the view of the *Sēp̄er ha-Yiḥûḏ* (late thirteenth century C.E.), discussed below on p. 167, which maintains that the letters of the Torah are the forms of God.

175. The other contending interpretation vocalizes *ʾāmôn* as *ʾāmûn* (Qal passive participle from *ʾāman*, "to nurse") or *ʾᵉmûn* (noun), "nursling, darling." For the details of the scholarly debate see Gerhard von Rad, *Wisdom in Israel*, translated by James D. Martin (London: SCM Press Ltd., 1972), 152; R. N. Whybray, *Wisdom in Proverbs: The Concept of Wisdom in Proverbs 1–9* (London: SCM Press Ltd., 1965), 101–2; Martin Hengel, *Judaism and Hellenism: Studies in Their Encounter in Palestine during the Early Hellenistic Period*, vol. 1, translated by John Bowden (Philadelphia: Fortress Press, 1974), 153 with n. 291; R. B. Y. Scott, "Wisdom in Creation: The *ʾāmôn* of Proverbs VIII 30," *Vetus Testamentum* 10 (1960): 213–23. For a brief discussion of the concept of primordial wisdom in Proverbs 8.22–31 and the subsequent development of this notion in the wisdom books of the Apocrypha and the philosophy of Aristobulus and Philo, see Holdrege, *Veda and Torah*, chapter 2, "Torah and Creation in Pre-Rabbinic Texts."

176. See, for example, Sip̄rê Deut. §37; Gen. R. I.1; Gen. R. I.4; Gen. R. I.8; Lev. R. XIX.1; Song R. V.11, §1; Ned. 39b; Pes. 54a; Tanḥ., ed. Buber, Bᵉrēʾšîṯ §5; PRE §3, f. 6a.

177. See, for example, Gen. R. I.1; Gen. R. VIII.2; Lev. R. XIX.1; Song R. V.11, §1; Tanḥ., ed. Buber, Bᵉrēʾšîṯ §5; Tanḥ. Bᵉrēʾšîṯ §1; Exod. R. XXX.9.

178. See, for example, Gen. R. I.4; Song R. V.11, §4; Exod. R. XLVII.4; Tanḥ. Bᵉrēʾšîṯ §1. Regarding the role of wisdom in creation, with no explicit mention of the Torah, see Lev. R. XI.1; Ḥag. 12a; Ber. 55a; Tanḥ., ed. Buber, Bᵉrēʾšîṯ §15; Exod. R. XLVIII.4; PRE §3, f. 8b.

179. Gen. R. I.1.

180. The characterization of the Torah as God's "working instrument *(kᵉlî)*" in creation recalls earlier sayings, attributed to R. Akiba and R. Eleazar b. Zadok, respectively, in which the Torah is said to be the "instrument

(k^e lî) by means of which the world was created." See 'Ab. III.14; Sip̄rê Deut. §48.

181. As discussed in n. 185, the last portion of this pericope is replicated almost verbatim in Tanḥ., ed. Buber, B^e rē'šîṯ §5, where it is attributed to R. Judah b. Il^c ai. A similar conjunction of Genesis 1.1 and Proverbs 8.22 is found in Targum Neofiti 1 on Genesis 1.1, in which *b^e rē'šîṯ bārā' Elohim* is interpreted as *b^e-ḥoḵmāh bārā'*. Cf. Fragment Targums P and V on Genesis 1.1.
182. Exod. R. XLVII.4.
183. See, for example, Tanḥ. B^e rē'šîṯ §1; Tanḥ. P^e qûḏê §3.
184. Tanḥ. B^e rē'šîṯ §1.
185. Tanḥ., ed. Buber, B^e rē'šîṯ §5. This Midrash is nearly identical, verbatim, with the last portion of the opening proem of Genesis Rabbāh (I.1), discussed earlier. The two Midrashim clearly stem from a common tradition, with the Tanḥûmā''s version perhaps representing the earlier of the two, since it is shorter and does not contain the more developed image of the architect and blueprint that is found in Genesis Rabbāh. Moreover, if the attribution can be trusted, the Tanḥûmā' version is ascribed to an earlier sage, the Tanna R. Judah b. Il^c ai (ca. 150 C.E.), who lived nearly a century before R. Hoshaiah (ca. 225 C.E.), to whom the Genesis Rabbāh proem is attributed.
186. PRE §3, f. 6a.
187. PRE §3, f. 6b. As in Tanḥ. B^e rē'šîṯ §1, Proverbs 8.14 is invoked as a proof text, in which the figure of wisdom declares, "Counsel *(^c ēṣāh)* is mine and sound wisdom *(tûšiyyāh).*" Cf. PRE §11, f. 27b.
188. Zohar I.5a; I.47a; I.134a–134b; II.161a; III.35b; I.207a.
189. Zohar I.207a. While the Torah is generally identified with Ḥoḵmāh in the Zohar, it is also at times described as having its source in the supernal wisdom. See, for example, Zohar III.81a: "There is no Torah without wisdom and no wisdom without Torah, both being in the same grade, the root of the Torah being in the supernal Wisdom by which it is sustained." Cf. Zohar II.121a.
190. It should be noted, however, that the primordial Torah is at times associated with Bînāh as well as with Ḥoḵmāh. See, for example, Zohar II.85a, which suggests that the Torah is an emanation of both Ḥoḵmāh, the Father, and Bînāh, the Mother. Moreover, as will be discussed below, the Torah in its later stages of manifestation as the Written Torah and Oral Torah becomes identified, respectively, with Tip̄'ereṯ, the son (the sixth *s^e p̄îrāh*), and Malḵûṯ, the daughter (the tenth *s^e p̄îrāh,* which is the Shekhinah). The gender of the Torah in its various manifestations thus encompasses both male and female.
191. Zohar II.161a.
192. See Gen. R. I.1, cited on pp. 140–41. Cf. Tanḥ., ed. Buber, B^e rē'šîṯ §5, which replicates the last portion of the Genesis Rabbāh passage and describes God as "looking into" *(hibbîṭ)* the Torah to create the world, although this idea is not explicitly elaborated in terms of the image of a blueprint.

A number of scholars have noted the obvious parallels between Genesis Rabbāh's use of the blueprint analogy and the Alexandrian Jewish philosopher Philo's use of a similar image in which the architect is depicted as sketching the plan in his mind. Philo writes,

> [A] trained architect . . . first sketches in his own mind wellnigh all the parts of the city that is to be wrought out, temples, gymnasia, town-halls, market-places, harbours, docks, streets, walls to be built, dwelling-houses as well as public buildings to be set up. Thus after having received in his own soul, as it were in wax, the figures of these objects severally, he carries about the image of a city which is the creation of his mind. Then by his innate power of memory, he recalls the images of the various parts of this city, and imprints their types yet more distinctly in it: and like a good craftsman he begins to build the city of stones and timber, keeping his eye upon his pattern and making the visible and tangible objects correspond in each case to the incorporeal ideas. (Op. 17–18)

Similarly, Philo writes, when God began to create the world, "He conceived beforehand the models of its parts, and . . . out of these He constituted and brought to completion a world discernible only by the mind, and then, with that for a pattern, the world which our senses can perceive" (Op. 19). This world of archetypal ideas is the blueprint of creation contained in the mind of the architect, who, according to Philo, is the Logos (wisdom) (Op. 20, 24–25), the instrument employed by the King of all to bring forth manifest creation. The Logos is identified in other passages with the Torah, which as the ideal pattern of creation is "stamped with the seals of nature" and is "the most faithful picture of the world-polity" (II Mos. 14, 51; cf. Op. 3).

For a discussion of the parallels between the use of the blueprint analogy in Genesis Rabbāh and Philo, see George Foot Moore, *Judaism in the First Centuries of the Christian Era, the Age of the Tannaim,* vol. 1 (Cambridge: Harvard University Press, 1927), 267–68; Hengel, *Judaism and Hellenism,* vol. 1, 171; Urbach, *The Sages,* vol. 1, 198–200. Other scholars have noted the similarities between the opening Midrash of Genesis Rabbāh and Plato's *Timaeus* 27f. See, for example, Henry A. Fischel, "The Transformation of Wisdom in the World of Midrash," in *Aspects of Wisdom in Judaism and Early Christianity,* edited by Robert L. Wilken (Notre Dame: University of Notre Dame Press, 1975), 80. Maimonides, in his *Guide to the Perplexed,* wondered about the expression *histakkēl* ("to look at, contemplate"), which corresponds to the expression *hibbîṭ* used in the Midrash attributed to R. Hoshaiah, and remarked that this very expression is used by Plato when he states that God contemplates the world of Ideas and thus produces existing beings. Moses Maimonides, *Guide for the Perplexed,* pt. 2, chap. 6. See Urbach, *The Sages,* vol. 1, 199 with n. 69.

Scholars are not in agreement concerning the extent to which Genesis Rabbāh's depiction of the Torah as the architect and blueprint of creation reflects the doctrine of Platonic Ideas, particularly as expressed in Philo's concept of the Logos. Ephraim Urbach has argued against such a hasty conclusion and has emphasized the essential differences in the language and imagery used by R. Hoshaiah and Philo to express the analogy of the blueprint.

> R. Hoshaᶜia's homily contains not the slightest reference to the world of Ideas or to the location of the Ideas. In the analogy, "the architect does not plan the building in his head, but he makes use of rolls and tablets"—a fact that Philo carefully refrained from mentioning, because it contradicted his purpose in adducing the analogy. Like the architect who looks at the rolls and tablets, so the Holy One, blessed be He, looked in the Torah, but it contains no forms and sketches of temples, gymnasia, markets and harbours, and this Torah is not a concept but the concrete Torah with its precepts and statutes, which are inscribed in letters.

Urbach goes on to assert that the analogy in R. Hoshaiah's Midrash is "only a literary embellishment." See Urbach, *The Sages,* vol. 1, 200.

Although Urbach is correct in pointing out the differences between Philo's depiction of the blueprint as a mental plan and Genesis Rabbāh's use of the more concrete imagery of "plans and tablets," he goes too far when he attempts to limit the proem's conception of Torah to the concrete Book of the Torah. Long before the redaction of Genesis Rabbāh, a suprahistorical dimension had been superimposed on the historical phenomenon of Torah through its identification with primordial wisdom. This identification is assumed in the homily attributed to R. Hoshaiah, and thus its use of the analogy of the architect and blueprint must be viewed against the background of a conception of Torah that encompassed supramundane as well as mundane dimensions. This does not mean to suggest that the author of the Genesis Rabbāh proem necessarily appropriated all of the Hellenistic elements that were incorporated into the Jewish conception of Torah/wisdom by the writers of the wisdom books of the Apocrypha and by the Alexandrian Jewish philosophers Aristobulus and Philo. In particular, it is highly unlikely that the author borrowed directly from Philo in his analogy of the blueprint. Indeed, he was probably not even aware of Philo's writings. The similarities between their uses of the analogy can better be explained by their access to a common tradition, which intermingled traditional Jewish wisdom speculation with Greek philosophical categories.

193. See, for example, Gen. R. I.13; Gen. R. XII.14; Tanḥ., ed. Buber, Bᵉrē'šîṯ §17; PRE §3, f. 5b–6a. None of these Midrashim explicitly connects the plan of creation with the Torah.
194. See pp. 137–38.
195. Hebrew text cited in Urbach, "Śᵉrîḏê Tanḥûmā' Yᵉlammᵉḏēnû," 20.

196. Lev. R. XXXV.4.
197. Pes. K. 12.1; Mak. 23b. "Members" refers to the joints, bones, or organs that are covered with flesh and sinews, excluding the teeth.
198. Zohar II.161a. This passage concludes the Zohar's discussion of the Torah's role as the architect and blueprint of creation cited earlier. God is similarly described elsewhere in the Zohar as "contemplating through seeing" *('istakkēl)* the Torah in order to create the world. See, for example, Zohar I.5a, mentioned below, and I.134a. Cf. I.90a (Sitrê Tôrāh).
199. Zohar I.5a.
200. Zohar I.207a. For the Torah's role in bringing forth creation, see also I.24b (Tîqqûnîm); II.200a; III.152a; and the references cited above in n. 188.
201. Zohar I.134b; cf. I.186b; II.25a (Rā ᶜăyā' Mᵉhêmnā').
202. Zohar II.162b; II.165b.
203. See p. 153.
204. For references see n. 158.
205. For references see n. 164.
206. See, for example, Mek., ed. Lauterbach, Šîrāṯā' §8, vol. 2, 62, 63; Mek., ed. Lauterbach, Šîrāṯā' §10, vol. 2, 78, 79; Mek., ed. Lauterbach, Wa-yassaᶜ §1, vol. 2, 92; Mek., ed. Lauterbach, Ba-ḥôḏeš §8, vol. 2, 263; Mek., ed. Lauterbach, Ba-ḥôḏeš §9, vol. 2, 275; Sip̄rê Deut. §307; Sip̄rê Deut. §343; Gen. R. IV.4; Gen. R. XXIV.2; Lev. R. III.7; Pes. K. Suppl. 1.15; Esth. R. I.12; Song R. IV.5, §1; ᶜErub. 13b; Meg. 13b; Sot. 10b; Qid. 30b; Qid. 31a; Sanh. 19a; Pes. R. 21.7.
207. This tradition appears twice, in Gen. R. XXXI.8 and Gen. R. XVIII.4, where it is attributed to R. Phinehas and R. Hezekiah (or R. Ḥilkiah) in the name of R. Simon b. Pazzi. Cf. Tanḥ., ed. Buber, Nōaḥ §28.
208. See, for example, *Sēp̄er Yᵉṣîrāh* 2.2: "Twenty-two letters are the foundation: He engraved them, He hewed them out, He combined them, He weighed them, and He set them at opposites, and He formed through them everything that is formed and everything that is destined to be formed." For a brief discussion of the *Sēp̄er Yᵉṣîrāh,* see Gershom Scholem, "The Sefer Yeẓirah," in his *Kabbalah,* Library of Jewish Knowledge (Jerusalem: Keter, 1974), 23–30; idem, "The Name of God and the Linguistic Theory of the Kabbala," pt. 1, 72–76. For a translation and commentary on the text, see David R. Blumenthal, "*Sefer Yetsira:* Text and Commentary," chapter 3 of his *Understanding Jewish Mysticism: A Source Reader. The Merkabah Tradition and the Zoharic Tradition,* The Library of Judaic Learning, vol. 2 (New York: Ktav, 1978), 15–44.
209. Ber. 55a.
210. See Urbach, "Śᵉrîḏê Tanḥûmā' Yᵉlammᵉḏēnû," 20. This passage appears at the end of the Midrash cited above, on pp. 143–44, which links the Torah to the plan of creation conceived in God's mind.
211. See, for example, Gen. R. I.10; Pes. K. 12.24; Song R. V.11, §4; Pes. R. 21.21.
212. See, for example, Gen. R. XII.10; Men. 29b; Pes. R. 21.21; Tanḥ., ed. Buber, Bᵉrē'šîṯ §16.

213. Mek., ed. Lauterbach, Šîrāṯā' §10, vol. 2, 78–79; Mek., ed. Lauterbach, Baḥôḏeš §7, vol. 2, 255; Gen. R. III.2; Gen. R. IV.6; Gen. R. XII.10; Gen. R. XXVII.1; Šab. 119b; Pes. R. 49.10; Pes. R. 27.4; Pes. R. 23.5; Tanḥ., ed. Buber, Bᵉrē'šîṯ §11; Deut. R. V.13; PRE §7, f. 15b.
214. See, for example, Ber. 57b.
215. 'Ab. V.1.
216. Gen. R. XVII.1; RH 32a; Meg. 21b; Pes. R. 21.19; Pes. R. 40.5; PRE §3, f. 8b; PRE §32, f. 74a.
217. Gen. 1.1, 2, 3, 6, 9, 11, 14–15, 20, 24, 26. Alternative enumerations of the ten words, found in Gen. R. XVII.1 as well as in later rabbinic texts, generally exclude *bᵉrē'šîṯ* and/or the spirit/voice of God upon the waters and include instead one or both of the two additional commands "And God said" in Genesis 1.29 and 2.18. See Gen. R. XVII.1; RH 32a; Meg. 21b; Pes. R. 21.19; PRE §3, f. 8b.
218. In a variant of this tradition found in the Talmud, in RH 32a and Meg. 21b, the role of *bᵉrē'šîṯ* as the first ot the ten words is substantiated through reference to Psalm 33.6, "By the word *(dāḇār)* of the Lord were the heavens made, and all their host by the breath of His mouth." Hence, Genesis 1.1, "*Bᵉrē'šîṯ* God created heaven and earth," is interpreted to mean "By means of the word God created heaven and earth (= 'their host')."
219. See Gen. R. I.1, discussed on pp. 140–41. Cf. Tanḥ., ed. Buber, Bᵉrē'šîṯ §5.
220. The spirit *(rûaḥ)* of God moving upon the face of the waters in Genesis 1.2 is interpreted in light of Psalm 29.3, "The voice *(qôl)* of the Lord is upon the waters," to mean the voice of God.
221. Gen. 1.3, 6, 9, 11, 14–15, 20, 24, 26.
222. Zohar I.2a; I.3b; I.15a; I.18a.
223. As will be discussed below, this primordial point is identified in the Zohar with Ḥoḵmāh, the second *sᵉp̄îrāh*, who is designated as *rē'šîṯ*. See Zohar I.3b; I.15a–15b; I.29b; I.30b; I.31b; cf. I.24b (Tîqqûnîm); I.145a.
224. See, for example, Zohar II.20a (Midrash ha-Neᶜĕlām): "When it arose in thought before the Holy One, blessed be He, to create His world, all the worlds arose in one thought and with this thought they were all created. This is the meaning of 'With wisdom have You made them all' [Ps. 104.24]. And with this thought, which is wisdom, this world and the world above were created." See also I.29a; I.3b; I.21a; III.5b; cf. III.42b–43a.
225. Zohar I.15a.
226. Zohar I.15a–15b.
227. Zohar I.15a–15b.
228. See, for example, Zohar I.22a (Tîqqûnîm); III.290a ('Iḏrā' Zûṭā').
229. Zohar I.50b; I.29a; cf. I.39b; II.85b.
230. See, for example, Zohar I.74a; I.50b. See also I.246b, which emphasizes that the four stages in the unfoldment of the divine language are ultimately one.
231. Zohar I.50b; cf. I.141b.
232. See, for example, Zohar I.15a; I.31b. 'Ên-Sôp̄ is understood to be the unmanifest subject of the sentence.

233. Zohar I.16b.
234. Zohar I.50b; cf. I.141b.
235. Zohar I.16b.
236. Gen. 1.3, 6–7.
237. Zohar III.32b; I.17b; I.29b; I.46a–46b.
238. Gen. 1.11–27.
239. See pp. 147–48.
240. Zohar III.5b; III.261a.
241. See, for example, Zohar I.15b; I.16b.
242. Zohar I.47b.
243. Zohar I.17b; I.47b; cf. I.71b–72a.
244. Zohar II.238b; II.205b–206a.
245. Zohar II.161b; II.205b.
246. Zohar III.113a; II.161b.
247. Zohar II.200a.
248. Zohar II.205b.
249. See, for example, Zohar II.85a.
250. Zohar II.60a,60b.
251. This doctrine is first developed in *Lîmmûḏê 'Ăṣîlûṯ* (Munkács: Samuel Kahn, 1897), f. 3a, 15a–15b, 21d–22a, which is printed under the name of Ḥayyim Vital but in Scholem's view was undoubtedly written by Israel Sarug. Cf. Menaḥem Azariah of Fano, *Šiḇ ͑îm û-Štayim Yᵉḏî ͑ôṯ* (Lvov, 1867); Naphtali Bacharach, *͑Ēmeq ha-Meleḵ* (Amsterdam, 1648; reprint, Bene Berak: Yahadut, 1973), chap. 1, esp. end of §4. See Scholem's discussion in "The Name of God and the Linguistic Theory of the Kabbala," pt. 2, 181–82, and in "The Meaning of the Torah in Jewish Mysticism," 73–74.
252. BP III.12.34,37.
253. Zohar II.161a.
254. For a discussion of the phenomenology of Vedic cognition as described in Vedic and post-Vedic texts, see Holdrege, *Veda and Torah,* chapter 3. See also J. Gonda, *The Vision of the Vedic Poets,* Disputationes Rheno-Trajectinae, vol. 8 (The Hague: Mouton, 1963).
255. Mek., ed. Lauterbach, Ba-ḥôḏeš §9, vol. 2, 266; cf. Pes. R. 33.10; PRE §41, f. 98a.
256. Zohar II.81a–81b; II.146a; II.93b–94a. For a discussion of the phenomenology of the Sinai revelation as described in rabbinic texts and in the Zohar, see Holdrege, *Veda and Torah,* chapter 4. For an analysis of the Zohar's treatment of the Sinai theophany as a visionary experience, see Wolfson, "The Hermeneutics of Visionary Experience: Revelation and Interpretation in the *Zohar.*"
257. For a more detailed discussion of practices associated with the Vedic Saṃhitās and the Written Torah, see Holdrege, *Veda and Torah,* chapters 5 and 6.
258. See Graham, "Scripture as Spoken Word: The Indian Paradigm," chapter 6 of his *Beyond the Written Word,* 67–80, esp. 68.

259. Staal, *Nambudiri Veda Recitation,* 11–17; idem, "The Concept of Scripture in the Indian Tradition"; idem, *Rules Without Meaning,* esp. 191–311. Coburn, " 'Scripture' in India." See also Walther Eidlitz, *Der Glaube und die heiligen Schriften der Inder* (Olten and Freiburg: Walter-Verlag, 1957), 11–29; Renou, *The Destiny of the Veda in India,* 23–26; Jan Gonda, *Vedic Literature (Saṃhitās and Brāhmaṇas),* A History of Indian Literature, vol. 1, pt. 1 (Wiesbaden: Otto Harrassowitz, 1975), 43–45.
260. Among the six Vedāṅgas, *śikṣā* ("instruction") is concerned with the proper articulation and pronunciation of the Vedic sounds; *chandas* ("meter") includes texts on the various prescribed meters used in reciting the *mantras*; *vyākaraṇa* ("analysis and derivation"), in addition to grammatical works describing and analyzing the Vedic language, includes the various *prātiśākhyas*, which prescribe the methods of pronunciation that prevail in the different Vedic *śākhās* or schools; and *kalpa* ("ritual") includes the Śrauta-Sūtras and Gṛhya-Sūtras, which are concerned with the proper performance of the Vedic sacrifices and domestic rituals, in which recitation of the *mantras* assumes a central role.
261. For a description of the *pāṭhas* and other recitative techniques, one may refer to K. V. Abhyankar and G. V. Devasthali, *Vedavikṛtilakṣaṇa-Saṁgraha: A Collection of Twelve Tracts on Vedavikṛtis and Allied Topics,* Research Unit Publications, no. 5 (Poona: Bhandarkar Oriental Research Institute, 1978), esp. xvii–xlix; Staal, *Nambudiri Veda Recitation,* esp. 21–30, 40–52; N. A. Jairazbhoy, "Le chant védique," in *Encyclopédie des musiques sacrées,* edited by Jacques Porte, vol. 1 (Paris: Labergie, 1968), 144–61.
262. Pāṇinīya Śikṣā 52; cf. Nāradīya Śikṣā I.1.5.
263. ᶜErub. 13a.
264. For references see n. 167.
265. Ezra b. Solomon, MS Leiden, Warner 32, f. 23a; Azriel, *Pêrûš hā-'Aggāḏôṯ,* 37–38. Cited in Scholem, "The Meaning of the Torah in Jewish Mysticism," 44–45.
266. MS Milano-Ambrosiana 62, f. 113b. Cited in Idel, "Infinities of Torah in Kabbalah," 145. See Idel's discussion of this passage in his "Tᵉp̄îsaṯ ha-Tôrāh bᵉ-Sip̄rûṯ ha-Hêḵālôṯ wᵉ-Gilgûlêhā ba-Qabbālāh," 62–64.
267. MS Milano-Ambrosiana 62, f. 113b. Cited in Idel, *Kabbalah,* 188.
268. The brahmanical focus on the phonology and syntax of the Vedic Saṃhitās, with corresponding neglect of semantics, has led Staal to conclude that the Vedic *mantras* are in the final analysis meaningless and thus do not constitute linguistic utterances. He maintains that the Vedic *mantras* may be more fruitfully understood in relation to the structures of music than to the structures of language. See Staal, *Rules Without Meaning,* 191–311. Staal's comparison of the *mantras* with music resonates with the brahmanical tradition's own characterization of the *mantras* as the primordial rhythms of creation. However, in the traditional brahmanical perspective, as expressed both in mythological speculations and in the philosophical formulations of the Mīmāṃsakas, the fact that

the discursive meaning of the *mantras* is not emphasized does not necessarily imply that they are meaningless. Rather, the *mantras* are held to have another type of meaning, which may be termed "constitutive meaning," as will be discussed below.

269. As discussed below, the hermeneutical discussions of the formal schools of Vedic exegesis, Pūrva-Mīmāṃsā and Vedānta, focus on the Brāhmaṇa and Upaniṣadic portions of the Vedas, respectively, and thus do not provide many substantive interpretations of the *mantras* that are the core *śruti* texts. It is not until the fourteenth century that we have the first comprehensive commentaries on the Ṛg-Veda and other Saṃhitās by Sāyaṇa. There were apparently commentators on the Saṃhitās prior to Sāyaṇa's time, but none of them dates to earlier than the tenth century. For a discussion of the commentaries of Sāyaṇa as well as of earlier and later commentators, see Ram Gopal, *The History and Principles of Vedic Interpretation* (New Delhi: Concept Publishing Company, 1983), 94–140. Coburn has suggested that even the commentaries of Sāyaṇa, who flourished during the Muslim period in India, may not reflect an entirely indigenous Indian impulse but rather may have been inspired by the Islamic tradition that sacred texts are to be exegeted as well as recited. See Coburn, " 'Scripture' in India," 454–55.
270. For a discussion of the various arguments used in Pūrva-Mīmāṃsā to establish the authority of the Veda *(veda-prāmāṇya),* see Holdrege, *Veda and Torah,* chapter 1, "Pūrva-Mīmāṃsā."
271. For a range of essays discussing the principles and characteristics of Midrash, as well as the interrelationship between Midrash, halakhah, and aggadah, see Howard Eilberg-Schwartz, "Who's Kidding Whom? A Serious Reading of Rabbinic Word Plays," *Journal of the American Academy of Religion* 55, no. 4 (1987): 765–88; Judah Goldin, "From Text to Interpretation and from Experience to the Interpreted Text," *Prooftexts* 3, no. 2 (1983): 157–68; idem, "The Freedom and Restraint of Haggadah," in *Midrash and Literature,* edited by Hartman and Budick, 57–76; William Scott Green, "Romancing the Tome: Rabbinic Hermeneutics and the Theory of Literature," in *Text and Textuality,* edited by Charles E. Winquist, *Semeia* 40 (1987): 147–68; Susan A. Handelman, *The Slayers of Moses: The Emergence of Rabbinic Interpretation in Modern Literary Theory* (Albany: SUNY Press, 1982), 27–82; Joseph Heinemann, "The Nature of the Aggadah," in *Midrash and Literature,* edited by Hartman and Budick, 41–55; Barry W. Holtz, "Midrash," in *Back to the Sources: Reading the Classic Jewish Texts,* edited by Barry W. Holtz (New York: Summit Books, 1984), 177–211; James Kugel, "Two Introductions to Midrash," *Prooftexts* 3, no. 2 (1983): 131–55; reprinted in *Midrash and Literature,* edited by Hartman and Budick, 77–103; Roger Le Déaut, "A propos d'une définition du midrash," *Biblica* 50, no. 3 (1969): 395–413; Gary G. Porton, "Defining Midrash," in *The Study of Ancient Judaism,* edited by Jacob Neusner,

vol. 1 (New York: Ktav, 1981), 55–92. In addition to the essays noted above by Goldin, Heinemann, and Kugel, Hartman and Budick's collection, *Midrash and Literature*, contains a number of essays that examine the relationship of Midrash to a variety of literary genres. The various forms of "midrashic imagination" are further explored in the more recent collection edited by Michael Fishbane, *The Midrashic Imagination: Jewish Exegesis, Thought, and History* (Albany: State University of New York Press, 1993).

272. The *karma-kāṇḍa,* the section of the Vedas that pertains to action (*karman*), includes not only the earliest sacrificial traditions found in the Saṃhitās and Brāhmaṇas, but also the Kalpa-Sūtras (ca. 600–200 B.C.E.), which form one of the six Vedāṅgas. The Kalpa-Sūtras comprise three types of texts: the Śrauta-Sūtras, which give detailed instructions for the performance of the *śrauta* sacrifices, based on the Saṃhitās and Brāhmaṇas as well as on actual practice; the Gṛhya-Sūtras, which describe the domestic rites that regulate the various aspects of family life; and the Dharma-Sūtras, which prescribe the ritual and social duties of *varṇāśrama-dharma* that are to performed by members of the four social classes (*varṇas*) at different stages of their lives (*āśramas*). In the post-Vedic period from 200 B.C.E. onward the ritual and social obligations prescribed in the *karma-kāṇḍa* were further crystallized and expanded in the form of elaborate law codes, the Dharma-Śāstras.

273. For a more detailed exposition of these theurgic conceptions, as formulated in brahmanical texts and in rabbinic and kabbalistic texts, see Holdrege, *Veda and Torah,* chapters 5 and 6. See also Idel's discussion of kabbalistic theurgy and its antecedents in rabbinic literature in his *Kabbalah,* 156–99.

274. See, for example, SB II.1.4.11–12. For an analysis of the ways in which the *varṇas* are connected to the three Vedas and to the Vedic meters in the hierarchical taxonomy of the Brāhmaṇas, see Brian K. Smith, "Canonical Authority and Social Classification: Veda and *Varṇa* in Ancient Indian Texts," in *History of Religions* 32, no. 2 (1992): 103–25; idem, "The Veda and the Authority of Class: Reduplicating the Structures of Veda and *Varṇa* in Indian Texts," in *Authority, Anxiety, and Canon: Essays in Vedic Interpretation,* edited by Laurie L. Patton (Albany: SUNY Press, 1994). See also idem, *Classifying the Universe: The Ancient Indian Varṇa System and the Origins of Caste* (New York and Oxford: Oxford University Press, forthcoming).

275. See, for example, the famous parable of the damsel in the palace, Zohar II.99a–99b, which vividly describes the stage-by-stage process through which the hermeneutical experience unfolds until it finally culminates in divine communion between the interpreter and his bride, the Torah. For a discussion of this and other relevant Zoharic passages, see Holdrege, *Veda and Torah,* chapter 6.

276. The *jñāna-kāṇḍa* is the section of the Vedas that pertains to knowledge *(jñāna),* as distinct from the *karma-kāṇḍa,* the section that pertains to

action. While the *jñāna-kāṇḍa* consists primarily of the metaphysical speculations of the Upaniṣads, I am using the term here in a broader sense to refer to those strands of the brahmanical tradition that, in accordance with the Upaniṣadic sages, emphasize the importance of knowledge—in the sense of both intellectual understanding and direct experience—of ultimate reality as a means of gaining liberation *(mokṣa)* from the cycle of birth and death.

277. A number of Upaniṣads recommend using the syllable Om as a vehicle in meditation. See, for example, MU II.2.4,6; Praśna V.1–7; SU I.13–14; Maitri VI.22–26,28. Such conceptions are further elaborated in later Yoga and tantric traditions, which advocate the practice of meditation techniques that use as a vehicle specially designated *mantras* that are thought to possess sacred power. These *mantras* are frequently monosyllabic or disyllabic and are not necessarily Vedic in origin, but they are generally modeled on the prototype of Om and are upheld as potent sound-vibrations by means of which one may come to experience directly that transcendent level of reality which is the ultimate source and abode of Śabdabrahman, the Veda. For discussions of the role of *mantras* in various aspects of Indian thought and practice, see Harvey P. Alper, ed., *Mantra* (Albany: SUNY Press, 1989); J. Gonda, "The Indian Mantra," *Oriens* 16 (1963): 244–97; Shashi Bhusan Dasgupta, "The Role of Mantra in Indian Religion," in his *Aspects of Indian Religious Thought* (Calcutta: A. Mukherjee, 1957), 22–41; Alex Wayṃan, "The Significance of Mantra-s, from the Veda Down to Buddhist Tantric Practice," *The Adyar Library Bulletin* 39 (1975): 65–89; Padoux, "The Mantra," chapter 7 of his *Vāc*, 372–426; idem, ed., *Mantras et diagrammes rituels dans l'Hindouisme* (Paris: Éditions du Centre National de la Recherche Scientifique, 1986).

278. For a detailed exposition of Abulafia's hermeneutical methods and ecstatic techniques and their historical antecedents in philosophical and mystical sources, see Idel, *Language, Torah, and Hermeneutics in Abraham Abulafia;* idem, *The Mystical Experience in Abraham Abulafia,* translated by Jonathan Chipman (Albany: SUNY Press, 1988); idem, "Abraham Abulafia and *Unio Mystica,*" chapter 1 of his *Studies in Ecstatic Kabbalah* (Albany: SUNY Press, 1988); idem, *Kabbalah,* 97–103. Idel has emphasized that although there may be superficial similarities between Abulafia's techniques and yogic practices, there are significant points of divergence. See Idel, *The Mystical Experience in Abraham Abulafia,* 39–40; idem, *Kabbalah,* 97.

For a discussion of the relationship between the hermeneutical approaches of the theosophical kabbalists and Abulafia, see ibid., 200–49. See also Scholem's discussions of Abulafia in "The Name of God and the Linguistic Theory of the Kabbala," pt. 2, 184–93; "Abraham Abulafia and the Doctrine of Prophetic Kabbalism," chapter 4 of his *Major Trends in Jewish Mysticism,* 119–55.

279. Smith, "Scripture as Form and Concept: Their Emergence for the Western World," in *Rethinking Scripture,* edited by Levering, 45.

280. The "Aryans" and the "people of Israel" are not of course strictly delineated, closed ethnic groups, as the brahmanical tradition has absorbed various non-Aryan groups within its fold in the course of its history, just as the Jewish community has admitted gentiles through conversion and has even undertaken proselytizing efforts in certain periods. Rather, these collective designations represent *idealized categories* in which tradition-identity is assigned first and foremost through birth into a community that defines itself in terms of blood descent.

281. The sociocultural taxonomies of any community are inscribed in the bodies of its constituent members through practice, transforming the biological body into a socialized body that has internalized the symbolic schemes and values of the culture. See Catherine Bell, "The Ritual Body and the Dynamics of Ritual Power," in *Ritual and Power*, edited by Holdrege, *Journal of Ritual Studies* 4, no. 2 (1990): 299–313. Bell's essay draws on the insights of Pierre Bourdieu, *Outline of a Theory of Practice*, translated by R. Nice (Cambridge: Cambridge University Press, 1977), and Michel Foucault, *Discipline and Punish*, translated by Alan Sheridan (New York: Random House, Vintage Books, 1979). See also Bell's *Ritual Theory, Ritual Practice* (New York: Oxford University Press, 1992).

282. For an extended discussion of my thesis concerning the "embodied" nature of the brahmanical and rabbinic traditions, see my concluding remarks in *Veda and Torah*, in which I contrast this paradigm of "religious tradition" with three traditions that are missionary in orientation and that develop categories of tradition-identity that diverge from the ethnic-based model: "Christianities," "Buddhisms," and "Islams."

Note on Translation and Transliteration

The translations of all Sanskrit passages are my own. The transliteration of Sanskrit terms generally follows the scientific system adopted by the *Journal of the American Oriental Society*.

The translations of passages from rabbinic texts are my own. With respect to biblical verses, my translations generally follow the standard translation, Herbert G. May and Bruce M. Metzger, eds., *The New Oxford Annotated Bible with the Apocrypha. Revised Standard Version* (New York: Oxford University Press, 1977). However, I have at times rendered the verse to accord with the Midrashist's interpretation. The translations of passages from the Zohar, unless otherwise indicated, are cited either from Isaiah Tishby and Fischel Lachower, eds., *The Wisdom of the Zohar: An Anthology of Texts*, translated by David Goldstein, 3 vols. (Oxford: Oxford University Press, 1989) or from Harry Sperling, Maurice Simon, and Paul P. Levertoff, trans., *The Zohar*, 2nd ed., 5 vols. (London: Soncino Press, 1984). In the case of the Zohar and other medieval kabbalistic texts in which I have cited the translations of other scholars, I have consulted the original text myself, with the exception of several manuscripts that were not available to me.

The transliteration of Hebrew terms generally follows the scientific system adopted by the *Journal of Biblical Literature,* with two exceptions: (1) spirantized *b*^{e}*ḡaḏk*^{e}*p̄aṯ* letters have been marked; and (2) a hyphen has been inserted after the definite article *ha-* (with consequent loss of doubling), the prepositions *b*^{e}*-*, *l*^{e}*-*, and *k*^{e}*-*, and the conjunction *w*^{e}*-*, in order to facilitate reading by the nonspecialist. In the case of well-known Hebrew terms (for example, Shekhinah, Kabbalah) and texts (for example, Torah, Mishnah, Talmud) the common conventional spelling has been retained. The rendering of names of rabbis (for example, Akiba, Hoshaiah) and kabbalistic scholars (for example, Ezra b. Solomon, Azriel b. Menaḥem) also follows conventional usage wherever possible, although it is sometimes difficult to determine what constitutes the most common convention with respect to proper names.

Notes to Chapter 9

Abbreviations: *AHDO*—Archives d'Histoire du Droit Oriental; *ANET*—J. B. Pritchard, ed., *Ancient Near Eastern Texts Relating to the Old Testament* (1969); *CRAI—Comptes Rendues de l'Académie des Inscriptions et Belles-Lettres; Enc. Jud.—Encyclopedia Judaica* (1973); *HUCA—Hebrew Union College Annual; Isr. L.R.—Israel Law Review; JAOS—Journal of the American Oriental Society; JCS—Journal of Cuneiform Studies; JJS—Journal of Jewish Studies; JNES—Journal of Near Eastern Studies; JRS—Journal of Roman Studies;* LE—Laws of Eshnunna; LH—Laws of Hammurabi; *RIDA—Revue Internationale des Droits de l'Antiquité; TvR—Tijdschrift voor Rechtsgeschiedenis.*

1. The original French edition of Robert Lingat's *Classical Law of India* appeared in 1967 under the title *Les Sources du Droit dans le Système Traditionel de l'Inde.* The present edition, published by the University of California Press in 1973, has been significantly enhanced by the translator, Professor J. D. M. Derrett, who has revised the bibliography and provided his own preface, appendix, and numerous notes, as well as Lingat's curriculum vitae and a list of his publications. Derrett has himself contributed to the study of the classical Indian sources along similar lines, most recently in *Dharmasastra and Juridical Literature* (1973) (from Gonda, ed., *A History of Indian Literature,* vol. 4), and *History of Indian Law* (1973) (from Spuler, ed., *Handbuch der Orientalistik,* 2 abt., III Bd., 1).
2. Manu's minute regulation of everyday conduct, such as diet (Lingat, *Classical Law,* 80; cf. rabbinic and Islamic law); the development of the Brahmins from priests and spiritual preceptors to jurists (Lingat, *Classical Law,* 65; cf. the early juristic role attributed to the Roman *pontifices,* a comparison suggested by Lingat himself on page 143, n. 1); the relatively late development of the attribution of texts to the deity (page 25; cf., probably, the process leading to the canonization of the Pentateuch); the interpretation of Vedic, narrative texts (page 8f.; cf. rabbinic exegesis of Genesis);

"The succession to property is a corollary of succession to sacra, or the religious obligations of the family" (page 58, hinting, by the use of this terminology, at the parallel with Roman succession under the *ius civile);* the use of rules relating to succession at death to meet the absence of a law governing succession to the throne (page 213; cf. the mediaeval succession struggles described by Maine, *Dissertations on Early Law and Custom,* chap. 5 (1901); the notions of *kṣatra* and *svāmin,* in which ownership and power are not differentiated (page 212; cf. the Roman *dominium,* etc.); the gradations of expulsion from caste (page 53; cf. the rules of the Qumran sect); the apparent development of penance from punishment, rather than vice versa (page 63ff.; cf. the development within biblical law); the administrative system, envisaging central appointment of officers responsible for units of 10 (20), 100, and 1000 (page 81; cf. Exodus 18.21, 25); the theory of kingship (page 207; cf. some biblical traditions).

A number of linguistic parallels may also be noted: The idea that knowledge and inspiration derive from sight underlies both the Sanskrit *veda,* which has the same root as the Latin *video* (page 7, n. 11), and the biblical use of *ro'eh* for a prophet; the term for "Good Custom" is *acara,* "the way of life" (page 198, cf. the Hebrew *dherekh* and *halakhah* and the Islamic *tariqah* and *shari'ah.* Indeed, it is not inconceivable that *dharma, dherekh,* and *tariqah* may all ultimately descend from an original biliteral root *dh-r*); humanity, *manava,* takes its name from its progenitor, Manu (page 87, cf. the biblical "name" given to the progenitor of mankind, which is simply the normal word for man, *'adam*).

In listing these parallels, I imply no judgment regarding either the exactitude of the similarities or the significance, if any, to be attached to them.

3. The phrase is used as the title to part two.
4. E.g. Pollock in note A to Maine's *Ancient Law,* 19 (1906), against Maine; Seagle, *The History of Law,* 106–7 (1946). Cf. Kraus, "Ein zentrales Problem des altmesopotamischen Rechtes: Was ist der Codex Hammu-rabi?," *Geneva* 8 (1960): 289–90.
5. Much discussed and with differing results in the context of the various ancient Near Eastern collections. See, for example, Cardascia, *Les lois assyriennes,* 37–38 (1969); in general, Diamond, *Primitive Law, Past and Present,* 46 (1971).
6. Also much discussed in the literature on the ancient Near Eastern collections.
7. It may be noted that Lingat places considerable weight upon comparison of the phenomena of legal science for the purpose of relative dating. See especially the argument at 92–96, and cf., earlier, Maine, *Lectures on the Early History of Institutions,* 14–15 (1875); idem, *Dissertations on Early Law and Custom,* 9–11 (1901).
8. Maine, *Ancient Law,* 15 (edited by Pollock, 1906); cf. his *Village Communities in the East and West,* 219 (4th ed., 1881), on the caste regulations.
9. An exception: the publication under royal commission of ancient, repealed or superseded laws, such as the *Ancient Laws of Ireland* (1865).

10. Driver and Miles, *The Babylonian Laws,* vol. 1, 53, 401 (1952). See further Kraus, "Ein zentrales Problem"; Klima, "La Perspective historique des lois hammourabiennes," *CRAI,* 1972: 308.
11. *The Babylonian Laws,* vol. 1, 53 (1952). The interpretative function for which Szlechter, "L'Interprétation des lois babyloniennes," *RIDA* 17: 107ff. (1970), contends falls far short of the verbal interpretation denied by Driver and Miles.
12. See Borger, "Marduk-zakir-sumi I und der Kodex Hammurapi," *Orientalia* 34 (1965): 168–69.
13. Kraus, "Ein zentrales Problem"; Finkelstein, "Ammisaduqa's Edict and the Babylonian 'Law Codes,' " *JCS* 15 (1961): 100–104. See also Paul, *Studies in the Book of the Covenant in the Light of Biblical and Cuneiform Law* 24–25 (1970), and literature there cited.
14. Preiser, "Zur rechtlichen Natur der altorientalischen 'Gesetze,' " *Festschrift für Karl Engisch,* 17–36 (1969).
15. Klima, "La Perspective historique," 312.
16. "The Middle Assyrian Laws and the Bible," *Biblica* 51 (1970): 553; disputed by Loewenstamm, "The Phrase X (or) X plus one in Biblical and Old Oriental Laws," *Biblica* 53 (1972): 543; and see further Jackson, *Essays in Jewish and Comparative Legal History,* chap. 6 (1975).
17. E.g., Greenberg, "Some Postulates of Biblical Criminal Law," *Yehezkel Kaufmann Jubilee Volume 18,* n. 25 (1960); Finkelstein, "The Goring Ox: Some Historical Perspectives on Deodands, Forfeitures, Wrongful Death and the Western Notion of Sovereignty," *Temple Law Quarterly* 46 (1973): 258 n. 276, 270 n. 312.
18. Weinfeld, *Deuteronomy and the Deuteronomic School* (1972).
19. Indeed dharma is applied to the physical laws of the universe as well as the norms of society. In Kelsen's terms, it combines the principles of causality and imputation.
20. See especially Lingat, *Classical Law,* xii–xiii, 257ff., and note Radhakrishnan's definition on p. 258 n. 3.
21. Ibid., 176f., 180ff., 259.
22. Ibid., part 2, chap. 2.
23. Ibid., 68.
24. Ibid., 207–8.
25. Ibid., 225–26.
26. Ibid., 229–30.
27. Ibid., 71–72.
28. *Oxford Lectures and Other Discourses,* 30–33 (1890), comparing also the relationship of English common law to the laws of the American states. Cf. also Lingat, *Classical Law,* 204.
29. Wilson, "Authority and Law in Ancient Egypt," *JAOS* 17 (1954, suppl.): 6–7.
30. *Studies in the Book of the Covenant,* 5.
31. Speiser, "Authority and Law in Mesopotamia," *JAOS* 17 (1954, suppl.): 13, stressing the distinction between the two terms. This view seems preferable to that of Driver and Miles (*The Babylonian Laws,* vol. 1, 23), who

virtually take the phrase as a hendiadys and suggest that it corresponds to "something like law and order."

32. Speiser, "Authority and Law." See further Landsberger, "Die babylonischen Termini für Gesetz und Recht," *Symbolae ad iura orientis antiqui pertinentes Paulo Koschaker dedicatae,* 219–34 (1939); Greenberg, "Some Postulates of Biblical Criminal Law," *Yehezkel Kaufmann Jubilee Volume* 9 (1960).
33. Prologue to LH, col. 5a, lines 14–24. The rules themselves, to which the term *mesharum* is applied, are also said to be commanded by Shamash, col. 24b, lines 84–8. For the interpretation of the relief on the stele as an investiture of the king by Shamash, see Paul, *Studies in the Book of the Covenant,* 7–8.
34. Paul, *Studies in the Book of the Covenant,* 6.
35. Ibid., 10.
36. Kraus, "Ein zentrales Problem," esp. 290; Paul, *Studies in the Book of the Covenant,* 24 n. 1; Weinfeld, *Deuteronomy,* 151 n. 1.
37. Greenberg, "Some Postulates," 11, though other aspects of the differences between biblical and Mesopotamian concepts there proposed are more contentious (see Jackson, "Reflections on Biblical Criminal Law," *JJS* 24 [1973]: 8–38, esp. 26–29). There are however some interesting parallels between the biblical and Babylonian idioms for justice. Deuteronomy 6.18 *hatov weh-ayashar* is sometimes regarded as an equivalent to LH's *kittum u mesharum, yashar* and *mesharum* deriving from a common root. Weinfeld (*Deuteronomy,* 150f.) now suggests that Deuteronomy 4.8 *mishpatim tsedokim* is a (hostile) allusion to LH's *dinat misharim.*
38. From the root *yarah.* At Exodus 24.12 God bids Moses receive "the tablets of stone . . . which I have written for their instruction."
39. Weinfeld, *Deuteronomy,* passim, esp. 3—approving Klostermann, *Der Pentateuch,* 344 (1907)—151 n. 1, 298–306; Falk, "On the Study of Jewish Law," *Dine Israel* 4 (1973): v–vi.
40. *The Laws of Eshnunna,* 69 (1969).
41. For biblical law, the classical example is Deut. 24. 1–4, where the institution of divorce by delivery of a written document is presupposed. This example is all the more striking if one accepts the view that sources such as Hos. 2.4 reflect an earlier procedure, by uttering *solemnia verba.* On the Deuteronomic provision, see most recently Toeg, "Does Deuteronomy XXIV, 1–4 Incorporate a General Law on Divorce?," v–xxiv.
42. I.e., a conditional protasis [introduced by *shumma* (Akk.), *ki* (Heb.), *si* (Lat.)] in which the issue is set forth, followed by an apodosis containing the legal solution.
43. A good illustration of the promulgation of a casuistic law as a result of a decided case is Numbers 27.1–11, which combines the following components: (*a*) The daughters of Zelafhad, whose father has died without leaving a son, complain that according to the law as it then stood they would be excluded from the inheritance, vv. 1–4; (*b*) Moses seeks an oracular decision on their claim. Judgment is given for the daughters of Zelafhad, vv. 6–7; (*c*)

Moses is thereupon instructed to proclaim the law to the Israelites as a precedent. The terms of the law so to be declared are expressed in one of the normal, casuistic forms (*'ish ki . . . ; we'im . . . ; we'im. . . .* Cf. Leviticus 27.1–8; Numbers 5.5–8, 11–28; 30.2–16). In fact the passage may well not be unitary: for in (*a*) and (*b*) the daughters only claim, and are only granted, a share in the estate along with their father's brothers, while in (*c*) the right of brothers is (as in Roman law) deferred; moreover, (*a*) and (*b*) are concerned only with succession in the absence of sons, while (*c*) sets forth a complete system of intestate succession. Nevertheless, the literary construction itself suggests an awareness that decided cases could give rise to proclamations of generally applicable law couched in casuistic form.

44. See Kraus, "Ein zentrales Problem," 288.
45. Here, it is typically found subordinated to a more general form, e.g. Gaius, *Inst.* 1.28–9; 3.139–40. Cf., earlier, Plato, Laws IX.915d; XI.923c; Demosth. in *Macart.* 57.
46. "Gewohnheitsrecht," *Reallexikon der Assyriologie und vorderasiatischen Archäologie,* edited by Ebeling, Meissner, Weidner, vol. 3, 322–23 (1968).
47. See the conclusion of Driver and Miles (*The Babylonian Laws,* vol. 1, 24) that the practice documents "exhibit neither close correspondence nor striking differences" to the laws. For a frequently cited example of divergence in the theft laws, see Jackson, "Principles and Cases: The Theft Laws of Hammurabi," *The Irish Jurist* 7 (1972): 161–70. For ancient Israel there is virtually no documentary evidence independent of the Bible itself (on the Elephantine Papyri, see Yaron, *Introduction to the Law of the Aramaic Papyri,* 115f. [1961]). The fourfold penalty for theft and slaughter of a lamb (Exodus 21.37) is reflected in 2 Samuel 12.6 (see Jackson, *Theft in Early Jewish Law,* 144–48 [1972]); on execution against the person of the debtor or a member of his household, see 2 Kings 4.1; Job 24.9; Elon, *Herut haperat bedarkhei geviyat hov bamishpat ha'ivri,* 1–9 (1964).
48. Greengus, "A Textbook Case of Adultery in Ancient Mesopotamia," *HUCA* 40–41 (1969–70): 43, and literature there cited.
49. The common translation, which has Hammurabi assert that he has established *kittum* and *mesharum* "in the language of the land" (col. 5a, line 22) is not universally adopted. See Jackson, "Reflections," 10–11 n. 21.
50. On the relationship of (the Sumerian) Lipit-Ishtar 10 to LH 59, see Driver and Miles, *The Babylonian Laws,* vol. 1, 161–62 n. 4; Jackson, "Reflections," 162; on that of (the Akkadian) LE 53–55 to LH 250–52, Yaron, "The Goring Ox in Near Eastern Laws," *Isr. L.R.* 1 (1966): 396–406.
51. Lingat, *Classical Law,* 195–206. See also 189–95.
52. Falk, *Introduction to Jewish Law of the Second Commonwealth,* 16–17 (1972). For the traditional restrictions, see Elon, "The Sources and Nature of Jewish Law and Its Application in the State of Israel," *Isr. L.R.* 2 (1967): 547–48; idem, *Jewish Law* (Heb.) 2 (1973): 732–37.
53. For a criticism of the traditional common law denial of desuetude, see Harari, "Desuetude," *JJS* 25 (1974): 112–13 (*Studies in Jewish Legal History in honour of David Daube,* Jackson ed.).

54. *Classical Law,* 83.
55. "Ein zentrales Problem."
56. *Deuteronomy,* passim, esp. 5, 164, 170–71. Cf., earlier, Mendelsohn, "Authority and Law in Canaan-Israel," *JAOS* 17 (1954 suppl.): 31. Weinfeld's identification of the immediate source of much of Deuteronomy as the court scribe has attracted some criticism from McCarthy in his review in *Biblica* 54 (1973): 451–52, but the latter's suggestion that "the educated man or group in Judah who knew the political situation in his country might have produced a work which showed knowledge of the treaties and the wisdom themes" begs the questions (*a*) whether there were such men outside the court; and (*b*) whether such circles, if they existed, are as likely as the court scribe to have enjoyed the kind of authority which the historical books suggest the king gave to Deuteronomy. One may note that the importance of circles akin to those posited by Weinfeld is not peculiar to early antiquity. Fischel, *Rabbinic Literature and Greco-Roman Philosophy,* 34 (1973), observes the existence of an "academic tradition of scholar-bureaucracies which resembled each other to a certain degree and were in contact with each other in the classical, Christian, and Jewish worlds in the first two to three centuries of Roman Imperial times." We may add that the development of Sanskrit studies in the West in the nineteenth century was itself, in large measure, the work of a comparable elite.
57. Kraus, *Ein Edikt des Königs Ammisaduqa von Babylon* (1958); Finkelstein, "Ammisaduqa's Edict," 91–104 and in *ANET,* 526. The principal text derives from a later king of Hammurabi's dynasty, but the genre is attested also by other fragments and references in contemporary documents.
58. Esp. the use of the passive, e.g., "The arrears . . . are herewith remitted" (2). For some correspondences between the proclamations in LE and the edict, see Yaron, *The Laws of Eshnunna,* 68, 69.
59. Cf. Finkelstein, "Ammisaduqa's Edict," 103.
60. § 20, in *ANET,* 528.
61. In the light of this the frequent ancient Near Eastern and biblical theme of the king's duty to protect the widow, orphan, and poor may well be considered more than pious hope. See Mendelsohn, "Authority and Law," 26, on the Canaanite Keret and Aqhat legends; Fensham, "Widow, Orphan and the Poor in Ancient Near Eastern Legal and Wisdom Literature," *JNES* 21 (1962): 129–39.
62. *CRAI,* 1972: 312–13.
63. *The Laws of Eshnunna,* 59–71. The variety of forms in LE leads Finkelstein to distinguish this collection from the "law-codes" and assign it to a category intermediate between them and the edict (the latter being itself considered an *expostfacto* literary presentation rather than an original, authoritative text of the edict actually proclaimed). See *JCS* 15 (1961): 102.
64. I refer here not to the grammatical forms by which Yaron and others distinguish various *Sitzen im Leben* but to the minutiae of drafting within the forms, by which he seeks further to identify the origins of particular laws in

statute or precedent. On p. 70 he observes: "The combination of equivalents indicates the 'statutory' origin of a provision, or at least reformulation by the compiler," and cites the unnecessary cumulation of masculine and feminine as an example. The formula "X or (X + 1)" (on which see literature cited above, note 16) falls into the same category. In this latter case the biblical occurrences of the formula outside the Pentateuch occur chiefly in sources associated with wisdom and its identification as a wisdom trait seems more likely than the conclusion that it derives from an ancient parliamentary draftsman. A systematic examination of wisdom language along these lines is clearly needed. For the moment, see Roth, *Numerical Sayings in the Old Testament,* 88ff., 99 (1965); Whybray, *The Intellectual Tradition in the Old Testament,* 73 (1974), and literature there cited.

65. As, most likely, in the account of the Josianic reformation.
66. *Deuteronomy,* 153–54, 385.
67. Lewy, "The Biblical Institution of *derror* in the light of Akkadian Documents," *Eretz Israel* 5 (1958): 21–31 on Jeremiah 34 (in which the temporary nature of the effects of Zedekiah's measure is central). See also Finkelstein, "Ammisaduqa's Edict," 104; Weinfeld, *Deuteronomy,* 153 n. 1.
68. § 20, in *ANET,* 528.
69. Zakovitch, "Some Remnants of Ancient Laws in the Deuteronomic Code," *Isr. L.R.* 9 (1974): 349–51, citing also Isaiah 16.14 (MT) and 21.16 (Qumran MS).
70. Finkelstein, "Ammisaduqa's Edict," 104 n. 19.
71. Gurney, *The Hittites,* 89 (1952).
72. Güterbock, "Authority and Law in the Hittite Kingdom," *JAOS* 23 (1954, suppl. 17).
73. Neufeld, *The Hittite Laws,* 153 (1951).
74. Jackson, *Essays,* 154–55.
75. For discussion of the nature of the Hittite Laws, see Neufeld, *Hittite Laws,* 107ff.; Imparati, *Le leggi ittite,* 3–4 (1964), and literature there cited.
76. Despite the view of the history of the Hittite Laws expressed by Neufeld, *Hittite Laws,* 109; Gaudemet, *Institutions de l'Antiquité* 86 (1967). The popularity of the text does not necessarily indicate its legally binding nature, as the history of the LH shows.
77. 2 Kings 22.8–23.25. But even here there is no indication that the text of the rediscovered book was given to the judiciary.
78. Ezra 7.10, though the emphasis on teaching is still very prominent. Falk, *Introduction to Jewish Law,* 5.
79. E.g., ibid., 6.
80. Silver, *Maimonidean Criticism and the Maimonidean Controversy 1186–1240* (1965); *Enc. Jud.,* vol. 5, 638ff.
81. For the Mishnah, see Neusner, ed., *The Modern Study of the Mishnah* (1973); for the Babylonian Talmud, see, e.g., *Enc. Jud.,* vol. 15, 764.
82. This article was originally published in the *American Journal of Comparative Law* 23 (1975): 490–508. The last two pages, which consider the extent to which Lingat's theory is applicable also to Roman law, are not here reproduced.

Notes to Chapter 10

1. For a global understanding of Hinduism, see Madeleine Biardeau, *L'hindouisme: anthropologie d'une civilisation* (Paris: Flammarion, 1981). I thank my husband, Dr. Sunthar Visuvalingam, for all his help in elaborating the theoretical framework around my earlier French draft of this paper. I thank the University Grants Commission, New Delhi, for having supported my fieldwork in India; and the French Foreign Office for the Bourse Romain Rolland in Benares, and now the Lavoisier Fellowship to continue my research at the Department of Sanskrit and Indian Studies, Harvard University, under Prof. Michael Witzel. I am grateful also to the Bourse de la Vocation, of which I am a laureate since December 1980, for their generous grant towards a computer.
2. Translated by Jean Varenne (Paris: Seuil, 1981), 94–95.
3. Much of the material in this paper had been presented from a more anthropological perspective, focusing rather on the underlying ideology of transgression, in my as yet unpublished (in English) paper on "Adepts of Bhairava in the Hindu Tradition," presented to the Assembly of the World's Religions, 15–21 November 1985 (New York).
4. For this school, refer to the works of Lilian Silburn published by DeBoccard (Paris: Institut de Civilisation Indienne). Also to the *Tantrāloka* of Abhinavagupta with the commentary of Jayaratha, The Kashmir Series of Texts and Studies (KSTS), 12 vols., edited by Madhusudan Kaul Shastri (Srinagar: 1918–1938); translated into Italian by Raniero Gnoli, *Luce delle Sacre Scritture (Tantrāloka) di Abhinavagupta* (Torino: U.T.E.T, 1972). Finally, for an overview of the historical and anthropological background of the system, see A. Sanderson, "Śaivism and the Tantric Traditions," in *The World's Religions,* edited by Stuart Sutherland et al. (London: Routledge, 1988), 660–704.
5. Sunthar Visuvalingam, "Transgressive Sacrality in the Hindu Tradition," paper presented to the Assembly of the World's Religions (see note 3); see also his section on "A Semiotic Definition of Transgressive Sacrality," in *Criminal Gods and Demon Devotees,* edited by Alf Hiltebeitel (Albany: SUNY Press, 1989), 427–34.
6. L. Silburn, *Kuṇḍalinī: Energy of the Depths* (Albany: SUNY Press, 1988). Chap. 29 of *Tantrāloka,* KSTS no. 57 (Bombay: 1936), vol. 11 is also discussed in K. C. Pandey, *Abhinavagupta: An Historical and Philosophical Study,* 2nd ed. (Varanasi: Chowkhamba, 1963), 607–23. For the anthropological background, see also my "Bhairava's Royal Brahminicide," esp. 195–98, in *Criminal Gods and Demon Devotees,* edited by Alf Hiltebeitel (Albany: SUNY Press, 1989).
7. Biardeau, *L'hindouisme,* 167.
8. For the better-known system of *cakras,* see Mircea Eliade, *Yoga: Immortality and Freedom,* 2nd ed., Bollingen Series 56 (Princeton: Princeton University Press, 1969), 236–41; also Tara Michael, transl. with Introduction and Notes, *Hathayogapradīpikā* (Paris: Fayard, 1974). For the specificity of the Trika, see L. Silburn, *Kuṇḍalinī,* 25–33.

9. See W. D. O'Flaherty, *Sexual Metaphors and Animal Symbols in Indian Mythology* (Delhi: Motilal Banarsidass, 1981), 296, 317.
10. Silburn, *Kuṇḍalinī,* 87–103.
11. See Michel Hulin, *Le principe de l'égo dans la pensée indienne classique: la notion d'ahamkāra* (Paris: Institut de Civilisation Indienne, 1978), especially 281–358.
12. I am partially summarizing from my Ph.D. thesis; see Elizabeth Chalier, "Unmatta Bhairava in the Āgamic Tradition of North India: A Study of Two Manuscripts, *Unmattākhyakramapaddhati* and Unmattabhairavapañcānga (University of Paris–X, June 1981), 388–89.
13. It may be noted that the zodiacal sign of the twins is designated in Sanskrit by the term *"maithuna"* (coupling or a sexed couple).
14. See "Between Mecca and Benares: The Marriage of Lat Bhairava and Gazi Miyan" by Sunthar Visuvalingam and Elizabeth Chalier-Visuvalingam (forthcoming).
15. For the *triśūlābja-maṇḍala* as a visual representation of the supremacy of Trika doctrine over the other sister-doctrines encompassed within it, see Alexis Sanderson, "Maṇḍala and Āgamic Identity in the Trika of Kashmir," in *Mantras et diagrammes rituels dans l'hindouisme* (Paris: Editions du C.N.R.S., 1986), 169–214.
16. "Purity and Power among the Brahmans of Kashmir," in *The Category of the Person: Anthropology, Philosophy, History,* edited by M. Carrithers, S. Collins, and S. Lukes (Cambridge: Cambridge University Press, 1986), 190–216.
17. See Elizabeth Visuvalingam, "Bhairava: Kotwāl of Vārāṇasī," in *Vārānasī Through the Ages,* edited by T. P. Verma et al., Bhāratīya Itihāsa Saṅkalan Samiti Publ., no. 4 (Vārāṇasī: BISS, 1986), 241–60; and my contribution to *Criminal Gods and Demon Devotees,* edited by Alf Hiltebertel (Albany: SUNY Press, 1989), esp. 177–91.
18. The term *vāmāmṛta-paripluta* "sprinkled with the nectar of woman" (*Tantrāloka* 29.10) could allude to menstrual blood over and above the less shocking meaning of "wine" (*vāma* = "left" instead of *vāmā* = "woman").
19. It is not the wife but "another's" *(parakīyā)* woman who is the natural object of eroticism in popular Tantricism and it is likewise the adulterous woman *(abhisārikā)* who is lavished with abundant sensuality in classical Sanskrit poetry and in the Kṛṣṇa-*bhakti* of the cow-herdesses.
20. On the notion of sacrifice, see S. Lévi, *Le sacrifice dans les Brāhmaṇa* (Paris: P.U.F., 1966); M. Biardeau and Charles Malamoud, *Le sacrifice dans l'Inde ancienne* (Paris: P.U.F., 1976).
21. Biardeau and Malamoud, ibid., pp. 7–8.
22. Lévi, *Le sacrifice,* 12.
23. Malamoud, "Village et forêt dans l'idéologie de l'Inde brahmanique," *Archives européennes de sociologie* 17 (1976): 8.
24. Malamoud, *Svādhyāya, récitation personnelle du Veda, Taittirīya Āraṇyaka livre II* (Paris: Institut de Civilisation Indienne, 1977); 68.
25. Biardeau, *L'hindouisme,* 163 and n. 1.
26. Eliade, *Yoga,* 255ff. This especially concerns Brahmanism, but as Biardeau says: "Tantrism does not invent anything, it merely appropriates the

established values in inverse, by rereading the tradition on an esoteric register" (Biardeau, *L'hindouisme,* 164). The same series of homologizations has been further elaborated and adapted to the *kulayāga* in a verse cited by the commentary on *Tantrāloka* 29.110; see Silburn, *Kuṇḍalinī,* 184.

27. See M. Biardeau, *Dictionnaire de Mythologies* (offprint; Paris: Flammarion, 1981), 89–90, 109–13; and *Histoires de poteaux: Variations védiques autours de la Déesse hindoue* (Paris: École Française d'Extrême Orient, 1989), 38–44, 49.
28. For a systematic analysis, see my "Adepts of Bhairava," and especially Kathleen M. Erndl, "Rapist or Bodyguard, Demon or Devotee? Images of Bhairo in the Mythology and Cult of Vaisno Devi," in *Criminal Gods,* 239–50. The variations of the same paradigm in the Newar Kumāri, and in the Ankālamman and Kāttavarāyan cults of Tamil Nadu, have been interpreted in my own and Sunthar Visuvalingam's contributions to *Criminal Gods.* David Shulman, *Tamil Temple Myths: Sacrifice and Divine Marriage in the South Indian Saiva Tradition* (Princeton: Princeton University Press, 1980) has demonstrated how this paradigm of the Vedic preclassical sacrifice still underlies the temple-cult of the otherwise purified Śaiva Siddhānta theology. The pervasiveness of the embryogonic theme throughout Asia, irrespective of differing doctrinal and cultural contexts, has been surveyed by Rolf A. Stein in his magistral article, "Les grottes matrices et lieux saints de la déesse en asie orientale," *Bulletin de l'École Française de l'Extrême-Orient,* vol. 151 (Paris: École Française d'Extrême-Orient, 1988), 1–106.
29. Shulman, *Tamil Temple Myths,* 294–316.
30. Biardeau, *Histoires de poteaux,* 50–62.
31. Silburn, *Kuṇḍalinī,* 88, 143–44.
32. S. Visuvalingam, "Transgressive Sacrality," 9. Materials on the Patan Agnihotra are drawn from the seminars by Prof. Michael Witzel at the Collège de France in May 1989 on the continuity between the Vedic and the Tantric *agnihotra,* the manner in which the original core is encapsulated within the later framework. For the project of "cooking the world" *(loka-pakti)* in the Brahmanical sacrifice and a more systematic study of the Vedic symbolism of fire, see Charles Malamoud, *Cuire le monde: rite et pensée dans l'inde ancienne* (Paris: Editions la Découverte, 1989), 35–70.

Notes to Chapter 11

1. *Shegel ha-Qodesh,* edited by Greenup (London, 1911; reprinted Jerusalem, 1969), 104.
2. *Méirat Enayim,* edited by Erlanger (Jerusalem, 1981), 275.
3. *Sefer Tashak,* edited by Jeremy Zwelling (Ann Arbor, MI, 1975), 118.
4. *Tikkunei ha-Zohar,* edited in Zohar I, 22b, and see our translation in *Zohar,* vol. 1, 129.

5. *Tikkunim of Zohar Hadash* (Jerusalem, 1978), 103a.
6. *Sheqel ha-Qodesh,* 20.
7. *Sefer ha-Yihud,* Ms Paris 799, fol. 22b.
8. Ibid., fol. 23b.
9. Ibid.
10. Henri Corbin, *Le paradoxe du monothéisme* (Paris, 1981), 32.
11. *Tefillah le-Moshe,* 70a.
12. *Commentary on the Sha'are Ora,* 11b n. 3.
13. "Commentary on the Torah," edited by Israel Weinstock, in *Temirin* 2 (1981): 245.
14. Commentary attributed to R. Israel, in *Tefillah le-Moshe,* commentary on the prayer of R. Moses Cordovero (Prezmysl, 1891), 69b–70a, 70b.
15. *Kabbalah: New Perspectives* (New Haven, 1958), 195.
16. *Sefer Sod ha-Sodot,* edited by J. Dan, in *The Circles of the First Kabbalists* (in Hebrew), Akademon, Hebrew University (Jerusalem, 1986), 131.
17. *Sha-are Orah,* 41b.
18. *Traité d'histoire des religions,* 352–53.
19. Cited by J. Dan, *The Circles of the First Kabbalists* (in Hebrew), 153.
20. *Explanation of the Commentary of Nahmanides* (Warsaw, 1875), 32b.
21. *Méirat Enayim,* 271–72.
22. *Commentary on the Torah,* trans. and annotated by Chavel. (New York: Shilo, 1971–1976), vol. 3, 277.
23. *Halakhot G'dolot,* edited by S. Jerusalmi, vol. 2 (Jerusalem, 1969), 44.
24. *Tefillah le-Moshe,* vol. 1, 213b.
25. Mircea Eliade, "Spirit, Light and Semen," in *Occultisme, sorcellerie et modes culturelles* (Paris, 1976), 134ff.
26. *Introduction aux voie de Yoga* (Monaco, 1980), 210.
27. Ibid.
28. Ibid., 211.
29. Ibid.
30. Ibid., 216.
31. Text cited in ibid., 216 n. 34.
32. *Tefillah le-Moshe,* 213a.
33. Ibid.

Notes to Chapter 12

1. Vol. 2, 561. Quoted in Ben Zion Bokser, ed. and trans., *Abraham Isaac Kook* (New York: Paulist Press, 1978), 231.
2. I am grateful to Rabbi Alan Unterman of Getley, Manchester, for some of these details and for certain other material provided in the text. He is, of course, not responsible for my interpretations. I am also very grateful to Professor Yehuda Gellman of Ben-Gurion University of the Negev for some specific textual references generously provided by him.
3. Quoted by Zvi Zinger in *Encyclopedia Judaica,* vol. 10, 1184.

4. See my *The Religious Spectrum: Studies in an Indian Context* (New Delhi: Allied Publishers Ltd., 1984), and *The Concept of Spirituality* (New Delhi: Allied, 1988). The latter work includes a short discussion of Kook's work in the contexts of tree symbolism.
5. Ṛg Veda III 22.3.
6. *Mystics as a Force for Change* (Wheaton: Theosophical Publishing House, 1981).
7. The first of these appeared in *Arya,* in 1916.
8. *Sri Aurobindo Birth Centenary Library (SABCL),* vol. 13 (Pondicherry: Sri Aurobindo Ashram, 1970), 41.
9. *Tikkunei Zohar,* second introduction, 12b. Quoted in Louis Jacobs, *Principles of the Jewish Faith* (New York: Basic Books, 1964), 125–26.
10. *Peraquim Be-Mahashebeth Yisrael,* edited by S. Israeli (Israel, 1982), 77–78. Quoted in Jacobs, *Principles,* 126.
11. Cf. the "forward and backward movement, like the appearance of a flash of lightning" mentioned in Ezek. 1.14.
12. *Teshuvah* literally means "return."
13. *The Lights of Holiness,* vol. 1, 15, quoted in Bokser, *Abraham Isaac Kook,* 204.
14. Some think that Kook can be described as a "pantheist" (cf. Samuel Hugo Bergman, *Faith and Reason: Modern Jewish Thought,* translated by Alfred Jospe (New York: Schocken Books, 1966), 124. A similar line is taken by Nathan Rotenstreich, *Jewish Philosophy in Modern Times* (New York: Holt, Reinhart, and Winston, 1968), 221. Whether or not we use this label, this is an aspect of his thought which comes close to that of Rabbi Shneur Zalman of Liadi.
15. Mahatma Gandhi was not a mystic, but for him too, religious consciousness issued in insight into what was *to be done.* See my *Gandhi's Religious Thought* (Notre Dame: Macmillan, 1983).
16. I draw on remarks made by Rabbi Bokser in Delhi.
17. *Social and Political Thought,* vol. 15 of *SABCL,* 159.
18. He refers to the "danger" of nature as the "confused play of the three gunas of Prakṛti in their eternal entangled twining and wrestling." *Essays on the Gīta,* 134.
19. *The Synthesis of Yoga I,* vol. 20 of *SABCL,* 141.
20. *Letters on Yoga I,* vol. 22 of *SABCL,* 278.
21. Ibid., 281.
22. Sisirkumar Ghose, *Sri Aurobindo: Poet* (Calcutta: Transition Books, 1972), 41.
23. Ibid., 38.
24. Ibid., 34.
25. Ibid., 33–34.
26. Ibid., 55.
27. Ibid., 56.
28. Ibid., 58.
29. Ibid., 64.
30. Ibid., 64.
31. Bokser, *Abraham Isaac Kook,* 375.

32. Ibid., 381. Espousal imagery abounds in the Kabbalah no less than in Sri Aurobindo's work.
33. Ibid., 374.
34. Ibid., 380.
35. Ibid., 81. Gandhi used to refer to "a sense of expansion" as an indication that we were on the right track. The "oceanic circle" metaphor which vividly expresses his conception of a transformed society likewise is conceived to grow. See my *Gandhi's Religious Thought.*
36. *Lights of Holiness,* vol. 2, 555, 355–56, quoted in Bokser, *Abraham Isaac Kook,* 221, 223.
37. *Lights of Holiness,* vol. 1, 66–67, quoted in Bokser, *Abraham Isaac Kook,* 206–7.
38. *Lights of Holiness,* vol. 2, 484, quoted in Bokser, *Abraham Isaac Kook,* 21.
39. *Orot ha-Kodesh,* vol. 2 (Jerusalem: Mosad Harav Kook, 1963), in Bokser, *Abraham Isaac Kook,* 10.
40. "Derekh Hatehiah," in ibid. 292.
41. See *Yismah Lev on Shabbat, Pesahim.*
42. Bokser, *Abraham Isaac Kook,* chap. 12, p. 86ff.
43. "Avraham Yitzhak ha-Cohen Kook," in *Guardians of our Heritage,* edited by Leo Jung (New York, 1958), 497.
44. Cf. Samuel Hugo Bergman: "All creatures are fragments of the one world-soul which is the source of all being and orders the world with wisdom. The higher the degree of evolution, the more does the organic character of the world become manifest: and the evolutionary process will have reached its goal when all men will unite their will with the will of God." *Faith and Reason: Modern Jewish Thought,* 129–30.
45. "Talele Orot," *Takhemoni* (1910), 17ff, quoted in Bokser, *Abraham Isaac Kook,* 311.
46. *The Life Divine* (New York: E. P. Dutton, 1949), 590.
47. Vol. 29 of *SABCL,* 502.
48. *Sādhanā* is the ascesis through which perfection is sought; the *sādhaka* is the seeker or *yogin.*
49. *The Synthesis of Yoga,* vol. 20 of *SABCL,* 40.
50. Ibid., 42.
51. *Bhavani Mandir.*
52. Article in *Bande Mataram,* 2 August 1907.
53. Letter to C. R. Das dated November 1922.
54. *The Human Cycle* (Pondicherry: Sri Aurobindo Ashram, 1962).
55. There are Śaivite overtones in this last phase. He was at this time particularly disillusioned with socialist "formulas."
56. There is much in Sri Aurobindo's belief in an interfusion of human faculties which resembles Dilthey's writings on this theme. This is again a striking coincidence of viewpoints without any possibility of influence. Parallel to Sri Aurobindo's belief in a possible harmony of psychic powers, we have the frequent theme in Kook's writings that revelation is inherent in all the faculties and all constitute one unified whole.

57. *The Human Cycle,* 273.
58. While Sri Aurobindo's prose writings attach considerable importance to the evolution of a superman (fortunately minus the Nietzschean overtones), his poetry suggests a rather different kind of "saviour," the Rishi or prophetic-poetic visionary. Cf. the word *kavirāja,* which literally means king of poets and also means "healer."
59. *The Future Poetry,* vol. 9 of *SABCL,* 35.
60. *Essays on the Gita,* 385.
61. Rivka Schatz, of the Hebrew University in Jerusalem, stresses the discontinuity between Kook's thinking and the Zohar or Lurianic Kabbalah. The latter were not concerned with the problems of the modern world, above all with the crying need to close the gap between secular and sacred, flesh and spirit, Kook's mysticism, however, is very much rooted in that world and does not seek to fly away from it. He witnesses the deep congruence between being in the world and yet not of it, between being rooted and putting forth branches, flowers and fruit.
62. Rotenstreich, *Jewish Philosophy in Modern Times,* 223.
63. Bergman, *Faith and Reason: Modern Jewish Thought,* 131–32.
64. In the extended sense not only of origin but of having a special calling and destiny.

Index